WEST HIGHLAND STEAMERS

First printed	– –	1935
Second edition	– –	1950
Third edition	– –	1967
Fourth edition	– –	1987

ISBN 0 85174 505 9

© 1987 Brown, Son & Ferguson, Ltd., Glasgow G41 2SD
Made and Printed in Great Britain

Frontispiece

P.S. *Columba* (I)

From Painting by John Nicholson

WEST HIGHLAND STEAMERS

Fourth Edition

By

CHRISTIAN LESLIE DYCE DUCKWORTH
B.Sc., M.I.C.E., A.M.I.N.A.

AND

GRAHAM EASTON LANGMUIR
M.A., LL.B.

CONTENTS

LIST OF ILLUSTRATIONS

Coloured Illustrations

ABBREVIATIONS

P.S.	:	Paddle steamship.
S.S.	:	Single-screw steamship.
T.S.S.	:	Twin-screw steamship.
Tr.S.S.	:	Triple-screw steamship.
M.V.	:	Single-screw motor vessel.
T.S.M.V.	:	Twin-screw motor vessel.
Tr.S.M.V.	:	Triple-screw motor vessel.
D.S.M.V.	:	Double-screw motor-vessel (i.e., with propellers fore
	:	and aft).
Len.	:	Lengthened.
O.L.	:	Overall length.
L.	:	Lever engines.
St.	:	Steeple engines.
O.	:	Oscillating engines.
D.	:	Diagonal engines.
H.	:	Horizontal engines.
S.	:	Simple engines.
C.	:	Compound engines.
T.	:	Triple-expansion engines.
Q.	:	Quadruple-expansion engines.
N.C.	:	Non-condensing.
S.B.	:	Scotch boiler(s).
H.B.	:	Haystack boiler(s)
Hor. B.	:	Horizontal boiler(s).
S.E.	:	Single-ended boiler(s).
D.E.	:	Double-ended boiler(s).
W.T.B.	:	Water-tube boiler(s).
M.N.	:	Machinery Numeral (Lloyd's).
N.B.	:	New boiler(s).
N.E.	:	New engines.
D.D.	:	Direct drive.
S.R.G.	:	Single-reduction gearing.
D.R.G.	:	Double-reduction gearing.
S.C.	:	Stroke cycle.
S.A.	:	Single-acting.
Thw. fwd.	:	Thwart-ship propeller(s) forward
Dir. Prop(s)	:	Directional propeller(s)
Cont.-pitch Prop(s)	:	Controllable-pitch propellers
D.A.	:	Double-acting.
T.B.	:	Tons burthen.
Ren.	:	Re-named.
B.H.P.	:	Brake horsepower.
I.H.P.	:	Indicated horsepower.
N.H.P.	:	Nominal horsepower.
R.H.P.	:	Registered horsepower.

"C.R.O.S."	:	"Clyde River & Other Steamers", published by Brown, Son & Ferguson, Ltd., Glasgow, 1937: Second Edition, 1946: Third Edition 1972 and Supplement 1980.
"C.C.S."	:	"Clyde & Other Coastal Steamers", published by Brown, Son & Ferguson, Ltd., Glasgow, 1939: Second Edition published by T. Stephenson & Sons Ltd., Prescot, Merseyside 1977.
"R.O.S."	:	"Railway & Other Steamers", published by Shipping Histories Ltd., Glasgow, 1948: Second Edition by T. Stephenson & Sons Ltd. 1968.
"W.C.S."	:	"West Coast Steamers", published by T. Stephenson & Sons Ltd. Third Edition 1966.

PREFACE

Readers who are familiar with the first (1935), second (1950) and third (1966) editions of this book will notice that there are substantial additions in this fourth edition, not only towards the end, where we have included what has happened during the intervening years, but also throughout the book. Much additional information has come to light, and is incorporated where appropriate.

On account of the unique position and prestige held by the *Columba*, which no other ship has achieved before or since (and is never likely to do again), we retain her as our frontispiece.

A volume of this nature involves little or no creative work; it is merely the concentration in convenient form of a mass of information and data, much of which is available to the general public if it is known where to seek it.

We owe a great deal to previous writers over the last hundred and fifty years, whose labours are acknowledged gratefully; because, with the very best intentions, it is impossible to avoid using the results of others' investigations.

We acknowledge the assistance of all those who have contributed information and photographs, without which the record would have been less detailed; and, in particular David MacBrayne Limited and Caledonian MacBrayne Limited, their Directors and staff; Mr. R. B. Boyd; Mr. David Fenton; Mr. Alasdair Fraser; Mr. Jack Kernahan; Mr. James F. McEwan; Mr. Iain C. MacArthur; Mr. Fraser G. MacHaffie; Mr. Ian McCorie; Mr. A. W. McRobb; Mr. Ian N. Mallinson; Mr. John Nicholson; Mrs. C. Oxford; Mr. J. G. L. Pate; Mr. Alan J. S. Paterson; Mr. Fred Plant; Mrs. Ramsay; Mr. John Robertson; Mr Donald Robertson; Mr. Wm. McC. Russell; Mr. J. Aikman Smith; Mr. R. N. W. Smith; Mr. George M. Stromier; Mr. Leo J. Vogt; also the late Mr. David Campbell, Mr. William Connell, Rev. Wm. C. Galbraith; Mr. A. Ernest Glen; Rev. Canon J. N. Mallinson; Mr. George Moore; Mr. J. B. Macgeorge; Mr. Andrew McQueen; Mr. C. J. L. Romanes; Mr. John Thorburn; Mr. J. C. Tod; Mr. G. F. Whiteway; and Mr R. B. McKim: also the late Mr. James Ainslie of Fort William for the very useful additions on the steamers and coaches owned by members of his family over 140 years ago.

In the early days, when the personal touch meant so much more than it does nowadays, the chief of a concern was able to carry in his head most of the relevant facts of his business. As a result, in the case of the older vessels, there is a great dearth of reliable data on record for posterity; and we, like others who have trodden a similar path of steamship research, have been severely handicapped in this direction. Where ships have been registered, the main particulars at least are available.

We should have preferred to avoid, if possible, using the suffixes (I), (II), (III), etc. for distinguishing between ships of the same name, because in some quarters this practice might be interpreted—wrongly—to mean that the vessel concerned actually bore names and numbers. As, however, we have failed to discover any convenient alternative mode of distinction, we have again followed the above practice. Unless stated otherwise, readers are asked to note that no vessels bore numbers in addition to their names. The word "steamer" in the title has been retained though no steam-propelled vessel remains in the Clyde or West Highland fleet today, except P.S. *Waverley*, which has visited the West Highlands in the last four years.

In the chapters descriptive of the ships and in the fleet lists, the sequence adopted is based on the dates of acquisition by the Company regardless of the classes of vessels and their age. It will be appreciated that this arrangement gives the development of the fleet in chronological order.

It has fallen to me alone to make the necessary revisions for the third and fourth editions, on account of the sad death of Mr. C. L. D. Duckworth in 1953.

It is difficult to realise just how great have been the changes during the fifty years since the first edition appeared, or even in the twenty years since the third edition was published. The greatest of these arose from the introduction of vehicle ferry vessels (lift-loading) in 1964, followed by drive through ships from 1969.

Glasgow,
January, 1987   GRAHAM E. LANGMUIR.

CHAPTER I

THE PREDECESSORS OF DAVID HUTCHESON & CO.
1812-1851

City of Glasgow Steam Packet Company
Thomson & MacConnell

IN 1831 the City of Glasgow Steam Packet Company (first of the name) was founded to carry on trade between Glasgow and Liverpool, the partners being James Donaldson, Robert Ure, David Chapman, Robert Napier and James Thomson. The firm of Thomson & MacConnell (consisting initially of James Thomson and Archibald MacConnell, afterwards of the latter and David Chapman) were the Glasgow agents from 1834.

The first member of this fleet was *City of Glasgow* (I), which had been built in 1822, and which was joined by the new steamer *John Wood* (named after the famous Port Glasgow shipbuilder) in 1832. *Vulcan* followed in 1833; and, after about five years on the Liverpool station, she was transferred to the West Highland route from Glasgow. A second *City of Glasgow* appeared in 1835, followed by *Commodore* and *Admiral* in 1837 and 1839 respectively. These were large ships for their day, and the last to be built of wood for this fleet.

In 1828 Messrs. J. & A. Gairdner had placed on the Glasgow-Belfast route the steamer *Frolic*, in opposition to Messrs. Burns' *Fingal*. She continued in service for a year or two, and then was sold to ply between Pembroke and Haverfordwest; she went ashore near Swansea on 19th March, 1831. *Toward Castle* (originally one of the "Castle" fleet), built in 1822 and to a large extent reconstructed in 1831, succeeded *Frolic* in 1832, and from 1834 was owned by the Clyde Steam Navigation Company (first of that name), of which the partners then were James Donaldson, James Thomson and Archibald MacConnell, the agents being Messrs. Thomson & MacConnell. In 1838 she exchanged engines with Robert Napier's *Brenda*, and was transferred to the West Highland trade, which her owners had in that year entered. She sailed at first to Inverness along with Robert Napier's *Staffa*, and in 1842 was operating from Glasgow to Portree every second Monday, leaving Glasgow on Tuesdays in the alternate weeks for Port Ellen or Port Askaig; and on these runs she made connection at West Loch Tarbert with the "Castle" steamers trading to Loch Fyne, her place on the Portree and Islay service being taken from March, 1842 by *Foyle*. From 1844 the *Brenda* belonged to the City of Glasgow S.P. Co. and was sailing from Glasgow on Mondays for Islay, Oban, Lochaline, Salen, Tobermory and Portree. In 1849 she went to the east coast for service between Leith and Peterhead as a schooner, owned by Robert Bell & Co., Dumbarton, and in January, 1850 was for sale, lying in Bramley Moore Dock, Liverpool. She was sold to T. Fletcher, Goole in March that year.

Other vessels owned by the Clyde S.N. Co. were *Arab*, placed on the Belfast run in 1835, followed by *Tartar*, early in 1837. The former was sold to the Dublin & Glasgow Sailing & Steam Packet Company after a little more than a year, but the latter lasted till the end of 1850, being latterly on the West Highland services from Glasgow. *Circassian*, of 1837, was sold to foreign owners about the end of 1838, as also was *Vulcan* in 1840: she had been among the first steamships to visit St. Kilda.

Messrs. Thomson & MacConnell themselves in April, 1838, took over the wooden paddle steamer *Tobermory*, which had been placed in service at the end of November, 1836, having been built that year for a "body of enterprising gentlemen, consisting of landed proprietors, tacksmen and merchants connected with Mull, Morven and Ardnamurchan". She was registered originally at Greenock, and Mr. McEachern was the Glasgow agent from 1836 to 1838. The Clyde steamer *Royal Victoria* was owned by Messrs. Thomson & MacConnell for about a year in 1840-1, and in May of the latter year they took over Robert Napier's *Shandon*, to which further reference will be made later in this chapter.

To trace the origin of steam navigation in the West Highlands we must go back as far as the *Comet* but, before doing so, reference will be made to the West Highland steamers of Robert Napier, which were operated as part of the Thomson & MacConnell fleet from 1838, and which were absorbed by the City of Glasgow Steam Packet Company (second of the name) in 1844. The old concern of the same name had been taken over by G. & J. Burns in 1840 and absorbed into the Clyde Steam Navigation Company, by that time owned by them, Thomson & MacConnell, continuing as agents till the end of 1850. The partners of the new City of Glasgow Company were James Donaldson, David Chapman, Archibald MacConnell, David MacIver and Charles MacIver. Under the 1840 agreement, trade could be carried on under the names of the former companies, hence the formation of the new City of Glasgow S.P. Co.

Robert Napier

The famous marine engineer Robert Napier ran a service of steamers to the Gareloch in the 1830s, the first on record being the wooden steamer *Clarence*, followed in 1836 by *Brenda*, in 1839 by *Shandon* and in 1840-1 by *James Oswald* and *Royal Victoria*.

On 31st December, 1835, he took over the West Highland fleet then operated by D. Wright & Co., previously under the agency of

Archibald McEachern, which had itself absorbed the fleet of Henry Bell, Thomson and others, dating from the *Comet* of 1812.

After a period on the Firth of Clyde, the pioneer *Comet* (I) was transferred to the Firth of Forth, to sail between Grangemouth and Newhaven, but in 1819 she returned to the West Coast; and, after an extensive overhaul, which included lengthening, she started a service to Fort William *via* the Crinan Canal, becoming thus the first West Highland steamer. Unfortunately she was wrecked on 13th December, 1820 at the Dorus Mòr, near Craignish.

To take the place of *Comet* on the Firth of Forth a small steamer named *Stirling Castle* was acquired in 1820. A weekly service was then instituted between Edinburgh and Fort William, by coach to Newhaven, steamer to Grangemouth, coach to Lock No. 16 on the Forth and Clyde Canal, and canal boat to Port Dundas. The journey from Glasgow to Fort William was completed by *Comet*, and the fare for the whole journey was 34s. first cabin or 20s. second cabin. On the opening of the eastern portion of the Caledonian Canal from Inverness to Fort Augustus in 1820, *Stirling Castle* was transferred thither from the Forth; and at a later date she was sailing between Glasgow and Inverness by way of the Canal, which was opened throughout on 23rd October, 1822. On that occasion the boat described as "the small steam yacht which plies on Loch Ness (probably the *Stirling Castle*, followed by the sloop *Caledonia* of the Canal Commissioners was met by the *Comet* steam yacht coming from the west. The use of the word "yacht" for a passenger steamer is noteworthy, this being perpetuated to the present time in the English Lake District. In January, 1828 she went ashore at Inverscadail, near Ardgour, and a butler to the Chief of Glengarry and Clanranald was drowned; while the Chief himself in landing sustained such injuries as caused his death. He was 17th of the dynasty of Mac Mhic Alasdair, and was long spoken of as "the last of the Chiefs". His portrait by Raeburn is in the National Gallery, Edinburgh.

P.S. *Highland Chieftain*, acquired in 1820, was the old Dumbarton Company's steamer *Duke of Wellington* re-named. She sailed on 28th November, 1820, *via* the Crinan Canal to Isle Ornsay, which was reached in thirty-five hours from Glasgow. On the loss of *Comet*, *Highland Chieftain* took up the Fort William sailings till the appearance of *Comet* (II), after which she plied on the Dumfries—Liverpool and Glasgow—Stranraer routes (having been sold to R. Stewart about May, 1822) till about the end of 1824. She then re-appeared in the West Highlands as consort to *Ben Nevis* as after-mentioned. Next year she passed to J. McColl & Co. and in 1826 to Highland Chieftain Steamboat Company, and then to Archibald MacConnell in March, 1828, later going to John Laird, Archibald MacConnell and Alex. Laird. She returned to her former fleet in 1828 to take the place of the wrecked *Stirling Castle*, then was sold in April, 1832 to W. Young, being again sold in 1834, when the engine was removed and she became a schooner till broken up at Glasgow in 1838.

The second *Comet* made her debut on the Fort William station on 6th July, 1821, her passage occupying twenty-six hours, which was reckoned good steaming. Henry Bell may not have been interested in the ownership of this vessel, which was named as a memorial to him and his pioneer steamship. On the opening of the Caledonian Canal in 1824 the voyages of *Comet* (II) were extended to Inverness. In the morning of 25th October, 1825 *Comet*, homeward bound, was run down by Messrs. Burns' *Ayr* off Gourock, and sunk with considerable loss of life. She was afterwards raised, and sailed as the schooner *Ann* till 1876.

In March, 1822 P.S. *Highlander* was placed on the Fort William route as consort to *Comet*, and thus a twice-weekly service was given; but not for long, as in May of the same year *Highlander* was transferred to the Tobermory station, to begin a regular passenger and freight service between Glasgow and the Sound of Mull, calling at Loch Aline, (which was a port of call for the Glasgow-Tobermory ships from 1822-55, thereafter by those on the Glasgow-Stornoway run). Later in 1822 she gave sailings from the Broomielaw to Icolumkill (Iona) and Staffa, calling at Lochgilphead, Easdale, Oban, Loch Don, Aros and Tobermory. Her sailings at a later date were prolonged to Skye, and for a time she ran also to Strontian.

The agency for the steamers of this fleet was in the hands of Mr. Alexander Laird till it passed in 1832 to Mr. A. McEachern, already established as an agent for ships in the Highland trade, having succeeded Mr. John McLeod in 1828. The latter had commenced in April, 1824, with the little wooden paddle vessel *Ben Nevis* (I) which plied between Glasgow and Inverness by way of the Caledonian Canal, along with *Commodore* (I). In March, 1827, she was auctioned, but resumed her sailings in June. She was wrecked at Carskey, twelve miles south of Campbeltown, on 18th August, 1831, while homeward bound from Stornoway.

Towards the end of 1824 the owners of *Ben Nevis* acquired *Highland Chieftain* and were thus able at the beginning of 1825 to start a weekly service to Inverness.

At the beginning of 1827 *Maid of Morven* was acquired; she plied on the Glasgow-Tobermory and Glasgow-Fort William stations in alternate weeks. In 1834-5 her sailings were extended to Cromarty, Invergordon and Burghead. She passed to Robert Napier in December, 1835 and sailed for Thomson & MacConnell in 1838 to Oban, Tobermory and Skye. In 1841 she was sold to Alex. McKenzie, Jr., Kessock Ferry, and in 1846 was re-registered at Glasgow, becoming the property of Wm. Ainslie.

The schooner-rigged steamer *Benlomond* appeared in the West Highlands about 1828. On 18th June in that year the sailings for the season were announced in the *Glasgow Herald*, thus:—

HIGHLANDER from Glasgow every Monday for Oban, Tobermory and Staffa; and from Tobermory every Friday for Oban and Glasgow.

MAID OF MORVEN from Glasgow every Thursday for Oban
and Inverness; and from Inverness every Monday for Oban and
Glasgow.
BENLOMOND will leave Tobermory every Monday for Strontian and the celebrated Spar Cave in Skye alternately; and
BEN NEVIS is also appointed to sail in conjunction with the other
vessels betwixt Glasgow and Stornoway. The Ben Nevis will
therefore leave the Broomielaw every alternate Tuesday and
Stornoway every intervening Tuesday.

Benlomond was advertised to sail to Staffa and Iona in August
1829 and (under Capt. Turner) in June 1831 for Oban, Tobermory and
the Spar Cave in Skye. She was sold by auction on 1st April, 1833 and
set to ply between Newhaven and Stirling, being damaged by fire near
the former port on 4th June, 1833 and sold to Newcastle owners in 1836.

In 1832 two steamers were added, *Staffa* (I) and *Inverness*, the
latter making her first trip in February, 1833, to the town from which
she took her name. She was sold in 1834 to Archd. Ferguson, shortly
afterwards passing to Mr. Young, and in 1835 became the joint
property of the latter and Messrs. Burns. *Staffa* also was on the
Inverness station, making calls in addition at Cromarty and Invergordon for a time in 1834-5.

A steamer named *Colonsay*, built by Messrs. Duncan at Port
Glasgow in 1834, has been associated both with the West Highland and
with the Belfast route, but her exact service is doubtful. In 1834 a
notable addition to the fleet was made, viz. *Glen Albyn*, which was
much larger and more powerful than her predecessors. She was the
property of the Glen Albyn Steamboat Co. of Tobermory, composed
of landowners and merchants in the North and West Highlands, and
was placed in service along with *Staffa*, *Maid of Morven* and *Highlander*. This was the first steam vessel to call at St. Kilda, in 1835; and in
April, 1837, she was sold to the Trustees of the North British S.N. Co.,
a subsidiary of Messrs. Burns.

On 31st December, 1835, Messrs. Wright's steamers *Highlander*,
Maid of Morven and *Staffa*—were taken over by Robert Napier, who in
the following year added the *Brenda*, described in the "King of
Saxony's Journey", as sailing from Banavie to Tobermory (then a ferry
call).

The steamers remaining in the Napier fleet in 1838 appear to have
been *Maid of Morven*, *Staffa*, *Brenda* and *Toward Castle*, which
thenceforth came under the management of Messrs. Thomson &
MacConnell. To these was added also in 1838 the steamer *Tobermory*
already mentioned.

A track-boat *Thornwood* was introduced on the Crinan Canal in
1838, giving a much better service than had been possible by using the
steamers sailing from the Clyde to the West Highlands for the passage
through the canal.

According to the Transactions of the Agricultural Society of Scotland, 1878, in an article by Duncan Clerk, Writer, Oban, the *Maid of Morven*, *Highlander* and *Highland Chieftain* were fondly remembered by those who knew them in early life; and, at a later date, the *Rob Roy* (Captain Duncan), *Helen McGregor* (Captain Turner), *Toward Castle* (Captain Macdonald) and *Dolphin* (Captain McKillop) were regular and welcome visitors. The *Maid of Morven* was a great favourite and better known by her Gaelic name, *A'Mhaighdean Mhorairneach*.

Brenda exchanged engines with *Toward Castle* about 1838, and became the first vessel on the Glasgow-Lochgilphead station in connexion with the through route to the West Highlands, afterwards known as the "Royal Route" and maintained, latterly in modified form, by David MacBrayne, Ltd. and finally by The Caledonian S.P. Co. Ltd. In 1840 *Brenda* was placed on the Crinan-Oban route in succession to Messrs. Burns' *Helen McGregor*; while in 1842 she sailed from Glasgow to Oban, Fort William and Inverness. Originally single-masted, she was given a mainmast in 1844, and in the following year was broken up at Greenock.

P.S. "Shandon." This steamer, at first the property of Robert Napier and Richard B. Clelland, when new plied on the Gareloch route. She was built of wood in 1839, when iron steamships were still regarded as somewhat of a novelty and took part in a race against the iron steamer *Superb*; the result was a victory for the iron ship. (The *Superb* had been built in 1839 for the Stirling, Alloa & Kincardine Steamboat Co., but drew too much water and was sold to the Shandon & Glasgow Steam Packet Company (Robert Napier), being sold in 1850 to the Jersey S.N. Co. In 1840 the *Shandon* was lengthened on the "waveline" principle, and was reported to have gone much faster thereafter. Her side lever engine took steam from two "wagon" boilers.

In May, 1841 *Shandon* was registered in names of Archibald MacConnell and David Chapman, the then partners of the firm of Thomson & MacConnell, the ownership being transferred in March, 1844 to themselves together with Charles MacIver and David MacIver of Liverpool, the Trustees of the City of Glasgow Steam Packet Company.

From 1841 *Shandon* was employed on the various services operated by the joint Thomson & MacConnell and Burns organisation, including those to Ardrishaig in 1841 and to Dunoon and Kilmun in 1842, when she was advertised to sail every Monday, Wednesday, Thursday and Saturday at 9 o'clock, and Saturday also at 6 p.m. On Tuesdays and Fridays she sailed, with passengers only, from Glasgow to Lochgilphead direct. It was further added: "Passengers will be taken through the Crinan Canal, as on former seasons, in swift track-boats, and by steamers from the Canal to Oban, Fort

William and Tobermory the same day, and to Inverness and Portree on the afternoon of the following days". She was employed in excursions to Loch Riddon, Lochlonghead, Arran and Kyles of Bute.

Carvel-built, with sloop stem and standing bowsprit, *Shandon* was square-rigged, originally single-masted, but was given a second mast in the spring of 1844.

She was taken over by Messrs. Hutcheson as one of the ten original vessels so transferred, and was registered in their name in May, 1851; but with them her career was short. She was stationed at Oban in summer, performing the Crinan-Oban service, but the commissioning of *Mountaineer* (I) in 1852 rendered her redundant, as *Pioneer* (I) was then relieved from the Ardrishaig route to succeed *Shandon* at Oban.

In May, 1853 a certain John Anderson became the owner and master of *Shandon*, eight shares in her being transferred in October of that year to James Whyte of Rothesay and William Boyd McAllister of Liverpool. In 1853 Captain Anderson sailed the ship—with paddle-wheels removed—to Melbourne, where the shares owned by Messrs. Whyte and McAllister were sold to Wharton, Caird & Co., Merchants, of Melbourne, who in turn sold them to Crawford Maine of Melbourne. It is understood that Captain Anderson steamed *Shandon* from Australian waters to Singapore, and sold her to a Chinese merchant, who sent her to North China. She was broken up in April, 1865.

The red funnel with black top is said to have been adopted first of all by Robert Napier on *Shandon*, which introduced it to the West Highlands on her transfer thither. It thus passed to Messrs. Thomson & MacConnell and was transmitted to the Hutcheson/MacBrayne fleet, of which it remained the distinguishing mark. It would be almost impossible to think of the West Highlands without red funnels; and these are so much a feature of the district that Neil Munro confessed that he was sixteen years old before he discovered that all the steamers in the world had not red funnels with black tops!

The house-flags used by Messrs. Thomson & MacConnell and the City of Glasgow Steam Packet Company consisted of a blue pennant bearing a white St. Andrew's cross, flown above a red pennant. Messrs. Hutcheson combined these by adopting a blue pennant bearing a red cross superimposed over, but offset from the white cross, which remained the house-flag of David MacBrayne, Ltd., but is not at present in use, this being a dormant company not owning or operating any ships. Caledonian MacBrayne retained the red funnel (of a slightly darker shade) with black top, adding on the red portion a yellow disc, bearing the red lion rampant of the Caledonian Company. For the house-flag a similar disc and lion were added to the blue portion of the MacBrayne flag, but this emblem, when on a blue ground, was held to be a heraldic infringement, and was abandoned in favour of a pennant which is simply a repeat of the funnel marking.

William Young & Others

George Burns & William Young, 1835–1835

George Burns, 1835-1844

G. & J. Burns, 1844-1851

For the early history of this firm readers are directed to "C.C.S." It is proposed here to deal only with its ships employed in the various West Highland services.

In 1835 Mr. Burns learned that Mr. Young, who owned several small vessels engaged in the West Highland trade, was anxious for him to accept the agency for them in Glasgow. This was refused, but a counter offer was made to Mr. Young to acquire a half-share in his ships, on condition that it contained an option to purchase the remaining half on a later date. The offer was accepted, and there followed a period of intense development. Mr. Young's two steamers, *Inverness* and *Rob Roy* were taken over wholly by Mr. George Burns in September, 1835, being in August, 1844, transferred to James Burns and others, Trustees of the Glasgow & Liverpool Steamship Company, in whose name Messrs. Burns' Highland steamers were thenceforth registered.

Both were small steamers, short enough to use the Crinan Canal; and from Crinan their route was to Oban and Fort William, thence through the Caledonian Canal to Inverness. In 1834 their sailings were extended to Cromarty and Invergordon, but this did not last long. *Inverness* in 1835 received a thorough overhaul, being fitted with new cabins and machinery. She was then placed on the Mull, Ulva, and Strontian route under the Burns flag. In July, 1838 *Rob Roy* was sailing to Staffa and Iona from Oban every Tuesday and Friday afternoon, returning the following evening; at this time the Glasgow-Inverness service was being maintained by *Inverness*. In 1846 the latter was sold to Samuel Bromhead and Samuel Hemming, London-derry, and was broken up by December, 1851. *Rob Roy* became spare on completion of *Lapwing* in 1848, and was scrapped by November, 1850.

In May, 1835 there was added the paddle steamer *Helen McGregor*, which had probably been laid down for the previous owners of *Inverness* and *Rob Roy*.

In April, 1837, the steamer *Glen Albyn* was taken over by Jas. Martin, Jas. Burns and George Burns, Trustees of the North British Steam Navigation Company of Glasgow, and was sold in the following year to the General Shipping Company, Berwick-on-Tweed. There-after Messrs. Burns' *Antelope*, built in 1833, was operated by the North British S.N. Co. on West Highland routes till about the end of 1845.

When through services *via* Loch Fyne were introduced in 1839, *Helen McGregor* was stationed at Oban for the Crinan-Oban service. About a year later she returned to the Glasgow-Inverness route: and a few days before the end of 1843 she enjoyed the distinction of being the first steamer to sink in the Crinan Canal! She was at once raised, but was too badly damaged to proceed on her voyage, so had to be taken back to Glasgow for repairs. She remained on the Inverness station till broken up in 1848 on the advent of *Cygnet* (I).

For the joint through working between Glasgow and the West Highlands instituted in 1839 by Messrs. Burns and Messrs. Thomson & MacConnell, the latter firm provided the means of transport between Glasgow and Lochgilphead by P.S. *Brenda*, and by the trackboat *Thornwood* on the Crinan Canal. The last-named was brought from the Monkland Canal, and was horse-drawn. The

Crinan-Oban station was filled by *Helen McGregor*. The use of company-owned rowing ferryboats for landing at Iona and Staffa dates back to about this period, these being painted red (at least in later times). The normal procedure was to have one or more based at Iona for landing there, and one which was rowed across from Gometra to Staffa to tender to the steamer and land at or near Fingal's Cave.

An event of significance in West Highland steamer history was the constitution from 1st October, 1840 of The Clyde Steam Navigation Company, under a Contract of Co-partnery between The Glasgow and Liverpool Steam Shipping Company and The City of Glasgow Steam Packet Company and respective subscribers, amalgamating the fleets of these two concerns, but providing for their trade being conducted under the new name or either of the old names. Previous contracts were superseded by the new one, the ships contributed being as follows:—

> By the G. & L.S.S. Co.—*Actaeon*, *Achilles*;
> By The City of Glasgow S.P. Co.—*City of Glasgow*, *Commodore*, *Admiral*
> all on the Glasgow-Liverpool trade;
> By The City of Glasgow S.P. Co. or some of its subscribers:—*Tartar*, *Aurora*, *Antelope*, engaged in the Clyde and Belfast trade; *Toward Castle*, *Inverness*, *Rob Roy*, *Helen McGregor*, *Brenda*, *Maid of Morven*, *Staffa* and *Victoria* and the track-boat *Thornwood*, engaged in the Clyde and Highland trade and local trade on the Clyde.

Agents appointed were James Martin, Thomas Martin, James Burns, George Burns, James Donaldson, David MacIver, Charles MacIver and Archibald MacConnell and David Chapman, from which it would appear that the firms of agents concerned would be Messrs. Burns & MacIver in Liverpool; G. & J. Burns in Glasgow; and Thomson & MacConnell in Glasgow.

The reference to the steamer *Victoria* is presumably to the ship registered as *Royal Victoria*, the first ship built at Paisley.

P.S. "Dolphin" (I). Launched on 27th June, 1844, for Messrs. G. & J. Burns, this was the first iron steamer in their fleet, and the first specifically built by them for the West Highland trade. Originally three-masted, she had a square stern, and a dolphin and cupid figurehead. She plied from Oban on various routes, including that to Staffa and Iona, and passed to Messrs. Hutcheson in 1851. During the summer of that year her service was from Oban to Staffa and Iona on three days of the week and up Loch Linnhe to Fort William on the remaining three days alternately. In 1853 (on 1st and 8th August) she was advertised to give a day trip from Oban to Loch Corriskin (Loch Coruisk) and the Coolin Hills. In 1855 she was on the Glasgow-Stornoway, etc. run in company with the *Clansman*, in place of the wrecked *Chevalier*. After Messrs. Hutcheson had taken over the Loch Fyne trade in 1857, she was associated with *Mary Jane* and *Inverary Castle* on that route, her first trip to Inveraray having been made on 17th February, 1857. On 8th August, 1861 she took to Ardrishaig passengers and mails from the *Iona* (I), which had broken down in the Kyles of Bute.

Dolphin was sold in 1862 to W. R. Grazebrook, Liverpool, for the American blockade, and was captured by the Federals in 1863. Taken as a prize to New York, she was sold in July, 1864 and immediately resold to the Confederates. Under the name *Ruby* she was intercepted near Key West: again taken to New York, she was used as a patrol vessel, then sold in 1867 to an owner in Memphis, Tennessee, and wrecked in a gale in 1874.

. . . .

Dating from 1845 (the centenary of the rising which ended in the next year with the battle of Culloden), the steamer *Culloden*, built for the Kilmun trade of Messrs. Burns, also sailed for them on the Caledonian Canal till succeeded by *Curlew* in 1849. In 1847 she was employed for a time from Oban to Loch Etive and Glencoe, through coach excursions being arranged. She was clipper-bowed, with one funnel aft; and in an old print she is shown with a Castle Company funnel. Messrs. Denny purchased her in 1851, after which she put in some service between Newhaven and Dieppe, then on Belfast Lough, returning to the Clyde, which she finally left, rigged as a schooner, in January, 1853, for Melbourne, being transferred to Hobart Town and registry cancelled on 27th April, 1866.

The following were the arrangements of the West Highland services in 1846:—*Culloden*, *Dolphin* and *Shandon* were advertised to sail between Glasgow and Inverness (presumably not each of them the whole way!) while *Rob Roy* was on the Glasgow-Fort William-Corpach station. *Shandon*, *Dolphin* and *Tartar* were advertised also to sail from Glasgow to Ardrishaig, Oban, Tobermory and Portree; while on Wednesdays *Dolphin* performed a day excursion from Oban to Staffa and Iona. In the following year the arrangements were similar, and it was stated that a "smart boat" was "stationed at Oban for excursions to Staffa and Iona".

An important development in the Burns fleet was the acquisition in June, 1846 of the Glasgow Castle Steam Packet Company, whose steamers continued to be advertised separately till 1848. They were registered in name of the Trustees of the Glasgow & Liverpool Steamship Company from June, 1846.

Castle Steam Packet Company, 1832-1842
Glasgow Castle Steam Packet Company, 1842-1846

The exact origin of the Castle Steam Packet Company is doubtful, though it is thought that the first member of the fleet was *Inverary Castle* (I), built in 1814, just two years after the *Comet*. For a time there was a separate company for each ship in the fleet, and in 1832 the vessels then remaining were transferred to the Castle Steam Packet Company, of which the Trustees then were John Watson and Alexander King, Merchants, and Alexander Miller, Broker of Glasgow, together with Kirkman Finlay, James Ewing, Merchants, and Robert Thom, Cotton Spinner of Rothesay. The company was re-constituted in April, 1842, when the name was changed to Glasgow Castle Steam Packet Company, the Trustees of which were Alexander Struthers Finlay, Merchant, Glasgow, William Campbell of Tulliche-wan and James Hunter of Hafton, Argyle, with John Watson, Merchant.

The principal runs of the Castle steamers were to Rothesay and Loch Fyne; and it was on account of the latter service that Messrs. Burns consolidated, and so were able to transmit to Messrs. Hutche-son in 1851, the Glasgow-Ardrishaig passenger trade, part of the important "Royal Route" to the Highlands, operated by Messrs. MacBrayne; and the Glasgow-Lochfyne cargo service which went to D. Roxburgh & Co. then in 1857 to Hutcheson/MacBrayne and to Clyde Cargo Steamers Ltd. from 1916.

The funnel-colouring of the Castle steamers was black with a white band, and this was retained even after they had entered the Burns' fleet: in fact, according to some old drawings, it appears to have been adopted by Messrs. Burns for their Clyde steamers. It passed, also, with some of the vessels sold in 1851 to other owners, from whom it was ultimately inherited by both the Buchanan and Williamson Clyde fleets. Details of Castle steamers will be found in the fleet-lists. In addition the following may be noted.

In 1815 was built *Dumbarton Castle*, said to have been the first steamer in the Rothesay trade, her route being later extended to Inveraray, to which she was sailing in 1818. The following year she took up service between Leith, Newhaven and Grangemouth, being similarly employed also in 1820 and broken up at Leith in 1841. *Rothesay Castle* of 1816 was sold in 1830 and in August of the following year was wrecked off Beaumaris. The second *Inverary Castle* appeared in 1820, and operated on the Glasgow-Rothesay-Loch Fyne station, though in 1828 she sailed to Rothesay on certain days and from Glasgow to Brodick, Island of Arran on Thursdays, returning to Glasgow on Fridays, and making the usual calls. Her machinery was of the side lever type, steam being supplied by two copper flue-boilers. In 1836 she was stationed at Oban, sailing to Staffa and Iona *via* Tobermory, then owned by Alexander Barlas.

Toward Castle of 1822 was first owned by the Toward Castle Steam Boat Company, and was employed on the Loch Fyne route in company with *Inverary Castle* (II). In 1831 she was sold, and three years later became a member of Messrs. Thomson & MacConnell's

Belfast fleet, later trading to West Highland ports. *Dunoon Castle*, first of her name on the Clyde, was an old-fashioned wooden paddle steamer, with two masts, and one funnel, (aft). Owned initially by Alexander Patrick and others, Trustees of the Dunoon Castle Steam Packet Company, she was transferred on 1st March, 1831, to James Ewing, Merchant, Glasgow, from whom she passed to the Castle Steam Packet Company a year later. She remained in the Loch Fyne trade after the absorption of the Castle fleet by Messrs. Burns, and was sold, with several others of the Burns fleet, to Messrs. Denny in February, 1851. She was, however, in September of that year, acquired from them by the Glasgow & Lochfyne Steam Packet Company (D. Roxburgh & Co.).

Arran Castle of 1830, is said to have been on the Rothesay station along with *Inverary Castle* (II), etc. Another member of the Castle fleet, engaged in the Loch Fyne trade, was *Tarbert Castle* (I), superseded in 1838 on account of the appearance of a rival vessel, *Argyle*, which necessitated an improved service. She was then sold to the Montrose & Forth S.N. Co. (later to Dundee, Alloa and, as a sailing vessel, to Australia), while the first *Edinburgh Castle*, built in 1835, was sold in the spring of 1838 to Mr. C. H. Frewen, Rye.

To meet the opposition of the Bute Steam Packet Company's *Isle of Bute* and *Maid of Bute* on the Rothesay station, the Castle Company had the second *Rothsay Castle* built in 1837. This was, when new, a very fine steamer, the first built of iron for this fleet, and described by a writer fifty years later as "quite the *Columba* of her day". She ran in summer only, being taken out of the water on Hedderwick's slip at the end of each season and kept there all winter out of danger. She sailed to Lochfyne on certain days, making connexion (*via* Tarbert) with *Toward Castle* and other steamers calling at West Loch Tarbert; and, in the summer of 1842, she sailed daily at 6 a.m. from Glasgow to Greenock, Dunoon, Rothesay, Tarbert and Lochgilphead, proceeding on Saturdays to Inveraray. In 1849-50 she was for a time sailing from Inverness to Little Ferry, with occasional trips from Cromarty and also relieving *Edinburgh Castle* on the Banavie-Inverness run. She was also at various times on the Lochfyne station, on which she remained, on charter to Messrs. Hutcheson, till early in March, 1851. On 1st March in that year, however, it was announced that she would shortly be withdrawn and a first-class steamer put in her place. She was sold in May to Henry P. Maples and Wm. Denny & Bros., and plied between Newhaven and Dieppe in connection with the L.B. & S.C. and Paris & Dieppe Railways. At the end of the season she returned to the Clyde, Mr. Maples having transferred his half-share in her to Messrs. Denny; and she was then registered at Port Glasgow. In 1853 she was wrecked while on her way to take up service at Demerara.

Two additions to the Castle fleet occurred in 1838, viz. *Tarbert Castle* (II) and *Windsor Castle* (II). The former of these was the steamer built specially to oppose the *Argyle* on the Lochfyne station, and was launched in April from the yard of Messrs. Hedderwick & Rankin, then a short distance below the Broomielaw. Known as "the long *Tarbert*", she was a fine three-masted iron steamer, and unfortunately had a very short career, being wrecked in a storm on the Silver Rocks, Ardmarnock Beach, Kilfinan Bay, Loch Fyne on 17th January, 1839. The crew of *Argyle* went to assist, but found her a wreck, though all on board had been saved. Though the ship was salved and towed to the Broomielaw, it was found impracticable to make any further use of her hull; but the engine was fitted into the new *Inverary Castle*, where it gave exceptionally long service, lasting till the early 'nineties.

Windsor Castle of 1838 was rather a handsome iron steamer, with a fine figurehead of Queen Victoria with a gold crown on her head. The ship was, however, rather cranky; and, to steady her, she had heavy wooden "wings" fixed along her hull at the waterline. She had also a connexion from the bridge to the controls of the engine, by means of which the engine could be manoeuvred without signalling to the engineer. Sold for the Granton-Newcastle and Granton-Dundee trade of Andrew Greig and others, she left Broomielaw on 1st August, 1844. Unfortunately she was lost on the North Carr, off St. Andrews in October, 1844.

Registered originally in the names of Kirkman Finlay, John Watson, Alexander Miller, James Ewing and Robert Thom, the then Trustees of the Castle Steam Packet Company, *Inverary Castle* (III) was the first steamer built by Messrs. Tod & McGregor in their yard at Greenlaw (where General Terminus Quay now is). She received the steeple engine from the wrecked *Tarbert Castle* (II) mentioned above. She passed to the Glasgow Castle Steam Packet Co. in September, 1842 and to the Glasgow & Liverpool Steamship Company on 3rd June, 1846. In February, 1851, she was sold to Messrs. Wm. Denny & Bros., Dumbarton, continuing on the Lochfyne station, under charter till sold on 20th August, 1851 to the Glasgow & Lochfyne Steam Packet Company.

P.S. "Duntroon Castle." It was in 1841 that the Glasgow, Paisley & Greenock Railway was opened. The Railway Company endeavoured to make arrangements for the carrying of passengers and goods in connection with the trains; but the steamboat owners, disliking the idea of competition from a railway, did everything in their power to keep the trade to themselves. The Railway Company, accordingly, through its subsidiary company, obtained steamers of its own; and, to compete with these, several fine ships were built for the private owners, among them being *Duntroon Castle* for the Castle Company, in 1842. She was fitted with a two-cylinder steeple engine taking steam from a horizontal boiler, and had one funnel abaft the paddle-boxes, and two masts, square-rigged. Originally carrying a woman figurehead, this was altered in July, 1858 to a billet-head.

Her original run was to Rothesay and Loch Fyne. After she had entered the Burns fleet, however, she was transferred to the West Highland trade. An advertisement of 1850 stated that she had lately undergone considerable improvement to hull and machinery, having been furnished with new boilers, and would be found from her well-known speed an eligible conveyance for goods and passengers. Her route then was from Glasgow to Oban, Tobermory and Portree, with extension to Gairloch in June. On this she remained for Messrs. Hutcheson, in whose name she was registered on 4th April, 1851. She was succeeded by the first *Chevalier* in 1853, when she was sold to Messrs. Maples & Mories and others, being registered at London in May of that year. After various changes of ownership she passed at the end of 1859 to Thomas Chiltern, the younger, and Matthew M. Miller, and on 16th July, 1863 her register was closed, on her being sold to a foreigner. She was, however, re-registered at Cork on 27th July that year, in name of Ernest Drouke, her owner having become a natura-lised British subject. She was lost later the same year.

.   .   .   .

In 1844 there were added to the Castle fleet the *Cardiff Castle* and *Craignish Castle*, which, though large and comfortable steamers, were too slow to compete successfully with the railway boats. They were the first ships built for passenger service on the Clyde with diagonal engines (simple, of course). *Cardiff Castle* was a square-sterned clincher-built iron vessel, rigged as a two-masted schooner. She went to Messrs. Denny in 1851, and sailed under the management of W. F. Johnstone on the Rothesay station, being owned by Buchanan & Williamson from April, 1854 for a period, and in 1861 by A. Watson. She was ultimately broken up. *Craignish Castle* was launched on 26th June, 1844 and was conspicuous by having the longest funnel of any Clyde steamer of her period. After sailing for Messrs. Denny under W. F. Johnstone's management, and for the Lochfine Company, she was sold in 1862 to W. J. Grazebrook, Liverpool, for blockade-running, being re-named *Adler*.

P.S. "Edinburgh Castle" (II)/**"Glengarry."** This ship was built in 1844 for the Holy Loch service, her first registered owners being Messrs. Campbell, Watson, Finlay and Hunter, the then Trustees of the Glasgow Castle Steam Packet Company. After only two seasons on the Clyde she was, early in 1846, transferred to oppose Messrs. Ainslie's *Glencoe* on the Caledonian Canal, where the remainder of her long life was spent; and latterly she was a veteran of the first order. From June, 1846, she was the property of the Glasgow & Liverpool Steamship Com-pany, and was advertised by Messrs. Thomson & MacConnell until the end of 1850. She passed into the Hutcheson fleet in February, 1851.

On 18th March, 1860 she was sold to Robert Curle and James Hamilton, Shipbuilders, Glasgow, who re-sold her to foreign owners. Evidently she was not delivered, for she was re-purchased by Messrs. Hutcheson on 28th March, 1860.

Fitted with a steeple engine, which propelled her till the end, she originally had a slanting stem and square stern, the funnel being abaft the paddle-boxes. She also had the small poop-deck, which was a characteristic of the other Castle steamers of the period, and which she retained throughout. (This poop-deck is not mentioned in the registers until 1875, but this was probably an omission.) In the spring of 1875 she underwent very considerable alterations, the hull being lengthened, a straight stem fitted, and short deck saloons erected forward and aft. At the same time the funnel was moved forward of the machinery space, presumably to enable the boiler's weight to balance that of the engine, in the lengthened hull. She was re-named *Glengarry* and as such became very well known on the Canal.

In a guide-book published by Maclure & Macdonald in 1866 *Edinburgh Castle* is advertised as working the Inverness-Banavie service in conjunction with the new *Gondolier*, the two ships between them giving a daily service in each direction. This arrangement continued for a number of years, though while *Gairlochy* was on the run, the sailings of *Glengarry* were normally confined to the mail route from Inverness to Fort Augustus, with some additional cruises on Loch Ness in summer. She was sometimes referred to as *Edinburgh*.

Her ancient steeple engine presented some special features of interest in that pride of craftmanship showed itself in ornamental cast-iron work in such a utilitarian object as the long starting-bar, which was highly embellished with fancy designs. There were four piston rods fitted to the single cylinder.

A golden eagle model adorned the companion-way to the dining saloon which was situated near the stern, as was the custom when *Glengarry* was built.

Glengarry was one of the last MacBrayne steamers to carry a black hoop on her funnel, maintaining thus the tradition of early days.

The last extensive refit of the ship occurred in 1919-20, and is referred to in Mr. McQueen's "Echoes of Old Clyde Paddle Wheels", in that delightful chapter "By Heid Mark". She thenceforth reverted to the Banavie-Inverness run till 10th June, 1927, carrying on the Lochness mail run till 29th October.

Her end came in December, 1927, when, at the age of eighty-three years, she was generally acclaimed to be the oldest steamer in the world. She was broken up at the Rose Street Foundry, Inverness, which port had been her home for so many years. Subsequently a rumour gained currency to the effect that she had become a house-boat on the Norfolk Broads; but Mr. F. Burtt, author of "Cross-Channel and Coastal Paddle Steamers", as a result of a personal visit, was able to ascertain that this *Glengarry* house-boat was none other than the Southern Railway Company's P.S. *Lymington*, and in no way connected with the veteran of the Caledonian Canal.

.   .   .   .

In 1845 Messrs. Tod & McGregor built for the Castles Company the third *Windsor Castle*, followed in 1846 by *Dunrobin Castle*. The former was launched by Miss Mary Gillies Thomson on 24th May, 1845 and performed her first run from Glasgow to Gourock, Dunoon and Rothesay on Saturday, 28th June, 1845. She was known as "the fastest on the Clyde" and sailed from Rothesay to Glasgow in 2 hours, 28 minutes; but she was very tender, and was scrapped when quite new, her steeple engine being installed in *Dunrobin Castle* in 1846. The latter was an iron clipper-bowed paddle steamer, also said to have been "fast but cranky". Like so many others of this fleet she passed in 1851 to Messrs. Denny, and on 3rd June, 1853 was sold to Russian owners at Krondstadt, being re-named *Telegraph*.

Other additions to the Castle fleet were *Alert* and *Vale of Leven*, purchased in 1845 and *Maid of Islay* in July, 1846, the last-named having been operating for them from the previous year. The first-named generally maintained the West Loch Tarbert-Islay connexion, but in June, 1846 was advertised by Messrs. Burns to sail on the Clyde. *Vale of Leven* had been owned by the Dumbarton & Glasgow Steam Packet Company. All three left the fleet later in 1846, *Maid of Islay* being sold in October to William Cunningham Townley, Master Mariner, Liverpool.

G. & J. Burns (*contd.*)

In 1847 also Messrs. Burns acquired three steamers built three years earlier for the Glasgow, Paisley & Greenock Railway Company's subsidiary company, viz. *Pioneer*, *Pilot* and *Petrel*. *Pilot*, among other services for Messrs. Burns, performed that from Oban to Ballachulish and Fort William in 1849, and in 1850 was for a short time on Loch Lomond, the Caledonian & Dumbartonshire Junction Railway having been opened from Bowling to Balloch in July that year and leased by Messrs. Burns. The *Waterwitch* and *Prince Albert* of the Loch Lomond Steam Boat Company (in which Messrs. Burns also had an interest) also connected with the railway, these two steamers proceeding to Inverarnan with coach connexions in summer to Oban by Loch Awe; to Glencoe, Fort William and Inverness; and by Killin and Taymouth Castle to Aberfeldy, thence by Dunkeld to Perth. There were coaches from Tarbert also to Oban by Glen Croe and Inveraray, and from Inversnaid to join the steamer *Rob Roy* on Loch Katrine. After striking a submerged rock off Rowardennan she was raised, but was soon sold to Captain Gillies, who ran her between Glasgow and the Holy Loch till she was sold to Dublin owners. *Petrel* remained with Messrs. Burns till sold at the beginning of 1851 with some of the others of their steamers to Messrs. Denny, being then under the management of W. F. Johnstone. Later she became a Sunday breaker under Henry Sharp, and was broken up in 1886.

P.S. "Pioneer" (I). This was one of the three steamers above-mentioned; and after alterations she took up the Glasgow-Ardrishaig summer service following her transfer to Messrs. Hutcheson in 1851, in succession to *Merlin*. She continued thereon during that season.

She was a two-masted iron steamer, with slanting stem and one funnel aft, and like the other two members of the Greenock Railway fleet, had been built by Messrs. Barr & McNab at Paisley. She was fitted with a steeple engine.

When *Mountaineer* appeared in 1852, *Pioneer* was sent north to Oban for the Crinan, Mull, and Fort William services in succession to *Shandon*, but returned to her old route during the winter months at times. In the summers of 1862-4 she was on the Staffa and Iona run on Tuesdays, Thursdays and Saturdays, and on the Oban-Corpach service on Mondays, Wednesdays, and Fridays. She was also for a time on the Oban-Gairloch summer service instituted in 1875 which in later years became so closely identified with *Gael*.

In 1862 she went ashore at Silvercraigs, and on 14th March was towed to Messrs. Barclay, Curle's for overhaul. She was re-boilered, and about this time was given a beautiful clipper bow and decorated stern; in this condition she was an exceedingly attractive-looking craft. In May, 1868 she was given feathering floats. She lost her mainmast in the spring of 1872 and appears to have been lengthened by 27 feet in the winter of 1874-5: and at the same time the other major alterations were carried out, namely the substitution of slightly slanting straight stem, the addition of a second funnel and saloons. In this guise much of her former attractiveness had vanished, though it is difficult to resist the appeal of two funnels; and her interior arrangements had been much improved. From 1881 she was on the Sound of Mull service from Oban, in connexion with the railway then recently opened. Her career was a long and honourable one, and although she was stranded in Loch Sunart in 1888, she reached the ripe old age of fifty-one before being broken up in August, 1895, having been withdrawn from service two years earlier and laid up at Glasgow.

For the benefit of readers not very familiar with the West Highlands, it is appropriate to point out here that the original "Royal Route" embraced the journey from Glasgow to Inverness by way of the Crinan and Caledonian Canals, in stages thus: Glasgow to Ardrishaig by steamer *via* Kyles of Bute; Ardrishaig to Crinan (canal), originally by track-boat, later by steamer *Linnet*; Crinan to Oban and Corpach by steamer (in either one or two stages), coach from Corpach to Banavie, and finally Banavie to Inverness (canal) by steamer. The through service was operated in summer only, of course. With considerable modifications it continued in being for many years.

"Maid of Perth." Acquired in time for the 1847 season, this track-boat appears to have succeeded *Thornwood*. In an article in the *Greenock Advertiser* describing the damage to the Canal in 1859 was the following:—

> "Both the reaches of the Canal, at the east and at the west ends of the summit, each about four miles long, having remained uninjured, the Messrs. Hutcheson, ever anxious for the comfort of passengers by the "Royal Route", proceeded to disentangle the track-boat from the ruins of the house in which it had been laid up for the winter, along with an older colleague, long kept in reserve, and to convey them, one to each of the reaches, so as to continue the passenger accommodation on the same footing as formerly, an omnibus being intended to ply on the mile of road which intervenes, for parties unable or unwilling to walk."

"Sunbeam." This track-boat had cabins 20 feet by 12 feet and 12 feet by 6 feet as well as a canopy 18 feet by 10 feet, plate glass windows, draperies and curtains. She was stoutly built, the hull above the waterline being painted in oak graining and the deck cabin, which had large windows, done in white. A timber awning extended across the rear, supported on four pillars, surmounted by gilt crowns. A decorated scroll filigree style of panel extended the length of the cabin roof. These special fittings were for the visit of Queen Victoria to the Highlands in August, 1847, and the *Sunbeam* had the distinction of conveying Her Majesty through the Crinan Canal, which originated the title "The Royal Route".

The Queen commented on this part of her journey in "Leaves from our Journal of our Life in the Highlands" thus:

> "At five we reached Loch Gilp and all landed at Lochgilphead (Ardrishaig). We and our people drove through the village to the Crinan Canal, where we entered a most magnificently decorated barge, drawn by three horses ridden by postillions in scarlet."

The track-boats were succeeded by T.S.S. *Linnet* in 1866, but lay in the Canal near Crinan for a considerable number of years, *Sunbeam* being used on occasion as an overflow vessel at busy times.

P.S. "Cygnet" (I). Throughout the history of the fleet we know of only two cases of twin-sister-ships. *Cygnet* (I) and *Lapwing* (I) were the first pair, the second pair consisting of *Lochearn* and *Lochmor* of 1930; while *Hebrides* (II), *Clansman* (IV) and *Columba* (II) constitute the only "triplets". The first pair were rather odd-looking, their design

being governed mainly by the restrictions imposed by the dimensions
of the Crinan Canal locks. They traded between Glasgow and
Inverness, avoiding the circuitous route round the Mull of Kintyre.
Passengers were carried, but it may be assumed that cargo was their
mainstay. By 1851 *Cygnet* was performing some runs to Easdale,
Oban, Tobermory and Salen (Loch Sunart).

These ships had a rounded form of bow, to assist in nosing their
way through the canal lock-gates, this feature being noticeable also on
Linnet, Gondolier, Gairlochy, etc. Paddles were let in flush with the
bulwarks, and each ship had two masts, and a tall funnel (abaft the
paddles). The stern was round and originally a folding bowsprit was
fitted.

Although navigation round "the Mull" was avoided, experienced
travellers will remember that north of Crinan the sea can be quite
bad-tempered on occasion, and our two little friends must have given
their supporters some fun for their money until Oban was
approached.

Cygnet was launched as *Ben Nevis*, but never sailed as such, the
Burns influence having made itself manifest in the nomenclature of
the vessels just as this little steamer was being prepared for sea. In
1882 she was wrecked in Lochailort, to which she had been sent for a
cargo of wood.

P.S. "Lapwing" (I). As far as is ascertainable *Cygnet* and her
sister were similar in design and service, though *Lapwing* was slightly
longer, and inherited the engine and boiler from *Helen McGregor*.
She was lost comparatively early, being sunk in 1859 off Kintyre by
collision in a fog, with *Islesman*, then sailing for Mr. Orme.

.   .   .   .

In the same year in which the foregoing appeared there was also
added to the Burns fleet *Plover* (I), which formed the connecting link
between Glasgow and Bowling for passengers making the Loch
Lomond tour, there being at that time no railway between these
points. Messrs. Burns in 1850 disposed of their interests in the Loch
Lomond Steamboat Company and in the Caledonian & Dumbartonshire Junction Railway (from Bowling to Balloch), and so had no
longer any reason for providing a steamer service between Glasgow
and Bowling. *Plover* was therefore sold, and went to Wm. Denny &
Bros. She is best remembered on account of the explosion of one of
her boilers on 5th February, 1851. She was sold in August, 1852 to the
Lancashire & Furness Railway Co. for their Barrow trade. After
leaving the Clyde she was lost in 1861.

.   .   .   .

William Ainslie

Mr. William Ainslie, of Fort William, commenced to operate steamer and coach services to the West Highlands in December, 1845 and in August of the following year advertised the *Marquis of Breadalbane* Coach from Glasgow by the Clyde, Dumbarton, Lochlomond, Inverarnan Inn, Glenfalloch, Tyndrum, Dalmally, Glenorchy, Coalchurin Castle, Lochawe, Bencruichan, Bunaw, Taynailt, Lochetive, Connel, Dunstaffnage and Dunolly Castles to Oban. (The names are so spelt in the advertisment). The journey was accomplished by coach, and by steamer on Loch Lomond, in about twelve hours from Glasgow to Oban, from which there was a steamer connexion to Fort William. The New Swift Steamer *Queen of Beauty* was to sail from Fort William at 5 a.m. and from Oban at half-past 7 a.m. on Tuesdays, Thursdays and Saturdays, to Staffa and Iona returning to Oban and Fort William on the same evenings.

This vessel, dating from 1844, had been fitted with "Kibble's Patent Chain Floats", which were, however, unsuccessful. A pair of ordinary paddle-wheels was substituted in 1845, propelled by a side-lever engine, made by Robert Napier for the Dumbarton steamer *Leven* in 1824. This, his first marine engine, for many years could be seen at Dumbarton, erected on vacant ground at the foot of the Rock, as a monument to the builder: it is now in the Shopping Centre.

Along with the other two steamers of the Ainslie fleet, *Queen of Beauty* was acquired by Messrs. Burns in June, 1849, and was stated to have been re-named *Merlin*: but the registers show her as broken up without change of name.

The following from *Railway and Shipping Journal*, was quoted in the *Glasgow Herald*, of Monday, 22nd April, 1850:—

"The *Merlin*, a new steamer, has just been fitted out by Messrs. Thomas Wingate & Co., for Messrs. Burns to form part of the latter's system of Clyde steamers, and contains so many improvements and additions in the steamer to what have already been known on the Clyde, that we think a brief description will be interesting. The vessel is of the ordinary improved class of iron passage steamers that have been introduced to compete, as far as possible, with the swifter mode of conveyance, the railway. Instead, however, of being fitted with ordinary engines, she had had put in engines of a novel and peculiar modification in the mode of condensation and the method by which their pumps work. The condensation is effected by distillation by conducting the steam into horizontal tubes ten feet long each, that lie in iron boxes, placed in the bilges of the vessel, one each side of the engines, through which boxes a continuous rush of water takes place as the vessel moves along; and the emptying of these tubes is effected by small steam engines working the pumps, independent of and isolated from the main engines. Whether the vessel be moving or not, the vacuum in the condenser is kept perfect and the boilers supplied with distilled steam, as if the vessel herself were carrying on. This mode of condensation was contemplated by James Watt, attempted by Cartwright, experimented on by David Napier and patented by Hall, but never perfectly successful till now.

The other improvements introduced into the *Merlin* are the feathering paddle-floats, which give a greater propelling surface, and D. Napier's upright tubular boilers, which can be worked with the same security as if on freshwater, and free from brine, no matter how salt or dirty the fluid may be through which the vessel herself is obliged to pass. In addition the *Merlin* is steered from the platform betwixt the paddles: she has her cooking apparatus placed so that the smoke escapes by the main funnel: and she has all her windows, companion and cabin entrance so placed that the deck from stem to stern is altogether unbroken and uninterrupted, as a promenade. Her cabins are larger than usual, the saloon being capacious enough for 100 passengers, and the fore-cabin sufficiently large and roomy to give dining accommodation to thirty more. The *Merlin* is as perfect a specimen of a first-class Clyde steamer as could be desired. On Saturday last, with her spirited owner and friends she effected the eighty miles, Glasgow-Ardrishaig—eighty miles against the tide—in five-and-a-quarter hours."

The certificate from Thomas Wingate & Co. dated 2nd June, 1851 states she was built in 1850. Possibly parts of the *Queen of Beauty* may have been incorporated. *Merlin* remained with Messrs. Burns for less than a year, being sold for the Rothesay service under W. F. Johnstone's management. She was in collision at the Broomielaw on 18th October, 1853 and was sunk for a time at Napier's wharf. She ceased sailing after being damaged in a severe storm in 1856.

Readers will recollect that the old steamer *Maid of Morven* was sold in 1841. After being in the ownership of Mr. McKenzie of Kessock Ferry she was acquired by Mr. William Ainslie and in 1846 was advertised by Dugald McIntyre, his Agent in Glasgow, to sail to Fort William, calling at Easdale, Oban and Appin. She was one of the three steamers taken over from Mr. Ainslie by Messrs. Burns in June, 1849 and was broken up before the end of 1850.

P.S. "Curlew." The third of the Ainslie steamers taken over had a very interesting history. Built as *Loch Lomond* in 1837 by David Napier and placed by him in service on that loch, she was, on 7th March, 1846, purchased by Mr. William Ainslie, and transferred to the Caledonian Canal under the name *Glencoe*, operating from Gairlochy (in connexion with coaches from Fort William) to Dochgarroch for Inverness. For her entry to the Burns fleet (and first registration) she was re-named *Curlew* and became one of the members of the original Hutcheson fleet in 1851, when she was operating from Inverness to Cromarty, Invergordon, Burghead and Little Ferry twice weekly, as an extension to the Glasgow-Inverness sailings by *Cygnet* and *Lapwing*. She had one deck and a quarter deck, and two masts, one of which was removed in July, 1851. She had a standing bowsprit and figurehead, and square stern. She would appear not to have been in commission after 1853, and by 1855 had been sold to Liverpool owners, passing to Messrs. Willoughby for the Tranmere ferry about 1858: by them she was broken up in 1862.

G. & J. Burns (*contd.*)

The last addition to the Burns West Highland fleet appears to have been *Lochfine*, acquired in 1850 from Mr. William Roxburgh. This was the first screw steamer in their fleet, and the first in the West Highland trade, for which she had been built in 1847. She did not long remain with Messrs. Burns, being sold in June, 1851, to the Dumbarton Steamboat Company. Thereafter she sailed with cargo only (and without masts or bowsprit), between Glasgow and Dumbarton. Her career ended about 1896, when she was broken up following a collision with Glasgow Bridge.

During 1850 Messrs. Burns' passengers for Kilmun were being conveyed by the steamer *Express* by connexion from Kirn, and neither they nor their successors appear to have operated any subsequent Holy Loch service.

A general rearrangement of the Irish and West Highland services took place early in 1851. At the end of the previous year Messrs. Thomson & MacConnell retired from the Liverpool and Belfast trades. The West Highland services, which had been run by them and Messrs. Burns in association since 1839, passed to Messrs. G. & J. Burns alone, and this trade was handed over by them to Messrs. David Hutcheson & Co. from February, 1851.

CHAPTER II

DAVID HUTCHESON & COMPANY, 1851—1879

IT was in February, 1851, that the firm of David Hutcheson & Co. was formed, the partners being David and Alexander Hutcheson (who had been heads of departments with G. & J. Burns) and David MacBrayne, a nephew of the Messrs. Burns. The senior partner is commemorated by a monument on the Island of Kerrera, bearing the following inscription:—

"Erected by a grateful public in memory of David Hutcheson, by whose energy and enterprise the benefits of greatly improved steam communication were conferred on the West Highlands and Islands of Scotland."

He retired from business in 1876, and Alexander Hutcheson in 1878. David MacBrayne, whose name is so familiar, was an outstanding personality at the firm's headquarters at 119 (originally known as 83) Hope Street, Glasgow.

To the new firm was transferred the West Highland trade, together with eight steamers and two track-boats, viz. *Shandon*, *Dolphin*, *Pioneer*, *Duntroon Castle*, *Edinburgh Castle*, *Cygnet*, *Lapwing* and *Curlew*, together with the Crinan Canal track-boats *Maid of Perth* and *Sunbeam*.

For a few months *Inverary Castle* and *Rothsay Castle* were employed by Messrs. Hutcheson on the Lochfyne run on charter, but in April this trade was transferred to the Glasgow & Lochfine S.P. Co.

From 1879 Mr. MacBrayne operated the business in his own name. By this time nearly a dozen steamers, whose names had become household words, formed part of the fleet, including *Pioneer*, *Glengarry*, *Mountaineer*, *Glencoe*, *Clydesdale*, *Iona*, *Linnet*, *Chevalier*, *Gondolier*, *Clansman* and *Columba*. In 1902 Mr. MacBrayne's sons, Mr. David Hope MacBrayne and Mr. Laurence MacBrayne became partners with their father, receiving each a quarter share in the ships; and the shares of the younger son were transferred to the elder in December, 1905.

A private limited company was incorporated, operating from 1st January, 1906, with Mr. David Hope MacBrayne at its head. Mr. MacBrayne (senior) then retired but retained a half-share in the ships; and he survived only for another year, his death occurring in Glasgow on 26th January, 1907, when he was in his 93rd year. His executrix transferred to the Limited Company his shares in the ships.

In 1912 the fleet reached its maximum size, when thirty-six vessels were on the books.

The next change occurred in 1928 when circumstances demanded a reconstructive policy in connexion with the renewal of the mail contract which expired that year. The whole subject was brought up in Parliament, and as a result of much deliberation—during which various alternative schemes were made known and discussed—the London, Midland and Scottish Railway Co. and Coast Lines Ltd. acquired the business and formed a new Company, named David MacBrayne (1928) Ltd. In 1934 the name reverted to David Mac-Brayne Ltd., this being now a dormant Company.

It is not inappropriate to add here that the Company's claim to the title "The Royal Route" is based on the fact that her late Majesty Queen Victoria traversed it in part in 1847 and afterwards, on two different occasions, when visiting the Highlands, sailed in the firm's steamers. Again in 1902 their Majesties King Edward VII and Queen Alexandra cruised through the West Highlands in the Royal Yacht, visiting many of the scenes of interest.

The first mail contract appears to have been secured by the Company about 1855 and the title "Glasgow & Highland Royal Mail Steamers", which was so well known, was brought into use somewhat later.

It is of interest to note that in 1923 Mr. Laurence MacBrayne, younger son, gave to the University of Glasgow in memory of his father Mr. David MacBrayne the house in which the latter had lived. This is No. 11 Park Circus Place, Glasgow, now known as the MacBrayne Hall. It is used as a hall of residence for men students from the West Highlands and provides accommodation for about forty.

References to the "Company" mean the Hutcheson/MacBrayne organisation whether this was a company in a strict legal sense or otherwise.

P.S. "Mountaineer" (I). Messrs. Hutcheson, having by now taken stock of their position, decided at the close of their first season to provide a better steamer than *Pioneer* (I) for the Ardrishaig service. *Mountaineer* (I) was the result. Mr. McQueen gives us an excellent account of the new crack ship in the "Echoes of Old Clyde Paddle Wheels", and tells us that she was launched from the Govan yard of Messrs. J. & G. Thomson on 29th May, 1852 by Master David Hutcheson, nephew of two of the owners.

On trial on 22nd July she "ran the lights" (Cloch to Cumbrae) at a fraction below fifteen knots, which in those days was no mean performance.

The vessel was a very fine specimen in her day, flush decked with slanting stem finely decorated on each side with gilded carving of a Highlander in full costume holding a greyhound in leash, square stern also embellished, two funnels and a single mast. On the cover of the lower saloon companionway was a goat carved in wood.

Being primarily a passenger-carrying steamer, the *Mountaineer* was distinguished by the excellence of her accommodation and furnishings. The work of the artist and decorator was liberally incorporated. The result was that she at once became a popular vessel and traffic increased to such a marked degree on the Ardrishaig route that her place was taken by the first *Iona* after only three seasons.

Transferred to Oban in 1855 she maintained the Staffa and Iona and Fort William services in summer with the *Pioneer* and returned to the Ardrishaig route during the winter. Records show that in the early 'sixties the *Mountaineer* also ran to Crinan, while during 1855 she also performed some excursions from Oban to Loch Coruisk.

In the course of her life she was lengthened some twenty-one feet and in 1876 given deck saloons fore and aft.

Mention was made earlier of the association with the Oban-Gairloch route of the *Pioneer*. The *Mountaineer* was on this run for a time and it was when inward bound for Oban on 27th September, 1889 that she met her end through stranding on the Lady Rock near Duart Castle. The *Oban Times* referred to this disaster once or twice in August, 1933. From these accounts it appears that the weather thickened in the vicinity of the Lismore light and the vessel got off her course. Hitherto the generally accepted theory was that the ship went ashore as a result of a machinery breakdown. The hull was but little damaged and there was no loss of life, but before salvage could be effected bad weather set in; and on 7th October, 1889 she broke in two, and the after part sank in deep water. The crew had saved her paddles, funnels and part of her machinery.

·   ·   ·   ·   ·   ·   ·

A letter to the *Glasgow Herald* of 1st September, 1897 refers to a *screw* steamer *Culloden* sailing to Rothesay in the 1850s chartered to Messrs. D. Hutcheson & Co.

P.S. "Chevalier" (I). This steamer's career was very brief. She was launched on 25th March, 1853 and was described as "sleeping 50 cabin passengers and with decorations of a superior class, though quite in accordance with those of the *Mountaineer*, *Dolphin*, *Pioneer* and others". She had a raised quarterdeck, two masts, standing bowsprit and square stern, and was the first member of the Hutcheson fleet with oscillating engines. She worked during 1853-4 from Glasgow *via* Mull of Kintyre to Oban and Skye having *Islay* (I) by agreement as her opposite number, leaving Glasgow on Thursdays and making the same calls, but including Broadford. She was really the successor to *Duntroon Castle*. The passage from Oban to Broadford took twelve hours, and fourteen to Portree; and she seems to have been the first Hutcheson ship to include Stornoway and, on certain runs, Scrabster for Thurso. She was wrecked on Iron Rock, Sound of Jura on 24th

November, 1854. The decks were covered only at high water, and it was thought that the boilers, funnel and the greater part of the engines might be salved. The wreck was exposed for sale on 31st July, 1855.

Two Friends and **Robert**. These sailing vessels were registered in name of David Hutcheson & Co. in May, 1854. It is thought they may have been bought with cargoes of coal.

P.S. "Iona" (I). We have now reached the beginning of the famous *Iona* era. The story of the *Ionas* has been told before but we do not think any apology is called for in repeating it here, as these steamers became so famous and set up such a standard for the world to praise and admire. The first of the name was described as "the Queen of the Clyde steamers" in Hugh Macdonald's "Days at the Coast" (1857).

From what has been written above concerning the first *Pioneer* and *Mountaineer* readers will have gathered that, as a result of Messrs. Hutcheson's enterprise, the Ardrishaig route was developing rapidly and fast becoming, if it had not already been, the "star turn" of all their West Highland services.

We find, therefore, that after only three seasons the *Mountaineer*—crack ship and pride of the fleet—was relegated to less important work to make way for *Iona* (I), though reverting to the Ardrishaig station in spring and autumn.

The association of the Company with Messrs. J. & G. Thomson had already occurred with the building of the *Mountaineer* and this remained almost unbroken as far as the construction of the more famous ships was concerned right down to 1885, when the *Grenadier* appeared, a period of thirty-three years.

Thomsons therefore were entrusted with the order for the new vessel and produced a beautiful flush-decked craft having a curved slanting bow, square stern, two funnels and single mast. She was given oscillating engines, and these drove her on trial at some 17 knots.

In July, 1855 she was chartered for the ceremony of visiting the Clyde Lighthouses. She attained immediate success on the Ardrishaig summer service on which she spent eight seasons. In August, 1861 she broke down in Kyles of Bute, and the *Dolphin* from Ardrishaig soon took the passengers and mails there. Temporary repairs enabled the *Iona* to steam slowly back to Glasgow, being overtaken by the *Dolphin* on her inward run, near Port Glasgow. Had not the American Civil War intervened, it is probable that the career of the first *Iona* would have been a long one. Unfortunately the temptation to part with ships at that time at extraordinarily profitable prices proved too strong for Messrs. Hutcheson, and at the close of her eighth season *Iona* (I) was sold. On 2nd October, 1862, having left Glasgow about 2 p.m. for Nassau (for blockade-running), in ballast trim, fitted with a mainmast, and loaded with coals for her own consumption, she was, when approaching Gourock Bay struck on the starboard quarter abaft the paddles about 7 p.m., by S.S. *Chanticleer* returning from trials and sank stern foremost in deep water in about twenty minutes, fortunately without loss of life. The wreck has in recent years been located by divers.

P.S. "Clansman" (I). In the same year as *Iona* (I) came out, the first possessor of another illustrious name appeared from Thomson's yard. She was intended for more arduous duty than her contemporary, namely the Glasgow, Oban, Skye and Stornoway route in succession to the first *Chevalier*, and this service kept her less in the limelight. She was similar to *Chevalier* but three-masted. It is recorded that on her first voyage back from Stornoway *Clansman*'s speed averaged thirteen miles per hour. No better reading of the working conditions aboard *Clansman* is available than in Alexander Smith's "A Summer in Skye", where a fascinating account is given from first-hand knowledge and experience, with a delightful description of calling at Arisaig.

After fourteen years' service she went aground in thick fog on Deep Island, off Sanda, on 21st July, 1869, and became a total wreck.

Glasgow & Lochfine Steam Packet Company

In February, 1857 Messrs. Hutcheson took over the above concern, which had been formed in 1851 to carry on the Glasgow-Lochfyne cargo trade previously in the hands of Mr. William Roxburgh, and of Messrs. Burns. The partners in the new company were Thomas Brownlie, Merchant and Builder, Glasgow, and William Roxburgh, Merchant, there, the Glasgow agents being Messrs. D. Roxburgh & Co.

The first vessel on record owned by William Roxburgh was *Lochfine*, built of iron by Messrs. Denny in 1847. Schooner-rigged with bowsprit, but no figurehead, she had a length of only 74.5 feet, and so was able to make use of the Crinan Canal. Unfortunately, on her maiden voyage, in December, 1847, *Mary Jane* ran into her; and, as the damage appeared slight, she set out on her homeward run from Oban. She got only as far as the Cumbraes where, leaking badly, she was taken in tow by the tug *Defiance*, sinking in shallow water in Cartsdyke Bay. She was duly raised, and during 1848 was advertised by Captain Duncan Colquhoun to sail for Fort William *via* Greenock, Ardrishaig, Easdale, Oban, Appin and Corran and calling at intermediate ports and jetties, from Glasgow every Tuesday at 7 a.m. Each Thursday she fitted in a day excursion from Fort William at 5 a.m., arriving on Friday in Glasgow in time to load further cargo for sailing again on the following Tuesday. In 1850 she was sold to Messrs. Burns.

The Glasgow & Lochfine Company acquired from Sir James Matheson his steamer *Mary Jane* in August, 1851, followed by *Inverary Castle* and *Dunoon Castle* from Messrs. Denny, in August and September respectively.

Dunoon Castle was sold in November, 1854 to Michael McLachlan, Fish Merchant, Glasgow, who died on the 14th of the same month, the vessel then passing to his widow as his executrix. It is understood that the *Dunoon Castle* was wrecked and broken up several years prior to November, 1864, when her register was closed. The cross-head of her engine did duty for many years in the works of Messrs. Stewart & Sons, Paper-makers, McNeil Street, Glasgow.

P.S. "Mary Jane"/"Glencoe" (II). We have already paid homage to the veteran *Glengarry* and we now pass to a ship whose merit is not inferior. In the realm of seniority *Glencoe* existed, in all, two years longer than *Glengarry* and the longevity of both vessels—the difference being practically negligible—was amazing and spoke volumes for the quality of the material and soundness of workmanship which went to the making of ships about the middle of last century.

Mary Jane was built to the order of Mr. (afterwards Sir) James Matheson of Stornoway, being named after his wife. Some authorities thought that the ship was built as the *Windsor Castle* for the Castle Company, but further investigation has resulted in this surmise being negatived, although it is possible that some material from the other ship—scrapped when only a year old—was incorporated. The *Mary Jane* was registered at London till August, 1851.

The original rig was that of a flush decked steamer with fiddle-bow and bowsprit, and two masts, the engine being of the steeple type with single cylinder. She was originally steered by a wheel at the stern.

Her first voyage, on 18th June, 1846, was from Glasgow to Oban, Tobermory, Portree and off the intermediate ports to Armadale, Balmacarra (Lochalsh), Kyleakin, Broadford, etc. She plied also from Stornoway to Lochinver on alternate Mondays, then direct to Portree. It is interesting to note that the Stornoway traffic in the 'forties was in private hands; though it is significant that *Mary Jane* was sold by Sir James Matheson in April, 1851, just after Messrs. Hutcheson had taken over the Highland services. From 1849 Sir James had also the steamer *Marquis of Stafford*, launched on 29th September in the previous year, and for a time registered as owned by the Duke of Sutherland, which operated mainly between Stornoway and Poolewe in succession to various sailing vessels, as also did the later P.S. *Ondine*, between Stornoway and Ullapool, carrying the Stornoway mails.

Mary Jane passed into the ownership of the Glasgow & Lochfine Steam Packet Company in 1851 and entered the Hutcheson fleet in 1857. She continued with her new owners as consort to *Inverary Castle* running between Glasgow and Inveraray for eighteen years, and in

1875 was withdrawn for a higher calling. Alterations and additions were made; she was lengthened; and, when she re-appeared, it was without the mainmast and bowsprit, but with a slanting bow, detached deck-saloon aft, and the name *Glencoe*. It was in this guise that she became so well known all over the West Coast.

Emerging thus as a saloon steamer, she was able to take her place as an up-to-date passenger carrier and a few years later the saloon deck became continuous. Among the services allotted to her were the following:—Oban to Tobermory, Loch Scavaig, Coolin Hills, Portree and Gairloch, each way three times per week, a new route, which she inaugurated in June, 1875; Greenock-Ardrishaig mail service in winter; Portree mail service (from Strome Ferry, later from Kyle of Lochalsh); Oban-Fort William-Corpach. From 1890, on a threat of competition from a new company formed in Islay, she was transferred to West Loch Tarbert to succeed the *Fingal*, which had caused complaints, continuing there till herself succeeded by the *Pioneer* (II) in 1905, after which the *Glencoe* became the normal Portree mail steamer, by this time operating from Mallaig and Kyle of Lochalsh. On 17th September, 1909 she exceptionally re-visited Stornoway, taking the place of the *Gael* which had cylinder trouble at Mallaig when about to relieve the *Sheila*. In June-July, 1917 she was back on the Islay mail run. She then commenced a period of short charters, being with the G.& S.W. Railway Co. in November and December, for Ardrossan-Arran; then laid up till 15th April, 1918 when she went to the C.S.P. Co. Ltd. for services from Wemyss Bay and as stand-by boat. In July, 1918 she performed excursions at Oban, then in November and December, 1918 and again in February, 1920 was back on her old Lochfyne station, but for Clyde Cargo Steamers Ltd., relieving *Minard Castle*. In August and November, 1918 she was Portree Mail Steamer, and, 4th and 8th April, 1920, when she was Lochgoil Mail Steamer. Apart from being laid up for most of 1919 and early 1920, she continued on the Portree station for most of the remainder of her life, including in the 1920s the Loch Scavaig excursion.

It appears that she did not figure extensively at the "Mecca" of MacBrayne steamers—namely Oban—except in her early days as *Glencoe*. She was essentially an "all the year round" boat carrying mails, passengers, cargo, and live stock, whereas as is well known, the majority of the saloon paddlers usually hibernated at Bowling or Greenock for eight months of the year. This fact adds to the remarkable degree of longevity of the vessel, particularly when it is realised that such routes as Tarbert-Islay in winter entail at times pretty severe buffeting and anything but plain sailing.

The ship was obviously robust and a good sea boat, though a casual glance would not give that impression. It is not to be forgotten too that she had braved the terrors of the Minch for five years before passing into the Lochfine Company's hands.

The model of a golden eagle over the lower saloon entrance aft was always an object of admiration. It will be recalled that *Glengarry* carried a similar model, the main difference being that *Glengarry*'s eagle was represented with outstretched wings.

A note must be made concerning *Glencoe*'s engines and boilers. The accuracy of Lloyd's Register is rarely questioned, and rightly so. However, it has to be pointed out that the new engine reported by that official publication as having been fitted in 1880 is incorrectly stated. We are indebted again to Mr. McQueen for his investigations in this direction and in a letter to the *Glasgow Herald*, dated 2nd September, 1931, he explained that in 1880 a surface condenser was fitted in place of the original jet type, no other changes being made. This clears up a point which had been in dispute for some time, particularly as the steeple engine which propelled the vessel latterly would have been almost obsolete in 1880. It could scarcely have been new then, but could conceivably have been taken from another old steamer. We know now that this was not the case, but that instead the engine which lay in the basement of the Kelvingrove Art Gallery, but which was scrapped during the second war, was the one supplied by Tod & McGregor when the ship came out in 1846.

As regards boilers, the original horizontal one was replaced in 1883 by another which in 1901 was succeeded by the haystack boiler of *Fusilier* made in 1888. Probably it was from 1883 till 1901 that *Glencoe* carried a tall thin funnel. In 1928 a further re-boilering took place, this time with one of *Grenadier*'s haystacks of 1902. On account of the differences of pressure of the engine after the second re-boilering, two waste-steam pipes were carried—one forward and one aft of the funnel—taking the steam from the safety-valves and reducing valve set to the pressures corresponding to that of the boiler and that for which the engine was designed.

Glencoe's last duty was on the Portree mail service. Having completed her winter's work up north, she paddled away from Skye in May, 1931 to return no more. In June of that year she was brought up to the Broomielaw alongside the new Diesel-electric vessel *Lochfyne* for public exhibition, and great interest was shown in the contrast between the two ships. The *Glencoe* was sold to Ardrossan Dockyard Ltd. on 3rd August and was broken up in the autumn of 1931, with many regrets on the part of Highlanders with a sentimental feeling for the old craft and all that she had done over a period of eighty-five years.

At the time of her demise the old ship shared with the 1846 *Premier* of Weymouth the distinction of being the oldest in the world. *Premier* lasted till 1938; but her duties were far less arduous than those of her Highland contemporary.

P.S. "Inverary Castle"(III)/**"Inveraray Castle."** It is on record that the whole career of this ship was spent on the Glasgow-Inveraray cargo service for various owners, with the exception of part of 1859, when, owing to the closing of the Crinan Canal, she ran from Glasgow to Oban via Mull of Kintyre, and also sailed from Glasgow to Inverness (before lengthening) in April, 1862 and on occasion to Islay, e.g., in January, 1863. (The change in spelling of her name was registered in 1874, though it had appeared earlier in advertisements.) She had operated the Greenock-Ardrishaig mail service from October, 1855 to March, 1856 under the Lochfine Company's contract, as a stop-gap after withdrawal of Caird's Rothesay Castle, apparently employed by Messrs. Hutcheson (by sub-contract) under their first mail contract, on "Columba" timings, but with a call at Strone.

She was twice lengthened, in 1862 and 1873. Originally poop-decked and schooner-rigged, she became flush-decked in 1862 and latterly had a detached deck-saloon aft. She was fitted with feathering floats in May, 1868.

Since cargo carrying was her principal duty, it will be realised that speed was a matter of secondary importance. In fact the whole day from 6 a.m. was occupied in the single run to or from Inveraray. The trade in those days on this route must have been of fair proportions, because two steamers were continuously engaged in it for some eighteen years.

Inveraray Castle's consorts on this station were the famous *Mary Jane* (afterwards *Glencoe*) and, for a time, *Dolphin*. These boats were much employed carrying the celebrated Loch Fyne herring to Glasgow, but this trade decreased on account of the smart screw steamers introduced by the fish merchants, which followed the fishing-boats wherever they might be working and proceeded to the market whenever loaded, thus bringing about a reduction in the schedule services to the Loch Fyne ports. From February, 1875 a call was made by *Inveraray Castle* at Ormidale once a week in each direction; and about this time the service became restricted to three days per week each way.

Inveraray Castle was laid up at Bowling in 1889, after breaking her paddle-shaft on 14th May in that year. She resumed service on 20th June, 1889. In April, 1891 it was reported that she was to be fitted with the engine and boilers salved from *Mountaineer*, but by May, 1892 she was being broken up at Bowling, and her hull was still there in June, 1895, her register being closed on 24th September that year. One of her masts went to *Glencoe*.

P.S. "Duke of Argyll." This steamer was, like *Inverary Castle*, engaged originally in the Loch Fyne trade, her first sailing to Inveraray having taken place on 27th November, 1852. She was built for the Glasgow & Lochfine S.P. Company to take the place of *Dunoon Castle* (of 1826). Lengthened in 1855, *Duke of Argyll* came into the Hutcheson fleet in July 1857, and plied for these owners for about a year only, being accidentally sunk in the Sound of Mull on 12th January, 1858, *en route* to Stornoway. She was raised and beached alongside the pier at Salen on 15th March, 1858, ready for towing to the Clyde and was broken up by 1st December in that year.

Glasgow & Highland S.P. Co.

P.S. "Maid of Lorn"/"Plover" (II). In 1849 this iron steamer was built by Messrs. Wingate, similar in dimensions and general design to Messrs. Burns' *Cygnet* and *Lapwing*, though slightly larger. Like them, she traversed the Crinan Canal; and, on her being commissioned, there was advertised a "new line to the West Highlands" by the "splendid and powerful new steamship *Maid of Lorn*", on a weekly service between Broomielaw and Inverness. Her owners were Alexander Ainslie and others, Trustees of the Glasgow and Highland S.P. Co. From March, 1851 an Agreement with Messrs. Hutcheson regulated the number of voyages by the *Maid of Lorn*, *Cygnet* and *Lapwing*.

Maid of Lorn had a chapter of minor accidents in 1854. On 19th August she broke her shaft off the Treshnish Isles, but managed to reach Tobermory under sail, and was then towed to Glasgow. Later in the year she was twice sunk in the Crinan Canal, but appears to have been little the worse. In 1855 she was advertised also to sail to Oban, Tobermory, Coll, Tiree and Bunessan. On the 28th March, 1857, she entered the Hutcheson fleet and on 21st December, 1858, was sold to Barclay, Curle & Co., by whom she was resold to foreign owners at the beginning of the following year. In February, 1859, however, she was re-purchased by D. Hutcheson & Co., who had just lost *Lapwing*. She was then re-named *Plover*, and ran as consort to *Cygnet* between Glasgow and Inverness. In the Highlands she was nick-named the "Gun-boat". She occasionally appeared on the Loch Fyne cargo run, and is said to have been the last paddle steamer to sail through the Crinan Canal. For a time she operated a service to Loch Sunart, based at Oban (a regular call at Croggan being discontinued from 1877). She was again sold to foreign owners in 1879, but again she did not leave her native country, and her ownership reverted to David MacBrayne, who finally sold her on 1st February, 1883 to William Cumstie Williamson. Shorn of paddles and paddleboxes, she was, off Row (Rhu), Gareloch, moored as hulk, and was sold as such on 27th August, 1891 to Jamieson & Co.

David Hutcheson & Company (*contd.*)

P.S. "Stork." This steamer was built for Messrs. Burns' Liverpool service, and was later on the Belfast run. She was acquired by Messrs. Hutcheson and was sailing in August/September, 1857, from Oban to Portrush every Tuesday and Thursday, returning to Oban on the following day in each case. By 23rd September she had ceased for the season. In 1858 she was placed on the Glasgow-Stornoway service with *Clansman* (I). Her sojourn here was brief, as she was sold in 1861 to the Italian Government.

S.S. "Fingal" (I). This was the first screw steamer owned by Messrs. Hutcheson, for whom she was built in 1861, running for four months only, in succession to the *Stork*, on the Stornoway station along with *Clansman* (I). Her hull was similar in design to that of her immediate successor *Clydesdale* (I), but her tall funnel was placed forward of amidships. She was square-rigged. Like so many others of the coastal ships of the time, she was sold to run the American blockade; and, after capture, she became the Federal gunboat *U.S.S. Atlanta*. Her hull was armour-plated and she was quite unrecognisable as a former West Highland steamer. During part of 1861-2 the Dublin & Glasgow Company's former steamer *Ariel* (at this time owned by Messrs. J. & G. Thomson) was chartered to take the place of *Fingal* on the Stornoway route.

P.S. "Fairy." The twin-hulled P.S. *Alliance* ran on the Caledonian Canal in July, 1861, presumably on charter, until this new vessel should be ready.

This was the first of normal design to have a deck saloon, and was built to run on the Caledonian Canal along with *Edinburgh Castle*, which, since the departure of *Curlew*, had been maintaining the service alone, except while *Alliance* was there. It would appear that there was not at that time sufficient traffic for the two steamers; for it is recorded that in 1862 *Fairy*, being too large for the canal servcice (then three times a week each way, but supplemented by *Cygnet* and *Plover*), was placed on the Staffa and Iona run from Oban; and in September of that year she took up the Glasgow-Ardrishaig sailings in succession to *Iona* (II), just withdrawn to be sold for blockade-running.

The *Fairy* was similar to *Gondolier* as built, i.e., without the navigating bridge, but without a mast.

She was sold in November, 1863 to J. Proudfoot and M. Gray, Glasgow, and her gross tonnage was, for foreign trade, increased to 210, by inclusion of the saloon previously exempt. She may have been engaged in blockade-running. In August, 1866 she was sold in Montevideo to a foreigner and her register was closed.

S.S. "Clydesdale" (I). This handsome steamer was built for the Glasgow-Stornoway bi-weekly cargo and passenger service to take the place of *Fingal* in running alternately with *Clansman* (I), which she did for many years. Launched by Messrs. Thomson in the spring of 1862, she was fitted by them with inverted-cylinder, surface-condensing engines.

She was re-boilered in 1869 and again in 1893, when she received a double-ended boiler in place of (presumably) two single-ended boilers, and at the same time the machinery was compounded by Messrs. Hutson & Son, Glasgow. Two funnels were then fitted instead of one, so that the ship's appearance was altered materially. She always carried two masts, originally with gaffs and latterly with short cross-trees; and her clipper bow and bowsprit gave a beautiful finish to the hull.

The advent of the *Claymore* in 1881 did not mark the end of the association of *Clydesdale* with the Glasgow-Stornoway route, though thereafter she was usually there in the capacity of a relief. In 1882 she was on the Glasgow-Islay route and also on various occasions later, e.g. June-July, 1896. She carried on the Stornoway mail service from about 1886 from Strome Ferry (Kyle of Lochalsh from 1897). (The Portree mail service from Strome Ferry had been taken over by Mr. MacBrayne from the Highland Railway Company in 1880.) From the early 1850s the Stornoway sailings were on certain occasions extended to Scrabster for Thurso, and in 1885 this was operated by the *Clydesdale* as a separate service from Glasgow. From 1889 *Clydesdale* was working from Oban to the Outer Islands, and it was during this period that she visited St. Kilda on certain trips.

The career of *Clydesdale* came to an end in January, 1905, when she stranded on the Lady Rock, and was afterwards dismantled.

P.S. "Iona" (II). Resuming the *Iona* story once more, Messrs. Hutcheson had perforce to take action in time to provide a suitable steamer for the summer service of 1863, since the first *Iona* had passed out of their hands the previous autumn. It would have been a retrograde move to bring back *Mountaineer*, and, in any case, another steamer was wanted somewhere; so *Iona* (II) duly came into being from Thomson's yard. Following generally the lines of her predecessor, she was, however, a saloon steamer and had greater speed, being understood to have attained 18 knots on trial on 24th June, 1863.

The following is an excerpt from the *Illustrated London News:*—

"The new *Iona*, the property of Messrs. David Hutcheson and Co., of Glasgow, was launched from the building-yard of Messrs. J. and G. Thomson, Govan, about a month ago. She was constructed to ply between Glasgow and Ardrishaig, the south-eastern terminus of the Crinan Canal. She had her engines fitted in and was finished at Lancefield. Recently she made a trial-trip over the usual course, between the Cumbrae and Cloch Light-houses, with great success. She is built of iron. Her actual length is 245 ft., and her breadth of beam 25 ft. She has a depth of 9 ft., and she draws little more than 4 ft. of water. Her engine-room, which is uninclosed on three sides save by rails, is a little palace in its airiness and perfect cleanliness. Everything is formed after the newest and most excellent models, her engines being of the oscillating species, and fitted up with tubular boilers, super-heaters, and every new and well-tried improvement. The paddle-wheels, 20 ft. in diameter, are most skilfully constructed, and are furnished with patent feathering floats. But the most singular and attractive feature which distinguishes the new *Iona* is the extensive and comfortable accommodation provided for passengers throughout the whole extent of the vessel. The cabin end of the steamer is fitted up and finished in the most magnificent style of art, combining indeed the beauty, comfort, and all the facilities of a perfectly furnished private mansion. The dining-room is 75 ft. in length. The steerage end of the vessel, although necessarily fitted up in a less luxurious style of art, is nevertheless, correspondingly furnished with all requisite comforts. But the original feature in the new *Iona* is the deck-saloon, some 180 ft. in length, which affords sheltered accommodation for vast numbers of first and second-class passengers. The cabin portion of the deck-saloon is furnished and finished in the richest and most superb style. A range of white and gold pillars runs through the centre; and the windows, which are curtained, are constructed so as to be capable of being opened or shut at will, according to the condition of the weather. The steerage-saloon is also furnished with taste and comfort. There is a post office on board, in front of the saloon. The roof of the saloon, or what might be called the upper deck, forms a safe and splendid promenade. In good sea weather this lofty and extensive observatory will be as luxurious a lounge as the saloons beneath will be in weather of a rainy or tempestuous character. In brief, the new *Iona* is a floating mansion in which a person may go to sea without losing the sense of home."

Once again a promising career was cut short; and, after a short summer season only, purchasers snapped her up for the American Blockade. Her saloons were taken off and succeeded by temporary deckhouses, and she was given a mainmast. She was registered in name of D. McNutt, being re-sold to Charles Hopkins Boster, of Richmond, Virginia. She was not, however, much more fortunate than her predecessor, being sunk near Lundy Island on 2nd February, 1864, while *en route* to U.S.A.

Her place on the Ardrishaig station was temporarily filled by the *Fairy* in September, 1863.

S.S. "Staffa" (II). In April, 1863 a report appeared in the *Glasgow Herald* to the effect that the new screw steamer *Ossian*, building for Messrs. Hutcheson, was getting into frames, but would not be launched for several months. So far no further trace of a ship under this name has been found, and it seems likely that she was re-named before completion. *Staffa* was a small screw steamer, two-masted, single-funnelled, and having a straight stem and round stern. Originally flush-decked, she later was decked to the bow; and a navigating bridge was then provided, forward of the funnel. The arrangement of her accommodation was, after these alterations, similar to that of *Clydesdale*, though she was, of course, considerably smaller. In 1866 she was advertised on the Glasgow-Oban run *via* Mull of Kintyre, together with *Clansman* (I) and *Clydesdale* (I); but whereas these carried on northwestwards, it was to Inverness that *Staffa* went. During her overhaul in November, 1877 her relief was the then new *Lochiel*.

On the Glasgow-Inverness service, in 1884 she had as consort the new *Cavalier*. She ran aground on Cathsgeir Rock outside the west of Gigha, on 23rd August, 1886, and the passengers were safely landed. Next day she broke in two and foundered.

P.S. "Iona" (III). On the sale of *Iona* (II) no time was lost in placing the order with Messrs. J. & G. Thomson and the laying down of *Iona* (III), the *Iona* which became so well known and latterly the oldest member of the fleet. In those days Clydeside must have been thinking that this idea of one *Iona* per annum was about to become a habit! However, as things turned out, the necessity for another vessel of the name did not arise for a period of seventy-two years after the third of the name assumed duty. The fourth was a mere lighter, re-named to preserve the name *Iona*; and the fifth and sixth motor launches.

The subject of our writing was launched on 10th May, 1864 described as the *New Iona* and on trial gave a good account of herself, though it is narrated that her speed was a shade less than that of her predecessor. Her appearance was beautiful in every way, and she was a joy to the eye. The characteristic curved slanting bow was fitted, and alleyways extended right round the deck saloons. It is on record that she inherited the saloons, together with some of the furnishings, from *Iona* (II), since these items were still new and were not required for the service the latter was destined to, but never did, perform.

Originally fitted with short funnels, and without a bridge, she was very similar to *Iona* (II). A navigating bridge was erected between the paddle-boxes during the winter of 1870-1 and Chadburn's telegraphs and steam steering-gear were installed in 1873, the *Iona* being one of the first ships so fitted. The first and second sets of boilers were horizontal. The latter dating from 1875 were succeeded in 1891 by a pair of haystacks, which served her for the remainder of her career. The simple oscillating engines underwent little change, other than the provision of a surface condenser by Messrs. Hutson & Corbett, during the 1891 reboilering, in place of the original jet type. Steel paddle-floats took the place of wooden ones.

Iona (III) was, of course, put on the Ardrishaig summer service, and settled down to this for fourteen years, when the great *Columba* appeared and took pride of place. *Iona*, however, remained on the same route for a year or two, giving an additional service. In 1880 she was transferred to Oban in preparation for additional traffic for the opening of the railway, and was given a considerable re-fit, including an oil-gas lighting installation: and she had an extra lifeboat on the starboard quarter near the bow, for the more exposed route from Crinan to Oban and Corpach.

The season of 1886 found her back on the Clyde, running from Ardrishaig in the morning to Broomielaw, which she left, on the return journey, at 1.30 p.m. She provided, therefore, with *Columba*, a double daily service, which indicates that the passenger traffic at that period must have been extensive.

It must be borne in mind that in pre motor-car days road traffic was but the merest fraction of what it is today, and in the West Highlands in particular, with very scanty railway connexions, passengers naturally travelled on the steamers and took full advantage of all the facilities offered. Early in the present century we find the summer traffic demanding even more from the *Iona*, and from 1904 she was hard put to it, as the following daily itinerary shows. Leaving Ardrishaig at about 5.45 in the morning (not infrequently with a flock of sheep on board occupying the whole of the promenade deck, to the passengers' amazement!) she proceeded to Wemyss Bay, putting in calls at Tarbert and the Kyles of Bute. She then returned to Ardrishaig non-stop, leaving Wemyss Bay at 10.40 and arriving more or less simultaneously with the *Columba* at 12.50. That completed half the day's work. Next followed, on one or two days a week only, a short trip to Otter Ferry in Loch Fyne and back to Ardrishaig, whence she left again for Wemyss Bay, and returned finally to Ardrishaig about 10 p.m.—altogether a 17-hour day.

During the first war, she remained on the Clyde, operating on the Ardrishaig route from Wemyss Bay, till relieved in this by *Columba* in August, 1916. She was at that time painted grey all over. Thereafter she was chartered to The Caledonian Steam Packet Co., Ltd., sailing between Wemyss Bay and Rothesay, etc., having for a short period the buff funnels of the Caledonian Company.

During the winter of 1918-19 new saloons were fitted, the fore saloon thereafter extending about ten feet farther forward than previously. She was employed for a number of years on the Lochgoilhead and Arrochar service until 1927, when she returned to Oban for the Fort William route. She continued to be stationed at Oban in summer each season, but took the Ardrishaig service from Greenock for a short period at the beginning and end of each season. In the winter she was laid up at Greenock, though for many years prior to the formation of the 1928 company her destination was Bowling. She was a noble craft with a world-wide reputation, in spite of the number of years she had to play second fiddle to *Columba*.

After her long career of seventy-two years, she was sold in April, 1936 to Arnott, Young & Co. (Shipbreakers) Ltd., and was broken up at Dalmuir, alongside *Columba*. Her deckhouse was afterwards owned by the late Mr. A. B. Murdoch, who had it successively at Tollcross, Kilmacolm and Giffnock. The bell from the *Iona* is now in the "Puffer Aground" restaurant at Salen, Mull.

P.S. "Gondolier." This steamer was built in 1866 for the service she performed for over seventy years, namely that on the Caledonian Canal between Inverness and Banavie. The selection of her name seems to have been a particularly happy one. Of the various steamers which have served the Company in these waters, she was perhaps best known to the travelling public, with the possible exception of *Glengarry*, whose term of years there was longer, but whose route was for a long time a subsidiary one.

The *Gondolier*, was chartered for the funeral of the Duchess of Argyle in May, 1878, and called at both Wemyss Bay and Rosneath, with her funnel painted black for the sad occasion.

In appearance, while being a very handsome and well-finished vessel, she lacked the beautiful lines of her contemporaries, the bow and stern in particular tending to spoil her. The reason for the peculiarly-shaped bow was doubtless to facilitate the working in and out of the canal locks, and the stern was designed with the same end in view.

In common with other steamers of the period such as the second and third *Ionas* and *Chevalier* (II), she had alleyways round the aft saloon. (*Chevalier* and *Gondolier* had full-breadth saloons forward, but these were not part of the original design, which had a promenade deck forward, but with the sides unenclosed.) A navigating bridge was later fitted.

Her twin-cylinder oscillating engines were practically miniature reproductions of those fitted to *Iona* (III), *Chevalier* (II) and *Columba*, and were generally maintained in splendid order. Two loco-type boilers were originally supplied, the working pressure being latterly 22 lb. per sq. in. In November, 1929 the boilers were condemned, but it was decided to try to get an extension of the certificate for one year (presumably on reduced pressure) and to build a new paddle steamer as her successor. In February, 1930, however, this was abandoned, and it was decided to instal one haystack boiler, made in 1902, from the *Grenadier*, which had in 1929 been broken up. This was done in April, 1930, at Ardrossan. The pressure of this boiler was then 90 lb., and two waste steam-pipes were fitted for the safety-valves of differing pressures, as on *Glencoe*; but in the case of *Gondolier*, both were aft of the funnel. Normal docking and refitting were carried out at Inverness, though in her earlier years she was several times on the Clyde for overhaul. In 1935 she was given new saloons with large windows (the aft one still with alleyways) and in 1936 a deckhouse was provided over her saloon companion-way, this being done at Ardrossan.

With the withdrawal of this ship late in 1939 the Company bade farewell to the oscillating engine. The vessel was taken over by the Admiralty early in 1940; engines, boiler, sponsons, paddle boxes and saloons were removed at Inverness and her generator went to the *Pioneer*; and the hull was towed to Scapa Flow for sinking to block a passage. Thus ended another long career. The agreement was for an equivalent vessel to be built when conditions should permit, but this did not eventuate.

The engine-room telegraphs, made by Messrs. Chadburn, bore their name, followed by "Makers to H.R.H. The Prince Consort"— an interesting historical association, particularly towards the end of the *Gondolier*'s long existence.

P.S. "Chevalier" (II). In design and appearance this ship was virtually a small edition of the third *Iona*, which was two years her senior. She was one of three steamers built for the Hutcheson fleet in 1866 for tourist services, viz. *Gondolier*, *Chevalier* and *Linnet*. It is probable that she was intended for the Staffa and Iona route round Mull, which, with the expanding tourist traffic, would now be becoming a popular excursion from Oban.

We have already seen that in 1886 *Iona* was taken off the Corpach-Crinan service, *Grenadier* having appeared on the scene in 1885; and from about this time *Chevalier* became closely identified with the Crinan route.

At that time there was an early morning start from Corpach with calls at Fort William, Ballachulish and elsewhere to Oban where the bulk of the southbound and day trip passengers would embark. At Crinan the steamer had a few hours' rest before the return journey, but apparently the crew were not idle. This spell in the middle of the day was the only suitable opportunity available for getting the ship and her men into the condition insisted upon. Decks had to be scrubbed, paint work washed, brass polished, boots cleaned, etc. To the credit of all concerned let it be recorded that the result was magnificent, as the ship was a delight to the eye, with her beautiful hull and lines, flaming red funnels and polished copper steam pipes, gleaming in the sun. The men took great pride in their ship and returned to her season after season.

On 9th October, 1909 on account of having had a fire in the dining-saloon, the *Chevalier* was unable to perform the Ardrishaig mail run; and the Caledonian *Duchess of Fife* was chartered to take her place.

For parts of 1913 and 1914 she was on the Broomielaw-Lochgoil-head route, this service having come into Messrs. MacBrayne's hands on taking over in 1912 along with Turbine Steamers, Ltd., the trade of the two Clyde steamers of the Lochgoil & Inveraray Steamboat Co. Ltd., to which further reference will be made later. *Chevalier* remained on the Clyde also during the first war, and was for a time on charter to The Caledonian Steam Packet Co., Ltd., who employed her on the runs to Millport or Rothesay from Wemyss Bay.

Originally supplied with horizontal boilers, the ship was reboilered in 1886, and in 1901 was given a new pair of haystacks by Messrs. Hutson, a surface condenser being then fitted. Electric light was installed in 1919 during re-conditioning after a fire, which occurred on board while the steamer was laid up at Greenock. Another alteration effected at this latter time was in the position of the dining saloon entrance in the upper saloon; this was formerly aft, as had been the practice in the days before deck-saloons were fitted, but was then moved forward, thereby conforming to the usual practice in later ships of this class, and also to that of *Iona*. (*Gondolier*, it should be noted, retained hers aft till the end.) The doors from the alleyways into the saloon near the stern were then converted into windows and steel bulwarks were fitted.

Normally laid up at Greenock in winter, *Chevalier* took up the Ardrishaig service on occasion; and it was while thus engaged that she came to grief on 25th March, 1927 through the fracture of the starboard paddle-wheel in a gale, when on the passage from Tarbert to Ardrishaig. The anchors did not hold; and, before any active measures could be taken, the ship drifted helplessly on to the rocks at the south-east corner of Barmore Island. The boats were lowered, and twenty passengers, mails and luggage, etc. were brought safely ashore at Stonefield. The vessel then began to fill, and had to be left for several days before she proceeded unaided to Greenock for examination and possible repair. The result of survey must have shown that economic repair was not feasible, and she was broken up at Troon after sixty-one years' service.

T.S.S. "Linnet." This quaint little vessel was the Crinan Canal passenger steamer during the whole of her long career with the Company. Her advent in 1866 occurred shortly after the re-opening of the Canal on one of its periodic closures, when the track-boats *Maid of Perth* and *Sunbeam* were considered to be too slow and inadequate for the rapidly increasing summer tourist traffic, and constituted a most important, if diminutive, connecting link in the Company's "Royal Route" from Glasgow to Oban and the North. The scarlet-coated postillions of the track boats vanished and became transformed into the *Linnet*'s red funnel!

She was a comic little ship, resembling a sort of floating steam tram if such can be visualised. The hull, though completely dwarfed by the superstructure, was finely modelled with a fascinating canoe-shaped bow, which could nose its way into opening lock gates.

The machinery consisted of two sets of 2-cylinder simple inverted engines, which drove the twin screws and exhausted up the funnel, producing the necessary draught for the fires just as in the case of locomotives. The engines were inclined slightly inwards so that all four cylinders were grouped together.

The loco-type boilers, located end-to-end athwart-ships supplied steam, and the furnaces were in the wings, engines and boilers being in a common compartment and attended by one man.

The machinery was controlled from the deck, and later from the bridge when this was added.

The ship steamed only about four months in the year, and made the double journey between Crinan and Ardrishaig daily, the night being spent at Crinan. The total daily mileage would amount to only about sixteen. In the winter she lay up under cover near Cairnbaan.

Linnet must have been known to hundreds of thousands of travellers from all over the world. It was always astounding how in the height of the season she absorbed the multitudes which disembarked at Ardrishaig from the *Columba* and *Iona* on their way north, even supposing some journeyed to Crinan by road, as the passengers' luggage always did. Anyway the feat was duly accomplished and, in a cloud of black smoke, the little steamer would set off crammed to bursting point with travellers for the initial run of four miles to Cairnbaan. The series of locks there was a good opportunity for stretching one's legs, and a large proportion of the passengers always availed themselves of it, while the *Linnet* manoeuvred herself in and out, and rose and fell with varying water levels. She presented a most attractive sight under these conditions; but the scene *par excellence* was yet to come, when on arriving at Crinan there was a spick-and-span *Chevalier* in all her glory of red, black, and gold, the two ships and scenery on a fine sunny day making a combination of colour without parallel. In time for the 1894 seasons she was given a deckhouse and navigating bridge, abaft the funnel, and new boilers.

Sold on 12th September, 1929, to the Glasgow Motor Boat Racing Club and stationed in the Gareloch at Shandon in June, 1930, for use as a club-house, without engines and boiler, but with a deckhouse from the *Lord of the Isles* erected on the upper deck, *Linnet* was finally wrecked in a storm in January, 1932.

P.S. "Dolphin" (II). As subsequently narrated, the *Islay* of 1849 was in February, 1868 bought by Messrs. Hutcheson and was given the name *Dolphin*. She is thought to have been on the Loch Fyne run, but in July the same year was sold to the Donaghadee & Port Patrick Short Sea Steam Packet Company. After about a year with them she passed to London owners.

.   .   .   .

In the autumn of 1869 Messrs. Burns' S.S. *Snipe* was advertised to sail on the Glasgow-Stornoway route with *Clydesdale* in place of the wrecked *Clansman*, but is understood to have been on charter only.

.   .   .   .

S.S. "Clansman" (II). This steamer was laid down after *Clansman* (I) had come to grief on Sanda. The new vessel was built by J. & G. Thomson, and was destined to become a well-known favourite on the Glasgow-Stornoway route for which she was designed. She spent her whole life thus, running all the year round. It might be thought that for a ship thus employed little consideration would be given to beauty of appearance and attention to detail; but in those days it was not so, and we find *Clansman* (II) a most attractive-looking two-masted ship with clipper bow, figurehead, and bowsprit with ornamental carving both at bow and stern. Electric lighting was installed in 1904.

Her career as far as is known was uneventful in that she escaped the perils of the sea during the forty odd years she was at work. She was unusual for a screw steamer in having her bridge abaft the funnel due to the very small space between the funnel and the forward hold.

When she was joined by her lovely consort *Claymore* in 1881 the two ships operated together for many years, the *Clansman* leaving Glasgow on Mondays and arriving back on Saturday mornings, while *Claymore* left on Thursdays and returned on Wednesdays.

Clansman was laid up at Bowling 1909-10, and was sold to William Reed, Tynemouth, just before being broken up in 1910.

Walter Frederick Campbell—later
John Ramsay and Others, Owners of the Glasgow—Islay Steamers

It was in September 1875 that the last survivor of this fleet—*Islay* (II)—passed under Messrs. Hutcheson's control. The Islay services dated from 1826, when P.S. *Maid of Islay* (previously *Waterloo* of 1815) opened a new route, making two trips weekly from West Loch Tarbet in connexion with the steamers on the Clyde to East Tarbert (Loch Fyne). On Tuesdays she sailed to Port Askaig and on Thursdays to Oban, Tobermory, Isleornsay and Portree. Two years later there appeared a vessel named *Maid of Islay No. 2* (the word "No." and the numeral formed part of her name in the advertisements though not in the registers). This ship was put on the above-mentioned run in succession to the previous steamer of the name, which was thenceforth known as *Maid of Islay No. 1*.

In March, 1827, we have the following notice:—

"ISLA, STAFFA and SKY (*sic*): The steam Packets 'Maid of Islay' No. 1 and No. 2 continue to ply for the Season between Glasgow, Tarbert, Islay, Staffa, Iona and Skye. (These packets exchange passengers at Tarbert.) No. 1 sails with passengers and goods from Glasgow every Tuesday morning for Isla, Staffa and Iona, and every Thursday morning for Portree, Tobermory, Isle Ornsay, etc. No. 2 leaves West Tarbert on Tuesday afternoon, arriving at Islay same night, and returns on Thursday, when she receives the passengers and goods for Skye, etc., reaching Oban that night, Tobermory Friday forenoon, and Portree in Skye same evening. Passengers leaving Islay on Thursday will be in Glasgow that night, or early the following morning. Those leaving Skye on Monday arrive in Glasgow Tuesday night or Wednesday morning.

No. 1 leaves Glasgow every Saturday for Rothesay, returning on Monday morning and regularly calls at Greenock and Rothesay in going to and returning from Tarbert. The comfortable accommodation on board these packets, No. 2 being fitted up with beds, their powerful engines and great speed being already well known to the public, do not now require particular note.''

They evidently did not sail on these routes in winter, as in the *Herald* of March 24, 1828, we read that "the Steam Packets 'Maid of Islay' No. 1 and No. 2 commence on Tuesday, 8th April to ply for the season between Glasgow, Tarbert, Islay and Skye, going to Portree first Thursday of every month, other days to Kyleakin."

In spite of the first sentence of the above advertisement, it appears from its later information that No. 2 was stationed at West Loch Tarbert, and operated therefrom to Islay, Oban, Tobermory and Skye; while No. 1 plied between Glasgow and Tarbert, Loch Fyne, probably making Rothesay her terminus on the days on which she did not require to connect with her namesake at Tarbert.

The summer service of *Maid of Islay No. 2* has been described when dealing with *No. 1*, but from an advertisement of February, 1827, it appears that *No. 2* sailed in winter from Greenock for Islay, West Tarbert, Oban, Tobermory, Isle Ornsay and Portree, calling at the intermediate ports. We may thus deduce that No. 1 was laid up in winter, and that the above reduced service was then carried on by No. 2, presumably *via* Mull of Kintyre.

In 1831 *Maid of Islay No. 1* left her old route, being advertised to sail to Lochgilphead in conjunction with *Toward Castle*. About this period the owners of *Maid of Islay No. 2* stated that their vessel sailed from West Loch Tarbert in conjunction with *St. Mun* to East Tarbert, while they disclaimed all connexion with *Maid of Islay No. 1* and *Toward Castle*. The owners of *Maid of Islay No. 2* at that time advertised also the steamers *James Ewing*, *Superb* and *Rothesay*, the agent being Alexander Graham.

The *Maid of Islay* which made the connexion at West Loch Tarbert in 1836 (presumably No. 2) sailed each week to Islay, and once to Oban, Tobermory and Portree. In 1845 the *Maid of Islay No. 2* became the property of the Castle Company, in July, 1846, absorbed by Messrs. Burns, and the other had by that time ceased to ply.

In 1842 the Castle Company advertised that one of its steamers would sail from Glasgow for Tarbert on Tuesdays at 6 a.m., to connect with the steamer *Maid of Islay* from West Loch Tarbert for Islay. The steamer *Falcon* (C. Morrison) was in August, 1845 advertised to sail from Ardrossan to Stornoway, calling at Campbeltown, Port Ellen, Oban, Tobermory and Portree, and later she alternated with *Maid of Galloway* on this route.

In 1846 a wooden paddle steamer named *Modern Athens*, built by Messrs. Adamson at Dundee in 1836 and previously owned by the Dundee & Leith Steam Packet Company, was placed on the station. She sailed from Glasgow on Mondays for Port Ellen, and made two trips thence to West Loch Tarbert and back, in connexion with the Clyde steamers to East Tarbert, before starting on her return journey to Glasgow on Fridays. In July, 1849 *Modern Athens* was advertised for sale, and was described as being owned by John Ramsay. She was purchased by Messrs. Tod & McGregor, presumably in part-payment of her successor.

In October, 1849 the first *Islay*, a new iron paddle steamer, described in the advertisements as "powerful and fast-sailing", was placed on the route, in succession to *Modern Athens*, which thereafter for a time maintained the West Loch Tarbert-Islay connexion. *Islay* was clipper-bowed with two masts, and one funnel abaft the paddle-boxes. In April, 1851, it was announced that *Islay* would extend her sailings to Skye and Lewis, and the change took place on Monday, 19th May, *Islay* sailing from the Broomielaw on that day and regularly every Monday thereafter. She left Glasgow in time to reach Oban at 7 a.m. next day, leaving Oban again at 9 a.m. for Skye. She called at many ports, but omitted Broadford. She left Portree on Thursday mornings for the return journey. This extension resulted from an agreement with Sir James Matheson, under which he withdrew the *Mary Jane* and *Marquis of Stafford* from the West Coast.

In 1853 *Islay* had *Glow Worm* of the Ardrossan S.N. Co. as her opposite number and in 1854 she traded in company with *Chevalier* (I) from Glasgow to Oban and Skye *via* Mull of Kintyre. In a sailing bill published by Messrs. Hutcheson in 1858 she is shown as sailing from Glasgow to Islay with a weekly call at West Loch Tarbert, connecting there with *Iona* (I). It would appear that a through service to Islay *via* Tarbert was provided by Messrs. Hutcheson and the owners of *Islay*.

Islay went ashore at Port Ellen a few days before the end of 1857, but was refloated and was back on the station within a fortnight. In 1866 she stranded, but was salved and became the second *Dolphin* in the Hutcheson fleet.

.   .   .   .

The screw steamer *City of Worcester*, built in 1850, was purchased from the Severn Shipping Company by John Ramsay, Thomas Buchanan, William Mutter and Walter Graham in July, 1853. She carried cargo mainly, but effected the West Loch Tarbert connexion for cargo and passengers. She was wrecked in 1855.

P.S. "Islay" (II). Built in 1867 as the successor to her namesake, the second *Islay* was owned by C. Morrison, T. G. Buchanan and John Ramsay, and had two funnels, two masts and a clipper bow, which was later during repairs altered to a straight stem. She sailed from Glasgow to Portrush and Islay; also occasionally to Jura. A painting shows her with black funnels and a house-flag consisting of a pennant divided vertically, blue at the hoist with white St. Andrew's Cross, the other portion being plain red. After being taken over in September 1875 by Messrs. Hutcheson she continued in the same trade (but after a short time without the call at Portrush). In 1882 she was advertised for the Oban-Gairloch service as alternative to *Pioneer*, the Glasgow-Islay station being then filled by *Clydesdale*, rendered surplus by the advent of *Claymore*. *Islay* suffered a broken paddle-shaft in March 1888 and went aground, her place being taken by the then new "herring-screw" *Kenilworth*. The *Islay* was wrecked in Red Bay, Cushendall, Co. Antrim in December, 1890, her place being taken temporarily by the chartered screw steamer *Speedwell* of 1884.

David Hutcheson & Co. (*contd.*)

S.S. "Queen of the Lake." About 1845 the Loch Lomond Steamboat Company was approached on the subject of running a steamer on Loch Awe; but, after due consideration, it was decided not to extend the field of operations. So far as can be ascertained, nothing was done in this direction till 1861, when the iron steamer *Eva*, built at Maryhill, was placed on the Loch. She was auctioned at Inveraray in October, 1862; and, in 1863, the new saloon steamer *Queen of the Lake* was built near Port Sonachan for Captain Duncan Young, and was advertised to commence sailing on 1st July in that year. She was propelled by two high-pressure diagonal direct-acting engines. Originally intended as a cargo carrier, she was later converted for the conveyance of passengers. She was advertised for sale in April, 1873 and in 1875 passed into the Hutcheson fleet, being withdrawn in 1882, and left as a hulk, still partially visible when the water is low.

S.S. "Lochawe." This little ship was ordered through Messrs. Muir & Caldwell from Messrs. A. & J. Inglis on 31st December, 1875, and was completed in the Pointhouse yard of the latter on 24th March, 1876. She was then taken (in sections) to Ford, where she was re-erected, and launched into Loch Awe, the naming ceremony being performed by Mrs. Richmond of Porran. The simple engine exhausted to atmosphere up the funnel, which at one time was bell-mouthed. The engine was deck controlled.

In the account of the little *Linnet* it was observed with wonder how she tucked away the crowds of passengers from *Columba* and *Iona* at Ardrishaig. It is appropriate to mention here that there was another outlet, though it never proved so popular as the genuine "Royal Route", namely *via* Loch Awe to Oban. Passengers drove from Ardrishaig to Ford at the south end of the Loch, took *Queen of the Lake* or *Lochawe* to the north end, and, till 1880, completed the journey by coach from Pass of Brander to Oban. From 1880 the northern terminus was Lochawe Pier, and the journey to Oban was completed by train. The steamer on Loch Awe called at New York *en route* (a name which always surprised tourists) and also at Port Sonachan and Cladich. The route involved an additional change of conveyance as compared with that by Crinan; but it was well-worth doing. Travellers sometimes went by one route and back by the other; and the two could be included in a day circular excursion from Oban. *Lochawe* performed her last run on 11th August, 1914 and was never re-commissioned, being laid up at Ford Pier till scrapped in 1924.

Though *Lochawe* ceased to exist, it should not be imagined that that was the end of steamer services on the Loch. In addition to the cargo vessels there were the passenger steamers *Kilchurn Castle* and *Caledonia*, and the steam launch *Sonachan*, belonging to Mr. Cameron of Port Sonachan, and *Countess of Breadalbane*, *Growley* and *Mona*, of Lochawe Hotel. Of these *Countess of Breadalbane* passed to The Caledonian Steam Packet Co. Ltd. in 1922 and was succeeded by a twin-screw motor vessel of the same name in 1936 which, after being laid up from 1940 to 1947, resumed sailing in 1948, and was afterwards on Clyde services, having been taken overland to Inveraray in 1952: she is now on Loch Lomond as *Countess Fiona*. These are, however, outside the strict scope of this book, and further reference to them will be found in "C.R.O.S.".

S.S. "Lochiel" (I). A two-masted craft with straight stem and single funnel, this was an all-the-year-round passenger and cargo carrier, built by Messrs. Inglis. She was ordered on 23rd October, 1876 and completed on 25th June, 1877. She was on the Lochness Mail Service till October, when she took up the Tobermory and Loch Sunart run. In 1878 the goodwill of the Loch Etive sailings was acquired and in that summer the *Lochiel* was supposed to have performed these, but evidence is lacking. Her owners seem to have carried out the sailings on this route by charter or contract till 1885, but abandoned from 1886, on the advent of the *Ossian* for a local owner. *Lochiel* was on the West Loch Tarbert-Islay route in 1879-81: on the Strome Ferry-Portree run from October, 1881. She was involved in 1883, when Sabbatarian riots occurred over the landing of fish at Strome Ferry, the other steamer concerned being William

McLachlan's *Rob Roy* of 1882, apparently chartered. In 1884 the *Lochiel* was fitted out for a three-months' cruise in the neighbourhood of Skye, with a gun-boat in attendance, with a view to suppressing the riots likely to arise as a consequence of the then recently initiated legislation introduced by the London Land Reform Association.

Lochiel was on the Stornoway Mail Service when its mainland terminal was changed from Ullapool to Strome Ferry on 2nd January, 1885; and she was, in the 'nineties, on the Dunvegan service from Portree *via* Harris and Lochmaddy, in which she was engaged at the time of the mishap which brought about her end in 1907: she then ran ashore at Portree, and was afterwards broken up.

The hull of this vessel, when new, was painted grey: it is rather a coincidence that this should have been done so long before 1929, and that the first seagoing steamer of the fleet to have a grey hull should also have had a "Loch" name.

S.S. "Fingal" (II). This was a contemporary and slightly smaller edition of *Lochiel*, also built by Messrs. Inglis from whom she was ordered on 18th November, 1876, being completed on 8th November, 1877. It would seem that there had been an intention of using "Loch" names, as this ship was launched as *Lochness*, but renamed while fitting out, possibly when it was realised that she would be required to operate on Loch Ness only about two months in each year, and would be used elsewhere during the remainder of the year. She had a single mast (at least during her later years) and was originally flush-decked, with a small dining saloon forward of the funnel, being later decked to the bow in the manner of *Staffa* (II). Intended for the Inverness-Fort Augustus mail run, she was found unsuited and from 1881 transferred to the Tarbert-Islay service in winter and from 1885 also in summer, till succeeded there by the *Glencoe* in 1890, though relieving on this route from time to time. Later Oban was her base, for the Bunessan route. She also relieved the *Ethel* during overhauls; and she worked the Glasgow-Loch Fyne cargo service as relieving steamer for *Cygnet* (II) or *Texa*, as occasion demanded.

In January, 1917 *Fingal* was sold to H. Flinn of Liverpool, and foundered in September of that year.

P.S. "Columba" (I). We have recounted how the traffic on the Ardrishaig summer service demanded progressively larger, faster, and better steamers and how Messrs. Hutcheson met that demand, even if they did not anticipate it, from the time *Pioneer* (I) came into their hands in 1851.

It will be recalled that the *Pioneer* was followed in 1852 by *Mountaineer* (I) which gave place to the *Ionas* in 1855 *et seq*.

But for the appearance of a formidable rival and the approaching completion of the Callander and Oban Railway it is possible that the laying down of the ship now under review would have been postponed for some years, because, by the close of 1877, *Iona* (III) had completed only fourteen seasons.

The opponent was the first *Lord of the Isles*, produced in 1877 for the Glasgow and Inveraray Steamboat Company. This steamer was the best equipped on the Clyde; and, though her destination in Loch Fyne was not Ardrishaig, nevertheless she covered (*en route* to Inveraray) a large proportion of the Hutcheson calling places. The *Iona* would, and probably did, suffer in consequence.

Mr. MacBrayne was now taking a leading part in the management of affairs, and it was felt that the time was ripe for bringing out a ship to eclipse all predecessors. Messrs. J. & G. Thomson again received the order to build, the agreed sum being in the region of £28,000 for a 19-knot vessel.

Many readers will recall the result of this contract; but few can have conjured up visions at the time of the fame and renown the vessel in question would secure for herself in the years that were to follow. Intended to take the famous name *Iona*, it was, however, as *Columba* that she was launched at Clydebank on 11th April, 1878; she was ready for service that season.

What shall we say of her?

Primarily we must guard against extravagant statements, because the dear old ship held such a warm place in our hearts that it would be easy to be over-eulogistic and our remarks would lose immediately half their weight.

The *Columba*'s first claim to distinction lies in the fact that she was built of steel. At the time this was deemed to be a bold venture, as this product was still in the experimental stage, in spite of its use in the construction of the Clyde steamer *Windsor Castle* in 1859.

Secondly, she was the largest steamer of the whole river fleet and has only within comparatively recent years been surpassed in tonnage, though never by any Clyde river vessel in length.

Thirdly, her general form and lines followed closely those of *Iona* (III), *i.e.*, a saloon steamer with ornamented curved slanting bow and square stern, two splendid funnels, and single mast; but the additional 50 per cent of gross tonnage coupled with extensive detailed finish and elaborate fittings gave the ship more than a proportionately greater dignity and beauty. These characteristics combined with the Company's standard colour scheme of black, red, cream, and gold were a delight to the eye and presented a gorgeous and majestic spectacle.

Fourthly, the steamer's accommodation was the last word in extent, equipment and furnishing according to the fashion of the time. The main saloon extended the full width of the hull and in this respect we record the main constructional divergence of the *Columba* from her predecessors.

A hairdressing saloon and a post office were provided on board. It is of interest to note that the small steam engine fitted up in the barber's shop for driving the now obsolete type of brushes was made

C

by Mr. David Hope MacBrayne when at Cambridge. The smoking room abaft the main companion way was not incorporated originally. There were also book and fruit stalls. The steerage accommodation forward was of a relatively high order for the period.

Those in charge of the catering department made a point of seeing that this service was in keeping with the crack ship of the fleet.

Fifthly, due largely to the *Columba*'s route and the lack of alternative modes of transport up to 1914 the steamer's patrons—from all over the world—differed, particularly in August and September, from those commonly in the habit of making use of the so-called "excursion steamer" whether we apply this term to ships on the Clyde, Thames, Mersey or elsewhere. In the height of the season the atmosphere on board was quite different. It must be appreciated that many of her passengers would be travelling *en route* to their residences and shooting lodges far north of the steamer's outward destination (Ardrishaig) and the quantity of luggage and bicycles carried in those days was amazing, including almost every kind of sporting equipment. In fact the *Daily Mail* on 2nd May, 1933, in a very apt article on the ship, described her as the "Society Boat" of years ago. This just hit the nail on the head.

There is no doubt that the *Columba* possessed great prestige. She represented the peak of daylight passenger travel and comfort.

The old days have now vanished, largely on account of road and air transport development, inexpensive travel all over Europe and beyond, and a general change in the mode of living, travelling and holidaying.

We have selected and drawn our readers' attention to five outstanding characteristics of the famous ship.

It is now time to pass on to the mechanical equipment of the steamer. The twin-cylinder simple oscillating engines followed orthodox lines and they were most impressive to watch. This is explained in a measure by the paddle shaft being relatively highly pitched, due to the vessel's light draught and large diameter wheels. The heavy crank webs gave the impression of tremendous power. Actually the maximum indicated horse power is understood to have been in the region of 2,200, but this figure was not developed in service, and a speed of 18 knots was not normally required on her daily schedule. Originally fitted with four "Navy" type boilers working at 50 lb., these were replaced in 1900 by a pair of "haystacks" with six furnaces each, and working at 55 lb. It is believed that this change resulted in a reduction of weight sufficient to raise the ship 5 in. in the water. The engine speed was increased from 36 to 40 r.p.m., and the speed of the ship from 18 knots to nearly 19½. Technically the *Columba* has been of immense interest to naval architects and others, on account of her fine lines and long light steel hull, carrying amidships such a massive machinery installation.

It is but reasonable to note a weak point, and that was the almost complete absence of daylight in the vicinity of the engine room. Actually conditions were improved in 1929 when a small electric light plant was fitted; but up to that time the areas in question remained in semi-darkness, which was inimical to cleanliness and inconvenient for passengers and crew. The ship was not unique in this respect because the same feature characterised, in varying degrees, all the oscillating-engined steamers. Down below in the engine room the conditions with respect to light were really bad in the old days.

The carving work and finish of the paddle boxes were superlatively good with the Hutcheson/MacBrayne standard fan-shaped vents in black and gold; in particular a thistle emanating from the letter "U" of the name was most artistic and pleasing. Steel floats replaced the original wooden ones and gave increased speed.

The latest navigating appliances of the time were incorporated in the ship's design and included steam steering gear and capstan, and engine-room telegraphs (these were not quite an innovation then).

The chief drawback, in common with all of her type, was the heavy coal consumption due to such thermally wasteful machinery working at what in her later days is a very low pressure. The coal used daily from Glasgow to Ardrishaig and back was 18 to 20 tons.

The steamer did not deviate from the route for which she was built except in a small degree. During the 1915 season she was laid up on account of impending restrictions, and *Iona* operated from Wemyss Bay to Ardrishaig, her place being taken by *Columba* from August, 1916. She then carried on her normal duty. From 1st February, 1919 sailings were resumed to Ardrishaig from Greenock and Gourock initially by *Chevalier*, and from about two months later by *Columba*, which later reverted to her old route from the Broomie-law. She was never selected for active service: the only other functions she performed were to act on occasion as club steamer during some of the Clyde Yacht Club meetings, and perhaps an occasional charter for bodies such as the Institution of Civil Engineers.

For eight months of the year she rested at Bowling until 1929, when Greenock was selected. It was during these periods that every reasonable precaution was taken to obviate deterioration of her hull and machinery, while all necessary overhaul work was pursued as far as practicable.

It is comparatively rare for alterations to a ship to improve her appearance, but we think this could be said of the subject of our present writing particularly in the lengthening, in the spring of 1884, of her first rather stumpy funnels. Certainly the external alterations effected were few, and appear to have been confined to new funnels in 1900 and the erection of the companion way cover in 1901, later extended by the addition of the smoke-room and upper deck on which two extra lifeboats (ex *Scout*) were placed in 1914. The removal of the gaff from the mast somewhat detracted from her appearance.

The Post Office service was withdrawn at the time of the first Great War and was not re-instituted; the office was adjacent to the engine room. The furnishing of the saloon presented an interesting contrast to the river steamer of later times. The questions of taste and ease of cleaning enter largely into this. At any rate the old ship certainly had some flesh on her bones, which is more than can be said of some of the more recent products of the shipyards.

In 1929 the effect of painting the ship grey was tried; but (as might have been expected) the result was so deplorable and the popular outcry so intense that after a month a reversion to black was made. It is noteworthy that the public took such an interest in the steamer. In spite of the modern craze for the latest and newest in everything it is gratifying to know that many were able to appreciate the old ship to the end, and no one will deny that the *Columba* was a firm favourite, in spite of any shortcomings according to up-to-date ideas, and had become absolutely an institution. She must have been known by millions from all parts of the globe, and her name was assuredly a household word. How many hotels and inns in the Highlands have chosen this magic name for their hostelry?

The selection of her name and that of *Iona* seemed extra-ordinarily appropriate; for just as those two names had such a far-flung influence in religious matters, so also had those vessels—not only because of their leading part in the conduct of the "Royal Route" but also on account of the great diversity of travellers who patronised them season by season. During the summer of 1935—the ship's 58th season—one heard in hushed whispers that the end was approaching. Could it be true? It was, and in April, 1936 she was sold to Arnott, Young & Co. (Shipbreakers) Ltd., and taken to Dalmuir, where hammer, chisel and oxy-acetylene flame reduced that lovely form to scrap; but not before the sympathetic and kindly Company had sent out many souvenirs to enthusiastic recipients. Our acquisitions on this occasion were one of the crankhead brass oil boxes, and a small chair from the saloon. We welcome information from others who secured relics from the old ship.

CHAPTER III

DAVID MACBRAYNE 1879-1905

FROM 1879 the business was carried on by Mr. MacBrayne in his own name. The first ship built for the fleet within this period was *Claymore*, which, on the Glasgow-Stornoway route, was the counterpart of *Columba* in a less obtrusive way.

S.S. "Claymore" (I). Launched on 14th July, 1881, this steamer ran trials on 1st October in that year. Her lines in general followed those of *Clansman* (II) and those with a true nautical eye agree that she was the prettier ship of the two. In fact she was a real beauty and lovely to look upon, with her admirably proportioned clipper bow, bowsprit, and hull surmounted with a pair of tall stately masts. Perhaps the diameter of the funnel was inclined to be a little too small in proportion to its height, but we find it hard to locate any serious fault in the profile of this noble craft.

It is not to be forgotten that the ship was no pretty butterfly flitting over placid summer seas in daylight with only a complement of passengers. Far from it; she worked all the year round, in fair weather and foul, facing every conceivable kind of weather the West Coast could produce, carrying passengers, cargo and livestock, and negotiating open sea, sound, loch and bay all as part of the routine, with numerous calls both by day and night.

This was arduous work for the crew too, especially when the difficult nature of the navigation of the north-west coast is realised. In fact it speaks volumes for the skill and care of the ship's officers that accidents were so few and far between when, with short daylight hours in winter, so much really intricate navigation was called for and successfully accomplished. Bear in mind too that at most unimportant points of call there might be complete absence of guiding lights, and nothing but precise local knowledge, coupled with caution, could prevent disaster.

It is not always appreciated nowadays to what an extent the local inhabitants of the smaller towns, villages, and hamlets depended on ships like the *Claymore* for the necessities, as well as the luxuries, of life prior to the multiplication of services by sea, rail, road and air as we know them today. To begin with, a large proportion of the very materials used to house the people themselves would be brought from Glasgow or elsewhere. In fact we wonder how many West-Coast villages were taken to their destination by the *Claymore* during her fifty years of existence!

Similarly with foodstuffs: southward bound the steamer would carry livestock for transfer or market, and practically all the products of the districts served.

In this way the local inhabitants would come to regard the steamers as part and parcel of their very existence. In these circumstances therefore the carrying of tourists in the summer was virtually a secondary, if profitable, undertaking.

Again, when the facilities for the exchange of local news and gossip were not what they are now, what was more suitable than the floating information bureau which travelled so widely and called at regular intervals?

Perhaps we have digressed overmuch and wandered from the point at issue to generalisation, but our excuse is that we do want to impress on readers that the ships were so much more, on the human side, than mere carriers of cargo and passengers. They were an essential to life in the West Highlands.

To return to the *Claymore* herself, the machinery consisted of a heavy two-cylinder compound engine supplied with steam from a pair of single-ended Scotch boilers. The full speed of the ship was supposed to be 15 knots, but nothing approaching this was attained on service except in grave emergency. The propeller shaft possessed a peculiarity in that it was prolonged past the screw and had a bearing in the rudder frame. We should think the advantage of this design would be more imaginary than real. Electric lighting was installed in 1904.

Engines and boilers saw the ship through her whole life unchanged. Particularly as far as the boilers are concerned, this was an amazing achievement, in view of their almost continuous duty.

Actually it was the condition of the boilers which sealed the ship's fate eventually, as replacement at that stage of her career would have been uneconomic.

Her only serious mishap occurred in January, 1910, when she went ashore on the rocks at the north end of Pabbay, near Broadford in Skye. For a time things looked bad, but she was towed to Broadford by the *Sheila* and beached. After a month she was temporarily patched and towed to Greenock, extensively repaired and refitted, and returned to duty in July.

The ship was camouflaged in 1918 when pursuing her ordinary duties, with a view to eluding submarines.

She was painted grey in 1929 temporarily. Apart from the widespread disapproval of this new colour scheme, one fact really settled it—we hope permanently. It is this: in misty or foggy weather a grey ship is almost invisible, while a black one might be faintly discerned. The risk of collision was increased, and so there was a reversion to black.

Latterly the old ship was laid up in Glasgow—moored off Lancefield Quay—in winter, and to this extent our earlier remarks concerning all the year round trading require qualification.

Mention should be made here of what might be called the "Claymore of Australasia". We have in mind the lovely S.S. *Rotomahana* of the Union S.S. Co. of New Zealand Ltd., whose demise in 1926 was as much a blow to the people of the Antipodes as was that of her Highland contemporary five years later to those in the West of Scotland. The *Rotomahana* was built by Denny in 1879 and was somewhat over twice the tonnage of the *Claymore*, though resembling her closely in appearance. She was reputed to be the first ocean-going steamer to be built of steel. With a speed of some 17 knots she became a great favourite with crews and passengers who sailed in her between New Zealand and Australia, the North and South Islands of New Zealand, and on the Melbourne-Launceston service at various times. Very interesting and appreciative accounts of this beautiful vessel will be found in *Australian Steamships* and *Pacific Steamers* by Dickson Gregory and Will Lawson respectively.

The proposed sale of *Claymore* was delayed and she was put through survey for 1930. In 1931 there was a suggestion of mooring her in a Scottish loch as a hotel, and to buy a second-hand ship to take her place. The hotel idea was, however, abandoned and she was sold on 5th May, 1931, and shortly afterwards left the Clyde on her last passage up the West Coast *en route* to Bo'ness on the Firth of Forth for breaking up. At least one of her lovers has gone into verse giving us details of this painful journey.

One of the authors of this book, who was in Burma at the time, got into touch with Messrs. Thomson & McGregor, the shipbreakers in Bo'ness, and asked for the top three feet of the ship's main waste steam pipe up the funnel. In due course this was delivered in Burma, caked thick with numerous coats of black and red paint—that dreadful practice of post-war days. It was then burnished and lacquered as the owner's umbrella stand in his London house and now is in the other author's house at Bearsden, having been bequeathed to him. The pipe itself is 9¾ inches in diameter, and at the top of the bell mouth measures 21 inches in diameter. The total weight of the piece is 72 lb., which surprises many people. Messrs. Thomson & McGregor advised that souvenirs of the ship had been sent all over Scotland and England, thus testifying to the regard a great many people must have had for her. It would be interesting to learn more details of these relics. We know that the beautiful figurehead found a new home in a Forfarshire garden, and that the panelling of the saloon is in Oban Municipal Buildings, but there must be many other items scattered up and down the country cherished by their present owners.

As late as February, 1933, the disruption of the steamer was not complete, but what was then left was a pathetic sight. The empty hull was in process of being cut down with oxy-acetylene apparatus and a mere fraction of the lovely clipper bow was still recognisable. It is safe to say that no prettier ship will ever thread the waters that lead from Glasgow to Lewis.

S.S. "Cavalier." This steamer was built for the Glasgow-Inverness service in 1883, and her comparatively stumpy appearance indicated that full use was made in her design of the maximum permissible length dictated by the dimensions of the locks of the Caledonian Canal. A straight stem was, of course, imperative. Actually she was a handsome ship, her profile being very well balanced. She is understood to have been the first steamer sailing from the Clyde with electric light installed. She was a splendid sea boat, but somewhat slow.

Cavalier was kept fairly constantly on the Inverness run in succession to *Cygnet* (I) and at first was accompanied by *Staffa* (II).

With such a comparatively deep-draught vessel, grounding in the Caledonian Canal was of fairly frequent occurrence. This route was a leisurely one by comparison with the other all-the-year-round services, as a week was allowed for the complete round trip, and a large proportion of the time was spent in sheltered waters.

Cavalier, however, did other work and was sometimes seen on the Glasgow-Islay and Glasgow-Stornoway routes in winter. She also at Fair Holiday times assisted on the Clyde, conveying passengers from Glasgow to Greenock to connect with *Iona* for Ardrishaig, being so advertised in 1897, while in 1900 at the Fair she sailed the whole way from Glasgow to Ardrishaig. She sometimes was overhauled without relief, but in 1898 *Tartar* took her place; next year *Trojan*, *Tartar* and *Marie* in turn,

With the falling-off of traffic on the Glasgow-Inverness route, it became uneconomic to operate a steamer thereon; and in 1919 *Cavalier* was sold to The North of Scotland & Orkney & Shetland Steam Navigation Co. Ltd., who re-named her *Fetlar*. In March, 1920 she was purchased by the Dundalk & Newry Steam Packet Co., Ltd., for their cattle traffic to Birkenhead, in which she finished her career. She was broken up in 1927.

P.S. "Grenadier." This well-known paddler—one of the few latterly to remain in commission throughout the year—was the last steamer built for the Company by Messrs. J. & G. Thomson, from whose yard at Clydebank she was launched on 19th March, 1885, trials being run on the 14th May, when she was credited with 18½ m.p.h.

Grenadier was unquestionably a very pretty ship, being a saloon steamer with clipper bow, bowsprit, two funnels and one mast, all in complete accordance with the MacBrayne tradition of the time.

The machinery was, strange to say, oscillating. This type of engine was practically obsolete in the 'eighties, so evidently conservatism was very strong. The outstanding feature of the engines was that they were compound, one h.p. and one l.p. cylinder being arranged exactly as in the case of the non-compound steamers [the *Ionas*, *Chevalier* (II), *Gondolier*, and *Columba*]. Looking down at the engines from the deck the differences in the cylinder diameters and space occupied were, however, very noticeable.

No doubt the compounding did something to mitigate the heavy fuel consumption so characteristic of the simple oscillating type, as a slightly higher boiler pressure could be used. This was 95 lb. in the case of the *Grenadier*, latterly reduced to 90. It must be remembered that pressures of 100 lb. and upwards were impracticable with oscillating cylinders on account of the difficulty of keeping the cylinder trunnions and glands steam tight. On the Staffa and Iona run round Mull from Oban the coal used was 10-11 tons.

The story of the boilers is rather interesting. Initially two Navy or locomotive type boilers were fitted with Howden's forced draught, which served until 1902, when a pair of haystack type was installed. These boilers saw the steamer through the remainder of her career—a period of twenty-five years—but were not considered fit to be condemned when the vessel was broken up. Accordingly in 1928 one went into the *Glencoe* and the other to the *Gondolier* in 1930. A study of the life of boilers shows that in nearly every case where reboilering of Clyde steamers was carried out, the second set gave far longer service than the first. There is no need to delve too deeply for technical explanations in this book, but it is very probable that, in the earlier days when the steamers were driven hard to get the last knot possible, the boilers were not only working to full capacity or over, but all kinds of malpractices were indulged in, knowingly or unknowingly, which were not permitted in later years. It is acknowledged that the scarcity of serious accidents is a great tribute to the design, material, and workmanship put into the boilers. Re-boilering is a costly undertaking and with the decline of racing the owners found that more rational treatment was worth while. Another factor was the more general use of surface condensers in place of the jet type.

As far as is known, *Grenadier* was intended for the summer service from Oban to Mull, Skye and Gairloch, on which route she was in 1885 advertised to operate. She became much more closely identified, however, with that to Staffa and Iona from Oban, which had been carried on by the *Chevalier* (II); and the Ardrishaig winter service from Greenock.

In the summer of 1903 she was on a service leaving Glasgow at 1.30 p.m. for Tighnabruaich, proceeding on Saturdays round Bute to Rothesay and Wemyss Bay and returning from Rothesay at 8.15 each morning for Glasgow. The steamer became very well known and a general favourite on the Iona and Ardrishaig routes, which she served practically throughout her career. A break occurred during the first war when she left the Highlands from 3rd July, 1916 to 23rd October, 1919 and took an active part in mine-sweeping in the North Sea as H.M.S. *Grenade*. She was the only MacBrayne paddle steamer employed on actual war service. Apart from damaging her bow by collision with a trawler off Grimsby, she escaped disaster, and returned to the West Coast and her old haunts.

The ship was never renowned for speed, but she was a good sea boat. Her economy in proportion to her size told in her favour, and this no doubt accounted largely for her selection year by year for the Ardrishaig winter service.

Her end came very suddenly and unexpectedly. A serious fire broke out on board in the dead of night when she was alongside the North Pier at Oban in September, 1927. The conflagration spread so rapidly that some of the crew lost their lives, among them being Captain McArthur who had commanded the ship for years.

The *Grenadier* was so damaged that repair was considered impracticable and she was subsequently broken up at Ardrossan, whither she had been towed on 10th May, 1928. Thus passed away another example of the lovely creations the Clyde produced in its heyday.

The only parts of the ship, the whereabouts of which are known, are the bow name boards and the figurehead, both of which are in the Transport Museum, Glasgow.

P.S. "Lochness" (I). Constructed in 1853 as the *Lochgoil* for the Loch Goil Company, this steamer had a rather ugly clipper bow and short bowsprit, one mast, and funnel abaft the paddles. She changed hands and was transferred to Londonderry under the name *Lough Foyle* for Messrs. Steel & McCaskill of Greenock (afterwards Steel & Bennie, Ltd.). Returning to the Clyde in 1877 she worked on the Gareloch route for George Iron of Clynder and later for Henry Sharp of Glasgow until Mr. MacBrayne purchased her in May, 1885 for service on the Caledonian Canal. Prior to her taking up this duty, certain alterations were made including shortening, the fitting of a new bow and the addition of deck saloon accommodation.

Appearing then as *Lochness*, the steamer went north. Her run was mainly, if not entirely, between Inverness and Fort Augustus, where she succeeded *Fingal* (II), and was relieved by the *Glengarry* for many years, this service being a mail, passenger and cargo one operating all the year round.

She was sold in June, 1912 and scrapped after fifty-nine years' service.

S.S. "Ethel"/"Clansman" (III). Before passing into the Company's hands in 1885, this steamer had had a varied career. She was a Belfast product and was registered there initially in 1880, belonging to A. McMullin of Ballymena, Co. Antrim. In the 1882-3 Lloyd's Register we find no owner given, but under port of registry "France". During the next three years her owners are of the name of Banks, and port of registry either not given, or Swansea.

From the date of building the steamer is registered as *Ethel*, and it is understood that the name *Obokh* was borne only for the very short period in which she was under the French flag. She should therefore be described as *Ethel* ex *Obokh* ex *Ethel*.

The Company employed her on the Glasgow-Inverness service, no doubt as a successor to *Staffa* (II). She worked in company with the *Cavalier*, but in all probability did not carry passengers. In 1905 she ran on the Glasgow-Islay service for a short time, actually in the interval between the loss of the *Glendale* in July and the transfer of *Clydesdale* (II) from the Inverness run in August. During this spell passengers were carried. She returned to the Inverness station again soon afterwards. During overhaul in May, 1895 she was relieved by the *Fingal* and in March, 1896 by the *Thetis*, which also, along with *Nellie*, relieved in March-April, 1897; and in April, 1898 the relief was *Rob Roy*.

About October, 1910, the *Ethel* became *Clansman* (III), the Company no doubt wishing to perpetuate and retain the right to so familiar a name until such times as opportunity arose for giving it to a worthy successor to *Clansman* (I) and (II). It was not till 1964 that the name was again used for one of the fleet. There is not much to note with regard to the vessel's appearance, as she followed the lines, more or less closely, of a good many general carriers of her size and class. The machinery and boilers were situated further aft than usual, but were not right aft. The tall masts gave an enhanced note to her profile, which on the whole was not at all unpleasing.

In 1915 her route was closed by Government regulations, and she was used on the run from Glasgow to Stornoway, from which she made a vogage (with a cargo of salt herrings) to Fécamp, during which she was sold to Alex. F. Blackater, Glasgow, in May, 1916; then in 1918 to Peter S. Cooper, Kirkwall; in 1920 to the Middleton S.S. Co. Ltd., and in 1921 to Small & Co., being registered at Lowestoft in 1923; the style of the firm was later T. Small & Co. (Great Yarmouth) Ltd. She foundered at sea in October, 1924.

S.S. "Handa." This little vessel came out as *Aros Castle* in 1878, for Mr. Orme (see page 129) and entered the MacBrayne fleet in March, 1887. She was a curiosity in some respects, mainly on account of the full lines and dimensions of the hull, which was of great beam and depth in proportion to its length. The bow was straight and so was the stern (at least nearly so!) and there were two tall masts and a single short funnel. With such lines it is to be wondered what sort of progress the *Handa* made in a strong head wind and sea. Her normal full speed was but eight knots. She must have been a stout old craft, as she is believed to have tackled the Minch on the Outer Islands service early in her career with the Company for whom she also plied for a time on each of the Glasgow-Tobermory, Loch Sunart, Oban-Coll-Tiree, and Portree-Harris routes. She was relieved in January, 1896 by the *Nellie* and also in January-March, 1897. In April that year she took the place of *Glencoe* on the West Loch Tarbert-Islay route, while *Handa*'s own Loch Sunart run was taken by *Nellie*, her own overhaul, in June, July and September-November being covered by *Countess of Kellie*. She performed the Glasgow-Inverness run during May-August, 1916 and from 18th October, 1916 to 23rd February, 1917. During part of her career she carried passengers. She was perhaps best known in her later days as consort to *Brenda*, operating the bi-weekly cargo service from Glasgow *via* the Crinan Canal to points on the Firth of Lorne, Oban, Mull, Loch Sunart and Loch Leven; and on account of her large cargo-carrying capacity in proportion to her size, she earned for herself the nick-name of "MacBrayne's Gladstone Bag".

She was sold to Thos. W. Ward, Ltd. of Sheffield and abandoned at sea on 24th December, 1917.

S.S. "Mabel." This small steamer was brought to Loch Maree in 1883 by Mr. Hornsby, then manager of the newly-built Gairloch Hotel, later proprietor of Loch Maree Hotel. He had previously had a long-boat operating from a small jetty at the foot of the navigable part of the River Ewe at Croft. A channel had to be scooped out to get her up, and the pier was built at Tollie. A twice-daily summer service was operated to the head of the Loch at Rudha 'n Fhomhair (Rhu Nohar)—the Giant's Point. It was said that the *Mabel* had been a private yacht in the Outer Islands. She was acquired in the spring of 1887 by Mr. MacBrayne.

The hull was of attractive appearance, but the steamer as a whole was spoiled by an absurd funnel (with slightly bell-mouthed top) and mast out of all proportion to the ship's size. As would be expected, the mechanical equipment was of the simplest description, the engine having a single vertical inverted cylinder which exhausted to atmosphere up the funnel, as in the case of *Linnet* and *Lochawe*. As all three steamers operated in fresh water, no difficulty was encountered in obtaining boiler feed. Similarly the engine was controlled by the captain on deck.

It will be understood that with a total length of only some forty-five feet the vessel's accommodation was strictly limited, but she actually possessed a saloon below the "promenade" deck, though its dimensions were not great!

Running in the season only, the *Mabel* normally traversed Loch Maree four times daily between Tollie Pier (erected 1883) and Rhu Nohar in connection with coaches at each end for Gairloch and Achnasheen respectively. Passengers to and from Gairloch *via* The Highland Railway could either take the steamer and connecting coaches, or drive the whole way to or from Achnasheen. *Mabel* called at various points on the loch, the principal one being at the Loch

Maree Hotel. When not engaged on her scheduled runs, she was available for private hire.

At the end of the 1911 season she was found to be unfit for further service, and though tickets were printed for the through bookings for 1912, they were not used. Her withdrawal from service coincided with a general falling off of passenger traffic in the North, and she never resumed duty after World War I. Hauled up on the beach near the Loch Maree Hotel, she presented, in 1927 and 1937 a sorry spectacle as she lay rusting away. Even with the revival of the tourist traffic in summer, it is unlikely that a successor could be run profitably, on account of the development of road travel. Loch Maree is particularly beautiful and the *Mabel*'s route permitted a great deal more to be seen than could be accomplished by road alone.

After the withdrawal of the *Mabel* an attempt was made by local owners to revive the service with a fast motor-boat, but it did not pay, and the war put an end to it.

S.S. "Countess of Kellie." The appropriate names of many members of the Company's fleet have already been commented upon, but there are exceptions to prove every rule. With such a dominating title, readers might expect to find a swift passenger ship on one of the "crack" runs, but will be surprised to find that the subject of our writing was virtually a coal barge! She resembled in many ways the familiar "puffer", and her duties coincided therewith in that the Company employed her carrying coal for their steamers from Glasgow to the north *via* the Crinan Canal, though she sometimes performed some of their cargo and even passenger runs. She had, however, an interesting history, having been built in 1870 as a paddle steamer for the Alloa Ferry service of the Caledonian Railway Company. She came into the MacBrayne fleet in October, 1887 and was converted to screw propulsion.

It is to be noted that the vessel's full name never appeared in any of the published fleet lists of the Company. They were content—presumably on the score of brevity—with *Countess*! She was sold in 1904 to John Donaldson, Glasgow, and after a period at Dundee was from about 1918 in service at Stockton-on-Tees. She was converted into a mooring-hulk for R.O.P. Ltd., on 27th January, 1934.

S.S. "Gladiator." In November, 1887 Mr. David MacBrayne bought this ship at Hamburg in a burnt condition. It was reported in the following January in the *Glasgow Herald* that she was then being refitted at Aitken & Mansel's yard and had been chartered to a London firm for cargo-carrying to the Continent. It would seem that she was engaged in cargo tramping and there is no evidence of her employment in the West Highlands.

The *Gladiator* had been built for T. & J. Harrison of Liverpool, and had passed to other Liverpool owners before she came into the

MacBrayne fleet. On a voyage from Mauritius to London, having replenished her bunkers at Gibraltar, she touched on the Cabezos Shoal on 12th December, 1893 and was beached to prevent sinking. The crew landed safely, but bad weather caused her to become a total wreck.

S.S. "Udea." This little vessel was owned in South Wales until Mr. MacBrayne purchased her, her port of registry originally being Llanelly. She was one of the members of the fleet normally employed in coastral tramping, though occasionally used on the Loch Fyne cargo run and other routes.

A new boiler was supplied in 1880 and new engines in 1892. The latter may have been a case of compounding the original set, as the piston stroke remained the same.

She stranded on Cath Sgeir Rocks, Isle of Gigha on Sunday, 8th April, 1894, and sank in deep water in 15 minutes; the crew got ashore safely. She had been on a voyage with coal and iron from Glasgow to Portness, Butt of Lewis.

S.S. "Staffa" (III). Built at Renfrew in 1861 for the River Tagus trade, this ship, then named *Adela*, was sold in 1882 to James Wingate, Liverpool and about three years later to H. Reeve, Great Yarmouth, from whom she passed to S. McKnight & Co., Shipbuilders, Ayr. She was bought in February, 1888 and was re-named *Staffa*.

From the eighteenth century the mails for the Outer Hebrides passed through North Uist, and by 1840 those for Barra, South Uist, Benbecula, and North Uist went via Lochmaddy, as also did those for Harris till 1840 from which year the latter had its separate packet, twice a week in summer, once in winter, from Uig. These mail services were provided by Government vessels such as the sloop *Perseverance*, plying fortnightly to Lochmaddy from Dunvegan, later increased to bi-weekly and tri-weekly by the *Skylark*, and from 1876 daily by the cutter *Dawn* between the same ports. The early mail contracts to and from the Outer Islands, held initially by the Highland Fisheries Co. Ltd. (who operated the chartered steamers *Tartar*, *Holly* and *Electric*), passed to the Company late in 1888 and *Staffa* was stationed at Oban for this service, first along with *Clydesdale* (I) and along with the *Flowerdale* a few years later. In 1891 she was shortened. She had a straight stem, an ugly stern, two tall masts and a tall funnel of small diameter. She was never in the limelight, and it is doubtful if she ever achieved any popularity.

She was absent for 2½ months in 1893, her place being taken by the screw tug *Neptune*, (chartered from Steel & Bennie Ltd.), whose speed was praised, though not her sea-keeping qualities. After stranding at Lochmaddy on 8th January, 1894, she returned to her towage duties on the Clyde. *Staffa* was on the Loch Fyne cargo service in July, 1904; and in 1909 was sold to Wm. J. Garscadden, Glasgow, being broken up after lying in Bowling for some months.

P.S. "Fusilier." According to *The Marine Engineer*, *Fusilier* was built for the Oban-Gairloch service, including a trip once a week to Lochinver: but in this she was succeeded from 1891 by the *Gael*.

McArthur of Paisley turned out a steamer which, excepting the single funnel forward of the large paddle boxes, bore a remarkable resemblance to the *Grenadier* on a slightly smaller scale. She was launched on 14th April and ran her trials on 27th June, both in the year 1888.

At long last a departure was made from the old oscillating type of machinery, but the engine was not, as might have been expected, a compound diagonal one with a pair of cranks. Instead a single cylinder and crank were fitted—condensing of course—and as is well known, the lack of balance of this arrangement gave rise to the cyclical pulsations so familiar in this and other similarly powered vessels. This engine, supplied by Hutson & Corbett was no doubt fitted to reduce the cost of the ship. It is understood that the all-in cost of the *Fusilier* was amazingly low. In spite of this, however, she was a sound job; and, though appearances do not suggest it, she ranked as a good sea boat of her type.

The original haystack boiler did duty for thirteen years and a new one was installed in 1901. The former was then transferred to *Glencoe*, where it carried on for twenty-seven years until 1928, when one of the *Grenadier*'s twenty-six-year-old boilers was installed. This story of the juggling of boilers must be almost unique in the annals of marine engineering!

Now as to the *Fusilier*'s work. It may be assumed that she was stationed at Oban in summer during the major portion of her career. From there she worked mainly on the Fort William service, with various cruises and excursions thrown in between the scheduled trips. She also worked the Crinan route, though she never became closely identified with it. During part of July and the whole of August, 1916, she provided excursions from Glasgow (Bridge Wharf) to Kilcreggan, Kirn and Dunoon, with calls at Govan, Renfrew and Bowling. Later in the first war period she was chartered by The Caledonian S.P. Co. Ltd. for service from Wemyss Bay, and carried their buff funnel for a time.

When the *Grenadier* was destroyed in September, 1927, *Fusilier* took her place on the Staffa and Iona run for the 1928 season, and carried this on each summer until the arrival of *Lochfyne* in 1931. Likewise she performed the Ardrishaig winter service for three years, just as *Grenadier* had done. This kept her in commission continuously. It will be seen therefore that latterly she became a general maid-of-all-work appropriate to her class, but her history is not yet complete, because we next find her in 1931 on the Mallaig-Kyle-Portree mail service after the demise of the *Glencoe*, though in winter *Plover* (III) relieved her.

Before closing our account mention must be made of the striking alterations made to the ship about 1926. Opportunity was then taken to heighten the funnel by the depth of the black top, to place the bridge forward of the funnel, and to add a new deckhouse covering the main companion way on the promenade deck, and sponson houses aft, with the boats raised to promenade-deck level. Whatever advantages and conveniences were obtained in these modifications—the new location of the bridge was no doubt an improvement from the navigational point of view—the appearance of the steamer was unquestionably changed (not for the better).

During the years the *Fusilier* was out of commission in the winter months, Greenock was usually her resting place, though she was sometimes to be found at Bowling.

She had the distinction of being the last vessel actually built for the Company in the 19th century.

With the arrival of the Diesel-electric *Lochnevis* in 1934 on the Portree route, the old ship became redundant; and, after a short spell in Ardrossan Harbour, she was sold on 25th July, 1934 to Redcliffe Shipping Co. Ltd. of Hull for service on the Firth of Forth, being sent *via* the North of Scotland to Leith. She operated from Granton, and her excursions included such objectives as Kirkcaldy, Elie Bay, Bass Rock, etc. She had a passenger certificate permitting her to go to Dundee, but is not known to have done so.

Compared with her new owners' other vessel, *Cruising Queen* (ex *Cleethorpes* of the G.C.R./L.N.E.R. Humber Ferry service), *Fusilier* was fast; and it was found that she frequently arrived back from excursions ahead of schedule, so her speed was restricted in order to give passengers full value!

One season on the Forth sufficed to show that *Fusilier* was too extravagant in fuel for this work, and she was, accordingly, sold. She returned to the West Coast, and during the summer of 1935 was employed by the Cambrian Shipping Co. Ltd. of Blackpool making trips between Llandudno and Menai Straits under the name *Lady Orme*. Her hull was then white, and the funnel buff with black top. The 1936 season found her operating from Ramsgate for the same owners, the funnel having reverted to red with black top. In 1937 she was back in North Wales, owned by Ormes Cruising Co. Ltd., with buff and black funnel, the hull being black to main deck level, above which it was white. In 1938 her name was changed to *Crestawave*, but her service as such was of short duration. She was laid up first at Liverpool, later at Barrow, and in October, 1939, was sold for scrapping.

So ended the career—as a fallen star—of *Fuslier*, after trading between points as far apart as Portree and Ramsgate.

S.S. "Pelican." This vessel was formerly with the City of Cork S.P. Co. Ltd. About 1889 it is believed she ran between Oban and Iceland and also carried sheep and ponies between Liverpool and Iceland. She later became a coal hulk, first at Portree and then at Tobermory, and was finally wrecked in a storm at Calve Island, Tobermory, in December, 1895.

S.S. "Falcon." A similar ship to the *Pelican*, and purchased along with her from the City of Cork S.P. Co. Ltd., *Falcon* was engaged along with *Gladiator* in charter work to the Mediterranean and Continent. She was abandoned in November, 1890, when on a voyage from Glasgow to America.

S.S. "Margaret." The date on which this small steamer was built is not recorded, but she was first registered in January, 1889. She was probably on coal-carrying duty for the Company's steamers much in the same way as the *Countess of Kellie* and *Udea*. Her capacity was 60 tons. She is recorded in the Kelvin in January, 1894. She was sold to Wm. H. Arnott, Newton-le-Willows, Lancashire, and in 1895 to Liverpool & Cardigan Bay S.S. Co. Ltd., later to a Cardiff owner.

S.S. "Texa." Beginning in 1884 as *James Mutter* with Messrs. W. & J. Mutter of Glasgow, this steamer was engaged in the Islay cargo service for Mr. Ramsey, M.P., till acquired by the Company in 1889. She was advertised to leave Glasgow on 2nd August that year for Inverness via the North of Scotland and in July, 1891 she was named along with *Battle Isle* for the thrice-weekly Lochfyne cargo run.

She seems to have been engaged on a northern route shortly after her acquisition and the 1903 Company guide book mentions Arisaig as one of her ports of call. It is understood that she was a regular visitor there during the construction of the Mallaig extension of the West Highland Railway, which was completed in 1901. She was engaged also in coastal tramping, being reported e.g. in 1894 at Thurso (for paving-stones), at Portrush and at Pembroke (for bricks).

The steamer was probably best known during the period she worked on the Loch Fyne cargo service in company with *Cygnet* (II). She used to leave Glasgow (Bridge Wharf, under the Caledonian Railway bridge) with funnel and mast down, at 6 a.m. on Tuesday, Thursday, and Saturday, for Ardrishaig, and the whole day was occupied in making the requisite calls, loading and discharging cargo. She lay at Ardrishaig pier over Sunday, returning to Glasgow on Monday, Wednesday and Friday without visiting Inveraray. [This *Cygnet* (II) did.]

Texa had her machinery aft, and after alterations she carried a single mast and independent cargo winch.

Texa was sold to Douglas Shipping Co., I.O.M., on 20th August, 1917, and to Samuel Gray of Belfast in 1932, being wrecked in April, 1932.

S.S. "Loanda." After a coal strike in the eighties, when the fleet had difficulties in obtaining coal, and in view of a threatened strike in 1890, this ship was purchased in 1889, fully loaded with German coal and was sent to Broadford Bay as a supply ship for the MacBrayne fleet, replensihing her holds as necessary by being sent to Germany or Poland as required until supplies returned to normal. Owned initially by the British & African S.N. Co., she was, until the advent of *Lochgarry*, the largest ship (in gross tonnage) owned by the Mac-Brayne organisation. She was for a time at Oban, which she left on 20th July, 1895 for the Gareloch to be laid up. She was scrapped in January, 1897.

T.S.S. "Flowerdale." Built as the *Recovery* and registered at Dover, the subject of our writing came into Mr. MacBrayne's hands from the Independence Marine Salvage & Steam Pump Co. Ltd., Liverpool, in the summer of 1889. She was his first twin-screw sea-going steamer.

She was a handsome ship, though from the nature of her early employment it is probable that alterations were made before she started sailing in Scottish waters. However, she never approached the standard of beauty seen in the *Clansman* (II) and *Claymore* (I), in spite of her clipper bow.

As far as we know, she was retained on the Oban-Outer Islands mail service, having *Staffa* (III) as her opposite number for quite a few years. It is curious that this service should have been maintained by two ships unequal in size and accommodation. The *Flowerdale* was two-and-half-times the tonnage of *Staffa* and presumably her passenger accommodation was superior. The former relieved also on the Glasgow-Stornoway service.

At this period and for some time afterwards the Outer Islands services were operated thus. Two steamers were stationed at Oban and each left on alternate weekday mornings, giving thus a daily service. The route was similar to the present one through the Sound of Mull, but thereafter the steamers proceeded to Barra, South and North Uist, Dunvegan and the West of Skye before returning to Oban the following afternoon. On the other three days they traversed practically the same route in the reverse direction. There was a third steamer, stationed at Portree, which worked round the north of Skye to Dunvegan *via* Tarbert (Harris) and Lochmaddy, outwards three days a week and inwards the remaining three, connecting with the Oban steamers. Kyle and Mallaig did not at that time figure in the Outer Islands services at all. The *Flowerdale* sometimes relieved on the Glasgow-Stornoway route.

When the *Flowerdale* was lost off Lismore in 1904, her machinery and boilers were salved and placed in the new hulls of *Plover* (III) and *Cygnet* (II), each ship receiving one engine and boiler. Reference will be made again to this later, under the ships concerned.

S.S. "Maud." In the summer of 1889 a drought rendered un-navigable the summit portion of the Caledonian Canal, for which reason Mr. MacBrayne chartered this small steam yacht (really a launch) from Mr. Robert Patrick of Greenock to connect between the passenger steamers at each end of the low-water section. In September it was reported that the vessel had been bought, and would be renamed *Highland Chieftain*; but no change of name seems to have taken place and the next news of the vessel was in the fleet-list in 1893, still as *Maud*.

Practically on the site of the later Shiel Bridge Lodge there was, in the 1890s, an hotel which was taken over by Mr. David MacBrayne; the latter put a manager in charge. He bought an old church of corrugated iron in Govan, transported it in sections and rebuilt it, except for the spire, as an annexe to the hotel.

The *Maud* lay near the old hotel and did one run weekly on Loch Shiel to Glenfinnan, but was available every day to tow fishers up the loch in their boats, often waiting to bring them back. She seems to have started in 1893 and ran during the summer thereafter until 1897.

In 1896-7 the estate was bought by Mr. Rudd, a colleague of Cecil Rhodes at Kimberley, who warned Mr. MacBrayne out, in order himself to build. This he did in 1899, but the old hotel (not the annexe) had been kept in front of the new lodge. On its completion, Mr. Rudd gave the workmen money for a dance and the result was a fire on 24th March, 1900, which started in the old hotel and raged for three days, completely destroying the new house: the later building was immediately commenced.

In May, 1898, the *Lady of the Lake*, which had up to that time been Lord Howard de Walden's yacht, was placed on the regular mail service on the Loch up and down daily, this being done after consultation with the other proprietors, particularly Mr. Rudd.

There had been talk of Mr. MacBrayne putting a better boat on the Loch and making the service a regular one; but this did not materialise. So in 1899 the *Clanranald* was put on by Lord Howard de Walden, but proved to draw rather much water, and was succeeded in 1900 by the T.S.S. *Clanranald II* which (along with *Lady of the Lake*, both later motor vessels) continued on the Loch for many years. There is doubt as to how long the *Maud* lay after she ceased sailing; but she did not run with the *Lady of the Lake*, as the hotel had been given up before the latter commenced in the passenger trade.

It was not till 1954 that there was again a MacBrayne vessel on Loch Shiel.

For the foregoing we are indebted to Mr. Alan J. S. Paterson and to the late Rev. William C. Galbraith.

P.S. "Hero"/"Mountainer" (II). It will have been observed that since the building of the *Fusilier* in 1888 all additional or replacement tonnage had been obtained by the purchase of craft from other owners. In fact it will be found that this process was carried on right down to 1903, when *Lapwing* (II) was built for the Company.

Hero began on the Clyde, where she was employed on the Glasgow, Rothesay, Arran and Gareloch routes at various times. She also spent two seasons at Belfast (where she was registered in 1861), returning to the Clyde in May, 1863, her registry reverting to Glasgow in 1868. Owned by Malcolm McIntyre, she passed to George Ferguson and on 30th January, 1876 to Hugh Keith, going with the rest of the Keith & Campbell fleet to Captain Buchanan in February, 1885. She spent at least one season on the River Tay; and she was on excursion work on the Clyde in 1889 for Mr. Orr. The following year she was acquired by Mr. MacBrayne; and, as *Iona* was out of commission awaiting re-boilering, *Hero* was placed on her run from Ardrishaig, terminating at Greenock instead of Glasgow, but having broken down, she was replaced by Captain Buchanan's *Elaine* on charter, and was withdrawn from service on 8th November, 1890. Originally an ordinary flush-decker (and two-funnelled in her early days), *Hero*, under the MacBrayne flag was in 1892 transformed into a handsome steamer with clipper bow and bowsprit, single funnel abaft the paddles and one mast: at the same time her name was changed to *Mountaineer*. Her machinery was altered by Messrs. Hutson & Corbett, this, no doubt, consisting of the substitution of a surface condenser for the original jet one.

She was stationed at Oban in summer and lay up for the remainder of the year—usually at Greenock. It appears that no definite service was allocated to her, but she ran on short excursions as occasion demanded. She was sometimes used on the early morning mail and newspaper run from Greenock to Rothesay, in which she was in April and May, 1894 relieved by the paddle tug *Champion*, chartered from Alex. McKinnon, Greenock. She was sold in 1909 for scrap.

P.S. "Islay" (III). After eighteen years as *Princess Louise* on the Larne-Stranraer route to Ireland, this vessel became a member of the MacBrayne fleet. She was placed on a Glasgow-Islay run *via* the Mull of Kintyre in succession to *Islay* (II), and probably made two round trips per week. This service, in which quite a number of different steamers have participated from time to time, embraced one or more calls in Jura as well as those in Islay, and operated all the year round for passengers and goods. Pictures of the vessel show her as of sea-going design, flush-decked with straight stem, two funnels, and masts with derricks for cargo handling. Both bow and stern were ornamented, and the designs on the paddle boxes were not changed to the MacBrayne standard form for some time after she had sailed under her new flag. During her absence from 8th May to 11th July, 1895 her place was taken by the chartered *Rossgull*; in May-June, 1897 her relief was S.S. *Honfleur* and in June, 1899 was *Madge Ballantyne*.

She stranded on a rock near Sheep Island, Port Ellen on 15th July, 1902 in a dense fog, and became a total loss.

P.S. "Great Western"/"Lovedale." Once again Mr. MacBrayne bought in tonnage, this time from the G.W.R., obtaining their *Great Western*. The steamer seems to have spent most of her time on the Milford-Waterford route which the railway company had operated for many years. From 1878-85 she was transferred to Weymouth and ran across the Channel to Cherbourg.

She came north in her original rig, which was that of a straight-stemmed two-masted and two funnelled cross-channel steamer, both funnels being abaft the paddle boxes. She had much freeboard, and very small paddle boxes.

The Company placed her on the Stornoway mail service from Strome Ferry which she maintained until she was withdrawn temporarily for alterations in 1893. These alterations changed her appearance, as the two funnels were removed, and the new single one which was substituted was located too far aft to give a nicely balanced profile: in fact her appearance was decidedly odd. The ship was re-boilered, the paddle boxes changed to the MacBrayne standard design, and she was given the name *Lovedale*, from the mission station in Africa commemorating Dr. Love of Anderston, who was at one time associated with Dr. Burns in the Barony Parish, Glasgow.

She returned to the Stornoway route; and, on the extension of the Skye Line of the Highland Railway from Strome Ferry to Kyle of Lochalsh in 1897, the latter place became the southern terminus of the mail service to Lewis. In 1900 she was apparently the Portree mail steamer from Kyle and on Saturdays in the season she extended her voyage northwards to convey the *Gael*'s and other passengers for the weekend at Lochinver. She also relieved on the Glasgow-Stornoway and Outer Islands routes.

In 1903 we find the *Lovedale* running from Glasgow to Islay for a short period, and it is thought that she probably operated thus between the loss of *Islay* (III) and the advent of *Glendale* on this route.

Not much is known about her performance at sea, but she was evidently able to cope with the Minch and the Mull of Kintyre satisfactorily in all weathers, as her routes involved continuous working summer and winter.

She was broken up in 1904.

P.S. "Gael." For the early history of this ship readers are referred to Chapter X. Two periods of the *Gael's* career have now closed and we open the third and last, namely, that under the MacBrayne flag. In 1892 her after cargo hold and mainmast were removed, and she was given a new full-breath saloon aft, being also re-boilered. As far as is known, on her return to the West Coast, she was placed on the Oban-Gairloch daylight summer service. Leaving Oban on Tuesdays, Thursdays and Saturdays at 7 a.m., she made her way northwards through the Sound of Mull, calling at Tobermory; thence round Ardnamurchan Point to Eigg and Arisaig (Malliag was substituted on its establishment in 1901) and once a week to Loch Scavaig. Continuing through the Sound of Sleat and touching at one or two points *en route*, she called at Kyleakin, Kyle of Lochalsh (from 1897) and then proceeded to Broadford and Portree, finally crossing back to the mainland at Gairloch in Ross-shire. This was a long day, but in fine weather a magnificent run from the scenic point of view. The return journey, following the same route, was made on Mondays, Wednesdays and Fridays. During a few seasons an extended trip to Lochinver was arranged at weekends. (It appears that *Gael* made Gairloch her terminal port on those occasions also, but passengers for Lochinver were conveyed thither by the *Lovedale* from Kyle, sleeping accommodation for the Saturday and Sunday nights being provided on board.) This service was withdrawn on the outbreak of the first war and has never been re-instated.

In the 1903 season the *Gael* worked the Staffa and Iona service from Oban and sometimes relieved on the Stornoway mail run. During the first war she was laid up at Bowling for a time and later carried on some of the Firth of Clyde sailings, including the Ardrossan-Arran service, which was maintained by her also during part of 1919.

After the first war we find her employed on such duty as the Ardrishaig mail service in winter, the Stornoway mail route from Kyle of Lochalsh, and as the Directors' ship while on tour in the summer. She was really without a permanent job latterly: and being a costly ship to run, coupled with advancing years, it was evident that the end was approaching.

A raised fo'castle was added in the early 1900s, and in 1920 a mainmast was again installed when the ship was equipped with wireless telegraphy. But 1922 she had a deckhouse on the aft promenade deck.

These modifications never very materially altered the appearance of the steamer, and she was easily recognisable at all times. She looked more like a cross-channel steamer than any of the river fleet, and in fact this is what she really was, although built for the Campbeltown route. It must be remembered, however, that this trade involved cargo-carrying and some heavy seas on occasion.

She was fitted with haystack boilers, which were renewed in 1879 and 1892. The machinery which served her all through was simple oscillating, with two cranks. A peculiarity was the provision of twin piston rods to each cylinder. It is understood that the crankshaft carried away on one occasion in her early days on the Campbeltown run, and later at Oban a cylinder cover was fractured, probably through incomplete draining while warming up.

She was sold in May, 1924 for breaking up and on the way to her final resting place spent a night at Campbeltown, the scene of her initial triumph in 1867. It is noteworthy that she retained her name through the vicissitudes of a long career.

P.S."**Cygnus**"/"**Brigadier.**" As originally built, this steamer had a clipper bow, two masts, and two tall funnels abaft the paddles. She seems to have changed ownership in the south more than once but the Weymouth & Channel Islands Steam Packet Co. ran her between Weymouth and the Channel Islands from 1857 to 1889. She is next reported as being sold to run between Liverpool and Isle of Man but this did not last long, as she came into Mr. MacBrayne's hands in October 1890.

It will be recalled that the old *Inveraray Castle* was by this time nearing her end: and the *Cygnus* was put on the Lochfyne cargo run as her successor, having as alternative the chartered *Battle Isle* in the summer of 1891. About 1892 the steamer was rebuilt, and emerged as *Brigadier*, in what we may call her proper MacBrayne uniform. The principal changes involved a new and more shapely swan bow and a single funnel (aft) instead of a pair. The designs on the paddle boxes were brought into line with those of other steamers of the fleet. The machinery was overhauled and the ship was re-boilered and generally modernised.

She then went on to the Glasgow-Inveraray cargo service, but she did not remain there long before being transferred to one of the northern routes. She filled the Oban-Loch Sunart station for a time, and went aground at Strome Ferry on 7th February, 1896, following which she was on the Clyde for repairs from 9th July, giving the extra sailings for Tarbert Fair on 29th idem. She relieved the *Lochiel* on the Outer Islands service from Portree, in which latter occupation she was wrecked on Duncan's Rock near Rodel, Harris, on 7th December, 1896.

P.S. "Carabinier." Purchased as the *Albert Edward* from the L. & S.W. and L.B. & S.C. Railways, by whom she had been employed on the Portsmouth-Isle of Wight joint railway service, this ship came north as a complete stranger to Scottish waters. She was built at Southampton, and had spent all her days in the South of England. She arrived on the Clyde on 22nd October, 1893 and took up service in the following February succeeding the *Gael*, which had been temporarily on the Sound of Mull run.

Apart from a straight stem and a cargo derrick on the mast she bore some resemblance to the *Fusilier* (before rebuilding), and was only a shade smaller in tonnage, though some 30 feet shorter. The machinery was different, being compound oscillating with two cylinders.

The *Carabinier*'s station was Tobermory. Having facilities for handling cargo, she was employed during the fifteen years she served her Scottish owners on the regular Oban-Sound of Mull-Tobermory-Loch Sunart service carrying passengers, mails and cargo all the year round.

She was sold to J. J. King & Sons, Garston—for about £750—to be broken up at Troon, and left Greenock on 15th December, 1908.

.   .   .   .   .   .

After the departure of the *Brigadier* from the Clyde, the Loch Fyne cargo runs were largely performed by chartered tonnage, including *Battle Isle* and *Rossgull* in 1893-4. The latter was a year of many charters. To relieve the *Cavalier* on the Glasgow-Inverness route the S.S. *Ben Nevis* was obtained from Wallace Bros. of Liverpool. Dating from 1884 she had originally been owned in Fort William and was no stranger to the route between her home port and Glasgow. She completed her charter on 4th January, 1894.

S.S. "Aggie." This was one of the ships chartered for so long and on so many occasions that she appeared in fleet-lists and was regarded as a member of the MacBrayne fleet and carried the Company's colours. She was employed principally on the Loch Fyne cargo run carrying a few passengers, and dated from 1893. She was a "herring screw" owned by McKinney & Rafferty, Fish Salesmen, Glasgow, as also were *Nellie* (1892) and *Marie* (1891), also employed on charter on the Loch Fyne route at various times including the summer of 1894. In February that year she had taken the place of the *Flowerdale* on the Oban-Barra service. The *Aggie* continued to be chartered till the 1900s.

S.S. "Hibernian." The *Hibernian* began in Irish waters, her first owners being Messrs. Paul & Mackenzie of Dublin. She seems to have remained with them for some five years and was then bought by Craig & Peterson of Middlesbrough, for whom she worked until Mr. MacBrayne obtained her in July, 1894 for use in the coasting trade. Since she was bought to take the place of the *Udea* it would seem that any sailing she did would be of the nature of tramping; and this is borne out by her having been lost in the Irish Sea off Douglas, I.O.M. following a collision with the I.O.M.S.P. Co.'s *Prince of Wales*, on

12th August, 1894, her period in the MacBrayne fleet being of only a month's duration.

P.S. "Gairlochy." This steamer appeared on the Clyde as the *Sultan* and was a flush-decked ship with straight slanting stem, single mast, and funnel forward of a particularly large pair of paddle boxes. The engine was that of the P.S. *Wellington* built in 1853 and was of steeple design.

Beginning on the Kilmun station with McKellar of the Helensburgh "green" boats, she changed hands in 1862 to Captain Alexander Williamson and for the next thirty years or so proved herself a highly successful steamer in the Glasgow, Rothesay, and Kyles of Bute trade. A new boiler was installed in 1877. Captain James Williamson in his well-known book *The Clyde Passenger Steamer*, published in 1904, records that the *Sultan* was his first command, when he was twenty years of age.

The steamer's next owners—from September, 1891—were the late Glasgow and South Western Railway Company which obtained her with the remainder of the Alexander Williamson fleet; but she did not fly their flag for long, and we find her, in March, 1893, in the hands of Captain John Williamson, son of the former owner, with the name changed to *Ardmore*. Again this ownership was of short duration.

The steamer was now thirty-four years old, and was about to enter the last lap of her career. Incidentally this "last lap" was prolonged for nearly another quarter of a century, but the trading conditions were easy.

Mr. MacBrayne acquired *Ardmore* late in 1894 and prepared her for service on the Caledonian Canal. This involved shortening the hull—nearly to the extent of 30 feet—and fitting the canoe type of bow, somewhat similar to that of the *Gondolier*, for easy negotiation of the canal locks. (The steamer had already had her bow rebuilt once before, following a collision.) A saloon was added; and, generally speaking, the *Gairlochy*, as she now became, was brought up to MacBrayne standards, such as we have referred to in the case of several others of the saloon paddle steamers.

The *Gairlochy* took up the summer run between Inverness and Banavie, being opposite number to the *Gondolier*. Both ships were normally laid up at Muirtown in winter.

The fate of the *Gairlochy* may be remembered by some, namely destruction by fire at Fort Augustus on 24th December, 1919. The steamer happened to be working the Inverness-Fort Augustus mail service when the accident occurred. Sooner or later *Gairlochy* would have been disposed of in the ordinary way had this fire not occurred, as the post-war traffic in passengers and goods showed a marked reduction. She will be remembered as the best looking of all the

Caledonian Canal steamers. Her keel is still visible from Fort Augustus Pier when the level of the loch is low.

S.S. "Jessie." It is believed that this craft was a small open launch employed at Tobermory in the 1890s in connexion with the Western Isles Hotel, which had then recently been built and was managed by the Company.

P.S. "Glendale." It was in 1902, following the loss of *Islay* (III), that a notable vessel came into the Company's fleet. Circumstances, however, decreed that her career with them should be brief; but within the two or three years of her sojourn in the West Highlands she made a fair name for herself on several routes.

The early history of the *Glendale* is not without interest.

In 1875 the L.B. & S.C. Railway took delivery from the Govan yard of Messrs. John Elder of the *Paris*, which was the second ship on their books to bear that name. The steamer was designed for the cross-channel service between Newhaven and Dieppe; but, as her story is revealed, she will be found working at places as far apart as Dieppe, North Wales, Hamburg and Stornoway at various times.

For thirteen years the ship plied between Newhaven and Dieppe and proved herself an excellent sea boat. Her main fault seems to have been with respect to speed, and it was this shortcoming that resulted in her relatively early displacement from Newhaven. Mr. Burtt relates that on one occasion only did the *Paris* make the passage under 5 hours, when 4 hours 50 minutes were taken, corresponding to a speed of 13½ knots only.

It will be readily understood that even in 1888, when this occurred, something more expeditious was expected on an important cross-channel service.

The Fairfield Company (successors to John Elder) purchased the ship back and re-boilered her, increasing the pressure from 60 to 80 lb. Between 1890 and 1892 she was registered under the name of R. Barnwell, managing director of the Fairfield Co. It was during this period that the steamer was run on the Liverpool and North Wales tourist and excursion routes, preparing the way for the formation of the Liverpool & North Wales S.S. Co. Ltd., promoted largely by the Fairfield Company.

She is next found as *Flamingo* registered under A. Ballin of the Hamburg-Amerika Line, for the Heligoland service between 1892 and 1895, when she returned to Fairfield ownership in name of R. Barnwell and from 1896 to 1902 in that of W. M. Rhodes of London. She was re-named *La Belgique* with registration in Glasgow for a Tilbury-Ostend service. *Paris/Flamingo/La Belgique* having sampled the English Channel, Irish Sea, North Sea, the Clyde, and the Thames over a period of twenty-seven years was then deemed to be sufficiently experienced to face the Minch and the Mull of Kintyre, and coming into the MacBrayne fleet was given her new uniform and sent out as *Glendale*. She is said to have been a remarkably steady ship even in rough weather.

At the time of acquisition, consequent on the loss of *Islay* (III), there had been some juggling round of steamers, as we find the *Lovedale* away from Stornoway and on the Islay route, the *Gael* doing Kyle of Lochalsh and Stornoway, and the *Glendale* on the Oban-Gairloch service with extensions to Ullapool on Thursdays and Lochinver on Saturdays. This was in 1903. The *Glendale* also worked the Stornoway mail service and finished her career between Glasgow and Islay. Her wreck on Deas Point, Kintyre, on 20th July, 1905, was due to an error of navigation. She was outward bound from Glasgow and for some reason or other, such as confusion between the Sanda and the Mull lights, the course was altered too soon, and the vessel was run upon the rocks before the error could be rectified. Neither she nor her cargo was salved, but there was no loss of life.

Some time after entering the MacBrayne fleet she was given new funnels, very tall and slender, in place of those she had carried as *La Belgique*. The position of her lifeboats, also, was altered.

S.S. "Lapwing" (II). Reviewing the fleet as it stood in 1902 we find it consisted of thirty steamers, sixteen of which were bought secondhand, and the average age of the whole fleet was a shade over thirty-two years. It will be recalled that the last paddle and screw vessels built for the Company were the *Fusilier* (1888) and *Cavalier* (1883) respectively, all subsequent ships having been purchased from other owners. In the course of the next three years seven new steamers were built, to be followed by a number of others until *Mountaineer* (III) appeared in 1910.

The first vessel of the new batch—of which three were approximately sisters—was *Lapwing* (II). She was a neat little screw steamer of 211 tons, turned out by Scott of Bowling and engined by Hutson. The design was no doubt drawn up to satisfy the conditions prevailing on the Outer Hebrides services operating throughout the year. These conditions demand a passenger and cargo sea-going vessel, with sleeping accommodation, which can be run with the maximum overall economy.

The days of ornamented bows and sterns and other embellishment had gone, and with her straight stem, two masts and single funnel we find a thoroughly serviceable profile. For five years the *Lapwing* (II) ran on the Oban-Outer Islands mail service in company first with the *Flowerdale* and then with her own quasi-sister *Plover* (III).

When *Lochiel* (II) came out, *Lapwing* (II) went further north, and from her headquarters at Portree worked the Outer Islands service to Harris and Lochmaddy with Dunvegan as her outward destination, in succession to *Lochiel* (I).

As far as is known she finished her work with the Company on this latter route, excepting such spells of relieving duty that she may have undertaken from time to time including some service on the Clyde cargo runs about 1915. She stranded on Rat Rock, Oban on 28th January, 1917 and thus ended her career in the MacBrayne fleet. She was salved and taken to Bowling a few months later and was sold on 23rd April, 1918, to Clyde Cargo Steamers Ltd. (see Chapter X).

S.S. "Sheila." The second steamer of the new MacBrayne family was the famous *Sheila*, which became so closely identified with Stornoway and the inhabitants of Lewis. This was a product of Inglis of Pointhouse, both hull and machinery; she had the distinction of being the first steamer in the fleet to be fitted with triple-expansion engines and very neat and trim they were.

The ship was launched at Pointhouse on 30th January, 1904. When finished she was a "good looker". It would be extravagance to apply the epithet "pretty" as in the case of the *Claymore*, because gone were the days of beautiful clipper bows, bowsprits, carving and ornamentation. Nevertheless her hull was finely modelled, and with well proportioned masts and funnel even this utility ship possessed a grace of outline not so often met with in vessels of her size and class. *Sheila* was named after a character in William Black's novel *A Princess of Thule*. Her trials were run on 9th March, 1904.

Probably few steamers of only 280 tons have fulfilled such an important role and been known and respected in the same way as *Sheila*. We use the word "respected" with deliberation, because for over twenty years this little ship fought and defied the Minch, summer and winter, on the passage between Kyle of Lochalsh and Stornoway with passengers, cargo and mails, and the occasions when "weather and circumstances" were so utterly outrageous that she did not venture out were few and far between.

All the credit for this does not of course rest with the ship, because without her gallant crew such consistent running would have been impossible. We have heard of the most fearsome passages undertaken on winters' nights with such wind and seas that, steaming to the utmost limit, practically no headway would be made at all for hours, but sooner or later the steamer would be alongside the pier preparing for her next trip, or return passage as the case might be.

The hours involved on this Stornoway run were arduous, and it is generally conceded—but not always realised by West Highland travellers—that the Stornoway mail steamer was the hardest worked of the whole fleet. The week-end rest at Stornoway was little more than twenty-four hours, namely from arrival on the Saturday night to the departure very early on Monday morning.

There will be some who look back on their passages in the *Sheila* as a painful memory, but they must be fair and admit that her daily crossings of the Minch—actually twice per twenty-four hours—in practically all weathers for over twenty years without mishap was no mean achievement. On many important cross-channel services the volume of traffic and financial side of the undertakings used to permit of sufficient vessels being maintained to allow each ship fairly long periods of rest in the course of the year for reconditioning. Such a condition was not, and is not possible in the West Highlands on the continuous mail services, so that the only rest given to the *Sheila* was a short spell each year for dry-docking and survey in Glasgow. Here was a prominent case of the outstanding reliability of steam machinery.

Readers who are interested in this ship will find two most impressive and amusing descriptions of the Minch crossing from the point of view of the passenger who is not too good a sailor in the *Stornoway Gazette* during May, 1933. These were written by Mr. J. N. McIver of Stornoway.

The *Sheila*'s time on this station was not entirely unbroken, as she was employed on the Kyle, Mallaig, and Outer Islands service in 1921, and was in Oban about the time the Great War concluded. (In 1921, when she was otherwise employed, the *Gael* was Stornoway mail steamer).

In all probability the *Sheila*, when new, relieved the *Gael* or *Glendale*, and the difference in running costs must have been very marked indeed.

The fate of the ship was tragic. Captain Cameron was away enjoying a few days of well-earned rest and the steamer was in the hands of another officer temporarily. Attention has already been drawn to the dangers of navigation on the West Coast and to the great rarity of mishaps on the whole, but it is human to err, and the mistake that was made on the inward passage from Stornoway in the early morning of Saturday, 1st January, 1927, sealed the fate of the poor *Sheila* and she never reached Kyle.

We do not know the details, but it is possible the officer of the watch never saw the South Rona light, and thinking he had run his distance, altered course with a view to making the Applecross call, and did not discover his error till too late. The result was that the unfortunate vessel ran ashore in darkness in Cuaig Bay just south of the mouth of Loch Torridon, very early on New Year's morning. No lives were lost.

The *Claymore* was in the vicinity of Kyle at the time and took up the *Sheila*'s sailings until such time as the *Clydesdale* (II) was available. The latter was then on the service for two and a half years until *Lochness* (III) came out.

S.S. "Plover" (III)/**"Loch Aline."** The next two steamers built— *Plover* (III) and *Cygnet* (II)—followed very closely the lines of *Lapwing* (II) but all three were different in various respects. For instance *Lapwing* and *Plover* were both equipped for passengers and cargo and had sleeping accommodation, whereas the *Cygnet* had at first no cabins and was used almost exclusively for cargo. She also carried a single mast and independent derrick, but her machinery was similar to that of the *Plover*. Of the three, *Plover* (III) was the handsomest and the longest lived. She was launched at Bowling on 17th May, 1904, and given a boiler and the port engine of the old *Flowerdale*. (The propeller was right-handed so it can be deduced that the *Flowerdale*'s engines turned "inwards" ahead which is rather unusual.) This case of old "wine" going into a new "bottle" certainly worked well, and many people may not have realised that the machinery and boiler exceeded the hull in age by no less than twenty-six years.

Plover was built for the Islands services and worked on them continuously from Oban, Mallaig and Kyle of Lochalsh with only occasional diversions elsewhere. Her sea-going qualities were proved time and time again, and her reputation in this respect stood as high as that of *Sheila*. On 29th July, 1918 while on the Oban to Castlebay run *Plover* was shelled by a German submarine when one hour past the "passage of Tiree". With one small gun at stern *Plover* started counter-attack. The master (Captain Neil MacDougall) decided to lower the two ship's boats with passengers; and the submarine submerged. *Plover* arrived at Barra at 7 p.m. and the first boat at Rhum during the night. The other boat followed the route taken by *Plover* to Castlebay, arriving at dawn.

The exceptional services rendered were sheep-carrying from Ardrishaig occasionally, the Mallaig-Portree mail service for a period about 1933, and as private vessel for the Directors when on tour, in which duty she succeeded *Gael*. With regard to the last duty, early in 1934, the *Plover* went to Ardrossan for alterations, and created general surprise in the Highlands by re-appearing in August with a new buff-coloured funnel, extended promenade deck aft, the hull painted half white and bearing the name *Loch Aline* (the first "loch" name to be expressed as two words). A small motor dinghy was acquired for use with her. She remained a merchantman, however, and not a yacht; and during the winter months she undertook general relieving duty on the Islands services. During certain seasons, also, she performed local excursions from Oban: when on these duties she carried the normal MacBrayne funnel colouring. During the second war she was requisitioned on 8th December, 1939 and served as an examination vessel at Rothesay from 1940 to 1945. She was transferred to Burns & Laird Lines, Ltd. in March, 1946. Laid up at Ardrossan, she was sold in October, 1947 to H. Harper, Glasgow, for T. Heiton & Co. Ltd., Dublin, who altered her for cargo and coal-carrying and re-named her *Saint Fintan*. As such she was for a short period running from Dublin to Silloth. She was sold to E. G. Rees Ltd., Llanelly for scrap, arriving there on 2nd July, 1951.

S.S. "Cygnet" (II). This steamer was launched from Inglis' Yard at Pointhouse on Tuesday, 14th June, 1904 by Miss Ruby MacBrayne and in due course received the other boiler of the *Flowerdale* and the starboard engine. The *Cygnet's* propeller was left-handed.

As delivered, and for a number of years afterwards, she was employed almost solely on cargo duties, her route being the Glasgow-Inveraray one which in years gone by had been conducted by the *Inveraray Castle, Mary Jane, Dolphin* and *Brigadier*. However, for a portion of the winter she often went north to relieve the Outer Islands steamers when their turns came round for docking and survey.

The accommodation for passengers was much more limited than in the case of *Lapwing* (II) and *Plover* (III), but, during the time she functioned on these northern routes, the number of passengers travelling would be almost negligible.

Cygnet's rig was different from that of her two quasi-sisters in that a single hinged mast was fitted, and an independent cargo winch. The funnel was also hinged, the reason being that her berth in Glasgow was underneath the Caledonian Railway bridge on the north side of the river and at high water the head room was strictly limited. It will be recalled that *Texa* also used this berth. These two steamers ran turn about for a long time but only *Cygnet* proceeded as far as Inveraray. A curious mishap occurred at Bridge Wharf on 7th June, 1906, when, owing to a mistake, a sea-cock was left open and the ship sank.

After the Great War the various changes that had occurred necessitated the permanent transfer of the *Cygnet* to the Islands routes, and some additions were made to her, such as more accommodation for passengers, and the provision of wireless apparatus, which required a mainmast to be added. Actually these modifications detracted from the steamer's appearance, strange to say, and she never looked as well as *Plover* in her latter days.

She was then based at Oban while *Plover* was at Kyle, and between them they conducted the Islands mail services until the advent of the new motor vessels in 1930.

The Outer Islands services were inaugurated after the first Great War, and required two steamers instead of three (*vide* T.S.S. *Flowerdale*). One operated from Oban (outwards on Mondays, Wednesdays, and Fridays) to Coll, Tiree, Castlebay and Lochboisdale, and the other from Kyle working both north and south of Skye *via* Mallaig and embracing Eigg, Rum, Canna, Lochboisdale, Lochmaddy and Tarbert (Harris).

In concluding these notes on the *Plover* and *Cygnet* a word should be added on the old engines of the *Flowerdale*, which drove ships ploughing Hebridean waters for so long. They were two-cylinder compound with massive parts and bearings of ample proportions; and what struck an observer was the extraordinary rough and ready finish, so different from the finish of practically all the older sets of machinery. If our memory is not at fault the eccentric rods, for instance, were simply rough unmachined forgings, except of course at the ends. However, no one can deny the remarkable solidity of these engines and their absolute dependability.

Cygnet was sold on 17th September, 1930 to T. W. Ward Ltd. and broken up at Barrow in May, 1931.

S.S. "Brenda" (II). This chubby little steamer constituted the fifth new addition to the fleet between 1903 and 1905, and was launched by Scott of Bowling on Saturday, 29th October, 1904. She received a set of second-hand yacht engines which had been built in 1888, and the boiler was that which had previously served as donkey-boiler on *Flowerdale*. Her name revived that of one of the early Thomson & MacConnell steamers.

The *Brenda*, a compact-looking craft, was built for cargo work only and designed to run through the Crinan Canal on the Glasgow-Mull, etc. trade as consort to the *Handa*. She was the last vessel on the Glasgow-Inverness run, though her sailings were latterly curtailed to Fort William.

It is to be noted that with the disappearance of *Brenda* the service she performed was modified to the extent that the Crinan Canal was no longer used, her successor, *Lochshiel*, running round the Mull of Kintyre.

Brenda was sold on 11th December, 1929 to the West of Scotland Shipbreaking Co. Ltd. and scrapped at Troon.

P.S."Pioneer" (II). This was another Inglis product and having been launched in February, 1905, she ran trials on 25th March when a maximum speed of 14 knots was obtained. Service conditions would not require this speed.

The ship, built for the Islay mail service from West Loch Tarbert, was materially different from any of her predecessors, and struck a distinctly modern note. The hull was plated up forward to the promenade deck, and the paddle boxes did not project above this deck. The single funnel was well forward and the bridge abaft it. The engines were diagonal compound and the design was such that small and light parts, running at relatively high revolutions were the dominant features. The paddles consequently were very small.

Light draught is an important feature on this service, not because it is a fair weather sheltered route, as in the winter high seas have to be encountered, but because with the West Loch Tarbert pier being so far up the loch, there is little water there at spring tides. This made the problem of design much more difficult than it would otherwise have been, and no doubt accounted for the selection of a haystack boiler, it being well known that the evaporative capacity of this type, in relation to size and cost, is high. The working pressure was 120 lb. which we think is about the maximum for such a boiler.

The *Pioneer* came on to the Islay route in April, 1905, taking the place of the *Glencoe*. We are uncertain if she ever worked elsewhere,

THE MISSES GRAY BY COURTESY OF ALASDAIR FRASER

1   P.S. *Inveraray Castle*
At Tarbert

STROMIER-VOGT COLLECTION

2   P.S. *Glengarry* ex *Edinburgh Castle*
Near Fort Augustus

3   P.S. *Pioneer* (I)

At North Pier, Oban, c. 1869

4   P.S. *Pioneer* (I)

As altered in 1874-75. At Corpach.

5   *Sunbeam*

In Crinan Canal at Ardrishaig

6   P.S. *Cygnet* (I)

In Oban Bay

7   P.S. *Mountaineer* (I) as built

At Corpach

8   P.S. *Mountaineer* (I) as altered

In Oban Bay

9   P.S. *Glencoe* and T.S.M.V. *Lochfyne*

At Broomielaw, Glasgow, during Civic Week, June 1931

10   S.S. *Clydesdale* (I)

At St. Kilda

11 P.S. *Gondolier*
At Muirtown Wharf, Inverness, 8/1899
S.S. *Ethel* beyond and P.S. *Glengarry* on right

12 P.S. *Chevalier* (II)
At Crinan, 1913

13 T.S.S. *Linnet,* with P.S. *Chevalier* (II) beyond and S.S. *Countess of Kellie*

Crinan

14 S.S. *Clansman* (II) and P.S. *Islay* (II)

At Customhouse Quay, Greenock

15 s.s. *Lochawe*

At Ford, 1913

16 s.s. *Lochiel* (I)

At West Loch Tarbert

A. ERNEST GLEN

17   s.s. *Fingal* (II)
At Rothesay, 1912

MCISAAC & RIDDLE

18   s.s. *Cavalier*

19　　　　　　　　　P.S. *Grenadier*

Off Iona

20　　　　　S.S. *Handa* ex *Aros Castle*

In Oban Bay

21

s.s. *Mabel*

Arriving at Tollie, Loch Maree, July, 1910

22

s.s. *Staffa* (III)

In Oban Bay

23   P.S. *Fusilier*

In Oban Bay, c.1920

24   S.S. *Pelican*

As coal-hulk, in Portree Bay, 1892

MCISAAC & RIDDLE

25   P.S. *Mountaineer* (II) ex *Hero*
Off Dunollie, Oban

JAMES JOHNSTON, BY COURTESY OF D. A. FENTON

26   P.S. *Islay* (III)
Off Port Glasgow

27   P.S. *Lovedale* ex *Great Western*

At Lochmaddy

28   P.S. *Gael*

Approaching Kyle of Lochalsh 8/1921

29   P.S. *Brigadier* ex *Cygnus*
In Oban Bay

30   P.S. *Carabinier*
In Oban Bay

31

P.S. *Gairlochy*
near Tomnahurich, Inverness

32

P.S. *Glendale*
At Portree, 7/1904

33   S.S. *Loch Aline* ex *Plover* (III)   J. B. MACGEORGE'S COLLECTION
In Oban Bay

34   S.S. *Cygnet* (II)   STROMIER-VOGT COLLECTION

35   S.S. *Brenda* (II)   C.L.D.D.
At Ardrishaig, 1913

36   P.S. *Pioneer* (II)

At West Loch Tarbert, 8/8/29

37   S.S. *Clydesdale* (II)

Off Gourock, 1937

38   T.S.M.V. *Comet* (III)

Leaving Gourock on last run to Lochgoilhead, 30/9/46

39   T.S.M.V. *Scout*

At Ballachulish Quarries

40   s.s. *Chieftain*
Off Gourock

I. N. MALLINSON

41   Tr.S.M.V. *Lochinvar*
At Oban, 17/8/39

42   S.S. *Lochiel* (II)

Off Gourock

43   S.S. *Dirk*

In Oban Bay

44   P.S. *Mountaineer* (III)

Arriving at Gourock, 1936

45   T.S.S. *Lochness* (III)

Leaving Kyle of Lochalsh

46   M.V. *Lochshiel* (I)
Off Dunglass, 10/7/39

47   T.S.M.V. *Lochearn*
Off Kyle of Lochalsh, 7/9/48

48 s.s. *Lochbroom* (I)

Off the Cloch, 8/1936

49 T.S.M.V. *Lochfyne*

Off Toward, 9/6/59

G.E.L.

50　　　　　　S.S. *Princess Louise*

Leaving Inverness, 24/7/35

G.E.L.

51　　　　　　T.S.M.V. *Lochnevis*

Arriving at Dunoon, 19/9/59

G.E.L.

52   Tr.s.s. *Saint Columba*
Arriving at Innellan, 6/6/36

G.E.L.

53   T.s.s. *King George V*
Off Iona, 7/6/50
with M.V. *Iona* (V) leaving jetty

G.E.L.

54
    s.s. *Lochgorm* (**II**)
Leaving Stornoway, 9/6/50

G.E.L.

55
    s.s. *Lochgarry*
Off the Cloch, 14/8/39

56 T.S.M.V. *Lochiel* (IV)

Arriving at Fort William, 1939

57 T.S.M.V. *Loch Seaforth*

Off Greenock, 28/3/54

58 s.s. *Hebridean*

At Dunvegan Pier

G.E.L.

59 s.s. *Hebrides* (I)

Arriving at Greenock, Customhouse Quay, 31/7/51

60   S.S. *Dunara Castle*

At Tarbert, Harris, in the 1880's (with two funnels)

G.E.L.

61   S.S. *Dunara Castle*

At Oban, 7/8/46 (with one funnel)

G.E.L.

62
           S.S. *Loch Frisa*
Off Erskine, 9/9/55

G.E.L.

63
           S.S. *Loch Carron*
Off Bowling, 5/6/51

G.E.L.

64 T.S.M.V. *Claymore* (II)

Arriving at Oban, 3/9/55

G.E.L.

65 M.V. *Loch Ard*

Leaving Greenock, Customhouse Quay, 2/4/56

66   T.S.S. *Robina*

Leaving Lochgoilhead, 22/7/47

67   T.S.M.V. *Hebridean Isles*

Leaving Stornoway for Ullapool, 13/12/85

68
s.s. *Davaar*
Leaving Lochranza, 22/8/39

69
s.s. *Dalriada*
Leaving Gourock, 19/8/39

but a picture of Mallaig in the Company's 1907 guide book shows a steamer which can be none other than the *Pioneer* (II), so it is possible she worked the Portree mail service for a time. At any rate this did not last long and she made her name—that of a reliable and dependable unit of the fleet—unquestionably on the passage between West Loch Tarbert and Port Ellen and Portaskaig. The former place used to be her destination four days a week and Portaskaig the remaining two; but, after World War I, she plied to each alternately, and always spent the week-end at Port Ellen. The call at Jura (Craighouse) was included on Portaskaig days, and Gigha on the other days; and in her earlier years she also proceeded to Bruichladdich on occasion, as her predecessor *Glencoe* had done.

During her short spells off duty for dry-docking, *Mountaineer* (III) acted as relief until her disposal, after which *Lochinvar* was usually employed in this capacity.

One minor alteration was made in *Pioneer*, namely the substitution, for the standard type of MacBrayne paddle-box fan-vents, of the horizontal slot type. This was the only instance of paddle boxes of non-standard type being used on a MacBrayne vessel for any great length of time.

In 1939 *Pioneer* was to be succeeded on the Islay mail run by the new motor vessel *Lochiel*, but the latter could not be regularly used until improvements to the pier were completed, and *Pioneer* continued, *Lochiel* being stationed at Oban till they exchanged places in the autumn. In the early part of the second war she returned to the Islay route during part of 1939 and till 15th November, 1940, *Lochiel* being then employed on the Clyde. In 1940 she received the generator from the *Gondolier*. She also relieved on the Portree route in 1939-40, and performed livestock ferrying in the Oban area in 1941-2, when she in addition acted as relief on the Sound of Mull station, then was laid up off Tighnabruaich till 9th March, 1942. After overhaul she was on the Sound of Mull run from 15th June, 1942, then was for a time laid up. On 21st March, 1944 she left Lochaline for Oban and the Clyde, having been requisitioned by the Admiralty.

Stationed off Fairlie, she was used as the headquarters of the submarine control for the North Atlantic, being later fitted out as a research ship under the Director of Submarine Warfare in connexion with under-water telephone work. She had much valuable equipment on board and was purchased and re-named *Harbinger* in 1945. In January, 1946 she was taken to Messrs. Inglis' yard, where the paddle wheels were removed to facilitate her being towed to the south coast. She was then anchored in Portland Harbour as a floating laboratory, and was seen in the Solent on 8th March, 1958 in tow for Rotterdam for scrapping.

S.S. "Clydesdale" (II). We now come to the seventh and last new steamer of the 1903-5 batch. *Clydesdale* (II) was designed and built for

D

the Glasgow-Inverness cargo and passenger traffic. She lasted forty-eight years and it is extremely doubtful if she visited Inverness more than two or three times. Circumstances decreed otherwise, as we shall see directly.

In appearance and size the steamer was almost an exact replica of the *Cavalier*, though in minor details and finish the latter was superior. The *Clydesdale*'s machinery was triple-expansion, and the engine room much more spacious than was that of her older colleague.

Named by Miss Evelyn MacBrayne when launched on the 18th May, 1905, *Clydesdale* joined *Cavalier* and the two ships provided a bi-weekly service to Inverness. This was during the early summer of 1905. Then came the loss of the *Glendale* in July; and, since no other suitable steamer was available, *Clydesdale* (II) came on to the Glasgow-Islay run almost immediately—the *Ethel* filling the gap in the Inverness schedule meantime—and remained on it almost continuously for fifteen years. Thus was her career to and from Inverness nipped in the bud.

Now *Clydesdale* (II) was not entirely wedded to Islay; on the contrary during her long existence she proved herself an invaluable member of the fleet for the Glasgow-West Coast cargo trade in the winter months when the traffic did not require a larger vessel. After the loss of the *Sheila* in 1927 she stepped into the breach a second time, and did duty as Stornoway mail steamer until the *Lochness* (III) was brought out in 1929. About 1926 a change was made respecting the Glasgow-Stornoway trade and instead of the *Claymore* [or *Clydesdale* (II) in winter] proceeding to Lewis, the steamer kept to the mainland and turned south from Lochinver or Loch Inchard according to traffic demands. The cargo for Stornoway was transported in another steamer, as will be seen when we are dealing with *Lochiel* (III) and *Lochdunvegan* (I), which maintained an independent weekly service, putting in a very limited number of intermediate calls. Simultaneously the old twice-weekly service was curtailed to one every ten days.

Clydesdale was a splendid sea boat and a familiar figure at West Highland ports. During the second war she served on the various cargo, passenger and mail services, and in October, 1946, acted as relief Stornoway steamer for cargo. She also performed sheep-ferrying from the islands to Oban and Kyle, passengers being rarely carried in her later years. Latterly she was on the *Claymore*'s old run from Glasgow. She was sold in February, 1953 for scrapping at Port Glasgow.

Chartered Vessels

Though it is not our usual practice to deal extensively with chartered vessels, there are a few instances where the charter has been of such duration as to give the ship concerned almost the character of a member of the fleet. One of the outstanding examples of this was the little screw steamer *Aggie*.

Normally chartered vessels did not receive the honour of having their names included in the Company's fleet-lists, but *Aggie* was an exception, as also was *Jura*. The latter's name was included in a list on a large board maintained by the Company in Fort William Station, over the exit to the Station Hotel, which remained there until at least 1927. It is believed that the *Jura* in question was a small iron screw steamer built in 1869, and owned originally by Archibald Mackechnie, Glasgow. In 1871 she was purchased by John Thomas Hay, Londonderry, in 1874 by James NcNeil, there and on 4th November, 1876, by David Wilson, Glasgow, Donald Dewar, Lochgilphead and Duncan Young, Glasgow. After various changes in ownership of shares in the vessel she was owned equally from August, 1885, by Donald Dewar and James E. MacLarty, ownership of the whole passing to Donald Dewar on 19th November, 1898. On 3rd April, 1913, she was sold to James Paterson Waldie, Glasgow, and on 18th December, 1916, to W. A. Massey & Sons, Ltd., Hull. She became a total loss in August, 1917, on being sunk near Stranraer. The date or dates when she functioned as a member of the MacBrayne fleet are not known.

Another vessel employed on the Lochfyne cargo run and elsewhere on charter, also in the Company's colours, was S.S. *Battle Isle*, a "herring screw" built by Scott & Co., Bowling, in 1885 and owned by C. F. Paton & Co. Ltd., Glasgow. During 1893-4 and possibly later, *Rossgull* was chartered from the Earl of Leitrim, as also was the same owner's *Melmore*.

After the withdrawal of the old paddle steamer *Plover*, the screw steamer *Rockabill*, of 277 tons gross, was chartered in 1882 as a stopgap and sailed along with P.S. *Cygnet* and S.S. *Staffa* on the Inverness station, being so advertised in July, 1882. She distinguished herself by hitting the lock-gates at Fort Augustus, and later stranded on Ballyshannon Bar on 25th July, 1884, being then sold for breaking up. She had been built in 1878 for the Clyde Shipping Company, and was sold in January, 1883, to John MacFarlane and Duncan Young, the latter's shares passing in February and March, 1884, to R. B. Ballantyne and John J. Lawson.

In May, 1897, S.S. *Honfleur* was chartered from Messrs. Paton & Hendry to take the place of P.S. *Islay*, and was wrecked on the Island of Sanda. She had been built at Dundee in 1875 for the L.B. & S.C.R. Co.

Another temporary place in the MacBrayne fleet on the Glasgow-Inverness station, along with *Cavalier*, was, in 1899 occupied by the chartered vessel, *Piscator*, owned by T. McLaren, Glasgow, for whom she had been built in 1886.

CHAPTER IV

DAVID MACBRAYNE, LTD., 1905—1928

AN important development in transport in the West Highlands occurred in 1906 with the introduction of a motor omnibus between Fort William and North Ballachulish, the beginning of a network of road services which ultimately took the place of steamer services on many routes. The internal combustion engine was not, however, confined to land use.

T.S.M.V. "Comet" (III). This small vessel, acquired in 1907, was the Company's first venture into the realms of international combustion machinery for marine propulsion; and, whatever her failings may have been, the fact that she served the owners for forty years indicates that she proved herself a sound investment.

An interesting feature was the revival of the name of the first steamboat on the Clyde; and, on account of the descent of the MacBrayne fleet from that of Henry Bell, we feel justified in referring to the subject under description as *Comet* (III).

Built by Robertson of Canning Town, London, and engined by Gardner of Manchester, the ship was virtually a large launch of 43 tons with considerable covered-in accommodation in proportion to her size. No one could call her beautiful by any stretch of imagination. Her career with the Company was spent partly between Ballachulish and Kinlochleven, on the Crinan Canal, and mainly on the Firth of Clyde.

Travelling on board was a very different experience from that on a steamer, as the engine noises were apt to be rather tiresome. Early in her service the popping of the exhaust was dreadful, but this was afterwards largely rectified by improved silencing.

Comet had an accident near Fort Matilda about 1927-8 and went ashore; but the damage was not extensive. She was re-engined in 1928. She was damaged by collision with the Diesel-electric *Talisman* in August, 1936 and, after repair, returned to her normal route, having been engaged almost continuously as the "Lochgoil Mail Steamer" from about 1917.

She spent a short period in 1919 operating between Ardrishaig and Inveraray in connexion with *Columba*, calling at Otterferry, Crarae and Strachur. Requisitioned on 5th September, 1939 she was returned to her owners after four days only. She made her last run to Lochgoilhead on 1st October, 1946, and thus terminated one of the oldest continuously-operated passenger services in the world. Motor buses were substituted by Messrs. MacBrayne, running from Carrick Castle to Lochgoilhead and Arrochar & Tarbet Station, connecting with the trains on the West Highland Railway; but this route was found difficult to operate in winter; and in summer it was inadequate for the passenger traffic, so in June, 1947, a steamer was again put on—this time the T.S.S. *Robina*, chartered by Messrs. MacBrayne from Coast Lines, Ltd.

Comet (III) was sold in May, 1947, to Lady Bee Co. Ltd., and registered at London, later at Shoreham, being re-named *Gradely* on 8th June, 1948. She was used for short trips and as her owners' private yacht, and, on being sold, reverted to the name *Comet*. She became a houseboat in Shoreham Harbour, without machinery.

T.S.M.V. "Scout." This was the second motor vessel added to the fleet. In appearance she resembled closely a steamer for passenger and cargo traffic in sheltered waters by day, minus a funnel. She carried two masts, an independent cargo winch, and possessed extensive promenade space on two decks for a vessel of 82 tons gross. A small funnel was added after she had been in commission for some time. Her machinery was designed to use Scottish crude oil.

Placed on the Ballachulish-Kinlochleven route she worked for six years, until destroyed by a disastrous fire on board, caused by a blow-back from the engines, on 19th August, 1913. Her lifeboats gave further service on the *Columba* (I) and *King George V*.

S.S. "Chieftain." It would appear that either the Glasgow-Stornoway traffic was increasing sufficiently to justify a new cruise steamer or it was felt that *Clansman* (II) was becoming too old for this trade. Both circumstances may have urged Mr. David Hope MacBrayne to invite tenders for a new vessel at this time; and accordingly in due course there appeared in 1907 a vision of beauty which in some respects seemed to be a complete anachronism. We refer to the *Chieftain*'s lovely yacht-like lines and clipper bow, which had not been seen in a new ship of that type since *Claymore* came out in 1881. Æsthetically this was altogether a great triumph, in view of the fashions of the time.

With one exception only, as far as we are aware, nothing approaching the lines of the *Chieftain* has been attempted since in the case of a coasting merchant vessel. The exception—an East Coast product—was the 1931 *St. Sunniva* of the North of Scotland & Orkney & Shetland Steam Navigation Company, which company deserved much credit for building such a fine specimen in days when ugliness seems to be at a premium. Both steamers were about the same size.

The *Chieftain* was a noble ship with a noble name. Launched from the Ailsa Company's yard at Ayr by Mrs. D. Hope MacBrayne on 11th May, 1907, she was a shade over 1,000 tons gross with clipper bow, single funnel, two masts and extensive up-to-date passenger accommodation. The main engines were triple-expansion, and the cargo was worked by silent electric winches.

She was one of the largest steamers in gross tonnage ever built for the Company, though it will be recalled that the *Lochgarry*—purchased secondhand—was actually the largest owned up to that time, this honour having, prior to that date, been held by *Loanda* and now surpassed by the large vehicle-carriers such as *Hebrides* (II), *Clansman* (IV) and *Columba* (II), and more recently by *Isle of Arran* and *Hebridean Isles*.

Everything pointed to a long and successful career, but times were changing; and, though the *Chieftain* will long be remembered all the way from Glasgow to Stornoway and the Sutherland coast, the fact remains that—looking back on her performances—she was not an unqualified success. It is believed that the holds and winches were so arranged as to render the cargo handling difficult on her trade, and this trade demanded peculiar consideration in this respect; secondly she was a costly steamer to run; thirdly the passenger traffic which had promised so well began to decline after she had been running for a few years; and lastly came the First Great War.

It was unusual for this ship to be kept in commission all the year round, but she had to be brought out of winter quarters in a hurry when the *Claymore* came to grief at Broadford in January, 1910. The following August it was the *Chieftain*'s turn to go aground, on Raasay, fortunately without serious consequences.

When the *Clansman* (II) was withdrawn in 1909, the *Chieftain* and *Claymore* worked together in the summer months, while the *Cavalier* usually did duty for the former in the winter.

After the 1st Great War it was apparent that the traffic would not bear the cost of both the *Chieftain* and *Claymore*, and it is significant that the newer and larger vessel was selected for disposal, while the elderly *Claymore* was chosen to carry on with her time-honoured duties, though these were modified to the extent of excluding Stornoway, and the round trip was arranged to occupy in all ten days.

It is impossible not to look back with regrets on *Chieftain*'s career with the Company. Had fate decreed otherwise, she would have reigned long as the "chieftain" of the fleet, sharing the honours with *Columba* in her particular sphere; but it was not to be.

Her disposal occurred in June, 1919, on her sale to The North of Scotland & Orkney & Shetland Steam Navigation Co. Ltd., who re-named her *St. Margaret*. In 1925 she was purchased by Canadian National Steamship Co. Ltd., and registered as *Prince Charles* in name of Prince Charles, Ltd. (later Canadian National Steamships) to operate from Prince Rupert, B.C. Her beautiful clipper bow was then changed into a slanting stem, and various other alterations were made. About July, 1940, she was sold to Union Steamships, Ltd., Vancouver, and re-named *Camosun*; in December, 1945, to Oriental Navigation Co. Ltd., Tel Aviv, transferred to the Palestinian flag and re-named *Cairo*, operating as a passenger ship carrying 194 passengers in the Mediterranean trade. In 1947 she was sold to Zarati S.S. Co.,

Ltd., and registered at Panama under the Panamanian flag trading between Marseilles and Beira until June, 1948, when she went on a voyage to the West Indies. Laid up at Marseilles from 5th April, 1950 she arrived at Spezia on 8th January, 1952 and was broken up there.

Tr.S.M.V./T.S.M.V. "Lochinvar." The third motor vessel to be borne on the Company's books was designed and built as a successor to P.S. *Carabinier* on the Oban-Sound of Mull mail service. Though having comparatively fine lines and a well-designed hull, *Lochinvar* was no beauty, but had good, though restricted, passenger accommodation, the dining saloon being decorated with eight panels painted by J. Carey, representing the adventures of Young Lochinvar.

Originally she came out with a single tall thin funnel near the stern, and a cargo winch and crane amidships. Forward of the bridge was a single pole mast. Later a separate exhaust pipe was provided for each of the three sets of engines; finally these pipes were diverted and carried into a short large-diameter funnel forward of the cargo space. At the same time an electric crane made by Chambers, Scott & Co., Motherwell, was fitted in place of the original, and worked over the top of the funnel.

Her career with the Company was spent on the same route, namely Oban-Sound of Mull-Tobermory, carrying passengers, mails and cargo all the year round, apart from occasional relieving duties on the Tarbert-Islay or Lochgoil mail routes. She was on the latter in October-November, 1942, February-March, 1943, July-August, 1944 and January-March, 1945. She lived long enough to have become endeared to many folk in Argyllshire for her consistently good work on the service for which she was specially designed.

She was re-engined in 1926 and 1949, becoming twin-screw in the latter year. The machinery then fitted consisted of two sets of six-cylinder Davey Paxman motors with dimensions the same as those of the twelve-cylinder motors fitted in that year to *Lochearn* and *Lochmor*, and with parts interchangeable with theirs. (As in their case, a spare complete engine was kept ashore for *Lochinvar*, ready to be installed when either of those in use required an overhaul.) She had a very extensive refit, including new decks, an observation shelter, a wheelhouse and considerable renewal of hull plating, and resumed the Sound of Mull run in October, 1949. A mainmast was fitted in 1952. From 1955 she became spare, and performed short excursions from Oban, relieving in winter, and some years laid up in summer. In March, 1956 she went aground near Sanda when returning to Tobermory from the Clyde. Her service was then maintained by *Lochmor*, supplemented by *Lochbuie* and *Lochnell*. In February, 1958 it was agreed to base her at Inverness for cruises to Loch Ness as an experiment, but this idea was abandoned to keep her in reserve to cover wherever required. Then in 1959 she was placed on the Portree mail run where she was not particularly well received. On

23rd March, 1960 it was agreed to dispose of her for scrap as soon as fleet. overhauls would be completed. On 28th May, 1960 she performed her final MacBrayne run, from Tobermory to Oban, and was sold on 3rd June to Timbacraft Ltd., Shandon, at whose yard she lay till after her sale to an owner in the south. She returned to Greenock in October and had the words "*Brighton Belle*" painted on bow and stern, evidently without authority; and her old name had been restored when she left Greenock on 28th October. She opened a service between Sheerness and Southend, under the name *Anzio I* which lasted till the end of the 1963 season, after which she was laid up on the Thames. In the spring of 1966 she was on her way back to Scotland to run for Cromarty Cruises Limited, between Inverness and Invergordon, but met with disaster by being wrecked at Donna Nook, south of the Humber on 3rd April, 1966, with the loss of her whole crew including some of the directors of her new owners.

S.S. "Lochiel" (II). This handsome ship of 241 tons was intermediate in size between the *Sheila* and *Plover* (III) and in appearance very similar to them. Her promenade deck space was particularly good, and it was generally agreed that she was a thoroughly smart and trim little ship.

A notable feature of *Lochiel* (II) was the gyromechanism on board to eliminate, or at least reduce, rolling. This apparatus was operated by a motor which proved not sufficiently powerful to render it effective in really heavy weather. The apparatus was transferred in 1909 to the smaller *Dirk*.

The route allotted to *Lochiel* (II) gave ample scope, especially in winter, for trying out anti-rolling, pitching, twisting and every other kind of similar device, because she went on to the Oban-Islands mail service in place of the *Lapwing* (II). The latter then succeeded the *Lochiel* (I) on the Portree-Outer Islands run. *Lochiel* (II) ran on the Islands route with *Plover* (III) for a number of years. She was taken up by the Admiralty on 12th January, 1917, during the 1st Great War, and went from Oban to Grimsby, being afterwards blown up in July, 1918, while acting as a fleet runner in the Bristol Channel.

S.S. "Nellie"/"Staffa" (IV). This little cargo vessel was built for McKinney & Rafferty of Glasgow, and remained in their hands until 1904, when she was acquired by J. W. McIntyre, also of Glasgow. We have recollections of the *Nellie* lying in the Crinan Canal basin at Ardrishaig, mainly over week-ends, in the summer of 1906. She was then employed in connexion with the Loch Fyne fishing industry and had already been on charter to the Company.

The Company purchased the *Nellie* 1908, but did not change her name till April, 1910. She ran with *Brenda*, and possibly with *Handa* too, on the Glasgow-Crinan Canal-Mull and Loch Leven cargo service. Never a prominent member of the fleet, she resembled *Texa* on a smaller scale, the engines and boiler being fairly well aft, with a single mast and cargo hold forward.

Staffa (IV) was sold in April, 1916 to F. Reid of Ardrossan with whom she remained till 1925, when she changed hands again, and went to the Isle of Man with J. B. Kee of Ramsey. Later she went further south to Osman J. N. Eyon of Angle, Pembroke, and was sold in 1939 to J. B. Le Page & Co. Ltd., Guernsey, being lost about 1947.

S.S. "Dirk." We now come to the last of the screw steamers built for the Company of the group which consisted of *Lapwing* (II), *Sheila*, *Plover* (III), *Cygnet* (II), *Lochiel* (II), and *Dirk*. Apart from being the smallest of the six, the *Dirk* possessed a very tall funnel, which kept her going pendulum fashion when she rolled; and it may have been to counteract this that her owners chose her for the experimental transfer of a gyroscope from *Lochiel* (II), as stated previously.

It is rather remarkable that in a vessel of only 181 tons it was possible to incorporate sleeping accommodation for a number of passengers, since the cargo holds and working spaces necessarily occupied a disproportionately large amount of room in such a small steamer. Needless to say, everything was on a diminutive scale.

The little *Dirk* was stationed at Tobermory and, as far as we are aware, worked the Oban, Coll, Tiree and Bunessan mail service continuously. She made the outward passage on Mondays, Wednesdays and Fridays from Tobermory to Bunessan, and returned from Bunessan on Tuesdays, Thursdays and Saturdays to Oban, and then proceeded back to Tobermory on these evenings. This service lapsed after the 1st Great War.

Dirk was blown up, while on war service, about 1918.

P.S. "Mountaineer" (III). This was the last paddle steamer constructed for the fleet. For light draught and quick manoeuvring the paddle steamer held her own against every other mode of propulsion; and, on services where these characteristics were of considerable import, it is not surprising to find this type of vessel supreme. Not many of the Company's services are such as to render paddle steamers essential, however, and it seems most unlikely that we shall ever again see a MacBrayne paddle vessel.

Mountaineer (III) was launched from Inglis' yard at Pointhouse on 10th February, 1910, and in many respects was similar to *Pioneer* (II). We believe that had Messrs. Inglis been given a freer hand they would have turned out an almost exact sister ship, particularly in view of the success of their former product of five years earlier. However the late Mr. D. H. MacBrayne wished to incorporate certain distinctive features in the design, among them being the boarding-in all round of the promenade deck. Presumably this was to afford protection to passengers without going to the expense of providing covered-in accommodation on this deck. The result was not satisfactory, as the additional surface exposed to wind added to the "tenderness" of the vessel, and the boarding round the promenade deck was removed about 1926, beneficially we think, and especially as regards the steamer's appearance.

The promenade deck was not carried forward to the bow as in the case of the *Pioneer*, but terminated just aft of the mast. There was a saloon (3rd class) with large windows below the forward portion of the promenade deck. The general feeling concerning this steamer was that, somehow or other, she just failed to be what she might have been, namely a more comfortable steamer for passengers generally.

The machinery was similar in the two ships, but the *Mountaineer*'s cylinders were each ½ in. larger in diameter, and she had an independent air pump.

The routes allocated to the steamer were various, but she was never identified closely with any particular one, unless it were the Oban-Fort William Service, where she started her career and worked intermittently afterwards.

She but rarely worked north of Fort William or Tobermory, but she did the Oban-Crinan service, Oban-Sound of Mull-Tobermory mail route relieving the *Lochinvar*, West Loch Tarbert-Islay and Jura relieving *Pioneer* (II), the Portree mail run relieving *Fusilier*, and a winter service among Rothesay, Greenock and Lochgoilhead which subsequently lapsed. She also relieved the *Comet* on the Lochgoil mail service. During World War I she ran on the Gareloch route on charter to the North British Railway Company.

Oban was her headquarters in summer without exception, and latterly she conducted excursions as required and maintained a scheduled service to and from Lismore.

Finally must be added a rather amusing remark which was made concerning the *Mountaineer* in no less a place than the House of Commons when the whole question of the future of the Company and the mail contract was being debated in May, 1928. On one occasion the steamer was referred to as the "flapper" of the fleet, being then eighteen! This comment was doubly apt in view of the sound of the paddle beats when at speed.

The "flapper" duly grew up, but was sold in September, 1938 to be broken up by Smith & Houston at Port Glasgow.

Loch Leven Shipping Company, Ltd.

For the following we are obliged to Mr. John P. Grant, of Glencoe.

The introduction of hydro-electric power and the erection of an aluminium factory at the head of Loch Leven in 1904 brought a considerable influx of population and consequent development of trade in the district. Houses and shops were erected, and the name

Kinlochleven was adopted for the new village. As there was no road on the south side of the loch, and only an indifferent one on the north side, transport was largely by water; but the shallowness of the loch at the Narrows precluded all but the smallest craft from reaching the head of the loch.

At the end of the summer of 1905 the owners of the shops commenced to run a 25-ft. open boat, named *Glencoe*, between Kinlochleven and Ballachulish, principally to carry goods for the shops, but taking passengers when required; and in the autumn a regular passenger service was instituted. This launch, built of wood by Messrs. Dickie at Tarbert, was engined at Paisley Harbour Sawmills with an Albion motor, adapted for marine work, and proceeded north *via* the Crinan Canal. She won the first motor-boat race at the Royal Highland Regatta at Oban. In 1908 she was sold to a Tighnabruaich owner.

M.V. "Cona." This somewhat larger boat was added in 1906. She was certified to carry thirty-five passengers, and was one of the first motor vessels in the Highlands to be passed by the Board of Trade. The two vessels were often crowded, particularly at week-ends, since many workmen from Ballachulish were employed at Kinlochleven, and desired to travel home. At busy times, each motor boat towed a small rowing-boat; and sometimes, if a strong current were running against them at the Narrows, the passengers of the latter disembarked, carried their boat to the other end of the Narrows, launched it, re-embarked and continued in tow of the motor boat.

· · · · · · ·

In 1907 the still larger launch *Dolphin*, capable of carrying thirty-four passengers, was chartered; but by the autumn of 1907 the channel had been dredged, and from November, David MacBrayne Ltd. operated a service with their larger ships, first with *Mountaineer* (II), and later with the twin-screw motor vessels *Comet* and *Scout*.

T.S.S. "Loch Leven Queen"/"Lochness" (II). To compete with these the owners of the Loch Leven launches, in May, 1908, bought the twin-screw steamer *Lough Neagh Queen*, originally *Clutha No. 12*. Purchased by Messrs. J. D. Sutherland, R. P. Grant and John P. Grant, she was transferred to the newly-formed Loch Leven Shipping Company, Ltd., and commenced sailing in June, 1908, being appropriately re-named *Loch Leven Queen*. A regular daily service was maintained, the first run being from Ballachulish at 5 a.m. so that the workers could be at the factory by 6 o'clock. Other sailings took place at 8, 10, 1, 3 and 7, and sometimes at 10 p.m., if there were a late train. In spite of the cheaper fares by the MacBrayne vessels, the local company got considerable support; but in 1911 the two ships then remaining—*Cona* and *Loch Leven Queen*—entered the MacBrayne fleet. The latter was transferred to the Fort Augustus mail run in 1912 in succession to the old paddle steamer *Lochness*, and was given this name. For various periods she returned to the Kinlochleven service, and was the last steamer employed on it when it ceased in 1923 (road transport being then substituted). She returned to the Fort Augustus station from June, 1923 to 10th September, 1928, when she was withdrawn. She was sold on 10th January, 1929, to Rose Street Foundry Co. Ltd., Inverness, for scrapping. *Lochness* (II) was essentially an inland water vessel with low freeboard. The Company did not alter her very substantially from her original condition, but a deckhouse was added abaft the funnel and the deck rails were enclosed.

David MacBrayne, Ltd. (*contd.*)

For the Glasgow-Inverness run the screw steamer *Argyll* was chartered in 1911.

In 1912 David MacBrayne, Ltd., became interested in the steamers *Lord of the Isles* and *Edinburgh Castle* on purchasing, in association with Turbine Steamers, Ltd., the goodwill of the Clyde services of the Lochgoil & Inveraray Steamboat Co. Ltd. which Company continued to provide the road link between Dunoon and Strachur for the Loch Eck Tour (an attempt to revive the sailings on that loch by the *Fairy Queen* having been made in 1919, but soon abandoned). The two ships were registered thereafter in the name of Turbine Steamers, Ltd. only, and so are not strictly members of the MacBrayne fleet. They retained their former funnel colouring of red, with two white bands divided by a black one, and black top. It was through this purchase that David MacBrayne, Ltd. acquired their connexion with the Lochgoil trade, though the other concern, or its associates, John Williamson & Co. or Williamson-Buchanan Steamers, Ltd., in certain seasons provided the steamer for the passenger run. *Edinburgh Castle* was withdrawn in 1913, and her place was at first taken by *Chevalier*, then by *Ivanhoe* and later by *Comet*. *Lord of the Isles* survived till 1928; and, during her last season, she was operated by David MacBrayne, Ltd., on the Lochgoil and Arrochar station, as R.M.S. *Lord of the Isles*.

S.S. "Countess of Mayo." It is understood that this vessel was employed on the Ballachulish-Kinlochleven route for Messrs. Mac-Brayne, presumably in succession to *Scout*. Records indicate that she was built for duty on the River Shannon in the West of Ireland, being then registered at Dublin. In 1908 she was registered at Newry, passing in 1914 to the MacBrayne fleet with registry at Glasgow.

In 1917 she was sold to the Cromarty Steamship Co. Ltd., for duty
on the Cromarty-Invergordon ferry service where, in August, 1919, she
collided with the pier. She was then acquired by R. & W. Hawthorn,
Leslie & Co. Ltd. for ferry service on the Tyne, and renamed *Walker*,
being afterwards owned by the Borough of Jarrow.

T.S.S. "Duke of Abercorn." In May, 1914, this twin-screw steamer
was acquired. She operated the Ballachulish-Kinlochleven run
between 9th and 18th November, 1914 but gave much trouble on
account of the condition of the boilers, which were not worth repairing.
Originally named *Britannia*, owned by J. Brown and registered at
Lancaster in 1888, she was subsequently owned by the Morecambe
Steamboat Co. Ltd. until sold in 1909 to the Duke Shipping Co. Ltd.,
Dublin, who re-named her as above. At a later period she had been
owned by the Southend S.P. Co. Ltd. On 22nd February, 1915, she was
sold for scrapping.

S.S. "Kate." About a month after the acquisition of the foregoing,
another little vessel found her way into the MacBrayne fleet. It is
understood that she did not operate on any of her new owners' services,
but was laid up till sold in 1917.

S.S. "Lochiel" (III). After the first war the Admiralty allotted to
David MacBrayne Ltd.; as a replacement for the lost *Lochiel* (II), the
steamer *Devonia*. This ship had belonged to the Anglo-French
Steamship Co. Ltd. of Devonport (Onesimus Dorey, Guernsey, Manager), and had been built and engined in 1906 by Scott of Kinghorn,
Ltd., Fife, for the cargo and passenger trade among Plymouth, Guernsey and St. Brieux. She was taken over by the Shipping Controller in
1918, and registered in the name of David MacBrayne, Ltd. in 1919,
being re-named *Lochiel* in the following year. She did not, however,
follow her namesakes' footsteps in respect of service.
   The steamer bore a striking resemblance to *Clydesdale* (II), but
was a shade smaller and had a more attractive overhanging stern. Her
passenger accommodation was more limited and, in fact, was only
occasionally required, as *Lochiel* (III) functioned mainly as a cargo and
livestock carrier, though retaining her passenger certificate till 1925,
when alterations were made which increased her gross tonnage to 318.
   She worked on the Glasgow-Stornoway direct cargo service and
also on the Glasgow-Islay weekly run when *Clydesdale* was required
elsewhere. When not engaged on either of these routes, she was held as
a general reserve cargo steamer, and proved herself particularly useful
for special seasonal traffic in connexion with the transport of livestock.
   She made a few runs for Clyde Cargo Steamers, Ltd. (on charter)
in the spring of 1936, and last appeared in MacBrayne's cargo sailing list
in February, 1937. Thereafter she was for a time laid up at Greenock

and was sold in October, 1938 to Guernsey & Alderney Trading Co. Ltd., being registered as *Isle of Alderney*. She was taken over in May, 1940 by Crete Shipping Co. Ltd. (Stelp & Leighton Ltd., Managers). After taking part in the evacuation of the Channel Islands, she was requisitioned by the Ministry of Transport and served mainly as a supply ship to L.C.T.s on the Clyde, based at Lamlash. In February, 1946, she was transferred to the Greek flag and re-named *Annoula*, owned by S. N. Angelos, Athens. About October, 1946, she was registered at Panama as *Monte Lirio*, owned by Compania Navigacion "Monte Lirio" S.A.

M.V. "C. & B. No. 1"/"Lochgorm" (I)/**"Iona"** (IV). Built at Ipswich in 1913, *C. & B. No. 1* had a gross tonnage of 37 and belonged to Messrs. Crosse & Blackwell of London, where she was employed by them as a motor lighter on the Thames. She was sold to the Aluminium Corporation, Ltd. in 1924 and in 1928 to David MacBrayne Ltd., being the last vessel acquired by them before the company was re-constituted. Stationed at Bowmore, Islay, the vessel functioned as a cargo-lighter (in succession to a sailing vessel) for the handling of goods to and from the Glasgow steamers, because the limited depth of water rendered it impossible for the latter to come alongside at Bowmore. The lighter had her machinery aft, with a short funnel. There was a tall mast and cargo derrick forward, the hold being amidships.

The name (if one can call it such) was changed to *Lochgorm* only in 1930. Early in February, 1934, she ran aground in Lochindaal and was disabled for about two months.

On the disposal of *Iona* (III) in 1936 the name *Iona* was given in October to the lighter *Lochgorm*, to preserve *Iona* for a worthy successor to the three famous paddle steamers. This however did not materialise till 1970.

It was eventually decided to introduce a road transport service between Bruichladdich and Bowmore; and *Iona* was, accordingly, withdrawn about 1937. After a period of idleness, the hull was sold in April 1938 (minus machinery) to Ardrossan Dockyard Ltd., being thereafter used as a support for staging for painting ships' hulls, etc.

. . . .

During the 1928 season, on account of the transference to Oban of *Iona* (III) to make up the deficiency there caused by the loss of *Grena-dier*, the Company chartered P.S. *Lord of the Isles* for the Glasgow-Lochgoilhead-Arrochar run in succession to *Iona*, having also made use of this vessel in the spring of that year on the Greenock-Ardrishaig service.

Vessels chartered during the 1920-1930 period include Messrs. J. Kennedy & Sons' S.S. *Welshman* and Messrs. J. & A. Gardner's *Saint*

Barchan and *Saint Enoch* and, in September, 1928, P.S. *Queen-Empress*, of Williamson-Buchanan Steamers, Ltd., which sailed on the Ardrishaig route from Glasgow at 7.11 a.m. on the Autumn Holiday in that year.

CHAPTER V

DAVID MACBRAYNE (1928) LTD.

DAVID MACBRAYNE LTD.

1928-1947

THE new Company, David MacBrayne (1928) Ltd. had come into being in 1928, with its obligation to build not fewer than four steamers within two years.

In January and February, 1929 it was resolved to sell the *Linnet* and *Brenda*, Ministry of Transport approval being obtained for the former, and also *Lochness* and *Mountaineer*. The sale of the last-named did not take place at that time. In May it was agreed to purchase the *Denbigh Coast* from Coast Lines Ltd.

S.S. "Lochdunvegan" (I). This vessel had been launched on 27th May, 1891, for Messrs. G. & J. Burns, and had traded as *Grouse* between Greenock and Ireland for many years, without passengers. After the first war she was on 31st October, 1922, sold to Grahamston Shipping Co. Ltd. (T. L. Duff & Co., Managers) and re-named *Kelvindale*, plying between Glasgow and Stranraer; and, this trade having been absorbed by Coast Lines, Ltd., she returned to Messrs. Burns' successors, Burns & Laird Lines, Ltd., on 31st October, 1923. The following year she was transferred to Coast Lines, Ltd., and became *Denbigh Coast*, remaining thus till transferred to David MacBrayne (1928) Ltd. in 1929 and again re-named, this time *Lochdunvegan*, in accordance with their then new standard nomenclature.

The steamer was not unpleasing in appearance, with good lines and originally a pair of tall masts; she was in some respects similar in looks to *Ethel*. The main-mast was removed during the second war.

The machinery was triple expansion, and the cylinders were rebored in March, 1923, and November, 1931. On the former occasion she was also re-boilered.

Lochdunvegan was employed mainly on the Glasgow-Stornoway direct weekly service, embracing calls at Tobermory and Portree only, as a rule. [It will be remembered that under the heading of *Clydesdale* (II) attention was drawn to the changes made with respect to the Glasgow-Stornoway traffic about 1926.] She was also on occasion on the Glasgow-Islay and Glasgow-Fort William, etc., cargo runs. On 8th April, 1948, she was withdrawn and laid up in the East India Harbour, Greenock. After a service of fifty-seven years she was sold to Metal

Industries Salvage Ltd., Glasgow, and was towed on 27th July, 1948, to Faslane, Gareloch, for scrapping.

T.S.S. "Lochness" (III). The first of the new vessels to be built and put into commission under the terms of the constitution of the new Company was *Lochness*, which was designed for the Mallaig-Kyle-Stornoway mail service. She was launched on 6th June and ran trials on 9th July, 1929 being accepted next day. She was of 777 tons—larger than the old *Claymore*—and was provided with good accommodation for two classes of passengers. Her appearance was in accordance with contemporary ideas—namely for utility only—but it cannot be denied that she was an imposing craft, and had all the appearance, inside and out, of a miniature liner. The hull was originally grey, but was afterwards black. (This scheme of grey hulls was initiated with the *Lochness* and the reasons for its abandonment are given under the *Columba* and *Claymore*.) The propelling machinery consisted of two sets of triple-expansion engines supplied by steam from two single-ended oil-fired Scotch boilers. These gave a full speed of about 14 knots.

The first service performed by *Lochness* was to Tarbert, Loch Fyne, at Glasgow Fair, 1929. She commenced on 1st August that year on the Stornoway run, for which she received her oil fuel at Kyle from a large stock tank specially erected for the purpose, quite a landmark in the vicinity of the railway station. As has already been pointed out in our notes on the *Sheila*, the Stornoway mail steamer is a hard worker, the *Lochness* (III) being no exception. Her week-end rest amounted to about 24 hours at Stornoway all the year round, excepting her annual period for docking and survey. She was a fine sea boat and as far as the comfort of her passengers and crew were concerned far excelled the *Sheila*. From about the end of November, 1940 she called three days a week at Raasay instead of every day at Applecross.

Shortly before the second war it was decided to provide an even finer ship for this service, though, on account of hostilities, nothing was done till 1945, when the order for the successor of *Lochness* was placed. Many questions were raised in Parliament regarding the alleged inadequacy of the accommodation of *Lochness*, particularly for third-class passengers; and, after very considerable delays, her successor, T.S.M.V. *Loch Seaforth*, duly took up the Stornoway sailings on Saturday, 6th December, 1947. *Lochness* was then transferred to the Islands route from Oban, so as to relieve *Lochearn* to be re-engined. She performed the run in record time, even though a call at Colonsay was added from January, 1948. During the summer of 1948 she made the Colonsay call on a special trip from Oban on Tuesdays, thus giving a day excursion for the benefit of people staying in Oban. This, however, was abandoned in 1949, when the Islay mail vessel commenced calling at Colonsay. After the return of *Lochearn*,

Lochness became spare steamer, till sold in July, 1955 to Lloyd Mediterraneo S.P.A., Rome, by whom she was re-named *Valmarina* and in 1958 she passed to S. Billinis & Co., Piraeus, becoming their *Myrtidiotissa*.

M.V. "Lochshiel" (I). This vessel was not one of the new batch required to be built by the Company, but was constructed to take over the modified duties of *Brenda*. It will be remembered that this cargo service was *via* the Crinan Canal to the Firth of Lorne, Mull, Loch Sunart and Loch Leven. It was now routed *via* the Mull of Kintyre and the Company gave up using the Crinan Canal entirely.

The *Lochshiel*, which was launched at Leith on 8th August, 1929, was a typical modern coasting cargo ship of small tonnage, with machinery aft and a cruiser stern. Utility and economy of operation were the keynotes of her design, and she could have been regarded as a reincarnation on a larger scale, of the *Brenda*, which she succeeded. She carried two masts and the propelling machinery consisted of a six-cylinder Gardner Diesel motor of 300 B.H.P., running up to 290 r.p.m. The ship's designed speed was 9 knots. There was a small auxiliary oil-fired boiler, which was used mainly for operating the steam cargo winch and capstans.

The savings in the operation of a vessel of this type, provided the price differential between coal and oil fuel is reasonable, must be substantial, particularly as standby losses when the ship is in port are reduced. *Lochshiel* had a cargo capacity of about 200 tons. Her first run commenced on 1st October, 1929.

In January, 1952 she was sold to Mr. Owen Ferris of Ruislip, Middlesex (managed by Mr. H. A. J. Ryeland, Dover); and, after one or two trips from Dover to Calais and to Folkestone, she was on 20th February, 1952 renamed *Eugene*. In 1954 she was sold by Admiralty Court order, to Belgian owners, and the following year it was reported that this was for breaking up.

T.S.M.V. "Lochearn." The order for the two twin-screw motor vessels was confirmed in November, 1929, to be built by Ardrossan Dockyard Ltd. These constituted a pair of genuine sister ships, *Lochearn* and *Lochmor*. Only once before had a pair of nearly identical vessels been owned, the *Cygnet* (I) and *Lapwing* (I), both of which were taken over by Messrs. Hutcheson from Messrs. Burns in 1851 as recorded previously.

Lochearn and *Lochmor* were the second and third additions to the fleet under the new contract which demanded that the Outer Islands services should be substantially improved as regards the passenger accommodation, coupled with lowered fares and freight charges.

The two ships in profile were different from anything dealt with so far. With straight stems, exceptionially ugly cruiser sterns, two masts, and single funnels, the vessels were quite imposing; but the *tout ensemble* was not pleasing, largely on account of the insufficient rake of masts and funnels and the form of the latter. Viewed from forward the ships looked well; but as broadside and aft views were obtained, their aspect became progressively worse, until when seen from aft they were definitely ugly. This was rarely the case with the old ships. We have heard statements to the effect that the *Lochearn* and *Lochmor* were like a pair of models bought at a toy shop, and this is frankly not far from the truth with respect to their external appearance! The best way of making it impossible to ascertain what a ship looks like in the water is to go on board, and this is what the vast majority of passengers do because it is of interest only to a very few individuals of odd habits—like ourselves—to know how the vessel appears!

Having arrived on board a whole host of pleasant surprises was at hand—particularly if the traveller retained vivid memories of the older ships on the route—because without fear of contradiction it can truthfully be stated that the passenger accommodation in both classes, bearing in mind the size of the vessels, was very good.

Within the limits of a little over 500 tons a total of 400 passengers could be carried. This was the extreme permissible figure and of course berthing facilities for such a number were not possible. The first-class cabins provided were on two decks, and were very well laid out with really comfortable bunks, reading lamps, and both hot and cold running water. For a passage of one or at most two nights on board nothing more could be desired.

The public rooms comprised a dining room with separate small tables, a lounge, and a smoking room, all tastefully and comfortably furnished. All this accommodation was amidships and was repeated on a plainer scale for third-class passengers aft. The latter accommodation was perhaps the more striking of the two as far as comparison with the old ships was concerned. All the sanitary arrangements and equipment were excellent. Another important and highly necessary feature was the provision of ample covered-in deck space, again for both classes of traveller.

The machinery in each case consisted of twin sets of six-cylinder Gardner heavy oil engines aggregating 600 B.H.P. together. Actually these engine sets were identical with the single one installed in the *Lochshiel*. These engines were unfortunately very noisy and this fact marred in a large measure the other amenities of the ship. The intention was to obtain a speed of 12½ knots, but, whether the engine power was insufficient, or the hull resistance greater than was anticipated, or both, we cannot say; but in practice it was found that neither vessel could be relied on to attain this speed. The service speed was in fact about 9-9½ knots; and in 1948 it was decided to re-engine both ships with a view to improving the speed.

Silent electric winches and capstans mean a great deal on vessels employed as these two are and they were accordingly fitted.

Both vessels came out initially with grey hulls.

The foregoing covers the main features common to this pair of sister ships, and we can now deal with them individually.

Lochearn, which was launched on 29th April, 1930, and, commencing on 1st August that year, was normally stationed at Oban for the Islands mail service, which included passengers, mails and cargo, outwards on Mondays, Wednesdays and Fridays. The route embraced calls at Tobermory, Coll, Tiree, Castlebay (Barra) and Lochboisdale (South Uist), returning similarly on the alternate days, Kilchoan being included until 1949. The ship also at times worked the service normally allotted to *Lochmor*.

Lochearn received her new machinery at Ardrossan and went on to the Outer Islands route from Kyle and Mallaig in July, 1948, returning to the Islands route from Oban in June, 1949.

Three interchangeable Paxman-Ricardo Diesel engines were provided, one set being kept ashore. Each engine had twelve cylinders, there being two banks of six cylinders in V formation, 1,000 r.p.m. being the normal full speed, when 330 B.H.P. was developed. To reduce noise these engines were enclosed in portable light-weight acoustic hoods, and the first impression on entering the engine room was that the engineers had been provided with a couple of air-raid shelters! The propeller speed of 300 r.p.m. was obtained with Modern Wheel Drive Ltd. SLM-type oil-operated gearing, the propeller shafting being about 15 inches below the engine shafting. The original propellers and shafting were retained. Another feature of interest was the construction of the funnel and adjacent engine hatch in aluminium alloy, to minimise top weight.

It is understood that at full S.H.P. of 600 a speed of 11·7 knots was obtained.

The ship was improved from the passengers' point of view in respect of noise, but she was still by no means as silent as a steamer. She was given a new funnel, shorter than the old, but of more pleasing appearance. In 1955 she succeeded *Lochinvar* on the Sound of Mull run and in the summer of 1964 maintained the Mull and Morven car ferry service, along with her twin sister, until *Columba* took over. *Lochearn* was sold on 26th August, 1964 along with *Lochmor* to Kastoulakis Co., Piraeus. After refitting they left Ardrossan re-named respectively *Amimoni* and *Naias*.

T.S.M.V. "Lochmor" (I). For general information common to this ship and her sister, readers are referred to the notes on *Lochearn* above. Gone for ever, it must be supposed, are the graceful lines of years ago; but what has been lost outwardly has been gained inwardly, the accommodation and economy of operation of these two vessels having been of a high order.

To reduce top weight the funnel of *Lochmor* was slightly shorter than that of *Lochearn*.

Lochmor, which entered the water at Ardrossan on 15th May, 1930, was usually stationed at Kyle of Lochalsh and performed the somewhat exacting Outer Islands mail service, involving the circuit of Skye in both directions, also Mallaig, Eigg, Rum, Lochboisdale (South Uist), Lochmaddy (North Uist) and Tarbert (Harris); but the schedule was different in summer and in winter, whereas the Oban service remained practically the same all the year round. Early in their careers, in March, 1931 the two sisters went aground at Kyleakin, the one endeavouring to pull the other off, but without success until the veteran *Glencoe* pulled them both clear and they were re-floated.

During 1933 and 1934 *Lochmor* took over part of the duties of the Portree mail steamer in addition to her own on Wednesdays, because the latter was diverted to make an excursion to Loch Scavaig in the afternoon. From 1947 *Lochmor* herself performed the Loch Scavaig excursions, giving cargo services to the Island of Soay at the same time, by means of the motor vessels *Islander* or *Western Isles* (owned by Mr. Bruce Watt, Mallaig) from the anchorage in Loch Scavaig.

In July, 1948, *Lochmor* was transferred to Oban for the Sound of Mull service during *Lochinvar*'s absence for overhaul; and, after the return of the latter, *Lochmor* performed various short cruises from Oban, and sheep-ferrying duties, etc., in the autumn. Her re-engining was carried out at Ardrossan, being completed in June, 1949, when she returned to the Outer Islands service. The new machinery was identical with that of *Lochearn*. The Outer Isles run ceased on 15th April, 1964 when the Hebridean car ferry run commenced and *Lochmor* then performed the Mallaig-Armadale ferry run (cars being lifted on board) till relieved on the advent of *Clansman*, when she joined her sister in similar duties at Oban. She was sold to Greek owners as mentioned above.

S.S. "Lochbroom" (I). After trading between Aberdeen and London for sixty years with the Aberdeen Steam Navigation Company as the *City of London*, this steamer was bought in 1931 as successor to the old *Claymore*, which was scrapped after fifty years' service.

At first sight it might be thought rather odd to spend money purchasing a ship ten years older than the one she was to replace, but much depends on what is obtained for the money expended. It will be recalled that one of the principal reasons for the demise of the *Claymore* was the condition of her boilers and in our account of her we drew attention to the astoundingly long service they had given without serious mishap. Now in the case of *City of London* a very different state of affairs existed, because she had been re-boilered in 1882 and again in 1901, as well as having been refitted and reconditioned in other directions. Nevertheless, *Lochbroom*, as she duly became, was an old steamer in 1931, but perfectly sea-worthy and sound.

She was built of iron by John Elder, the predecessor of the Fairfield Company, and in tonnage and length was almost identical with the *Chieftain*. A straight stem was fitted and a rather ugly stern. The tall masts and funnel were well proportioned, and the latter was almost encircled with an array of waste steam-pipes. On the whole the steamer was typical of the 1,000-ton passenger and cargo coaster of her time. The dining saloon possessed the customary long table capable of seating no fewer than forty-six people, with cabins opening out into the saloon. The cabins were modernised by the fitting of running water, and some of the cargo space was converted suitably into passenger accommodation.

The engines were two-cylinder compound, fitted originally with piston tail rods which were afterwards removed. Two single-ended Scotch boilers (1901) supplied steam at 70 lb. Several details of construction of the machinery were interesting as illustrating the high class of workmanship put into the job.

Lochbroom was engaged on the Glasgow-West Coast trade, the sailings from Glasgow occurring every ten days on alternate Mondays and Thursdays. She was usually fully booked with passengers making the round trip during the season, and could berth eighty-one. The outward passage usually terminated at Lochinver, but was extended to Loch Inchard (Loch Clash Pier) monthly. Stornoway was not visited.

The steamer generally was laid up in Greenock for five or six months of the year, as she was too large to keep in commission continuously.

A wireless set was maintained on board so that passengers could listen to the regular news and other programmes.

In July, 1937, she was sold to Smith & Houston, Ltd., Port Glasgow, and broken up after sixty-six years' service.

T.S.M.V. "Lochfyne." The laying down, completion, and initial running of this very notable vessel were of such importance in the history of marine engineering that a large volume of literature was published in the technical press concerning her.

Lochfyne was the last of the four new ships built under the 1928 agreement and from the very first she had aroused an immense amount of interest among the travelling public. The explanation of all this lies in the fact that she was the first British passenger vessel to have the propellers driven by direct-coupled electric motors which received their energy from generators deriving their power from Diesel engines; or in normal parlance she was a "Diesel-electric" ship.

This mode of propulsion should not be confused with the allied one which had been previously adopted elsewhere, namely the "Turbo-electric" drive. In this system steam turbines take the place of the Diesel engines, the rest of the equipment—in principle—being common to both drives. We will touch again on the mechanical equipment of the *Lochfyne* briefly after having explained some of the characteristics of the ship and her work.

No fewer than three firms were responsible for the vessel, namely, Messrs. Denny of Dumbarton who built her and were principal contractors, Davey, Paxman & Co. Ltd., of Colchester, the makers of the Diesel engines, and Metropolitan-Vickers, Ltd., who supplied the electrical machinery and equipment.

Lochfyne was launched on 20th March, 1931, and was on trial on 25th May. With a gross tonnage of 748, straight stem carrying a slight rake, cruiser stern, two funnels (the forward one being a dummy) and single mast the ship was a notable example of up-to-date naval architecture. The passenger accommodation was extensive and embraced virtually the whole ship other than the crew's and machinery spaces. There were no cargo holds. The public rooms were all in accordance with modern ideas, simplicity and easy cleaning being the keynotes of the whole scheme of furnishing.

One weak feature was the manner in which the promenade deck space was reduced from being really effective by various obstructions such as hatches and ventilators.

The arrangement of the accommodation was such that the vessel could perform the two distinct services for which she was designed, one of which was "one class" only, that from Oban to Staffa and Iona in summer. In winter *Lochfyne* took the Ardrishaig mail service commencing on 12th October, 1931 and on this carried passengers in two classes till the abolition of this distinction on the Clyde steamer services. Her routes, therefore coincided exactly with those of the old *Grenadier*.

As in the case of the three other new passenger vessels, the hull was painted grey at first. Shiplovers will have noted a resemblance creeping in with these new motor ships to the style of profile and painting peculiar to the Union-Castle Line. This similarity became less, when black hulls again became standard.

Just before taking up duty the *Lochfyne* was exhibited to the public at the Broomielaw in June, 1931, alongside the ancient *Glencoe*.

Resuming the subject of the machinery installation, the prime movers consisted of two sets of five-cylinder four-stroke Diesel engines running at 330 r.p.m. and developing a total of 2,000 I.H.P. Each set was coupled to a direct-current generator of 540 k.W. capacity at 500 volts. Lastly the two propelling motors, located in a separate compartment aft of the electric generating plant, were coupled direct to the port and starboard propeller shafts and developed a total of 1,340 S.H.P. at 430 r.p.m. In 1953 she was re-engined with British Polar machinery and in the winter of 1965-6 she had a very extensive overhaul, which included renewal of a considerable amount of her electrical equipment.

The full speed of *Lochfyne* was 16½ knots.

We have mentioned one drawback to the ship, namely the obstructions on the promenade deck, and there was another which had been the subject of much thought and investigation—the vibration and noise on board, whether the ship was at rest or in motion. The cause was no doubt to be found in the main Diesel engines, coupled with the inherent characteristics of the structure of the hull. The vibration was not serious, still less alarming, but its elimination was a goal to be achieved if at all possible. We shall refer to the success obtained in this direction shortly when dealing with *Lochnevis*.

Another innovation was the control of the propelling motors which could either be done in the engine room or on the bridge. When the latter was in operation, the bridge officer by working the engine telegraphs in the usual way actually controlled the movements of the motors without the intervention of the engine-room staff.

In the old paddle days access to the engine-room to watch the machinery was always extremely easy, and it was a happy thought to arrange matters on board the *Lochfyne* so that a fair view was obtainable of at least the Diesel engines from the main deck.

The extent of the passenger space arranged in the ship may be gauged roughly from the fact that she was licensed to carry about 1,200 people. Being a daylight ship only, there was no passenger sleeping accommodation.

Lochfyne was, from 1936, employed mainly on the Fort William route in summer and carried on the Ardrishaig service (from Wemyss Bay) during most of the second war period. In 1946 she had to do the Fort William and Iona runs on alternate days, the Oban excursions being in that season catered for by *Robina*. In 1947-9 she operated to Fort William, also doing cruises from Oban, including a new one to Port Ellen, Islay, once a week.

From 1936 *King George V* took her place on the Staffa and Iona run, except during 1946 and the war years. For the Loch Fyne mail service all the year round (which she took over after the withdrawal of *Saint Columba*) she had her upper deck extended aft. Her place was taken at times by *Lochnevis*, and in the early part of the summer she was often stationed at Oban for excursion work.

In 1953 she was re-engined, attaining 16.224 knots on three runs on the measured mile, two knots faster than her previous service speed (13.75). In that year also she was given a mainmast. In 1960 a cafeteria was installed.

Sold to Northern Slipway Ltd., Dublin in January, 1970, she spent some time at Faslane, Gareloch, providing electric power for the shipbreaking yard there, and after sale to Scottish & Newcastle Breweries Ltd. she was re-named *Old Lochfyne* and was dry-docked at Govan with a view to static use. She was, however, scrapped at Dalmuir, where her famous predecessors *Iona* (III) and *Columba* (I) had ended their careers. She was photographed there on 1st April,

1974, the day of the launch at Leith of the third *Pioneer*, thus making a further link with early history, in that the *Lochfyne* when new in 1931 was photographed alongside the veteran *Glencoe* of 1846.

M.V. "Mingary"/"Kilchoan." This motor ferryboat was employed at Kilchoan until the institution of the Tobermory-Mingary service. After this she was transferred to Glenelg, later to Rodel, at which she was the last MacBrayne vessel, the calls there ceasing on the withdrawal of the Outer Isles run in April, 1964. She was in that year sold to Mr. John Montgomerie, harbourmaster at Tarbert-Harris, who used her for attending to the lights.

"Dumb Barge No. 1." This large red rowing-boat was built in 1932 for service at Rodel, where she was used till about 1958, being then succeeded by a motor launch. She may latterly have been named *Rodel*. A ferryboat there was sold on 20th April, 1948.

M.V. "Staffa" (V). In 1932-3 two motor launches were acquired by the Company for the ferry service at Iona, to convey passengers from the steamer to the landing stage. The first of these was *Staffa* and it was pleasing to observe the revival of the traditional name, which had appeared in the West Highland fleet exactly one hundred years earlier.

This little boat had a passenger certificate for forty-eight, and was propelled by a 14-h.p. Kelvin engine. She is understood to have been sold in 1939 to Captain McInnes, of Iona. Along with some of Messrs. MacBrayne's small craft, she was engaged during the second war in diving operations on the Clyde and elsewhere.

M.V. "Fingal" (III). Another traditional name was selected for the sister of the foregoing, which appeared in 1933; both were appropriately named, considering their sphere of operations. Sold to the Ministry of War Transport in 1942, *Fingal* took part in the D-Day landings in Normandy, and having been re-purchased returned to Iona in time for the 1947 summer season. She foundered in September, 1961, wrecked by the tail-end of a hurricane.

"Dumb Barge No. 2." In 1933 a rowing-boat similar to No. 1 was built for use at Stockinish, remaining there till calls ceased.

M.V. "Glenelg." Ferry at Glenelg, acquired 1933, later at Rodel.

Alexander Paterson

S.S. "Princess Louise" (II). The above-named, of Oban, introduced "short sea trips" in 1892 with a small steam yacht named

Marchioness of Lorn, and two years later had built his first *Princess Louise* to take her place, the latter ship being sold to the Admiralty in 1898. To fill the gap on her departure, the wooden screw steamer *La Gloria* was chartered and commenced sailing at Oban in June, till the new steamer should be ready.

This was a handsome little craft, employed like her predecessors in local excursions from Oban to Kerrera, Loch Etive, etc., with service runs to Dunstaffnage and Connel Ferry, and on various livestock duties from the islands, including Colonsay. Her owner also for a time had the *Manx Lass* and *Countess of Bantry*. On the death of Mr. Paterson in 1920 the ship passed to his son, from whose representatives she was purchased by David MacBrayne Ltd. on 27th April, 1934, along with the goodwill of the trade. That season she remained at Oban as before, but next season was employed on cruises from Inverness to Loch Ness, later being on special livestock duty in the Oban district. After being laid up in Ardrossan for a time, she was sold in April, 1939, to Crete Shipping Co. Ltd. (Stelp & Leighton Ltd., Managers) and was re-named *Bluestone* in October, 1939. Her end came when she was totally destroyed by bombing, while in dry-dock at Greenock, on 7th May, 1941.

David MacBrayne (1928) Ltd. (*contd.*)
David MacBrayne Ltd.

T.S.M.V. "**Lochnevis.**" Modelled and engined much on the lines of *Lochfyne*, *Lochnevis* was the second Diesel-electric ship to be built for the Company. She was smaller, however, and carried one large oval funnel only. The same drawback with respect to the promenade deck space was apparent.

The firms engaged in the contract were the same, except in the case of the electrical equipment, which was carried out by the General Electric Company. There had been a proposal to transfer to her the engines of the *Lochfyne* but this was not done.

The *Lochnevis* was launched by Lady Read, wife of Sir Alfred Read, at Dumbarton on 15th May, 1934, and ran trials on 28th June, when her designed full speed of 15 knots was obtained.

The prime movers consisted of two sets of six-cylinder four-stroke Diesel engines running at 500 r.p.m. and developing a total of 1,300 B.H.P. Each set was coupled to a direct current generator of 420 kW capacity at 500 volts. Finally, the two propelling motors developed a total of 1,050 S.H.P. at 400 r.p.m. and were situated in a separate compartment further aft than in the case of the *Lochfyne*. Actually the generating and motor rooms in the *Lochnevis* were separated by the 1st class smoking room and bar on the lower deck. This arrangement involved shorter line shafting, as well as employing a portion of the ship for the motors which would not be of much use for anything else.

The propelling motors were controlled either from the bridge or generating room as desired.

All cargo was carried forward, and the derrick was located forward of the mast.

On board the *Lochnevis* engineering enthusiasts were denied a view of the machinery, which was perhaps unfortunate, but it is probable that by avoiding undue open spaces much noise could be kept out of the passengers' accommodation. There is no doubt that Diesel machinery is noisy, and on the top deck of the *Lochnevis* when these engines were running, much quieter conditions were desirable. On the other hand, vibration in the case of the *Lochnevis* was conspicuous by its absence, and its elimination was a matter of very great satisfaction. The Diesel engine bed plates had been mounted with a specially designed set of springs which absorbed very efficiently vibrations which would otherwise have been transmitted to the structure of the hull.

Though not wholly a passenger ship, the handling and stowage of cargo did not obtrude itself on the passenger accommodation, which was of a high order, originally in two classes, and comprised lounges, dining rooms, smoke rooms, and ample covered deck spaces. The sanitary equipment was admirable. There was no need for sleeping berths, because the vessel was on day service only.

Lochnevis was designed for the Mallaig, Kyle and Portree mail service operating all the year round; in fact she was really the successor to the aged and venerable *Glencoe* of 1846, though this veteran had departed three years previously. It is almost impossible to conceive a greater contrast between the two ships: the one paddle-driven, with the slow-running steeple engine of over a century ago, and the other equipped with electrically-driven twin screws.

In addition to her scheduled service during the season, cruises were made by the *Lochnevis* from Portree to Gairloch and Loch Torridon, and once a week she made a trip from Mallaig to Loch Scavaig, all which proved very successful.

During the second war she was from 1st January to 29th March, 1940, on the Ardrishaig mail service (then being operated from Wemyss Bay) and carried the Company's war-time colours of black funnel, black hull and "horizon yellow" superstructure. She was, however, requisitioned in December, 1940, and became a minelayer as H.M.S. *Lochnevis*, returning to her owners when she again was on the Ardrishaig mail route in June, 1944, and November, 1945. She was restored to her old station, the Portree mail route, but the Loch Scavaig excursion was in post-war years performed by the Outer Islands vessel.

In 1946 she received a third lifeboat to bring her up to Steam II standard, and in 1952 got a mainmast. In October, 1955 it was agreed to instal two inflatable rubber dinghies, and later that year to have her re-engined with National Gas & Oil Engine Company's machinery. In June, 1956 alterations were decided including fitting a flush hatch to increase the car-carrying capacity from 6 to 9.

With reduction in traffic on the Portree route she was transferred to Oban, returning to Portree for Saturdays only for the 1959 summer season, but thereafter remaining south except for relief work. In 1965 she performed the Islay mail run to permit *Lochiel* to provide a car ferry service to Islay; but for 1966 this was reduced to certain days only, so that she could operate Oban-Fort William and some of the Oban excursions the other days, instead of having an express bus service between Oban and Fort William as was done in 1965. She was also on the Greenock-Tarbert-Ardrishaig route for considerable periods.

She was sold to Dutch owners. She left the Clyde on 23rd and arrived at Holyhead on 25th March, 1970 and three days later was reported at A. G. Slooten in Wormer near Zaandam. It is understood she was broken up there in 1974.

.   .   .   .

In October, 1934 the Company agreed to buy Mishnish Pier, Tobermory, and in January next year to extend it.

On 27th July, 1934 it was agreed to drop "1928" from the name of the Company.

From 1st January, 1935 till 31st December, 1944 David Mac-Brayne Ltd. were lessees of the Kyle—Kyleakin Ferry and operated, but did not own the vessels employed thereon, which were the property of the L.M. & S. Railway Company. These included *Kyle* (which was taken into the MacBrayne fleet in 1938), *Skye*, *Kyleakin*, *Moil* and *Cuillin*.

.   .   .   .

M.V. "Soay." It is recorded that on 17th May, 1935 there was transferred to the Company from Coast Lines the motor launch *Ripple*, to which the name *Soay* was given. She was engaged in ferry service at Loch Scavaig, her dimensions and passenger complement being the same as those of *Fingal* and *Staffa*. Like them, she was employed during the second war on diving operations on the Clyde and elsewhere. In 1944 she was sold to the Ministry of Transport, but was re-purchased and returned in time for the summer of 1946, after which she served at Iona. Having succeeded the wrecked *Arinagour* as Coll Ferry, she obtained a passenger certificate for 50 in June, 1950, reduced to 12 in winter. After repairs at Dumbarton she was at Craignure in May and June, 1951, then at Glenelg from June to September and sheep-ferrying in Loch Sunart. Latterly she was at

Iona, mainly on the cargo service, until she broke adrift and was driven ashore on 22nd December, 1955, the engine and shafting being salved.

.   .   .   .

A proposal to take over Williamson-Buchanan Steamers Ltd. and Turbine Steamers Ltd., or part, began in January, 1933, but by January, 1934 this had become restricted to the acquisition of the assets. Negotiations for the purchase of the seven vessels, furnishings, goodwill and trades, together with 10,000 Ordinary Shares of £1 each in Clyde Cargo. Steamers Ltd. and 1,205 shares of £1 each in Campbeltown & Glasgow S.P.J.S. Co., Ltd. were reported in July, 1935, when it was resolved to acquire the two steamers of Turbine Steamers Ltd.—*Queen Alexandra* and *King George V*, with the goodwill of the trade between Greenock and Campbeltown, together with the above shares, the offer being later amended and settlement effected on 3rd October. A proposal to acquire the trade of Jack Bros. was not approved. (This actually went to McCallum, Orme & Co., Ltd.)

Tr.S.S. "Queen Alexandra"/"Saint Columba." On 3rd October, 1935, the assets and goodwill of the Williamson-Buchanan Steamers, Ltd. and Turbine Steamers, Ltd. were acquired by David MacBrayne, Ltd. in association with the L.M. & S. Railway Company. Of the steamers owned by the two Williamson concerns, the two belonging to Turbine Steamers, Ltd. were transferred to the MacBrayne fleet, one being *Queen Alexandra*, which dated from 1912.

As is well known, *King Edward* of 1901 was the first passenger ship to be fitted with Parsons' marine steam turbines, being followed in 1902 by the first *Queen Alexandra*. The latter was damaged by fire at Greenock in September, 1911, and was sold to the Canadian Pacific Railway Company, who re-named her *Princess Patricia*. To take her place, the steamer under review was constructed by Messrs. Denny in 1912, and was almost identical in design and dimensions with her predecessor. Like her she was propelled by direct-acting turbines on three screw shafts.

Placed initially on the Campbeltown run for Turbine Steamers, Ltd., she was requisitioned during the first war for transport work, in which she was engaged from 7th February, 1915, till 10th May, 1919. She rammed and sank a German submarine, in recognition of which her master, Captain Angus Keith, received the O.B.E. and Distinguished Service Cross.

After re-conditioning, *Queen Alexandra* resumed her place on the Firth, usually on the Inveraray run till restored to that to Campbeltown in 1927. In 1932 her upper deck was enclosed to form

an observation lounge as on the later steamers, and her accommodation was considerably improved.

It had been intended that the *Queen Alexandra* would be used
between Oban and Fort William and the *King George V* to
Ardrishaig, but the former would have required considerable modifications to get a certificate for the intended route; and there was a
suggestion of exchanging her for the *Atalanta*, former G. & S.W.R.
Clyde turbine steamer on charter for one year. This, however, did not
take place; and instead it was decided to give the *Queen Alexandra* an
extensive refit for the Ardrishaig service, and to use the *King George
V* at Oban for Iona, Fort William, etc.

At the time of her transfer to David MacBrayne, Ltd., *Queen
Alexandra* was laid up in the Albert Harbour, Greenock, and her
white funnels were forthwith painted red. She did not, however, sail
for her new owners in this condition; for, when she emerged from the
yard of James Lamont & Co. Ltd., in May, 1936, she was scarcely
recognisable, the upper deck having been extended aft, and a third
funnel and second mast added. Her name had in April, 1936, been
changed to *Saint Columba*, her owners desiring, no doubt, to perpetuate in some measure the name of her illustrious predecessor, but
wisely refraining from copying it exactly.

The three funnels, which were slightly "stepped" were shorter
than the old and elliptical. She was the first and so far the only Clyde
passenger vessel of normal design to carry three funnels.

It is noteworthy that until 1935 there had been no turbine ships in
the MacBrayne fleet; but the two vessels acquired in that year were
both propelled by this type of machinery.

Saint Columba was employed on the Glasgow-Ardrishaig run,
which was regarded as the most important of the MacBrayne summer
services. Like *Columba*, she left Bridge Wharf at 7.11 a.m. each day
(except Sundays), making calls at the usual ports.

She was in 1937 converted for burning oil fuel, being the second
steamer of the MacBrayne fleet so fitted, the first being *Lochness*
(III). She was the first Clyde steamer to burn oil, with the exception of
Caledonia (1889), which did so experimentally for a time.

Requisitioned in January, 1940 *Saint Columba* was an accommodation ship in East India Harbour, Greenock, for Boom Defence
personnel till 1946. In the spring of 1947 she re-appeared, again from
Messrs. Lamont's, having been reconditioned and, in a few respects,
altered. Plating round the stern in place of the open rail gave rather a
better finish, and created an impression of great length with the sweep
of one line from stem to stern. (Actually she was the longest Clyde
steamer, which distinction previously belonged to her predecessor,
Columba.) Her passenger accommodation was remodelled, and she
was again an excellent ship.

She was restored to the Ardrishaig station on 19th May, 1947,
though then operating from Gourock only, on account of the number

of hours which the crew would have had to work if she had sailed from Glasgow as in pre-war days.

With her three funnels *Saint Columba* was a most impressive ship, and one of the handsomest on the Clyde. In time for the 1952 season, her mainmast was lengthened, so that the masthead light would be in such a position as to comply with the new regulations. She went aground at Ettrick Bay, Bute, in August, 1953, but was little damaged. After the 1958 season her end came, when she was sold to British Iron & Steel Corporation, and was towed to Port Glasgow on 23rd December to be broken up, during the following year.

T.S.S."King George V." The other steamer taken over from Turbine Steamers, Ltd., was *King George V*, a twin-screw vessel with single-reduction geared turbines, and originally fitted with two high-pressure Yarrow water-tube boilers working at 550 lb. and with a steam temperature of 750 degrees Fahrenheit. The port set of machinery, consisting of four ahead turbines, worked on the principle of quadruple expansion. The starboard set worked triple expansion ahead, the first turbine on this side receiving its steam from the extra high-pressure one on the port side. Both sets operated identically when the machinery was reversed, two astern turbines being incorporated in each set. The original boilers were removed in 1929, Babcock & Wilcox boilers being then installed, and navy-tops fitted to the funnels. A change was made again in 1935, and the steamer thereafter had one ordinary double-ended Scotch boiler, working at 200 lb. pressure. The extra high-pressure turbine was taken out, and then both sets were similar and worked triple expansion ahead, each high-pressure turbine receiving boiler steam. New funnels of greater diameter than the old, and without navy-tops, were fitted at the same time.

The turbines were of Parsons' design, and were supplied, along with the single-reduction gearing, from that firm's establishment at Wallsend.

It was late in the 1926 season when *King George V* took her place in the Turbine fleet, and from the beginning of the following season she was employed on the Campbeltown or Inveraray service, more often on the latter, with the Lock Eck Tour in connexion.

Though similar in appearance to the previous Clyde turbine steamers, *King George V* nevertheless embodied many improvements. She was the first Clyde steamer to have part of the promenade deck enclosed, and also had her dining saloon on the main deck instead of below, as had previously been the usual practice.

On entering the MacBrayne fleet *King George V* was repainted in their colours, and in 1936 appeared on the Oban-Staffa-Iona service with six lifeboats instead of her previous four—the two extra lifeboats were inherited from *Columba* and had previously done duty on *Scout*. She was converted to burn oil fuel, in 1938.

In the second war *King George V* was employed as a tender on the Firth of Clyde; she also acted as a troop transport at Dunkirk, making six trips in all in May, 1940. In recognition of their services on these occasions her master, Captain MacLean and her chief engineer, Mr. W. Macgregor, were each awarded the D.S.O., and her bo'sun, Mr. Mackinnon, the D.S.M. She returned to the Clyde and served as a tender when Dominion and later American troops were being landed at Gourock; and she carried Mr. Winston Churchill to his battleship when on his way across the Atlantic.

Like her predecessors in the Oban tourist services, *King George V* appeared on the Ardrishaig run from time to time; and during the whole of the summer of 1946 she was employed thereon, *Saint Columba* not having been released in time. A motor was fitted to one lifeboat in the spring of 1948. The first post-war landing at Staffa was on 23rd May, 1950.

During the winter of 1950-1 *King George V* was converted by her builders to burn oil fuel, which resulted in an increase over her recent speed. In 1952 she received a mainmast, in preparation for the regulations regarding masthead lights about to be brought into force.

On acquiring inflatable dinghies in the spring of 1959, her lifeboats were again reduced to four, these being the new boats supplied to *Saint Columba* in 1947, and she lost the historic pair. It was agreed in March, 1959 to instal a buffet for coffee and sandwiches, and in January, 1960 to have a cafeteria. In time for the 1962 season her dining saloon was extended forward, the galley being transferred to the stern (with a tall chimney above), and the lavatories to the forward end of the boiler casing. The after ends of the deck shelter were enclosed, bringing G.T. up to 985. In May, 1970 she had her most caried itinerary, under charter to the Highlands & Islands Development Board for the Festival of the Countryside, when she set out from Oban for a week's cruising, first to Tobermory, round Ardnamurchan Point to the Sound of Sleat and to Kyle of Lochalsh for the first night; then to Portree and Aultbea, with an excursion from the latter back to Portree and then to Mellon Charles instead of Aultbea, on account of the condition of the pier; next day when prevented by storm from going to Tarbert (Harris), to Kyle of Lochalsh and back to Mellon Charles and on to Ullapool, where she spent the next day, stormbound (when she was supposed to go to Lochinver and round Handa); then back to Kyle for a trip to Rhum, where passengers landed, then to Mallaig, and ultimately back to Oban. This was a most ambitious programme, unfortunately marred by exceptionally stormy weather.

In 1973 she passed to Caledonian MacBrayne Holdings Ltd., having yellow discs on the funnels, with the red lions from the *Duchess of Hamilton*.

Withdrawn at the end of the 1974 season, she spent the winter as usual in East India Harbour, Greenock and was sold at 12 noon on 3rd

April, 1975 to Nationwide Transport Ltd. She was towed away from Greenock on 12th April by the tug *Mumbles*, a sad farewell to the last two-funnelled (fore and aft) MacBrayne ship—a feature of the Highland scene since the advent of the first *Mountaineer* in 1852. While undergoing conversion to a floating restaurant she was severely damaged by fire at Cardiff on 26th August, 1981, and in April, 1984 was left partly dismantled opposite Penarth to be broken up by the sea.

    .   .   .   .

In May, 1936 it had been agreed that David MacBrayne Ltd. would purchase the *Lairdsheather* from Burns & Laird Lines Ltd. and dispose of *Lochiel* (III); but in October, in view of the heavy expenditure required this was abandoned and instead it was decided to purchase *Lairdspool* and *Lairdsrock* from the same fleet, and to dispose of *Lochbroom*.

In August and September, 1936, the small motor launch *Port Star*, owned in Port Glasgow, was chartered for the Lochgoil mail run while the *Comet* was being repaired after her collision with the L.N.E.R. vessel *Talisman*.

S.S. "Lochgorm" (II). At the beginning of 1937 S.S. *Lairdspool* (ex *Lily*) was transferred from Burns & Laird Lines, Ltd. to David MacBrayne, Ltd., for the Glasgow-West Highland service, being placed on the Glasgow-Stornoway run from 2nd February that year.

Launched on 7th November, 1896, for the Laird Line, she had been employed on various routes, latterly on that from Glasgow to Sligo, Westport and Ballina. She was of the normal type of passenger and cargo steamer built in the 'nineties, and was tolerably handsome. She had been re-boilered in December, 1920.

After overhaul at Ardrossan she was re-named *Lochgorm*. From 1938 she began to carry a small number of passengers on the Stornoway run, but this ceased when the second war started. She was from March, 1942 to 1945 allocated by the Ministry of War Transport, to McCallum, Orme & Co. Ltd., and operated their services from Glasgow to Oban, Coll, Tiree, etc., in place of *Hebrides*, which was allocated to Messrs. MacBrayne for an additional service between Oban and Tiree, the latter ship having more extensive passenger accommodation than *Lochgorm*. In due course each ship reverted to its own owners' service, and in 1947 *Lochgorm* was altered in appearance by having the tops of her masts truncated, which spoiled her profile completely, and made her look like Messrs. Burns' *Lurcher* and *Setter* of 1906. She was sold on 5th June, 1951 and broken up at Port Glasgow.

E

S.S. "Lochgarry." Another steamer acquired by Messrs. Mac-Brayne in January, 1937, was *Lairdsrock*, also from Burns & Laird Lines, Ltd. As in the case of *Lairdspool*, this steamer had made a few runs for Messrs. MacBrayne on charter in the autumn of 1936; and like her too, on being transferred, she was sent to Ardrossan for overhaul. The alterations carried out were, however, much more extensive.

Launched as *Vulture* on 14th June, 1898, for the Burns fleet, this steamer went on her official trial trip on 5th October in that year, when a speed of 15½ knots was averaged on six runs between Cloch and Cumbrae lights. She was propelled by triple-expansion machinery, three new single-ended oil-fired boilers having been installed by Messrs. D. & W. Henderson & Co. Ltd. in 1924, in place of the original coal-fired boilers.

Vulture was employed principally on the Ardrossan-Belfast route, and was owned by Burns & Laird Lines, Ltd., from 1922, her name being changed to *Lairdsrock* in 1929. On the discontinuance of the Ardrossan-Belfast night passenger service at the end of August, 1936, she was laid up in Ardrossan Harbour till chartered, and ultimately transferred to David MacBrayne, Ltd., as above-mentioned. Her name was changed to *Lochgarry* at the end of January, 1937.

During reconstruction a very large oval funnel was fitted, at first painted scarlet with blue band and black top, but fortunately the blue band had disappeared by the time she entered service. The passenger accommodation was entirely remodelled, the alterations including the building of a completely new shade-deck and dining-saloon. She was a very fine ship for the West Highland summer cruises, in which she took the place of *Lochbroom* and her accommodation was a great advance over that of any of her predecessors. She was the largest ship (in gross tonnage) up to that time owned by the Hutcheson/MacBrayne concern.

But for the second war, *Lochgarry* would probably have had a long career in the fleet. Requisitioned in 1940, she took part in the evacuation of Dunkirk, and suffered some damage, but was back in service as a transport between Scotland and Iceland. Unfortunately she was lost on 21st January, 1942, by foundering off Rathlin Island while so engaged, with the loss of more than twenty-three members of her crew.

M.V. "Garry." This was a small motor launch, about 25 feet in length, engaged in 1937 in running short cruises from Fort William and conveying passengers to the shore from *Killarney*, *Ulster Prince* and *Lochgarry*, etc., when they called. With the other small craft, she was engaged in connexion with diving operations during the second war, and on returning she reposed for a considerable time in a shed at

Bridge Wharf (South Side), Glasgow. From 1948 to 1953 she was on ferry duties at Glenelg, except when laid up at Shandon, and thereafter was at Rodel till 1963. She then became the second boat on Loch Shiel and on cessation of the service on 30th September, 1967 was laid up at Acharacle. She was the last MacBrayne vessel there. She was sold to Mr. D. Henderson, Newton, Acharacle early in 1969 and the following March to Mr. Ewan Shaw of Onich.

M.V. "Kyle." In 1938 this member of the Kyle of Lochalsh-Kyleakin ferry fleet was acquired for ferry duties at Iona. After war service during the second war, she was stationed at Coll, to act as ferry to the Company's steamers calling there, and was sold in March, 1941.

T.S.M.V. "Lochbuie" (I). A complete departure from Mac-Brayne tradition occurred in 1937 with the ordering from Messrs. Nicolaas, Witsen & Vis., Alkmaas, Amsterdam, of a twin-screw motor passenger launch intended initially for use between Oban and Craignure, but from delivery in 1938 used for cruising from Fort William. This little ship duly appeared, bearing the name *Lochbuie*. Not only was the fact of her having been built in Holland a novelty, but her design was different from that of any previous member of the fleet. A welded steel hull with slanting stem (much flared) and curved transom stern, surmounted by a teak cabin (with alleyways along the sides) gave her the appearance of a small motor yacht. No passengers were allowed on deck (except at the stern); and the seating inside the cabin was reminiscent of that of a motor bus: she was, in fact, advertised as a "sea-coach". Everything was most compact, and there was a small saloon on the lower deck forward.

The machinery, supplied by M.A.N., Augsburg and Nuremberg, consisted of two sets of four-stroke cycle single-acting internal-combustion engines, giving a speed of $14\frac{1}{2}$ knots—a higher rate than might have been expected from a vessel of her type.

A curious feature was a letter "M", painted in red, on the front of the bow, in the place where a figurehead might be expected. This has not been repeated on subsequent members of the fleet, though in a comparable position *Loch Seaforth* had a Highlander. The hull of *Lochbuie* was white, with dark blue waterline; she had no funnel.

Lochbuie gave cruises from Fort William (in summer only) as follows:—In the forenoon to the head of Lochiel; in the afternoon on Mondays, Wednesdays, Fridays and Saturdays to Loch Corrie and Kingairloch; and in the afternoon on Tuesdays and Thursdays to Ballachulish and Kinlochleven. In addition evening cruises were run to Ballachulish Bay or the head of Lochiel. In winter she was laid up at Greenock. In the summer of 1939 she was based at Oban. On 6th September, 1939, she was requisitioned and served as a hospital launch on the Clyde under the name *Roundalay*. She was sold in March, 1947, to James Louis McEwan Miller, Alan John McCulloch

Miller and Kenneth Bruce Miller, and in August of that year was re-sold by them to British Channel Islands Shipping Co. Ltd., being next month re-named *Silver Coast* and registered at Poole. Early in 1950 she was sold to Lt. Col. M. Brooke-Hitching, London and became the yacht *Marlene*, passing in September, 1953 to Mr. Douglas H. Dobbs, who re-named her *Pirate Princess*.

T.S.M.V. "Lochiel" (IV). A further ship following approximately the lines of *Lochfyne* and *Lochnevis* was produced in 1939 by Messrs. Denny for the Company's West Loch Tarbert-Islay service. She different from the two mentioned above in having Diesel engines driving twin screws through reduction gearing, electrical transmission being absent.

It was on 4th April, 1939, that the new vessel was launched, and she revived a name of long standing in the fleet—*Lochiel*. She succeeded *Pioneer* on the Islay run, the older ship being then sent to Oban. It may be remarked that the first *Lochiel*, though not closely identified with the West Loch Tarbert-Islay route, was employed thereon for a time about 1879, and the revival of the name on a ship built specifically for this service is interesting.

Lochiel had a raked stem, cruiser stern, single funnel and steel mast, with one derrick for handling cargo from the hold, which is situated forward. On the main deck were first- and third-class dining saloons and smoke-rooms (latterly one class only), above this deck being a promenade deck with lounge, purser's room and ticket office. Above these, amidships is a shade deck, with the navigating bridge raised to the level of the rail as on *Lochfyne* and *Lochnevis*, and obstructing any view forward which passengers might otherwise have had. The lower deck, below the main deck, contained the officers' accommodation and a cold store, the crew being accommodated in the forecastle, on main deck level. On that deck was a large space forward, for the carriage of motor-cars or cattle. The first-class accommodation was to the starboard side of the ship, the third-class to port, as on *Lochnevis*.

The three lifeboats were slung on Welin, Maclachlan davits, and the deck machinery, which was electrically driven, included steering gear, capstan and windlass and a hoisting and slewing winch.

The propelling machinery, made by Davey, Paxman & Co. (Colchester), Ltd., consisted of two sets of eight-cylinder Paxman-Ricardo "Comet Head" vertical Diesel engines, of the four-stroke, single-acting totally enclosed, monobloc, forced-lubricated type, each giving 440 B.H.P. at 400 r.p.m. They were flexibly mounted to reduce noise and vibration. Each engine drove through an oil-operated reverse reduction gearbox, which allowed full advantage to be taken of the reduced size and weight of the Paxman-medium-speed engine, instead of using a heavy slow-speed direct reversing engine. The principal elements in the gear-boxes were constant-mesh helical gears,

oil-operated friction clutches and their control-cock. Of auxiliary
machinery mention may be made of one six-cylinder Paxman-Ricardo
engine running at 1,000 r.p.m. and direct-coupled to a generator of 40
kW. capacity at 220 volts. Another set of the same size drives a
Reavell compressor.

A speed of 14 knots on trial was obtained, though the service
speed required was 12 knots.

Though intended for the Islay run, *Lochiel* spent part of her first
season at Oban, performing the Fort William service, etc. After
extension of the pier at West Loch Tarbert she was able to take up the
service for which she was intended; and on this she was fairly
constantly employed, though she acted as Portree Mail Steamer from
3rd October, 1939 to 9th May, 1940 and from 5th to 14th June, 1940;
and she relieved on the Ardrishaig service in May, 1942, and June,
1943, being then painted grey all over. From 1949 her sailings were
extended to include Colonsay on the days of her call at Port Askaig.
In 1953 a mainmast was fitted. On 8th October, 1960 *Lochiel* struck
submerged rocks in West Loch Tarbert, and was out of service till the
following March.

She was superseded by *Arran* in January, 1970, and sold in March
to Norwest Shipping Ltd., Douglas, I.O.M. Renamed *Norwest Laird*,
she was employed on a service between Douglas and Fleetwood
during that season only. She was later sold to Courage (Western)
Ltd., Bristol late in 1974, and is now a floating restaurant at Bristol,
with the name *Lochiel* restored.

. . . .

During the second war, the Government contract was suspended:
twelve vessels in all of the MacBrayne fleet, with a combined gross
tonnage of under 5,000, were employed in Government service. The
Portree mail service was suspended, and the Company's other services
were maintained with the ships remaining. The Ardrishaig station was
filled mainly by *Lochfyne* though *Lochnevis* and *Lochiel* each operated there for a time. The route was from Wemyss Bay, since the
boom across the Clyde between the Cloch and Dunoon prevented the
use of Greenock or Gourock. The ships were in some instances given
black funnels, with "horizon yellow" superstructure, among those so
treated being *Pioneer*, *Clydesdale*, *Lochnevis*, *Lochfyne*, *Lochiel* and
Lochinvar. Later in the war they were grey, as in the first war.
Lochearn, on the other hand, retained her red and black funnel when
the others were black.

Through waters sometimes mined and submarine-infested, the
ships on the passenger, mail and cargo services to the Islands carried
on for six years of war without much opportunity for overhaul, and it
should be recorded that this was achieved without a single mishap
during the whole period.

No ships were acquired by the Company during the war period, but deficiencies were made up as far as possible by chartering, or by Ministry of War Transport allocations. Among the ships in the former category may be mentioned the single-screw steamer *Ulster Star* of the Belfast Steamship Co. Ltd., and among the latter *Hebrides*, of the McCallum, Orme fleet, which, as recorded elsewhere, carried on a special service for David MacBrayne, Ltd., between Oban and Tiree, there being a considerably increased traffic to the latter place on account of an aerodrome situated there.

S.S. "Ulster Star." This was a ship of many names, launched on 14th September, 1904, as *James Crombie* for the Aberdeen, Leith & Moray Firth Steam Shipping Co. Ltd., which concern was absorbed by Messrs. Langlands in 1914. In the following year, the vessel under review was sold to Laird Line, Ltd. and named *Broom*, passing on 1st March, 1922, to the City of Cork S.P. Co. Ltd., by whom she was named *Lismore*. On 30th September, 1922, she was transferred to the Belfast Steamship Co. Ltd., who named her *Dynamic*, changing this to *Ulster Star* in 1931. This ship was continuously on charter to David MacBrayne, Ltd., from about 1942 till July, 1947, and after the cessation of hostilities was painted in their colours. She was employed on the Glasgow to West Highlands cargo service, really taking the place of *Lochgarry*. Though she returned to her owners in September, 1947, she again appeared in MacBrayne colours in November of that year and remained with this Company on charter for the rest of her career. On 11th February, 1948, she went ashore at Bunessan but was refloated the next day. She was sold in February, 1949 to be scrapped at Troon. The steamer *Lothdale* was chartered from Charles B. Simpson of Helmsdale for about two months, though *Ulster Star* was back in service early in April. Others chartered during the war period were *Borneo*, *Empire Daffodil*, *Empire Tulip*, *Parkstone*, *Hawthorn* and *Snowcrete*.

T.S.S. "Robina." In 1946 a further charter occurred, of this passenger steamer built in 1914 for Messrs. W. A. & P. Cordingley, intended as successor to the former Clyde steamer *Isle of Bute* in the excursion traffic from Morecambe. In 1919 she operated at Blackpool; in 1920 she was on the Bristol Channel; and in 1923-4 she was again at Blackpool, all on charter. In January, 1925, she was sold to Mr. William T. McCalla for excursion and tender service at Belfast, in which she continued till the outbreak of the second war. Requisitioned by the Government, she was then placed under the management of The Caledonian S.P. Co. Ltd., and was one of the many tenders stationed at Gourock. In January, 1946, she was purchased by Coast Lines, Ltd., and her port of registry was changed to Falmouth, the intention being to employ her in excursion work there. That, however, did not materialise, and from 12th June, 1946, she was continuously on charter to David MacBrayne, Ltd., till the spring of 1948. She carried their funnel colouring and black hull, but with green waterline and cream-coloured saloons.

Elsewhere we have remarked that it was curious that on the Clyde there had never been a twin-screw steamer with reciprocating engines, such as had appeared in other localities between the paddle and turbine eras. This gap was then filled, for *Robina* was of this type, and during 1947 was employed in Clyde passenger service from Gourock to Lochgoilhead. She was rather an attractive little ship, of a somewhat old-fashioned design, with saloons fore and aft and alleyways, as on *Iona*, *Chevalier*, *Gondolier*, etc. The fore-saloon was a lounge, and the after one a dining saloon, so that there was really no third-class accommodation. With a speed of about 14 knots, she would have been able to maintain many different services when required, but was used only on three.

Her first employment in the MacBrayne fleet was in local excursions from Oban, during the summer of 1946, in which she was really successor to *Mountaineer*, *Princess Louise*, etc. She and *Lochfyne* were the only two vessels stationed at Oban that summer, *King George V* being then required on the Ardrishaig route. Her itineraries included Isles of the Sea, Loch Spelvie, Tobermory, Loch Sunart, Loch Creran, etc.

In the autumn of 1946 *Robina* was placed on the West Loch Tarbert-Islay mail run, relieving *Lochiel* for overhaul, after which she spent the winter at Ardrossan.

It was a pleasant surprise to many people to read the announcement in the Glasgow newspapers that between 2nd June and 13th September, 1947, *Robina* would provide a double daily return service between Gourock and Lochgoilhead, which she duly did. Though this was much appreciated, since the sea route is much more direct than that by road, and much more convenient, it was evidently not particularly well patronised. The next winter was spent at Greenock alongside *Saint Columba* and *King George V*, and, as it was decided not to resume the Lochgoil sailings, *Robina* in 1948 was chartered by her owners, Coast Lines, Ltd., to their subsidiary the Island Shipping Co. Ltd., Guernsey, Channel Islands. There she ran into and sank the latter company's *Herm Coast*, and damaged herself so severely that she was advertised for sale. She was purchased by the Southampton, Isle of Wight & South of England Royal Mail S.P. Co. Ltd. in August, 1948.

In March, 1952 she was reported sold to Italian owners, but the sale apparently did not take place, and she was later sold to Dutch ship-breakers, in August, 1958.

T.S.M.V. "Loch Seaforth." Under the Mail Contract dated 13th December, 1938, it was stipulated that the Company would provide two new vessels, one for the Islay mail service and one for that to

Stornoway. The former duly appeared in 1939, but the ordering of the latter had to be delayed on account of the outbreak of war. In February, 1945, the Provost of Stornoway announced that he had seen draft plans for the new ship, with the description of which the councillors were favourably impressed. A considerable agitation had occurred from time to time regarding the alleged inadequacy of the accommodation of *Lochness*, particularly in view of the additional numbers of passengers, including service personnel, travelling as a result of the war. The order for the ship was placed with Messrs. Denny later in 1945; and, after exceptional delays occasioned by shortage of supplies, etc., she was launched at Dumbarton on 19th May, 1947, to the accommpaniment of music provided by two pipers. During the period of about a year and a half, questions were continually being asked in Parliament as to when the new ship would be ready, on one of which occasions the Minister of Transport said she could not be ready for the winter of 1946-7, but would certainly be ready for that of 1947-8. When launched, it was thought the ship might be ready about August; but, on account of further delays in obtaining certain equipment, it was not till 6th December, 1947, that she was able to take her place on the Stornoway run; thus the Minister of Transport's forecast proved correct.

Loch Seaforth was much larger than her predecessors on the Stornoway mail service, with a gross tonnage of 1,089, and a length of 229 feet. She followed *Lochness* in design to the extent of having a large forecastle, a shade-deck and a cruiser stern; but her accommodation was much superior, the difference in the third-class rooms being particularly marked. There were cabins for both classes of passengers, and the third-class lounge was much superior to the first-class saloon of some of the older steamers. There were also cubicles for both classes of passengers.

With a raked stem, recessed anchors and two masts, the ship would have had quite a good appearance if she had been given a taller funnel; but the latter was so short as to be invisible from forward, and was elliptical, nearly perpendicular and with a slanting top, originally with very narrow black portion; and it was at first painted Burns-Laird red but fortunately later became MacBrayne red. In 1949 it was lengthened by the depth of the black top (as was done with *Iona* (III), *Columba*, *Fusilier*, etc.) and then the resulting deep black top changed to a narrow one in 1966, reverting to deep in 1972.

The ship differed from *Lochness* in having all her cargo accommodation forward, the foremast being provided with two derricks. The mainmast was a thin pole mast, for the purpose of carrying the wireless aerial.

The first-class lounge, situated in a large deck-house on the boat-deck level, under the bridge, was a magnificent room with large plate-glass windows, the officers' quarters being above this, level with and abaft the bridge. Four lifeboats were provided, slung on Welin Maclachlan davits.

A pleasing feature was a quasi-figurehead consisting of the well-known MacBrayne Highlander, originally designed by Mr. Tom Gilfillan, and used as a decoration on the Company's motor buses, sailing programmes, etc.

In accommodation the ship was a great advance over her predecessors on the Stornoway route, and in speed she was capable of leaving Stornoway at 12.15 a.m. and reaching Kyle and Mallaig in time for the mail trains; and this satisfied those who used to object strongly to the sailings of the former ships at 11.45 p.m. on Sundays.

The propelling machinery consisted of two sets of Sulzer engines made by the Swiss firm in Winterthur, and made an appalling noise. In May, 1949 Radar was installed, *Loch Seaforth* being the first member of the MacBrayne fleet to be so fitted.

Loch Seaforth had a series of mishaps. On 22nd October, 1971 she hit the island of Longay off Broadford, when the *Western Isles* took off her passengers, and she was later refloated. She continued on the Stornoway service till 28th January, 1972, when she left on what was expected to be her last run on that route; then she took up cargo runs from Oban to Coll, Tiree, Castlebay and Lochboisdale; but, following *Clansman* being involved in a collision, *Loch Seaforth* again took up the Stornoway service. From 29th May, 1972 she was on the Inner Islands run, which she had performed as relief previously: she included also Colonsay from Oban among her calls. On 22nd March, 1973 she ran aground on Cleit Rock in the Sound of Gunna. Three lifeboats were launched, one powered, which reached the Tiree shore, the other two being towed in by fishing-boats. After being refloated the *Loch Seaforth* was towed to Gott Bay, Tiree for inspection; and the *Columba* made a special run to Tiree till the *Claymore* took over the service. The puffer *Glencloy* was chartered to take cargo from Oban to Coll and Tiree. *Loch Seaforth* was pumped but next day shipped more water, and she blocked the pier, so that passengers had to be ferried ashore, using the ferryboat *Iona*. During April the pier continued to be blocked, the *Glencloy* kept up the service for general cargo, but vehicles and cattle could not be loaded. The Company then chartered the Dutch vessel *Johanna Buitalaar* for special cattle shipment from the Tiree sales, she being just able to squeeze in between the sunken vessel and the pier. On 11th May the giant floating crane *Magnus III* (chartered from Risdon Beasley of Southampton) arrived and on 10th lifted the *Loch Seaforth*, moving her to the beach. She was patched and refloated, then left in tow for Troon, where she was scrapped by the West of Scotland Shipbreaking Co., Ltd. So ended the career of one of the best ships of the Stornoway service.

T.S.M.V. "Lochnell." In terms of a further mail contract dated 3rd June, 1947, provision was made for a new twice-daily return service between Oban and Lismore, to be operated by motor launch, which also was to be utilised, when possible, for special passenger or excursion services. For this purpose there had been purchased in December, 1946 the former hospital launch *Galen*, which had been designed by Mr. John Bain, Joint Managing Director of James A. Silver, Ltd., Rosneath, who had built her in 1941 to the order of Glasgow Corporation, the acting body for the Port Health Authority. She had been used throughout the war in bringing stretcher cases ashore from the various ships in the Clyde anchorage, having as consort the former MacBrayne vessel *Lochbuie* (I), then named *Roundalay*. Re-named *Lochnell*, *Galen* was placed on the Oban-Lismore station and commenced on 30th June, 1947. (She is reported to have been officially re-named on 13th August, but is known to have carried the new name earlier than that date.) With a gross tonnage of 31, *Lochnell* was a smaller vessel than either *Comet* or *Lochbuie*. She could carry twenty-five passengers in summer, in winter twelve, and had a small cabin. Her hull was black, later light blue, then dark blue, and she had no funnel, the exhausts being through the sides of the hull. She had one mast, and was described as carvel-built of wood, with transom stern, and two watertight bulkheads. The additional facilities all the year round for travel between Oban and Lismore were appreciated by inhabitants of these neighbourhoods, and by visitors in summer. She was re-engined in November, 1958. Her usual relief was one of the red-hulled boats from Iona; but from 1965 she changed places with *Loch Toscaig* and performed the Toscaig run and forenoon cruise from Kyle of Lochalsh together with the Kylerhea mail run three days per week in succession to *Applecross*, till transferred to Tobermory for the Mingary service in May, 1968, in succession to *Lochbuie*. In this she was relieved on occasion by the *Vital Spark* from Maclean & MacRae of Kyle, and in July, 1969 by the local vessel *Elfrida*. From 7th December, 1976 she tendered to *Iona* on the winter run to Coll and Tiree, after it had been found difficult for the larger ship to call at the pier at Tobermory, this continuing till she was succeeded at Tobermory by *Staffa* on 7th March, 1981. *Lochnell* was then sold to T.B.J. Marine Ltd., Dumbarton, and delivered on 10th June, 1981, after having been laid up at Shandon since March.

CHAPTER VI

McCALLUM, ORME & CO. LTD.

IN November, 1947, it was announced that David MacBrayne, Ltd. had acquired the shares of McCallum, Orme & Co. Ltd. This company's business was absorbed completely with effect from 1st January, 1948, when its remaining vessels were taken into the MacBrayne fleet.

The company had been incorporated on 1st July, 1929, on the amalgamation of the firms of John McCallum & Company and Martin Orme & Company. It had, in 1935, absorbed the West Highland trade of Jack Bros.

Prior to 1929 both the McCallum and the Orme steamers were distinguished by a funnel-colouring of red with black top. The house-flag of the former was blue with a white disc bearing a thistle in natural colours, while that of the latter was the blue St. Andrew's saltire. At the amalgamation, a black hoop was added to the red funnels (to distinguish them from those of David MacBrayne, Ltd.). The new house-flag was a combination of the two old ones, viz., the saltire, with the disc and thistle superimposed.

John McCallum & Company

In 1871 Mr. Andrew Ross became the owner of a small steamer of the puffer type, named *Black Eagle*. At a slightly later period he became associated with Mr. John McCallum in the ownership of several ships trading to the West Highlands, the vessels of this fleet being registered variously in the names of Andrew Ross, Andrew McKenzie Ross and John McCallum, and, in later years, in those of William Young and Hugh Young.

The Western Isles Steam Packet Co. Ltd. was incorporated on 11th February, 1873 (Captain John McCallum being the owner of two shares) and commenced trading with the handsome paddle steamer *St. Clair of the Isles*, previously named *Lisboa* and owned by the Lusitania Steam Company, Lisbon. Built in 1860, she had been newly re-boilered when purchased by the Western Isles Company. The Glasgow agents for the owners were Messrs. Patrick Christie & Co., and the steamer plied on a weekly service from Glasgow on Thursdays to the Outer Hebrides and the more distant parts of Skye. The route was varied each week—on one trip Dunvegan and Uig were visted first, the steamer sailing thence to Lochmaddy and Lochboisdale, and on the following trip the calls were made in the reverse order, among the ports included being Port Charlotte, Bowmore, Small Isles (Jura),

Caol Ila, Barra and Port Phaedair; also Portrush on certain occasions. The start of the venture, which took place in July, 1873, was not an auspicious one; for, on her first trip, *St. Clair of the Isles* had to put into Campbeltown, unable to proceed on account of a machinery breakdown. Just a month later she struck a sunken rock in Loch Sunart and filled with water; but she got off, though so badly damaged that the service had to be suspended for some months while she was being repaired. At the beginning of April, 1874, the agency passed to Mr. A. Macpherson; and in the autumn of that year the sailings to the outlying parts of the Hebrides were discontinued. *St. Clair of the Isles*, which by this time had the screw steamer *Lady Ambrosine* as consort, was for a while transferred to a new route, making weekly trips to several of the smaller ports on Lough Swilly. In the summer of 1874 *St. Clair of the Isles* was sailing at 10 a.m. on Thursdays for the Hebridean ports above-mentioned, while *Lady Ambrosine* left on Mondays for Ardrishaig, Lochgilphead, Crinan Canal ports, Luing, Easdale, Oban, Lochaline, Salen (Mull), Tobermory, Kilchoan, Salen (Loch Sunart), Coll and Tiree, including Strontian or Carbost in alternate weeks.

The two steamers were auctioned in March, 1875, when *St. Clair of the Isles* was purchased by Messrs. Harris & Goodwin, Birmingham, and afterwards went abroad. She is known to have been surveyed at Singapore and to have been under the Dutch flag, but details of her subsequent career are lacking.

Lady Ambrosine was purchased by Captain McCallum, remaining in the Hebridean trade. Her sailings were arranged to avoid clashing with those of Mr. Orme's *Dunara Castle*, and twice-weekly sailings were thus provided to the Hebrides by the two ships.

Lady Ambrosine as originally designed was somewhat similar to Messrs. Orme's *Aros Castle*, her length being restricted so that she might use the Crinan Canal. In 1885, however, she was lengthened from 85 to 105 feet, which would preclude any further use of the Canal. She was sold in 1890 to Greek owners, and re-named in succession *Nicolaos* and *Olga*, being wrecked in February 1895.

Intended as a successor to *St. Clair of the Isles*, the screw steamer *St. Clair* was launched on 13th April, 1876, entering Messrs. McCallum's service in June. On 20th June, 1877, she was stranded in Loch Bracadale and after the lapse of a fortnight was re-floated. She went aground again on 25th September, 1878, this time at Salen (Loch Sunart); and, listing over, she filled with water. She was successfully raised, but her next disaster was her last, when she struck a submerged rock at Coll on 26th October, 1880, and sank. Her place was taken for a time by S.S. *Fern*, chartered from Messrs. Laird.

The *Hebridean*, the first ship designed by G. L. Watson, and a handsome vessel, was launched at Rutherglen on 30th April, 1881 for the McCallum fleet. She was well suited to the West Highland trade, and was long popular among passengers for summer cruises. She was for a time chartered to a Bristol firm, and on another occasion sailed to the Isle of Man on charter: she was really surplus during the summer months after the appearance of *Hebrides* in 1898, returning to the West Highland route each winter. In May, 1917, she was sold to Peter S. Cooper, Kirkwall, re-named *Express* and sank on 9th February, 1918. Like her predecessor she was relieved by the *Fern* of the Laird Line in March-April 1898.

The successor to *Lady Ambrosine*, purchased late in 1890, was *Quiraing*, which had originally been the Ardrossan Shipping Company's *South Western*, built in 1870. Having been sold in 1883 to Gustaf Gollcher, Malta, she became *La Valette*, receiving her third name after being purchased by Messrs. McCallum. Sailing from Glasgow to Iceland during August 1896, she was sold about the end of that year to the Ayr Steam Shipping Company, and carried the name *Merrick* for about two years, after which she was purchased by Messrs. McDowell & Barbour, Piraeus, who re-named her *Clio*. She was wrecked in 1904.

S.S. "Hebrides" (I). The Ailsa Shipbuilding Company, Ltd. built this steamer in 1898 for Messrs. McCallum's West Highland trade, as a successor to *Quiraing*. She was a fine ship of 585 tons gross, fitted with triple-expansion machinery, and like *Hebridean*, was designed by G. L. Watson. Her mean trial speed was 12·8 knots. She received a new boiler with three coal-fired furnaces in February, 1937. *Hebrides* also was a popular cruising steamer, being, like *Dunara Castle*, employed on extended summer trips to St. Kilda, etc. She passed into the McCallum, Orme fleet in 1929, and to David MacBrayne, Ltd. on 1st January, 1948, having been on charter to the latter for a time during the second war, sailing between Oban and Tiree. While on this route she ran aground, but was refloated, and was restored to McCallum, Orme & Co. Ltd. in 1946. During her absence from their fleet her place was taken by Messrs. MacBrayne's *Lochgorm* allocated by the Ministry of War Transport.

Early in 1948 the black hoop disappeared from the funnel of *Hebrides*: just when, for the first time in her career she was really entitled to it! In May, 1949, her deck-houses were painted white.

Latterly she carried cargo and livestock only, continuing on approximately her old route from Glasgow till 1952, with *Loch Frisa* on alternate runs thereafter with *Loch Carron*. Laid up at Greenock on the commissioning of *Loch Ard*, *Hebrides* was, on 1st August, 1955, taken to Messrs. Smith & Co.'s yard at Port Glasgow and scrapped.

.   .   .   .

The pier at Loch Eport, situated a considerable distance up the loch, was used by the first *Hebridean*, but was difficult of access for larger ships, and so a ferryboat was provided by Messrs. McCallum, the first being an open boat, propelled by oars and sail, of 12 to 15 tons. These boats went more than half-way down the loch, to Bruach an Eirich, to meet the *Hebrides*. There was a second boat, also, which was bought during the first war along with the *Sultan* of Fraserburgh (a Zulu, taking 20 tons or more); but, as she proved too big, the two were switched and *Sultan* remained till 1924, latterly with a Kelvin engine, giving a speed of 5-6 knots. She was succeeded by the second *Hebridean*, also a Zulu, from St. Monance, which was fitted with a 26-30 Kelvin engine giving a speed of 7 knots. She went ashore just below Locheport pier on New Year's night, 1926, after dragging her anchor, and broke her back. A smaller fishing-boat, *St. Bede*, was chartered from Finlay Mackenzie, Lochboisdale for about three months, until the acquisition of the *Respect*, carrying 40 tons and with a speed of 8-9 knots. She was brought from Anstruther through the Caledonian Canal in March, 1926. Her hull was painted with black tar, with a white water-line: the others were tar only. During the second war *Respect* was out of service for two or three trips with a broken shaft. About 1945 she was taken to Irvine for repairs and was absent for about a month; during these periods cargo went *via* Lochmaddy. She was caulked from stem to stern; but after about four years she began to leak, and being not worth repairing, she was beached at the pier, and sold in April, 1949 for £4:10/-.

Orme Bros. & Co.
William Lang—Martin Orme
Martin Orme & Co.

The earliest reference appeared in January, 1853, when Messrs. Orme Bros. & Co. advertised weekly sailings to Stornoway by the new steamer *Queen*. This was an iron three-masted screw vessel of 275 tons gross, with figurehead, bowsprit and square stern. She had sleeping accommodation for twenty-three passengers, and a speed of 12 knots. Her first owners were Messrs. James Orme, Martin Orme and Laurence Orme. As the Stornoway Harbour authorities considered themselves precluded from giving her berthage on account of their commitments with other owners, she was transferred to the Islay, Oban, Tobermory and Portree route, but ceased sailing about the middle of July. She was sold, and went to Melbourne, where she arrived some time before February, 1854.

Several of the steamers of this fleet were registered in the name of William Lang, of Groatholm, in the Parish of Kilwinning, Ayrshire, the first of which we have any record being *Queen of the Isles*, built of steel at Port Glasgow in 1860. For a time Mr. William Dick was the Glasgow agent, employing the small screw steamer *Cantie Queen* (built at Port Glasgow in 1859, and owned by Laurence Hill, Shipbuilder, there) from April, 1860, until the new *Queen of the Isles* should be ready. The latter was engaged for a short time in 1861 on the Limerick station, but soon returned to the West Highlands. She was sold on 12th December, 1862, to Mr. Wm. S. Crealock, of London, who transferred her registry to Aberystwyth; and she was wrecked on the Brest Rocks, near Aye, on 16th February, 1870.

Mr. William Dick originally of Oban was owner or agent in 1847 of the small screw steamer *Lochfine*, which sailed during 1848 with goods and passengers between Glasgow and Ardrishaig, later being placed on the Glasgow-Fort William route, and fitting in excursions from Fort William to Ballachulish on certain days. She passed to G. & J. Burns in 1850, then to Messrs. Denny, and finally to the Dumbarton & Glasgow Steam Packet Company, becoming well known in the carrying trade, with her high-bowed hull, derrick forward and piebald funnel aft. Her last exploit was an unsuccessful attempt to ram the Caledonian Railway Bridge.

Mr. Martin Orme was manager for the Great West of Scotland Fishery Co. Ltd., incorporated on 22nd April, 1857 (one of the shareholders in which was Mr. James R. Napier). For them the steamer *Islesman* was built in 1858 to provide communication between Glasgow and the various fishing ports, the Company having fishing stations at Stein, Glendale and Fraserburgh; and, when this ceased to be a profitable business, on account of changing conditions in the fishing grounds, the Company went into voluntary liquidation in 1860 and the ship was sold, being registered at Port Glasgow early in 1861 in the name of William Lang. (She had from October, 1860, been advertised by Mr. William Dick, presumably as agent.) Regular passenger services were then opened up from Glasgow to the Outer Hebrides, with calls at Oban, Bunessan, Coll, Tiree, Lochboisdale, Lochmaddy, Tarbert (Harris), Ullapool and Lochinver, and also at many other ports to which no regular services had previously been provided. The credit for this enterprise was largely due to Mr. Orme. Of a length originally of 107·7 feet, *Islesman* was in 1861 lengthened to 130·5 feet. In March, 1858, she had been altered so as to be able to berth above Glasgow Bridge. It is probably on account of her having been built by Robert Napier that the red and black funnel was adopted for the Orme fleet.

In 1868 *Islesman* was succeeded by *Dunvegan Castle*, and was then sold to Duncan Stewart, Engineer, Glasgow, who re-sold her later the same year to John Alleyne of Bridgetown, Barbados. She was lost in a gale at Martinique on 9th September, 1872.

The steamer *Chieftain*, built late in 1860, was registered in the name of William Lang early in 1861, and sailed as consort to *Islesman*. With them from time to time there also plied the steamer *Lancefield* (registered in name of James Robert Napier). This ship was sold on 18th December, 1865, to Robert McCracken of Liverpool and Archibald Armour of Birkenhead, returning to James R. Napier in 1866, and being re-sold on 26th April, 1867, to Thomas Henderson, Merchant, Glasgow, who on 1st July in that year transferred the registry to Malta, the vessel being owned from 1879 by Johan Gustaf Gollcher. She was broken up at Malta in October, 1886.

Chieftain struck a rock off the harbour of Coll in June, 1861. She was sold in March, 1863, to Hugh McLean of Tobermory and Robert Heron Steel (of Jas. Steel & Sons, afterwards Steel & Bennie), Broomielaw, Glasgow, and in the following year to Richard Rowe of Laxey, I.O.M., being lengthened to 114' in 1865, when her gross tonnage was increased to 127. In January, 1868, she was acquired by Thomas B. Morton, Great Yarmouth, and on 8th November, 1872, by Sir Edmond H. K. Lacon, Bart., Banker, there, who re-sold her on 26th September, 1874, to William Dawson, Merchant, Constantinople. Schooner-rigged with one deck and break, she was originally of a length of 85·4 feet, but in 1865 was lengthened to 110·8 feet.

Mr. Orme was joint owner, along with Mr. Alexander A. Laird, of the screw steamer *Scotia*, ex *Jamaica Packet*, which, transferred to the Glasgow & Londonderry S.P. Company in 1867, was re-named *Laurel*.

Dunvegan Castle, built in 1868, was a handsome little ship, with whale-back forecastle and accommodation for passengers and cargo. She remained on the Glasgow and Hebridean run till she went ashore at Dunvegan in 1875, following which she was refloated and sold by underwriters to W. McCulloch, Salvage Contractor, Glasgow, being later owned by J. Mawson, Barrow-in-Furness. Finally she sank after a collision in the Mersey on 26th April, 1889.

In 1871 the single-screw steamer *Talisman* was built for William Lang (Mr. Orme having 10 shares) by Messrs. Blackwood & Gordon of Port Glasgow, who also built *Dunvegan Castle* and the succeeding members of the fleet, *Dunara Castle* and *Aros Castle*. All were registered initially at Port Glasgow, and the builders retained certain shares in them.

Talisman was advertised in May, 1872, to sail from Glasgow every Thursday at 12 o'clock noon for Oban, Quinish, Dunvegan, Uig, Tarbert, Rodel, Lochmaddy, Kallin, Lochboisdale and Barra. The adventures of the Misses Astley from London visiting friends at Lochaline are described in the book "Morvern Transformed" by Philip Gaskell. They missed the *Clansman* at Customhouse Quay, Greenock and travelled on the *Talisman*, which was bound for Quinish and could not let them off at Lochaline, but ultimately landed them at Tobermory from which they hired a boat to reach their destination. At that time *Dunvegan Castle* was sailing on Mondays for Colonsay, Iona, Bunessan, Ulva, Tiree, Coll, Quinish, Kilchoan, Salen (Loch Sunart) and Strontian. *Talisman* was sold in 1874, being in 1875 registered in name of Wm. Fair, Liverpool and in the following year in that of J. D. Thomas, Tranmere. Later she was again sold, this time to South American owners and was seized as a prize by the Peruvian Government. After her departure from the Orme fleet, Messrs. Langlands' *Fairy Queen* was chartered for a time, and also carried on *Dunvegan Castle*'s service after the latter had gone ashore, until a new steamer could be built.

S.S. "Dunara Castle." Like her predecessors, this vessel came from Messrs. Blackwood & Gordon's yard at Port Glasgow. She entered the water about a week after *Dunvegan Castle* had gone ashore. On 21st June, 1875, she started on her maiden trip, and for a period of nearly seventy-three years she sailed almost continuously between Glasgow and the West Highlands. In peacetime the trips were extended, during summer, to St. Kilda, or to Loch Roag (Lewis), etc., thus providing extended tours for passengers. These, however, were discontinued in 1939 and have not been resumed. *Dunara Castle* took part in the evacuation of St. Kilda in 1930, and continued to call there on occasion during subsequent seasons.

Fitted for a time with two funnels, *Dunara Castle* was re-boilered in 1882 (when the machinery was compounded), and again in 1894, from which date she was single-funnelled. From time to time various improvements were made, such as the installation of electric light, wireless, etc.; and a small upper deck aft, was added about 1945. She was a handsome ship, and a fine sea boat.

Her name was taken from that of a ruined castle on the west coast of Mull, not far from Quinish, the residence of one of her original principal part-owners, William Lang.

She had various minor mishaps from time to time, as, for example, when she went ashore at the Battery Point, Greenock, in August, 1922; and in March, 1947, when she went aground near Bunessan, and remained fast for about a week, after which she was refloated (without the assistance of the tug which was standing by) and continued on her voyage.

Dunara Castle passed to the combined McCallum Orme fleet in 1929, and to David MacBrayne, Ltd., on 1st January, 1948. The cargo sailiings were then reorganised so as to dispense with one steamer, her calls being divided between *Hebrides* and *Ulster Star*; and *Dunara Castle* made her last voyage to the West Highlands from 19th to 27th January, 1948. She was thereafter laid up in the East India Harbour, Greenock, from 28th January and was sold to Smith & Houston, Ltd., being in April towed to Port Glasgow, and broken up during the summer of 1948.

. . . .

The last ship built for this fleet was *Aros Castle*, which appeared in 1878 and was registered in name of William Lang (then of Glengorm, Mull), later in that of Martin Orme. She was a very short boat—only 84·2 feet in length—and traded to Oban, Bunessan, etc.

via the Crinan Canal. In March, 1882, she stranded in the Sound of Jura, her position giving rise to some misgivings; and, about the same time, the steamer *Times*, which had been temporarily chartered to take the place of *Dunara Castle*, went ashore at Loch Carron. Fortunately both were successfully refloated. *Aros Castle*, however, went ashore again in 1887, this time near Iona, and was afterwards sold to Mr. MacBrayne, who re-named her *Handa* (see page 59).

Jack Bros.

In December, 1935, McCallum, Orme & Co. Ltd., took over the West Highland trade of Messrs. Jack Bros. This firm's association with these routes dated from about March,1927, and their steamers sailed from Kingston Dock, Glasgow, to various ports, including Castlebay, Northbay, Eriskay, Lochboisdale, Lochskipport, Petersport, Scotvin, Kallin, Lochmaddy, Leverburgh, Geocrab, Tarbert (Harris), Scalpay and Stein.

The ships first employed on these services were the wooden steam drifter *Rose Valley* and the iron steam trawlers *Sagittarius* and *Challenger*, the former of which was wrecked on the Kintyre coast in 1931, her place being taken by the small coaster *Burnside*: this vessel went on fire in Lochmaddy harbour on 13th March, 1933, and sank next morning. The funnel-colouring carried by Messrs. Jack's steamers was very varied, including buff with black top, red with black top, yellow with blue band and black top, yellow with very deep black top, light green with deep black top, yellow with black shield and black top, etc.

S.S. "Challenger." Originally owned by Thomas Devlin, Jnr., Trinity, Edinburgh, and registered at Granton, *Challenger* remained the property of his family till sold in 1926 to MacFarlane Bros., 22, Goosedubs, Glasgow. In 1929 she was purchased by James Jack; and, after spending about six years sailing for him, she entered the McCallum, Orme fleet in December, 1935. Thereafter she bore their standard colours. She carried cargo only, and sailed all the year round from Glasgow to Hebridean ports. From the time of the acquisition of the interest in the company by David MacBrayne, Ltd., her funnel was painted crimson, retaining the black hoop till about May, 1948. She with withdrawn in November, 1948, and sold to the British Iron & Steel Corporation (Salvage) Ltd. for scrap.

McCallum, Orme & Co. Ltd. (*contd.*)

The above Company owned various ferryboats at calling places without piers, including one motor vessel named *Thistle*, appropriately associated by name with one of the emblems in the houseflag. In 1931 Colonsay was served by a boat named *Nestor*, which may have been owned locally. The following entered the MacBrayne fleet following the acquisition of the shares in McCallum, Orme & Co., Ltd.—

M.V. "Arinagour." Used as the ferryboat at Coll, this member of the fleet was wrecked on 18th November, 1949, following engine failure.

M.V. "Nora." This boat appears to have served both McCallum Orme and MacBraynes, and was sold by the latter in March, 1949 to Mr. J. A. Cameron.

M.V. "Ardgoil"/"Eriskay" (I). This ferryboat was transferred to David MacBrayne Limited in December, 1947. She was employed latterly at Eriskay, till she foundered on 19th December, 1949, being afterwards raised, and slipped at Mallaig. She was sold in 1951 to Mr. MacKellaig, of Mallaig for £65, and £50 was paid to Alexander Maclennan (Mallaig) Ltd. for salvage.

There was also a rowing-boat at Finsbay, sold by David MacBrayne Ltd. in July, 1949 to J. Leslie Ltd.

M.V. "Glassard." Only two other vessels fall to be recorded in this fleet, and both were small craft. One was the motor launch *Glassard*, built in 1918, and previously named *Bounty*. By the company she was employed as a ferry at Colonsay. She foundered in April, 1949, and her engine was salved.

M.V. "Janet B." The last ship acquired was this salvage boat, purchased in Wales in 1944, somewhat smaller than *Respect*, which she succeeded. She was delayed at Colonsay for a while on her journey north, but in due course was stationed at Locheport. She passed to David MacBrayne, Ltd. in 1948, but did not sail for them, being at the time high and dry on the beach at Locheport. She was sold in October, 1948 to the Department of Agriculture to take stores to the new township at Loch Portan. Later she was used as a ferry to the MacBrayne steamers at Lochmaddy and in connexion with diving operations during the early stages of the rebuilding of the pier there. She eventually went aground in a gale, and never floated again. Her timbers were used for a Coronation night bonfire at Lochmaddy on 2nd June, 1953.

· · · · · · · ·

Vessels employed by McCallum, Orme & Co. Ltd., on charter

have included Messrs. J. Kennedy & Sons' *Welshman*, *Islesman*, *Cragsman*, *Naviedale*, *Snowcrete*; *Empire Tulip* in 1945, which broke down at Lochboisdale and was replaced by *Carlingford* for two voyages; also that year *Snowcrete* again, *Alouette*, *Borneo*, *Glas Island* and *Lochgorm*, the last-named from the MacBrayne fleet in exchange for *Hebrides*.

CHAPTER VII

DAVID MACBRAYNE, LTD. From 1948 to 1966

DURING 1948 various re-arrangements of the Hebridean and West Highland sailings took place. In December the run previously performed by *Challenger* was abandoned; and a new road transport service from Glasgow to the Great Glen together with additional local road services enabled *Lochshiel* to cease calling at Kingairloch, Kinlochleven, Glenborrodale and Glencripesdale: this allowed her instead to include Iona and Bunessan. The calls previously made by *Challenger* at Coll, Tiree, Uig, Dunvegan, Loch Pooltiel, Portnalong and Carbost were transferred to *Hebrides*, those at Soay and Elgol being omitted altogether. An additional service to Soay from Mallaig was provided by chartering the motor vessel *Islander*, which also acted as tender to the MacBrayne vessel at Loch Scavaig. After the withdrawal of *Dunara Castle*, the calls at Locheport, Finsbay, Leverburgh and Eriskay were taken by *Ulster Star*; but these also were given to *Hebrides* in December. In January, 1949, *Lochgorm* and *Hebrides* changed places, so that *Hebrides* then followed approximately the old *Claymore*'s route but then with Lochmaddy, Tarbert (Harris), Loch Skipport, Lochboisdale and Barra added, the calls in the north and west of Skye being later included with this run instead of those at the Outer Hebridean ports, which reverted to having their own ship operating from Glasgow. *Clydesdale* took up the service to the mainland and west Skye ports, and *Hebrides* was supposed to do the Hebridean run, but in fact spent a considerable portion of the spring of 1949 in relieving on the Inner Isles route from Oban.

Shortages in the fleet were made good by chartering, vessels so employed including *Ardachy* and *Ardchattan* in 1948, *Saint Rule* and *Saint Enoch* in 1949, also *Saint Oran*, *Saint Kearan*, *Saint Modan*, *Saint Aidan* and *Saint Bedan* all from J. & A. Gardner & Co. Ltd.; also in 1948 *Lothdale* from C. B. Simpson, Helmsdale.

Under the new contract, the same arrangements were continued as before for the Stornoway kipper service. During 1949 this was, as previously, maintained with chartered steamers, including *Naviedale*, belonging to Messrs. Simpson.

A change in the working of the Colonsay service took place in April, 1949, with the extension to that island of the Port Askaig sailings of *Lochiel*, two days per week in winter, and in summer four, to be performed twice in evenings, after her arrival at Port Askaig, and twice in mornings before her departure therefrom, thus giving a much better through connexion with Glasgow and the south than previously had been possible.

Further substitution of road transport and trans-shipment occurred, and regular cargo services direct from Glasgow by sea ceased
altogether to Kallin, Locheport, Finsbay, Leverburgh, Rodel, Stockinish, Canna and Rhum.

M.V. "Kallin." Two ferryboats came out to the *Hebrides* at
Kallin, one from Kyles Flodday, operated by three brothers named
Currie, and one from Kallin, operated by Mr. Nicholson. In 1948 the
Company took over the *Kallin*, which is distinguishable from the
other red boats in the fleet by having a white waterline. She was
stationed at Gramsdale, Benbecula, and latterly received cargo by
road from Lochboisdale or Lochmaddy. She was sold in 1968 to
Timbacraft Ltd.

M.V. "Marne." This ferryboat which had previously served
McCallum, Orme, was acquired for service at Gramsdale, later
transferred to Eriskay, where, after the cessation of calls by the cargo
steamers, she was used principally for cargo-carrying duties to and
from Ludaig Jetty, North Uist. Most of the passenger traffic there was
handled by Mr. Neil Campbell's boats, *St. Joseph*, *Lady of the Isles*,
etc., by arrangement with the Company. *Marne* was sold in 1967 to
Mr. A. Bell, Dumbarton.

M.V. "Lochbroom" (II). A new vessel intended initially for the
Glasgow-Stornoway route entered the MacBrayne service in
December, 1948. She had been built by Messrs. Scott & Sons at
Bowling during the war, intended as a coastal patrol vessel for the Far
East; but, with the cessation of hostilities, she was not required; and,
after being launched in 1946, as *Empire Maysong*, she lay in Bowling
Harbour till purchased in March, 1947. She was taken to Ardrossan,
stripped of her superstructure (which included a bridge close to the
bow), and fitted out as a cargo and cattle carrier for the West
Highland trade. A polar Diesel engine was supplied by British Polar
Engines, Ltd. and installed by the Ardrossan Dockyard, Ltd., instead
of the steam machinery, for which she had been intended. She had
two holds forward, served by derricks fore and aft of the single mast,
with the latest cargo-handling gear. The accommodation for officers
and crew was of a high order. The machinery was situated aft. The
first trip of *Lochbroom* was to Islay and Portree, and proved most
successful.

Latterly she became a spare cargo ship, appearing usually on the
Islay route relieving, or at Oban for sheep carrying. She was sold in
July 1971 to Focomar Shipping Co., Ltd. and re-named *Focomar*.

Tr.S.M.V./T.S.M.V. "Lochbuie" (II). In terms of the mail
contract of 1947, Messrs. MacBrayne agreed to operate a new service
between Tobermory and Mingary, as soon as possible after a suitable

motor launch had been acquired. An ex-R.A.F. rescue pinnace was fitted out by Marine Craft Construction Co. Ltd. and re-launched into the Leven at Dumbarton on 14th March, 1949. She was employed on a three-times daily service from Tobermory to Mingary, connecting at the former with the mail vessel from and to Oban; and the call of the Islands mail boat at Kilchoan was then abandoned. *Lochbuie* was extensively refitted, and had accommodation for thirty-six passengers and some cargo. For the handling of the latter she was fitted with a derrick, and had a small hold aft. She was re-engined in 1958. From 1965 she was for a time on the Lismore run in place of *Lochnell*, but soon was back on her old route till, after damage to her starboard side, her hull was found to be extensively affected by rot; and, after removal of her machinery, she was scrapped and burnt in May, 1968.

S.S. "Loch Frisa." In March, 1949, one of Messrs. MacBrayne's skippers went to Amsterdam to bring back a ship for the fleet, then named *Marleen*. This steamer had been built in Canada in 1946. She was one of a class of standard ships constructed for the Canadian Government, and sent to Britain on bareboat charter to the Ministry of War Transport (and initially a sister ship to the one which became *Lochbroom*), her original name being *Ottawa Maycliff*. Before completion she was sold to N.V. Motorschip Martha, later passing to N.V. Kustvaart-Reederij van Dudok de Wit & Co. (both of Amsterdam), from the latter of whom she was bought by Messrs. MacBrayne for the cargo services from Glasgow. After re-fitting at Irvine, she was re-named *Loch Frisa* (from the name of the largest inland loch in Mull); and, towards the end of June, 1949, commenced plying to the Hebridean ports alternately with *Hebrides*. The West of Skye calls were then made by these two ships, *Clydesdale*'s route reverting to that of the period before January, 1949. *Loch Frisa* was sold in July, 1963 to Constantine Skouras, Piraeus and renamed *George Skouras*.

"Dumb Barge No. 3." One of the lifeboats from *Marleen* became a dinghy at Iona.

.   .   .   .

From 6th April, 1950 all the sailings from Glasgow were from Kingston Dock.

.   .   .   .   .   .

M.V. "Craignure." In May, 1950 Mr. George Clyne, who operated the Craignure ferry intimated that he would cease to provide the service on account of the expense he would have to incur to bring the boat up to the requirements of the Ministry of Transport. Later that month, as a result of a petition signed by more than 500 residents in Mull and Iona, and meetings with Government officials, it was announced that Messrs. MacBrayne would provide a boat to enable the ferryman to continue, and would endeavour as soon as possible to secure one certificated to carry up to fifty passengers. The vessel chosen was *Silver Crest*, built in 1943, which had been acquired by the Company in 1950. To her the name *Craignure* was given, and she was thereafter employed mainly at that place, though occasionally on relief duties to Lismore while *Lochnell* had been off for overhaul. She was sold to Mr. Bruce Watt in 1964, and afterwards to Mr. Murdo McSween, Fort William, being brought back into the fleet (by this time of Caledonian MacBrayne Ltd.) in 1973 for the Iona-Fionnphort ferry. She was sold in August, 1979 to Gordon Grant Ltd., Iona, for transferring livestock to and from the Treshnish Isles.

M.V. "Iona" (V). Two new ferryboats were built in 1950 for service at Iona and Staffa, somewhat larger than those previously employed there. They were constructed by John Barr & Sons (Craigendoran) Ltd., in their Dumbarton yard, and fitted with Kelvin "J.2" engines. The first to appear was *Iona*, and she was the fifth powered vessel in the fleet to bear this famous name. She was on occasion employed as a relief on the Lismore service. Like *Fingal*, she was wrecked by the tail-end of a hurricane in September, 1961.

M.V. "Staffa" (VI). This was the sister to the foregoing, and like her had a certificate for fifty-five passengers, together with a crew of two; and *Staffa* was also a cargo-carrier. She has sometimes been used to relieve the *Lochbuie* or *Lochnell* on the Mingary or Lismore services, and from 3rd October, 1964 was stationed at Eigg for ferry duties, till transferred to Lochboisdale for use while the building of the extension to the pier was in progress during the winter of 1965-66. In the spring of 1967 she was sold to Messrs. MacLean & MacRae, Kyle of Lochalsh.

M.V. "Örnen"/"Lochdunvegan" (II). In August, 1950 the Company purchased from Hollands Angsbats A/B their motor vessel *Örnen*, which had been built at Gothenburg in 1946, and which was fitted with Atlas Polar engines made at Stockholm. After being overhauled at Flushing, this ship was handed over to the Company's representatives on 21st November, and sailed to Rotterdam, where a cargo was loaded for Dublin. After unloading, she proceeded to Glasgow under charter to Coast Lines, Ltd. It was proposed to name her *Lochalsh*, but in December she was given her new name as above and took up the Glasgow-Stornoway cargo run in succession to *Lochgorm*, which was then laid up, apart from some relief work. *Lochdunvegan* was unique in the MacBrayne sea-going fleet in being strengthened to withstand ice, and in having had a variable-pitch reversible propeller, until November, 1951. In the spring of that year she had a hold fitted with refrigerating apparatus for fish traffic from Stornoway, and was given accommodation for four passengers in deck cabins. She gave extra vehicle-carrying facilities to Tiree from Oban, and from Uig to Tarbert Harris on occasion. From early in 1972 she called at Kyle instead of Armadale, cargo going by the Kyle ferries and by road; but calls by cargo steamer at Kyle and Tobermory ceased, and the Stornoway call was transferred to *Loch Carron*'s roster in July, 1973, and *Lochdunvegan* was to be withdrawan in September. On an exceptional call at Lochboisdale she grounded on the rocks, and the Gardner ship *Saint Ronan* was chartered to take her place; and in June, 1974 the *Saint Kentigern* of the same fleet was chartered for one round trip in place of *Loch Carron*. *Lochdunvegan* was sold in November, 1973 to George Stavrou and Others, and re-named *Fanis*, under the Greek flag.

M.V. "Loch Carron." The order for the new cargo vessel required by the 1949 mail contract was placed with the Ardrossan Dockyard, Ltd., and the ship was launched by Mrs. T. F. Cameron as *Loch Carron* on 27th October, 1951. Several noteworthy features were incorporated in the design, which may be regarded as a development from that of *Lochbroom* (II), on a larger scale. The profile of the ship, for a modern one, was not unpleasing, showing raked stem, cruiser stern, one oval funnel (aft), with its top parallel to the line between the original tops of the two "stepped" masts. (In 1953 the mainmast was lengthened so as to carry the masthead light at the height above the forward light required by the regulations then introduced.

Good accommodation was provided for officers and crew, and also for four passengers. 148 cattle and four horses could be carried, in addition to cargo, the space for which was all forward, and was served by derricks forward and aft of the fore-mast, capable of handling 7½ and 5 tons respectively. This, at the time of commissioning, was the heaviest lifting gear in any of the Company's ships. It was operated by Mactaggart-Scott hydraulic auxiliary machinery in one circuit with that for the steering-gear, windlass, etc. She was the first ship of the fleet to be fitted with hydraulic machinery, and also the first to be built with a cellular double bottom. Radar was carried, as in the case of *Loch Seaforth*.

The main propelling machinery, situated aft, consisted of a standard M 46 M Polar six-cylinder Diesel, made by British Polar Engines, Ltd., Glasgow, giving a speed of 11 knots.

The *Loch Carron* was more or less regularly employed on the Outer Islands run from Glasgow, with *Hebrides* as her opposite number, until 1955, when the latter was succeeded by *Loch Ard*, *Loch Carron* being later alone on the weekly service. In 1970 her sailing day from Glasgow was brought forward from Friday to Thursday, to enable her to make an Oban-Lismore run; and she also made special sailings to Tiree for cars. In February, 1972 she performed the Stornoway cargo service, the *Loch Seaforth* taking her place for the transport of cargo to the Outer Islands, but operating from Oban.

When the latter had to return to the Stornoway mail run, the puffer *Glencloy* was chartered, but was unable to cope with the volume of traffic. On 31st July, 1975 formal intimation was given of the proposal to withdraw from 31st October next the cargo sailings from Glasgow, since most of the traffic was now going by road by MacBrayne Haulage vehicles and by those of private hauliers using the various ferry services. Arrangements had been made too for chartered vessels to convey cargo which could not be handled by the car ferries, such as petrol for Coll, Tiree, Barra, etc., and special livestock movements. As a result of objections this was not put into immediate effect; but a year later the T.U.C.C. agreed that no hardship would be occasioned, subject to monitoring the livestock movements. The *Loch Carron* had become the last regular coastal cargo ship operating from Glasgow. She was sold in January, 1977 to Kopsi Shipping Co., Ltd., Cyprus, and remained laid up at Springfield Quay, Glasgow till delivered to them in May. Her new name was *Georgis K.*

M.V. "Coll" (I). Two ferryboats similar to *Staffa* were built early in 1951, also by Messrs. Barr. They proceeded northward via the Crinan Canal to their respective ports of operation, the one now described being for service at Arinagour, Coll. She was superseded by the pier there, and was sold in 1967 to Mr. A. Cowie, Tobermory, later to owners of Isle of Coll Hotel; and re-named *Mhairi Anne*.

In April, 1970 a spare Paxman Ricardo engine was ordered for use in any of the ferryboats.

M.V. "Colonsay" (II)/"Eriskay" (II). The name of the sister to the foregoing revived that of one of the very early West Highland steamers, built in 1834. (See page 0.) When the new pier was opened at Scalasig, Colonsay, this ferryboat became redundant there, and was in 1965 transferred to Eriskay, being suitably re-named. The *Loch Carron* on 7th January, 1969 picked up the *Eriskay* at the Tail of the Bank and dropped her off next day at Lochmaddy for her new owner, Mr. Angus McAskill, Berneray, North Uist.

.   .   .   .

An important event in this period was the occurrence on 10th February, 1951 of the centenary of the formation of David Hutcheson & Co. To mark the occasion, eighteen MacBrayne vessels in harbour and at sea were dressed with bunting from stem to stern.

Further curtailments of cargo services by sea took place, the calls at ports on the mainland north of Kyle of Lochalsh—Aultbea, Baden-Tarbert, Gairloch, Loch Clash, Lochinver and Ullapool—being discontinued after the sailing of 20th August, 1951. This enabled the Company to dispense with one ship; and *Lochshiel* was the one to go, being sold at the beginning of 1952. Cargo continued to be accepted for Scorraig.

A new mail contract, the text of which was issued as a white paper on 9th April, 1952, provided for a subsidy to the Company of £360,000 per year, subject to certain conditions, including the construction of one new passenger and mail vessel, and one new cargo vessel, the duration of the agreement being from 1st January 1952 till 31st December, 1961.

On 30th July, 1952 it was announced that the Company had put forward a scheme to improve the cargo services, in particular by substituting road for sea transport to the West of Skye and West of Mull, which was commenced in principle by the Highland Panel to the local authorities in the area, the principal shippers and others interested.

The proposals involved six main changes, viz.:

(1)   Castlebay, Lochboisdale (also for Kallin, Flodda, Scotvin, Grimsay and Eriskay), Loch Skipport (also for Carnan and Petersport), Lochmaddy (also for Loch Eport), Scalpay and Tarbert (also for Finsbay and Leverburgh), would receive a ten-day service with one vessel, which would also serve Craignure, Salen (Mull) and Tobermory (also for Iona and Bunessan).

(2)   Eriskay would be served from Lochboisdale by Ludaig Jetty.

(3)   Coll and Tiree would be served by the Inner Islands vessel.

(4)   The West of Skye ports—Uig, Dunvegan, Loch Pooltiel, Portnalong and Carbost—and also Broadford and Kyleakin—would be served by road from Portree, where cargo would be landed by the Stornoway cargo steamer and also every ten days by the Inner Islands steamer.

(5)   The calls by the Inner Islands cargo steamer would be reduced to Colonsay, Luing, Oban (for Lismore), Lochaline, Coll, Tiree, Armadale (for Eigg), Glenelg, Portree (for Eigg and the West of Skye ports), with monthly calls at Ardlussa, Croggan, Ulva and Gometra, plus a call every second voyage at Scorraig, Loch Broom. (The services to Luing would be dropped when the Cuan vehicular ferry became usable and Scorraig would continue as a call only until the ferry at Badluachrach would be in commission.) The calls at Lismore, Fort William, Craignure, Salen, Tobermory, Mingary, Iona, Bunessan, Eigg, Mallaig, Armadale, Glenelg, Kyle of Lochalsh and Raasay by this steamer would accordingly cease.

(6)   Iona and Bunessan would be served by road from Tobermory, the former *via* Fionnphort and a MacBrayne ferryboat.

(7)   Goods for Bowmore would be landed at Port Ellen.

The above arrangements did not receive full effect, but in July, 1953 the services were re-arranged by the cessation of the Inner Islands cargo service from Glasgow, the two Outer Islands vessels being then planned to leave Glasgow on alternate Mondays, with calls at Colonsay, Craignure, Oban, Lochaline, Salen (Mull), Tobermory, Iona, Coll, Tiree, Barra, Lochboisdale, Lockskipport, Lochmaddy, Scalpay, Tarbert (Harris), Uig, Dunvegan and Carbost. At the same time further road transport and cargo trans-shipment was introduced so that Glasgow goods for Luing, Lismore and Croggan were conveyed via Oban; for Bunessan, Fionnphort and Mingary, *via* Tobermory; and Portnalong, *via* Carbost; for Struan, Colbost, Stein (Waternish) and Lochpooltiel, *via* Dunvegan; for Carnan and Petersport *via* Loch Skipport; for Kallin, Flodda, Scotvin, Grimsay and Eriskay, *via* Lochboisdale; for Locheport, *via* Lochmaddy; for Finsbay and Leverburgh, *via* Tarbert (Harris); and for Broadford, Kyleakin, Eigg and Rhum, *via* Armadale. Greenock goods for Armadale, Kyleakin, Broadford, Raasay and Portree were to be conveyed via Dunvegan; and for Eigg, Rhum and Rodel, *via* Lochboisdale. Calls were to be made at Ulva by special arrangement.

Again one ship was rendered redundant; but in preparation for the new arrangement, *Clydesdale* had been withdrawn early in 1953, the services being maintained with *Loch Frisa* or chartered ships until July. Thereafter *Loch Frisa* became spare, and was used as a relief, or for special runs carrying sheep, etc. The Scorraig call ceased in September, 1955.

M.V. "Rosalind"/"Lochshiel" (II). In 1951 the Highlands and Islands Advisory Panel recommended that, in order to maintain the service on Loch Shiel, Messrs. MacBrayne should be invited to take it over under arrangements to be made with the Ministry of Transport and the Scottish Home Department. The Loch Shiel Steamboat Service Co. Ltd., which was desirous of being relieved of carrying on the services, agreed to the proposal. Thus it was that the Company came to resume sailings on the loch, after having abandoned them about 1897. Orders were placed in January, 1953 with Messrs. Barr of Craigendoran for two motor launches to run on Loch Shiel, and the first of these—originally named *Rosalind*—was completed in October, 1953. She proceeded by the Crinan Canal and Sound of Mull to Salen, Loch Sunart, then was taken overland to Acharacle. After some difficulty, she was duly launched into the loch, and on 28th October made her first trip to Glenfinnan and back. In view of objections to the names proposed—*Rosalind* and *Celia*—*Lochaber* and *Lochshiel* were suggested; and, the former not being available the latter was selected.

This vessel was much faster than *Clanranald II*, and was able to perform the run of eighteen miles in two hours. She had a certificate for seventy-five passengers, being also equipped to carry cargo or cattle when required. Built with heavy scantlings to the design of Messrs. G. L. Watson & Co., Naval Architects, Glasgow, she was planked with mahogany on oak frames, and oak centre-framing. The planking was sheathed around the waterline for working in ice, which occurs frequently in winter time, the sheathing being faced with galvanised steel sheeting. She was protected by strong beltings. Seats for passengers were provided in the forward cabin, and on each side of the cargo space. The engine was a Kelvin Diesel type K.3, with electric starter and bilge-pump. Like most of the MacBrayne small craft, she had her hull painted red, the cabins having been varnished teak; and a small mast was carried. In June, 1962 she was brought from the Loch to Shandon where her passenger cabin and mast were removed, and she was thereafter at Iona, providing the link in the cargo service from Fionnphort and also acting as passenger ferry at Iona and Staffa to the *King George V*. While on a passage from Ardrishaig to Gareloch for overhaul, she was sunk by an unidentified vessel off Toward Point on 28th April, 1970, her crew being rescued.

M.V. "Lochailort." Names proposed for the second of the Loch Shiel launches (after *Celia*) were *Lochailort*, *Lochmoidart* and *Lochaline*, in order of preference, the first being accepted. This vessel, left Dumbarton on 1st June, 1954 under her own power to sail to Salen, whence she was transported to Acharacle, as in the case of the other. She was in many respects similar to *Lochshiel*, but had more covered accommodation for passengers and crew and was not designed specifically for cargo and cattle. She was at first used principally for passengers doing the circular tour, which could then be performed not only from Fort William *via* Glenfinnan to Acharacle and back by Ardgour, but also three days per week in summer from Oban. This tour, from Fort William, had for some years been operated by Messrs. MacBrayne, who ran the buses between Fort William and Glenfinnan on the one hand, and Acharacle and Ardgour on the other, through tickets being issued by them also to cover the sail by *Clanranald II* on Loch Shiel. In January, 1962 *Lochailort* sank near Acharacle after being holed by ice. Members of the Oban Sub Aqua Club were instrumental in effecting salvage by attaching 40-gallon oil drums to the keel and filling them with compressed air. After the departure of *Lochshiel* from the Loch, *Lochailort* carried on the service alone: and on account of limitation of accommodation, the circular tour no longer operated from Oban. She was relieved on occasion by the motor launch *Garry*. On the opening of the road from Lochailort to Kinlochmoidart the Loch Shiel sailings ceased, on 30th September, 1967. The *Lochailort* was laid up, but in the next year found a new occupation on the Toscaig service in succession to *Lochnell*. In 1969, however, the timber of her hull was found to be in poor condition, and she was disposed of by being burnt at Kyle of Lochalsh.

T.S.M.V. "Claymore" (II). A notable ship was launched for the fleet on 10th March, 1955, from the Dumbarton yard of Wm. Denny & Bros. Ltd. Ordered in accordance with the mail contract of 1952, this vessel was a great advance in many ways on *Lochearn*, her pre-decessor on the Islands route from Oban, and, with a gross tonnage of 1,024, was the second largest ship in the fleet. Her twin screws were driven by Sulzer engines supplied by the builders, and her speed was about 12½ knots.

With a raked stem and cruiser stern, she had an imposing appear-ance, in spite of her "smoke-dispelling" funnel, with very shallow top (only the domed portion being black) and with large vertical vents on the front. A light steel tripod mast was erected above the bridge, and a light mainmast aft; while near the bow there was a substantial Samson-post, supporting the 7½-ton derrick, the cargo hatch being situated between it and the forward end of the superstructure. Three lifeboats were carried, two on the starboard and one on the port side. Of these, one was motor driven.

Aids to navigation which were fitted in this ship included Radar, Decca Navigator Position Plotter, Echo Sounder and Wireless Tele-graphy.

The passenger accommodation comprised, on the promenade-deck, a first-class observation lounge and bar, second-class open lounge, two first-class de luxe staterooms and a hospital room; on the main-deck, the first- and second-class dining-saloons, divided by a sliding partition, on the middle line of the ship, and four first-class two-berth staterooms. On the lower deck were eight first-class single, and five first-class two-berth cubicles; also seven second-class two-berth cubicles. These are partitioned and fitted with doors.

On a Steam 2 certificate the ship could carry 494 passengers; and sleeping accommodation was provided for, in all, fifty-six, as compared with twenty-two on *Lochearn*. She could carry also about 100 tons of cargo, eleven motor cars, and twenty-six head of cattle.

The passenger accommodation was beautifully furnished. Inter-esting features were the marquetry panels, showing wild birds and scenes in the West Highlands, executed by a Swedish artist: and the engraving on the glass of the dining-saloon doors of the "MacBrayne Highlander" holding targe and claymore, which emblem appeared also on the bow, in colour.

The choice of the name for this fine ship was most interesting, showing something of the regard in which the previous *Claymore* was held. This was the first occasion, since the formation of the new com-pany in 1928, that a ship built for the MacBrayne fleet (apart from small craft) had received a name other than a "Loch".

In addition to serving on the route from Oban to Tobermory, Coll, Tiree, Castlebay and Lochboisdale three days per week in each direct-ion, *Claymore*, on certain afternoons in summer performed short cruises from Oban. During the summer of 1955 these were usually to the Isles of the Sea on Thursdays, and to Salen (Mull) on Saturdays, the latter being primarily for the transport of cars, supplementing the sailing on that day of *Lochinvar* on the Sound of Mull route.

During 1965, when *Lochnevis* was otherwise occupied, *Claymore* gave cruises from Oban to Fort William on Tuesdays (sometimes not landing), to Colonsay on Thursdays and to Tobermory on Saturdays. She also, on occasion, relieved *Loch Seaforth* on the Stornoway mail run prior to the advent of the car carriers.

Sold in April, 1976 to Canopus Shipping of Piraeus, she left the Clyde on 10th May under her new name, *City of Andros*, to join the former Clyde vessel *City of Piraeus* ex *Maid of Argyll*. When she entered service in Greece the name of the former *Claymore* had again been changed, this time to *City of Hydra*. She has become well known on day cruises to Hydra, Aegina and Poros.

M.V. "Loch Ard." The second of the ships built in terms of the 1952 mail contract was launched from the yard of Ferguson Bros. (Port Glasgow) Ltd., on 23rd May, 1955. After completion she entered service in June in succession to *Hebrides* on the fortnightly Outer Islands cargo run from Glasgow.

Somewhat similar to *Loch Carron* in many respects, the new ship had, however, certain innovations, the most obvious, externally, being the self-supporting bipod mast, with derricks fore and aft, capable of lifting five and ten tons respectively. (Previously *Loch Carron* had had the distinction of having the most powerful lifting gear of any of the Company's ships—7½ tons.) The reason for the increased lifting power was to be found in the heavy loads expected to be carried to the Outer Islands in the few years following her building, in connexion with engineering works for roads, bridges, etc.

Provision was made for carrying livestock, including 130 head of fat cattle, while there was also considerable space for the conveyance of deck cargo, including motor buses, lorries and cars. Four passengers could be accommodated, in two attractively-furnished two-berth staterooms. The Company's house-flag in metal was affixed to the front of the bridge superstructure—the first occasion on which this feature has appeared on any ships of the fleet. Navigational aids are provided as on *Claymore*. In January, 1957 it was agreed to instal a derrick with lifting capacity of 16½ tons.

From 1964 *Loch Ard* was employed principally on the Glasgow-Islay service. This ceased after the advent of the car ferry *Arran* on the West Loch Tarbert-Islay route; and *Loch Ard*, being redundant, was sold to the Irish & Scottish S.N. Co. on the basis of being bareboat chartered for six months; but this fell through and she was sold to Greek owners in April, 1971, leaving the Clyde as *Holborn*. Later she went to Spanish owners and was named *Candiera*, being sunk in the Mediterranean on 7th May, 1984.

M.V. "Loch Toscaig." In May, 1955 the Company acquired a motor fishing vessel *Irene Julia* to provide a service between Toscaig and Kyle of Lochalsh, the intention being to abandon the calls at Applecross given by the Stornoway mail vessel.

After re-fitting at Greenock, during which the fish-holds were converted to a cargo hold, and the crew's quarters and deckhouse into passenger accommodation, the ship was given the name *Loch Toscaig* and took up her sailings in May, 1956. In addition to her regular runs she gave forenoon cruises in summer from Kyle of Lochalsh to Loch Duich, Loch Carron, Loch Kishorn, Loch Toscaig, Broadford Bay or Raasay Narrows.

Originally black, her hull became light blue in 1960 and dark blue in 1963. From 1964 she was normally on the Oban-Lismore run. In mid-October, 1971 she returned after overhaul, her place having been taken by Mrs. Spencer's *Island Lass*. She was sold in November, 1975 to Mr. Gerrard of London, later used for fishing trips from Gourock. On 29th December, 1978 she was blown from her moorings and sank, then was raised and beached at Gourock, but was not restored and became a wreck, which was removed in September, 1986.

M.V. "Ulva." In 1956 this further addition was made to the fleet of small craft at Iona and Staffa, a boat similar to the others but with a small forecastle. She succeeded *Soay*, which had foundered during the previous winter. Originally varnished, she is now red like the other small craft. In recent years she has been at Eigg.

T.S.M.V. "Loch Arkaig." A wooden inshore minesweeper, of the type used to deal with hazards such as magnetic mines during the second war, was purchased by the Company in May, 1959. Intended to be named *Raasay*, it was as *Loch Arkaig* that she was commissioned. Stripped of her original deck fittings, she was given new light-weight metal superstructure by Jas. Lamont & Co. Ltd. at Greenock, and new Bergius engines. Her conversion for passenger work was completed by Timbacraft, Ltd. at Shandon and on 14th April, 1960 she was commissioned by Mrs. Cameron of Lochiel at Rosneath Pier as a member of the MacBrayne fleet. Her first service was on the Portree-Raasay-Kyle-Mallaig run in succession to *Lochinvar*, which had taken the place of *Lochnevis* there. In 1964 *Loch Arkaig* was herself succeeded on the Portree mail run by an even smaller ship, which did not normally operate south of Kyle, and was transferred to the Small Isles (or "Inshore Mail") service from Mallaig, for which she was fitted with a Samson post and an embarkation door in the bulwark, a ferry door in the deck lounge on the starboard side being added in June. She then also performed the Loch Scavaig excursion twice a week. By the next season the Small Isles service and the Portree run had been combined, operating on certain days only, and *Loch Arkaig* was the ship used on this, supplemented on Saturday afternoons on the Small Isles station by the *Western Isles* chartered from Mr. Bruce Watt. *Loch Arkaig* gave evening cruises in summer only from Portree in 1971-2, usually to Raasay, promoted by the Isle of Skye Tourist Association. In October, 1972 she relieved on the Lismore route, her own run being taken by *Sound of Islay* chartered from Western Ferries. When she returned, she included the Mallaig-Armadale calls previously given by *Loch Seaforth*. In 1974 she did not give evening cruises, since these were provided by the Portree-based *Clyde* owned by Mr. Kennedy. *Loch Arkaig* left Portree for the last time as mail steamer, on 17th March, 1975 after 14 years, thereafter serving only the Small Isles, with Mallaig-Kyle of Lochalsh added in summer and cruises to Loch Duich, Portree, etc.

On 28th March, 1979 the *Loch Arkaig* sank in Mallaig Harbour. In April she was declared to be a constructive total loss and in October it was reported that she had been sold to Ship and Yacht Consultants Ltd., London. After going to Spain she sank while undergoing trials, and was not to be salved, as reported on 28th October, 1985 from Cadiz.

T.S.M.V. "Loch Eynort." In December, 1961 the Company purchased the pilot boat *Valonia* from the Commissioners of Irish Lights and had her refitted by Timbacraft, Ltd. for the passenger, mail and cargo service from Portree to Raasay and Kyle. (She had initially been purchased with the intention of using her on the Small Isles run when the car ferries took over from *Lochmor*, but she proved unsuitable for this, though she was so used on occasion as a relief.) As she did not proceed to Mallaig, she was available for forenoon cruises from Kyle. She did not sail during the summer of 1965, and apart from a short spell of relief work, spent most of her time off duty in the Gareloch. Plans were prepared for an extensive reconstruction of her passenger accommodation, but did not receive effect. In 1970, when the *Clansman* was occupied on the Clyde, the *Loch Eynort* was used on the Mallaig-Armadale route (for passengers only), one run per day also for vehicles being given by *Loch Seaforth*. She also tendered to *King George V* from Mallaig on 22nd May, 1970 on her H.I.D.B. charter. In November she returned to Shandon to be laid up, having very little employment latterly. She was sold in October, 1971 to Francis A. W. Kirk, Newbury, Berkshire, later of Brixham, for use as a yacht, named *Skellig*.

M.V. "Iona" (VI). A successor to the fifth *Iona* was produced by Dickie of Tarbert, Ltd., in 1962 for ferry service at Iona and Staffa. She is similar to the others, and like them is painted red. She was relieving at Craignure when the new pier was opened there, and led in the *Lochearn* for the ceremonial opening. She was at Tobermory until the rebuilding of the pier and the substitution of a larger vessel for Mingary made her redundant, and she moved to Eigg.

F

M.V. "Applecross." With the intention of reducing the loss in operation of the service from Kyle of Lochalsh to Toscaig, the motor launch *Highlander*, which had previously belonged to Mr. Bruce Watt of Mallaig, thereafter to a Glenelg owner, was bought at the end of 1963, and in the following year appeared in the MacBrayne small-craft livery of red, and with a pale blue boot-top. Her name had been changed to *Applecross*, and in addition to performing the mail run to Toscaig (commencing on 20th January, 1964) she was available for forenoon cruises from Kyle three days per week, being engaged on the other three days in a new mail run to Kylerhea, taking the place of the call by the mail steamer at Glenelg. In the spring of 1965 she relieved on the Tobermory-Mingary station, her cabin having been somewhat shortened, and then went to join the fleet of small craft at Iona in place of the *Staffa*, which had gone to Eigg on the Company's taking over the ferry there. She was succeeded on the Toscaig run by Messrs. MacLean & MacRae's *Vital Spark* or *Puffin* on charter; and they ultimately contracted to provide the service, till it was withdrawn when road improvements had made transport by land practicable. *Applecross* was sold to Mr. Gibson of Fionnphort in 1969, and acquired by Caledonian MacBrayne Ltd. in 1973, following their having taken over from him the ferry service to Iona as from 1st October, 1972. Her cabin was removed entirely, but a wheelhouse was erected over the engine casing. From 1981 she became the regular vessel on the Tobermory-Mingary route, acting also as tender at Tobermory to the ships which could not call at the pier, and to all during the rebuilding of the pier in 1984-5. Being redundant from Tobermory-Mingary she was sold back to Mr. Alasdair Gibson, then of Lochbuie, Mull, for private use.

·   ·   ·   ·   ·   ·   ·

Armadale Pier, following reconstruction, from 17th June, 1957 was able to take car traffic.

Later that month it was decided to fit Radar to *Saint Columba*, *King George V*, *Lochfyne*, *Lochiel*, *Lochnevis* and *Lochinvar*.

In September, 1957 the Advisory Panel on the Highlands and Islands again considered the problem of sea services for the North Isles of Orkney and the implications of present and impending developments in the Hebrides as affecting the MacBrayne services. In August of the following year Lord Cameron, Chairman of the Panel, intimated the Company's proposals to withdraw the Portree mail steamer, and utilise the Stornoway mail ship for additional Mallaig-Armadale sailings, and with improvements in road transport on the Isle of Skye; but he emphasised that the proposed changes could not take effect without the consent of the Secretary of State for Scotland and of the Minister of Transport. Further proposals involved the withdrawal of the *Saint Columba*, the transfer of *Lochfyne* to the Clyde service all the year round, the transfer of *Lochnevis* to the

Sound of Mull mail run, and the withdrawal of the *Lochinvar*. Certain Skye bus services were taken over by the Company from 28th November, 1958. After opposition to the withdrawal of the Portree-Raasay-Kyle-Mallaig service it was agreed to keep this in operation for a further period of a year with the *Lochinvar*. Early next year the Advisory Panel approved withdrawal of the Portree mail steamer except in the tourist season, and the substitution of a ferry service to Raasay; but this was strongly opposed locally, and it was then disclosed that a new ship would be provided to succeed the *Lochinvar* on the run, and, if the sail south to Mallaig were omitted, this could also provide short cruises from Kyle of Lochalsh. In the summer of 1959 there was further agitation for a new ship to take the place of *Lochmor* on the Outer Islands run; but it was at the commissioning of the *Loch Arkaig* on 14th April, 1960 that Mr. C. B. Leith (General Manager from 1st May, 1959) announced the Company's far-reaching proposals for the introduction of three vehicle-carrying vessels to serve on the various Island routes, the intention being to shorten the journeys by sea, and increase the use of the roads. It was in that year that the double service to Islay was inaugurated, on Wednesdays to Port Askaig and on Saturdays to Port Ellen, during July and August, and mainly for the transport of cars. Later that year it became clear that the Company's proposals were for three main car-ferry routes, viz., Uig in Skye to Lochmaddy (North Uist) and Tarbert (Harris); Mallaig to Armadale (Skye); and Oban to Craignure (Mull) and Lochaline (Morvern). It should be noted that the North Ford causeway had been built, so that Benbecula and the two Uists became virtually one island, the South Ford causeway having been brought into use during the second war.

It was in 1961 that a new development occurred, viz.: combined motor coach and steamer tours in June and September from Glasgow to Benbecula, Eriskay and the Uists, and to Stornoway and the Outer Hebrides, using existing steamer services. These were greatly increased later, when the car ferry services became operative. The new pier at Craignure was expected to be ready for the spring of 1963 when also the first of the vehicle-carrying ships was expected; but it was the next year before they were ready for service. The direct cargo services to ports which included Greenock, Iona, Lismore, Scalpay, Lochskipport and Eriskay were to be withdrawn, and road transport substituted. There was opposition from these, in particular from Iona, where the arrangement was to be that cargo would be carried by lorry on the vehicle ferry to Craignure, then proceed to Fionnphort and be trans-shipped into the small ferryboat (to be provided by the company) for Iona.

In 1962 by mutual consent the call at Bunessan was abandoned, and road transport substituted; centralisation in Skye in 1961 resulted in the withdrawal of cargo calls at Uig, Carbost and Dunvegan.

A new Government contract for a further period of ten years was announced in December, 1961. The agreement had to be approved by the House of Commons in accordance with the Highlands and Islands

Shipping Services Act, 1960, which provided *inter alia* that the Secretary of State for Scotland should have power to build and charter ships; and it was stated this would be done if the plans for the new services involving three large vehicle-carrying vessels were approved.

The Greenock call was abandoned in June, 1962, and the item of Government investment towards the introduction of the new services was announced that month, with the invitation for tenders for the reconstruction of the pier at Uig, owned by the Department of Agriculture and Fisheries, involving its extension by almost fifty feet; and this in advance of Government approval of the proposals for the three car-carriers. Later the same month it was announced that the Government had invited tenders for the three vessels, from sixteen shipyards in Scotland and England. The specifications called for ships 230 ft. long and equipped to carry about fifty cars, and fitted with hydraulic lifts to enable vehicles to drive on at pier level at any state of tide. The total cost of the ships was expected to be about £2m., and they would be built for the Secretary of State under the powers given to him by the above-mentioned Act; they would be chartered to David MacBrayne Limited in terms of an agreement approved by Parliament last December. An attempt was made to reduce the proposed ships to two, for reasons of economy, but the then Secretary of State for Scotland, Mr. Michael Noble, refused to yield to Treasury pressure, and on 17th December, 1962 it was announced that the order for the three ships had been won by Messrs. Hall, Russell & Co. Ltd., Aberdeen, in competition with nine other shipyards in Scotland and England.

Proposals to withdraw the Tobermory-Mingary service and the Kyle-Applecross service were abandoned after opposition.

An extension for the pier at Lochaline was floated and towed to its site in the summer of 1963 in preparation for the introduction of the car ferry service the following year.

. . . .

T.S.M.V. "Hebrides" (II). After a short postponement on account of a strike, the first of the car-carrying ships was launched at Aberdeen, on 20th November, 1963, and named *Hebrides* by Mrs. Michael Noble. The revival of traditional names is noteworthy; all three are most attractive, and this one was a particularly appropriate choice, since she was intended for the Hebridean Ferry route from Uig to Lochmaddy and Tarbert. She was employed almost exclusively on that route, on which she commenced on 15th April, 1964. On the same day the Outer Isles mail service ceased, and *Lochmor* was transferred to operate the Mallaig-Armadale run until the second car-carrier should be ready. With a gross tonnage of 2,103·91 this was the largest ship up to that time to have been a member ·of the MacBrayne fleet. (The gross tonnage was subsequently reduced to 1420 on exclusion of the car-deck space in accordance with new regulations). Her passenger capacity was 600 in summer and 400 in winter, and there was sleeping accommodation for fifty-one. The garage space could accommodate fifty motor cars; and this could also be adapted for the transport of cattle. The main engines were of the Crossley Bros. type HRP 8/47 turbo-charged, two-stroke cycle, trunk-piston, airless injection, port scavenging type, and the service speed was 14½ knots. Denny/Brown stabilisers were fitted, and there was a Brown Bros. bow-thrust propeller to assist in manoeuvring at piers. The vehicle lift was operated by four hydraulic rams, one at each corner, supplied by MacTaggart, Scott & Co. Ltd., with a lifting capacity of 24 tons at a rate of 25 ft. per minute and with the ramps interlocked so that only one can be lowered at a time. Two 14-ft. diameter hand-operated turntables made by Francis Theakston (1933) Ltd. are arranged on the lift, and one of the same diameter in the garage space aft. Decca Marine Radar and Marconi Echo Sounder, Wireless Telegraphy and Radio Telephone were installed. The bell from S.S. *Hebrides* of 1898, given by Lord Strathcona, was hung in the saloon of the newer ship until she left the fleet.

The forward end of the vehicle deck was protected by two hydraulically operated vertically sliding MacGregor watertight doors. Height clearance at the forward end was 11 ft.; but, to give headroom in the engine room, the garage deck had a raised ramp about half-way along, reducing the headroom to 8 ft. 6 in.

All three ships were registered at Leith in name of the Secretary of State for Scotland, and were on long-term charter to the Company; but all were subsequently owned and their port of registry changed to Glasgow, *Hebrides* and *Columba* from 1973. As extra ship on the Ardrossan-Arran station the *Hebrides* had her first employment on Clyde passenger service at New Year, 1973. A mast was erected on the fore-deck in March, 1981 to carry the light, previously slung on the rigging, and in that summer she performed the Oban-Staffa-Iona excursion when *Columba* was elsewhere.

On the last night of *Hebrides* at Lochmaddy an "on board" ceilidh was held; and a live broadcast on Radio Highland was given as she lay at Uig for the last time. She was sold in 1985 to Torbay Seaways for service between Torquay and the Channel Islands, and left Greenock on Friday, 22nd November. She commenced her new duties in 1986, under the name *Devoniun* (being successor to the first vessel of that name, originally *Scillonian*, afterwards *Syllingar*). She is little altered in outward appearance, except for her dark blue funnel.

T.S.M.V. "Clansman" (IV). The second of the vehicle-carrying ships also suffered a postponement of her launch, on account of a damaged slipway. She was named by Lady Robinson on 14th January, 1964, and successfully launched on the following day. The white painting of her superstructure was carried a strake lower than on *Hebrides*, but this was changed before completion. Like her sister, she was dry-docked at Greenock, and after trials she entered the Mallaig-Armadale ferry service on 5th June, thus relieving *Lochmor* to assist on the Mull ferry run, carrying lifted cars. *Clansman* has relieved on the Stornoway mail run and also on the Hebridean Ferry run.

She was chartered to The Caledonian S.P. Co., Ltd. in the winter and spring of 1970 for the Gourock-Dunoon run, for which she was given a yellow funnel with black top, (without lions), reverting to red when she returned at the end of May to her usual run. From 1971 she was used on a run from Mallaig to Lochboisdale three nights and to Castlebay two nights, in addition to maintaining the Mallaig-Armadale service, making a 24-hour day five days per week, for which she had a double crew.

In 1973 very extensive alterations were made at Troon, including cutting both horizontally and vertically, and lengthening by about 30 feet forward of the superstructure and construction of a new bulbous bow; the heightening of the superstructure to give 5'6" more headroom in the car deck, (though 2½' lower forward than aft); the fitting of bow and stern doors and ramps to give drive-through operation; the removal of the lift: the conversion of the machinery to be fully bridge-controlled, and the installation of a 4-ton bow thruster in place of the 2-ton one originally fitted; and the substitution of twin rudders. In this condition the *Clansman* was placed on the Ullapool-Stornoway service in succession to the *Iona* in 1973; but her reduced speed following the conversion caused complaints, and she was superseded on that run by the Norwegian-built *Suilven*, though continuing to act as relief, as she did also each winter on the Scabster-Stromness crossing of the Pentland Firth in place of *St. Ola*, on charter to P. & O. Ferries. *Clansman* was the farthest-travelled of all the original vehicle carriers; she also visited London, as an exhibition ship.

She was on the Oban-Craignure run in the summer of 1975. Her summer employment in recent years has been on the Ardrossan-Brodick run, where her slow speed at sea was to a certain extent compensated by her speed in loading and unloading. Being succeeded in this in the spring of 1984, following a major breakdown, she was laid up for a time in James Watt Dock, Greenock, and on 14th August, 1984 was delivered to Torbay Seaways for a Torquay-Guernsey service, which however did not materialise on account of refusal of planning permission. She was accordingly re-sold, to Mira Shipping Line Ltd., Malta, who had just parted with their recently-acquired *Free Enterprise III* (which they had re-named *Tamira*) to the Isle of Man S.P. Co., Ltd. (who re-named her *Mona's Isle*); and the *Clansman* took the name *Tamira* for her Malta-Gozo run. She left the U.K. in December, 1984, and before long it was reported that she had been sold to Euch Zammit & Sons Ltd., also of Malta, by whom she was re-named *Al Hussein*. In February, 1986 she was sailing in the Gulf of Akabah.

T.S.M.V. "Columba" (II). The third of the vehicle ferry ships was launched by Lady Craigton, wife of the Minister of State, Scottish Office, on 12th March, 1964 and, having been caught by a strong gust of wind, she struck her sister-ship *Clansman* on the starboard side. Fortunately damage was slight; and, after dry-docking at Greenock and trials, *Columba* took up her service on the Oban-Craignure-Lochaline station on 30th July, 1964, relieving *Lochearn* and *Lochmor* which had been doing their best to cope with large numbers of cars which had to be lifted on board. The choice of the name of the most famous MacBrayne steamer of all time for the last of the three ships would seem to imply that this was regarded as the most important unit of the fleet. Like her beloved namesake, she has certain interesting features such as a small Iona cross on the bow jackstaff, and also painted on the lifebuoys at one side, balanced on the other side by the Company's crossed-flags emblem. The *Columba* has normally relieved the *Hebrides* on the Uig-Tarbert-Lochmaddy triangle during overhaul periods; and, commencing in December, 1972 she has relieved also on the Mallaig-Kyle-Stornoway route; in the summer of 1973 she took over the Mallaig-Armadale runs. When the *Iona* broke down, the *Columba* deputised for her on the Ullapool-Stornoway route.

From 1975 the *Columba* operated the summer service on Monday, Wednesday, Friday and Saturday to Coll and Tiree; to Iona on Tuesday and Thursday; and to Colonsay three times per week, and with three-day package mini-cruises, in which her sleeping accommodation was used. She gave an excursion from Gourock round the Mull of Kintyre to Oban in May, 1978 to celebrate the centenary of her namesake, and next year extended this to a two-night trip to St. Kilda, to celebrate the centenary of the use of the name David MacBrayne, repeating this trip also in 1980. In 1978, also, on a cattle run to Bruichladdich (the pier at Port Askaig being out of action) she took a party of members of the West Highland Steamer Club from Oban, the first passengers to land there for very many years.

M.V. "Scalpay,"(I). After the withdrawal of the Outer Isles mail steamer, the Island of Scalpay was served from Tarbert (Harris) by the locally-owned motor-fishing vessel *Catriona*, operated under contract. She in turn was superseded by the introduction of a turntable ferry-boat on the short run between Scalpay and Kyles Scalpay, Harris, in May, 1965. This little ship, the first of her type in the MacBrayne fleet, had been built at Fraserburgh in 1957 for the Ballachulish Ferry Co. Ltd., and had been named *Maid of Glencoe*. After a refit by Timbacraft Ltd. at Shandon she emerged with her new name, *Scalpay*, and painted in the MacBrayne small-craft livery of red with blue boot-top. She was taken over by Timbacraft Ltd. on 1st November, 1971 and her hull used as a floating pontoon, the engine being scrapped.

M.V. "Eigg" (I). During the building of the extension to the pier at Lochboisdale in the winter of 1965-6, a boat was required there to act as passenger ferry to *Claymore*. In order to release *Staffa* for these duties the Company purchased a vessel which had previously performed passenger excursions for Messrs. MacLean and MacRae from Kyle of Lochalsh to Eilean Donan Castle, etc., under the name *A' Mhaighdean Mhara*, and before that, as *Chieftain* she had been stationed by Mr. Bruce Watt of Mallaig on Loch Morar for that link of the Kyles Nevis circular tour. She was a double-bowed craft, originally a ship's lifeboat, with greater freeboard than the rest of the small red boats. On entering the MacBrayne fleet she was appropriately re-named for her new duties as ferryboat at the Island of Eigg. Withdrawn in September, 1974, she was scrapped early in 1978.

.   .   .   .

For the Toscaig service the small motor vessel *Vital Spark* (called after the puffer created by Neil Munro in the Para Handy tales) was chartered from Messrs. MacLean & MacRae of Kyle of Lochalsh, for duties as relief in 1968, and permanently from 1969, performing also the mail run to Kyle Rhea three times per week, till this was discontinued from 31st October, 1971. From 1969 she carried MacBrayne colours and had the wheelhouse from the *Lochbuie*. From 1st February, 1972 the service was operated by Messrs. MacLean & MacRae with a direct grant from the County. Their motor vessel *Puffin*, a former "Fairmile" launch, was used as relief.

T.S.M.V. "Arran" (V). The first of the "general purpose" ships of the Clyde fleet was transferred from The Caledonian S.P. Co., Ltd. to David MacBrayne Ltd. in November, 1969 for the West Loch Tarbert-Islay run where competition from the drive-on vehicle-carrying ship—*Sound of Islay*, of Western Ferries Ltd., had made it urgent to introduce a drive-on ship. Although loading by lift, the *Arran*, after an extensive overhaul, (which included the provision of watertight doors to the car deck, and new powered lifeboats) had great advantage over the derrick-loading *Lochiel*; and she took up the West Loch Tarbert-Islay run in full MacBrayne colours. She was sold back to The C.S.P. Co., Ltd., remaining on charter to David MacBrayne Ltd., serving Islay, Gigha and Jura.

At the end of 1972 she was sent to Barclay, Curle's for alterations, involving the removal of the lift and side-loading ramps, the removal of all superstructure abaft the lift (with consequent transfer of the mainmast to the upper deck), the installation of a stern ramp, and renewal of deck plates. A new bar was constructed in the saloon, and a new watertight door added at the entrance.

In this condition she returned to the Islay route, end-loading ramps having been installed at West Loch Tarbert and at Port Ellen (the MacBrayne service to Port Askaig having by that time been suspended). This continued till the advent of the *Pioneer* in 1974, after which the *Arran* was mainly employed on the Clyde, performing relief runs on Ardrossan-Brodick and Gourock-Dunoon-Kilcreggan—and doing some of the gas tanker runs from Gourock to Rothesay. (A side ramp was restored.) She acted also as relief in the West Highlands, including Mallaig-Kyle-Portree and Mallaig-Small Isles, Oban-Craignure and the special runs from Coll and Tiree, calling off Mingary for Tobermory Highland Games. During absence for overhaul the shortage of transport to Gigha was to a certain extent made good by chartering the puffer *Marsa*.

The *Arran* was sold to the same Greek owners who had purchased her sisters, but this sale fell through and following her withdrawal in 1979 she was laid up in East India Harbour, Greenock, till sold to Orisot Ltd. for use as a floating restaurant at Dublin, since closed.

T.S.M.V. "Iona" (VII). Intended for a passenger and vehicle service to Islay,. this ship is the first of drive-through design in the MacBrayne fleet (though not the first in service on any West Highland route, which was *Sound of Jura*, built in Norway in 1969 for Western Ferries Limited). The intention had been to use the new ship from a new pier near the entrance to West Loch Tarbert, but that was abandoned on account of expense, in favour of building a new pier at Escart Bay, this in turn being delayed on account of the expenditure of public money involved. Not being suitable for use at the existing pier at West Loch Tarbert, the new *Iona* was chartered to the C.S.P. Co. Ltd. for the Gourock-Dunoon run, and their *Arran* went to David MacBrayne Ltd. for the West Loch Tarbert-Islay run. The *Iona*, seventh of the name in the MacBrayne fleet (including small craft), is a fine passenger and vehicle-carrying ship, though with very little open deck space for passengers, but having a very pleasant lounge, seating 101 passengers, on the boat-deck forward, with chairs originally in shades of violet and blue, the cafeteria for 97 persons being at the after end of this deck. Her car space is the height of two decks, except for the "gallery" decks at the sides and she can carry 47 large cars, or 11 30-ft. vehicles and 7 cars. She has a hydraulically-operated stern ramp; the bow door and visor are combined; and she has also a lift and turntable system capable of moving 27·5 tons for side-loading at piers where end-loading facilities do not exist. Below the car deck is a smoke-room and bar for 50 persons, and also crew accommodation in two-berth cabins, while the officers have single-berth cabins on the gallery decks and in the house on the navigating bridge deck. Fitted with Denny-Brown retractable stabilisers, she has also a Diesel-driven 3-ton bow-thrust controllable pitch propeller; and the main machinery, consisting of twin Paxman engines each driving a fixed-pitch propeller through a gear, gives propeller speed of approximately

300 r.p.m., compared with the engine speed of 900 r.p.m., and a speed of 16 knots at 80 per cent continuous rating. On trials on the Skelmorlie measured mile she attained a speed of 17·51 knots. Control can be from the consoles in the engine-room, in the wheelhouse, in the bridge wings, or at the aft end of the navigation bridge deck, for astern working. Though commencing service in MacBrayne colours, she had her funnel changed to yellow with black top within a few days. After a spell on the Gourock-Dunoon run in Caledonian colours, the *Iona*, with red funnel restored, took up various West Highland services (Oban-Craignure; Mallaig-Kyle-Stornoway; Oban-Castlebay-Lochboisdale) and has also supplemented the Ardrossan-Brodick runs.

For the Lochboisdale service from Oban the *Iona* had certain alterations made by Robb Caledon at Leith, including the removal of the dummy funnel; the installation of a Radar scanner on a new support above the wheelhouse; the fitting of a gaff to the mainmast; the construction of a new deckhouse on the upper deck aft of the officers' accommodation; the fitting of a crane (3-ton) aft of the lift on the port side, the jib of this reaching to the stern; and the heightening of the engine exhausts by six feet, these being then painted as funnels with the red lion emblem on yellow disc on the outside of each. The deckhouse contained eight staterooms, toilets and shower, and a battery room (the batteries having been previously inside the dummy funnel). New seating was arranged in the cafeteria and saloon, the floor covering of which was renewed. After being succeeded on the Lochboisdale run by the *Claymore* in 1979, the *Iona* took up the Islay run for which she had been intended, but operating from Kennacraig to Port Ellen and (from 1980) also to Port Askaig. This is her normal occupation in summer; and also in winter, together with relieving on the Lochboisdale route.

Scottish Transport Group

Formed on 1st January, 1969 as a Public Authority under the Transport Act, 1968, this Group (which controls the Scottish Bus Group) took over from British Railways their interests in the Clyde and West Highland shipping services of The Caledonian Steam Packet Company Limited and David MacBrayne Limited. In the case of the latter this amounted to 50%, the other half being owned by Coast Lines Limited, from whom it was purchased in July the same year so that both shipping companies became wholly owned subsidiaries and wholly nationalised.

David MacBrayne Limited (*contd.*)

T.S.M.V. "Lochalsh II"/"Scalpay" (II). After use as relief at Scalpay, this vessel, having been succeeded by the third *Lochalsh*, was transferred to David MacBrayne, Ltd. and re-named *Scalpay*, for regular service there. She was herself relieved by the chartered *Glen Mallie* from Glenelg in 1971 and subsequently. In this she continued till succeeded by the *Kilbrannan* in 1977, after which she was spare, relieving for a time at Corran-Ardgour on charter. In November, 1979, she was sold to Ardmaleish Boat Building Company, Bute.

T.S.M.V. "Kilbrannan." In February, 1972, an association known as Caledonian MacBrayne Services was formed by The Caledonian S.P. Co., Ltd. and David MacBrayne, Ltd. to co-ordinate certain departments of the two companies, becoming the registered owners of the first and second small bow-loading ferry vessels. (Plans had also been prepared for a larger model, but in fact only the small version was built). Designed by Messrs. Burnett Corless, these were developed from the bow-loading converted *Coruisk*, but with a ramp slower in operation, to conform with Class II A requirements of a watertight seal. They are bridge-controlled; powered by twin Bergius Kelvin engines of type RS6, fresh-water cooled; with an electric start or hand start and with a Diesel-driven battery-charging unit, independent of the main engines. The one lifeboat is motor driven, to comply with II A regulations.

The first of the type—*Kilbrannan*—was launched for David MacBrayne, Ltd., intended for the new route between Lochranza and Claonaig, near Skipness, across the Kilbrannan Sound, taking the place of the Fairlie-Brodick-Tarbert relic of the Royal Route, inaugurated by the *Cowal*. She carried Caledonian colours initially. The route, operated in summer only, became popular, and a slightly larger ship of similar type has been employed on it since 1973, after which the *Kilbrannan* was on various routes, including relieving (on charter to Westeren Ferries, Ltd.) between Port Askaig and Feolin (Jura) and relieving at Largs. Since 1977 she has been normally on the Scalpay station.

T.S.M.V. "Morvern." Launched on 18th December, 1972, the sister-ship to the foregoing, destined for the Fishnish-Lochaline route (opened on 30th April, 1973 by Mrs. Spencer's *Island Queen* on charter) began on the Largs-Cumbrae Slip service, in full MacBrayne colours and flying their house-flag. Her upper deck was extended to accommodate the lifeboat. She was for a time engaged in tender duties at Ardyne and at Tarbert Loch Fyne during oil-rig construction, and later was on Oban-Lismore, Fishnish-Lochaline, etc., and now regularly on the Fionnphort-Iona run, where vehicles are limited to those of Iona residents or engaged in delivering goods to the island. When on purely passenger service, she has seats on the car-deck, these being removed when space is required for a vehicle. She was on the Colintraive-Rhubodach run in the spring of 1983.

CHAPTER VIII

THE CALEDONIAN STEAM PACKET CO. LTD.

WHEN railways were constructed to certain of the Clyde coast resorts during the earlier half of last century they were regarded by the steamboat owners as serious competitors, and at first no co-operation existed between them. It was not long, however, until the steamer proprietors realised that the railways had come to stay, and that it would be in their interest to make the best of things and run their vessels in connexion with the trains, rather than strive to compete against them.

The Glasgow, Paisley & Greenock Railway was opened from Glasgow (Bridge Street) to Greenock (Cathcart Street) in 1841, the steamers *Isle of Bute* and *Maid of Bute*, of the Bute S.P. Company, connecting with the trains, the *Royal Victoria* being added to the fleet about this time. In 1844 the company came under the control of the railway company, and purchased *Pilot*, *Pioneer* and *Petrel*: severe competition ensued between this concern and the private owners. The result was that in 1846 the Bute Steam Packet Company disposed of its steamers to Messrs. G. & J. Burns, and an arrangement was made with certain of the steamboat owners to provide connexions with the trains. In 1852-4 a further short-lived effort at steamboat-operation was made by the Railway Steam Packet Company, a subsidiary of the Caledonian Railway Company, which from 1847 had been the owners of the Glasgow, Paisley & Greenock Railway. Again the service was short-lived, and the trade reverted to private owners.

The Greenock & Wemyss Bay Railway Company, whose line was opened on 15th May, 1865, also tried shipowning through its subsidiary, the Wemyss Bay Steamboat Co. Ltd. Two saloon steamers had been ordered from Messrs. Caird & Co. of Greenock, and a smaller flush-decked one from Messrs. Wingate—*Largs*—which was launched in September, 1864. One of the larger ships was, before completion, sold for blockade-running in the American Civil War, and named *Hattie*; a replacement was ordered, the other original ship and this one becoming *Kyles* and *Bute*, launched respectively in October, 1864 and June, 1865. Pending their completion, various ships were chartered for the services from Wemyss Bay, including *Arran Castle*. A very ambitious programme of sailings was instituted including Ardrishaig in competition with Messrs. Hutcheson's well-established trade there, then maintained in summer by the third *Iona*. The venture was financially unsuccessful, and in January, 1866 the larger ships—*Kyles* and *Bute*—were sold for passenger sailings on the Thames, and the Ardrishaig runs were abandoned. Using the *Largs* together with the smaller *Victory* and *Argyle* purchased in May, 1865 and April, 1866 respectively, the Steamboat Company was able to maintain sailings to Millport and Rothesay. In 1869 the Company was unable to carry on business, and arrangements were made by the Railway Company for Captain J. Gillies and his son-in-law, Captain Alexander Campbell, to take over the *Largs* and *Argyle*, to which Captain Gillies added his own steamer *Venus*, the last survivor on the Clyde of the McKellar fleet. The Wemyss Bay services continued to be provided by Messrs. Gillies & Campbell till 1890, the fleet then consisting of *Lancelot*, *Adela*, *Arran* and *Victoria*, all disposed of soon after The Caledonian Steam Packet Company Limited had placed its own ships on the services from Wemyss Bay.

In time both the Glasgow, Paisley & Greenock and the Greenock & Wemyss Bay Railway Companies became absorbed by the Caledonian Railway Company, which in contemplation of the opening of its extension to Gourock had made tentative enquiries with a view to having steamer connexions provided by some of the existing private owners. Not being successful in this, and having failed to obtain parliamentary powers to run ships on the Clyde, it formed a subsidiary called The Caledonian Steam Packet Company (Limited), incorporated on 8th May, 1889. The colours adopted for the steamers were:—Funnels buff; hulls dark navy blue (later black) with broad white waterline and green underbody (later Indian red); saloons (outside) pale pink with pale blue panelling; and paddle-boxes white, with very beautiful decorations in gold. The flag was a yellow pennant bearing a red lion rampant, as on the Scottish Royal Standard. This emblem from the houseflag was added on the yellow portion of the funnel of *Glen Sannox* in 1964 and of most of the other ships from 1965.

The Greenock & Ayrshire Railway from Johnstone to Greenock, Albert Harbour (afterwards Princes Pier) was opened in 1869, and from 1870 the company obtained certain steamer services by contract. It was not till 1891, however, that that Company's successors, the Glasgow & South Western Railway Company, began to own its own ships.

On 1st January, 1923 the London, Midland & Scottish Railway Company was formed by the amalgamation of various English Companies and of the Glasgow & South Western Railway Company, the Caledonian Railway Company joining on 1st July. The Caledonian S.P. Co., Ltd. then became a subsidiary of the L.M. & S. Railway Co. and so ultimately of British Railways, till transferred to the Scottish Transport Group on 1st January, 1969. (Williamson-Buchanan Steamers Ltd. had been incorporated in the C.S.P. Co. Ltd. from October, 1935.) The S.T.G. also took over from British Railways the whole of David MacBrayne Ltd., 50% of which had belonged to the L.M.S. and the other 50% of which had been purchased by the Government from Coast Lines Ltd.

The history of The Caledonian Steam Packet Co., Ltd. will be found in "C.R.O.S." and other books, and here it is proposed to refer only to those ships of that fleet which remained on 1st January, 1973, when its name was changed to Caledonian MacBrayne Limited and certain ships were transferred to it from David MacBrayne Limited.

P.S. "Caledonia" (II). Launched at Dumbarton on 1st February, 1934, the *Caledonia*, a quasi-sister of the *Mercury*, attained a speed of 17.27 knots on trial. She took the name of the first vessel built for the C.S.P. Co., which had been withdrawn in 1933. She has been used for various services, among them being that from Wemyss Bay to Rothesay and Kyles of Bute, and also for general excursion work from Gourock, Greenock, Largs, Wemyss Bay, Rothesay, etc. In 1936 she was placed on the Arran run via Kyles of Bute, in succession to *Duchess of Argyll*.

Towards the end of 1939 the *Caledonia* was commissioned as a minesweeper, H.M.S. *Goatfell*, later a patrol vessel. Released in 1945 she was reconditioned by her builders and operated on various Clyde coast routes from Gourock or Wemyss Bay, and between 1954 and 1964 from Ayr, assisting to Arran at peak periods. In winter 1954-5 she was given a new oil-fired navy boiler at Troon, and from 1965 was stationed at Craigendoran. It was in 1969, however, that she justified inclusion as a West Highland steamer, being chartered by David MacBrayne Ltd. for the Tarbert mail service for ten days in April, and again on it for a few days at the beginning of October, but for her owners the C.S.P. Co., who had taken over the Lochfyne service from the first of that month. It was a very long time since this part of the Royal Route had been operated by a paddle steamer, and it was a fitting end to her active career. Early in 1970 she was sold to W. H. Arnott, Young & Co., Ltd., Dalmuir, by whom she was re-named *Old Caledonia*, being later re-sold to Bass Charrington Ltd. and moored near Waterloo Bridge on the Thames, as a floating restaurant. Unfortunately she was so badly damaged by fire on 27th April, 1980 that she was scrapped at Grays, Essex.

Tr.S.S. "Queen Mary"/"Queen Mary II"/"Queen Mary." This ship celebrated her fortieth birthday on Saturday, 5th May, 1973, by which time she was wearing the colours of Caledonian MacBrayne, Ltd. Her original name was restored at a ceremony on board on 6th May, 1976, the need for the numeral having gone with the demise of the Cunarder. She continued on excursions and charter sailings, including one on 4th September that year on the former Royal Route to Tarbert and Ardrishaig. She gave additional sailings to Brodick at peak holiday periods, supplementing the *Caledonia*, there, and also on the Wemyss Bay-Rothesay route on Saturdays. Her Glasgow berth was latterly at Springfield Quay. At the end of the 1977 season she was withdrawn and laid up in East India Harbour, Greenock, being subsequently sold to the City of Glasgow District Council to become a floating museum, but this idea was abandoned on account of the cutting of public expenditure. She was put on the market, being sold in 1980 to Euroyachts, Ltd. for yet another floating restaurant venture. Apart from a few days in drydock for underwater preservation, she remained in East India Harbour. In January, 1981, she was sold for similar use on the Thames, but so far has not been completed for her new role.

P.S. "Waverley" (IV). On 2nd October, 1946, a notable ship was launched by Messrs. Inglis for the L. & N.E.R. Clyde services, bearing the popular name *Waverley*. Her length is about the same as that of her predecessor, but she has about four feet more beam; and the propelling machinery is triple expansion, made by Messrs. Rankin & Blackmore, originally taking steam from a double-ended boiler, intended to be oil-fired but initially coal-fired. Externally there is a strong resemblance to *Jeanie Deans* (as altered), with two elliptical funnels forward, two masts, boats on upper decks, etc., and it is most pleasing to record that again the traditional North British type of paddle-boxes forms a feature of the design. With accommodation for about 1350 passengers, the ship was a great acquisition to the Craigendoran fleet, and was the first step towards making good the war losses suffered by the Clyde passenger fleet. She entered service early in the 1947 season, and was at first on the Arrochar station, being later on the Rothesay and Kyles of Bute or Round Bute run. For the 1947 season she carried L.N.E.R. colours, being repainted (along with *Lucy Ashton*, *Jeanie Deans* and *Talisman*) in B.R. colours in time for the 1948 summer season. She was transferred to the Caledonian S.P. Co. on 5th November, 1951. During the winter of 1956-7 she was converted to burn oil. From 1958 she succeeded *Marchioness of Graham* on the up-river excursions from Largs, Rothesay and Dunoon to Glasgow, once each week. Radar was fitted in 1960.

At the close of the 1973 season the *Waverley* was laid up in James Watt Dock, Greenock, then in 1974 was sold for a nominal sum to the Paddle Steamer Preservation Society, who transferred her to Waverley Steam Navigation Co., Ltd. Due to the wonderful efforts of members of that Society she was restored to passenger cruising, and has visited many places round the coasts of Britain giving excursions where none had been provided for very many years. Here, however, her ventures into the West Highlands require particular notice. It was in 1983 that the *Waverley*, on her circumnavigation of Great Britain, called at Kyle of Lochalsh, Oban, Fort William, etc., and gave excursion sailings to Iona; in 1984 also to Staffa, Tobermory, Craignure, Port Ellen; and in 1985 to Crinan, reviving memories of the *Chevalier*, *Mountaineer*, etc. and enabling one of the authors to complete by water his last missing link in the Royal Route (Glasgow-Inverness).

P.S. "Maid of the Loch." In July, 1950 the Railway Executive ordered from A. & J. Inglis Ltd. the ship, which has become the last paddle steamer built in Britain, for service on Loch Lomond. In accordance with tradition she had her dining saloon forward on the main deck, and deck shelters as on the later Clyde steamers, with upper deck above; and her paddle-boxes are of standard Loch Lomond design with horizontal slots, but having a most attractive Celtic interwoven decoration in silver paint, the name being in red on a blue background. On her bow she had the British Railways lion and wheel emblem. The hull is white, with green waterline, as on the other British Railways inland water ships, and the funnel, originally buff with black top, became plain buff shortly before her launch on 5th March, 1953. Her machinery is compound diagonal, rather like that installed by the same makers in *Kylemore* in 1897; and, like her, she takes steam from a navy boiler, but with three furnaces, having two oil burners to each, and with a working pressure of 120 lb. per sq. in. Her paddle-wheels have each eight floats, of American elm, thus following the N.B.R./L.N.E.R. practice of wooden floats. Her contract speed was 14 knots.

Owned since May, 1957 by The C.S.P. Co., Ltd., *Maid of the Loch* was from 1969 transferred (on paper) to Walter Alexander & Sons (Midland) Ltd., the bus operators, and, like the C.S.P. Co., a subsidiary of the Scottish Transport Group. This move, stated to be for administrative convenience and for "obscure legal and financial reasons", it was hoped, would provide sufficient resources to keep the service going, and produce some benefit from association with bus operators who have a large tourist traffic in Central Scotland, and who provide a considerable volume of trade for the *Sir Walter Scott* on Loch Katrine.

During the 1975 season the ship had a funnel of Caledonian-Mac-Brayne red with black top, but without the lion emblem, reverting to buff next season. She was sold in March, 1982 to a partnership of Ind Coope Alloa Brewery Co., Ltd. and Verigen Ltd. and registered in name of Maid of the Loch Limited, now wholly owned by the Alloa Company. She has been laid up at Balloch Pier awaiting a decision on possible future use. Her owners have plans to restore her to part-time passenger service, possibly with Diesel hydraulic machinery; but meantime she forms a landing stage for her successor in the Loch Lomond service, the *Countess Fiona*, better known previously as the *Countess of Breadalbane* and later *Gourockian* (see "C.R.O.S.").

.   .   .   .

In February, 1951 Lord Hurcomb, then Chairman of the British Transport Commission, announced a £1,000,000 plan to modernise Clyde steamer services. This involved the building of four passenger ships for shuttle ferry services, each carrying about 500 passengers and with a speed of 15 knots and three general purpose ships to carry 500 passengers and cargo, livestock and motor vehicles, to be fitted with electric lifts and ramps to enable speed of 16 knots.

T.S.M.V. "Maid of Ashton." The only Clyde passenger ship built by Yarrow & Co., Ltd., this was the first of the new Clyde fleet, and also the first to go, being sold in 1973 to the Yardarm Club of London, by whom she was re-named *Hispaniola II*, later without the numeral.

T.S.M.V. "Maid of Argyll.' This was the first of the two built at Pointhouse, from which had come so many North British and several MacBrayne ships. She entered the water on 4th March and became based at Craigendoran, performing the Dunoon and Rothesay services and also on Saturdays the Arrochar section of the Loch Lomond circular tour; and she alternated with the other *Maids* on the various services. Exceptional runs have included a charter by the Clyde River Steamer Club from Paisley to Dunoon and Loch Striven on 17th September, 1966; and in the spring of 1970 the Tarbert mail service, for which she received the locked mail-room partitions and shelter from her sister next mentioned. On 1st March, 1974 her sale was reported—to Cyclades Tourist Cruising Company, Piraeus, operating day excursions from Piraeus (Zea) to Hydra, Poros and Aegina under the name *City of Piraeus*, and being joined after one season by the *City of Hydra*, previously the *Claymore* of 1955.

T.S.M.V. "Maid of Skelmorlie." The other Inglis product was launched on 2nd April, and was identical with *Maid of Argyll*. In September, 1969 she was given small mail-rooms forward of the saloon, and had a temporary shelter above the galley for parcels and luggage, to make her more suitable for the winter service to Kyles of Bute and Tarbert, Loch Fyne, to which she was transferred next month following its having been taken over by the C.S.P. Co. Ltd. from David MacBrayne Ltd. on 1st October, 1969. This service lasted only eight months more, after which Tarbert was served from Fairlie by car ferry *via* Brodick; but that continued only for the 1970-71 summer seasons. Sold to Panamanian interests, this member of the fleet left Gourock, named *Ala*. She was subsequently registered in name of Felice Giuffe in 1977-8, and converted to a small car ferry, with stern-loading ramp and part of the after saloon and galley removed to make a flush car deck. In this condition she has been engaged in sailing to the Isle of Capri.

T.S.M.V. "Maid of Cumbrae." This was the only "Maid" to suffer major change while still on the Clyde. On account of urgency to obtain an additional end-loading vehicle carrier, she was sent to Barclay Curle's Elderslie Dockyard, where her galley and after saloon were, in March, 1972, cut away, clearing the main deck from the stern to a point just abaft the funnel, giving capacity for 15 cars and with both stern- and side-loading. A 13-ft. turntable was installed; and all passenger accommodation was crammed into the forward portion of the ship. She had a "capuchon" added to the funnel, and became a useful addition to the vehicle-carrying fleet. She was occasionally chartered, and on 30th April, 1977, became the only "Maid" to have visited Inveraray, on a charter to the Clyde River Steamer Club, with Loch Eck Tour in connexion. After a spell in James Watt Dock, she was sold and named *Hanseatic*, but later was registered in name of Navigazione Alto Tireno S.p.A. at Palermo under the Italian flag as *Noce di Cocco*, afterwards changed to *Capri Express*.

T.S.M.V. "Cowal" (II). The general purpose ships (except *Arran*) were built at Troon; and of these the *Cowal* was launched on 20th January, 1954. In 1970 she opened a new route from Fairlie to Brodick and Tarbert, (to take the place of the Gourock-Tarbert relic of the Royal Route) with morning and evening runs to Millport. The Fairlie-Brodick-Tarbert service ceased on the introduction of the vehicle ferry (summer only) between Lochranza and Claonaig in 1972. Thereafter the *Cowal* was employed on various Clyde routes, usually Wemyss Bay-Rothesay, and including calls at Ardyne until work ceased there and rendered *Cowal* redundant; and by July, 1977 she had retired to East India Harbour. She was sold to Greek interests ultimately reaching Piraeus.

T.S.M.V. "Bute" (VI). The last of the three general purpose vessels was launched at Troon on 28th September, 1954 and in December entered service on the Wemyss Bay-Rothesay station, being subsequently engaged on the other vehicle ferry routes on interchange with *Arran* and *Cowal*. She has relieved on the Oban-Craignure-Lochaline route in December, 1972 (in Caledonian colours, but with a MacBrayne houseflag) and next year (in Cal-Mac colours). She was altered in 1975 by the fitting of "horns" and the gear was raised to enable the lift to reach the higher level of the pier at Armadale, between which and Mallaig she provided the vehicle service in that and subsequent summers, re-appearing on Clyde reliefs during parts of the winter. She relieved *Loch Arkaig* on the Small Isles-Mallaig-Kyle run (for which a ferry door was cut in her ramp), also visiting Portree and peforming cattle runs from Iona to Oban and relieving on the Mull Ferry from Oban to Craignure. Laid up in James Watt Dock, she was sold to the same owners as *Cowal*—Thetouris Shipping. In April, 1980, she was arrested for non-payment of ship-keeping and watch duties; but ultimately this was withdrawn: named *Med-Sun* and flying the Greek flag, she set sail on 17th June, 1980 for Piraeus. It is understood that she did not enter service in Greece, but was broken up in 1985.

T.S.M.V. "Glen Sannox" (III). In April, 1955 an announcement was made of an impending order for a large vehicle-carrying ship for the Ardrossan or Fairlie to Brodick station. During that summer a vehicle service to Arran was provided on certain Saturdays by one of the smaller vessels, *Arran*, *Cowal* or *Bute*. The order for the new ship was in due course placed with the Ailsa Company; and she was launched at Troon on 30th April, 1957 bearing an illustrious name associated from 1892 with the Arran service. In design she was a much enlarged and improved version of *Arran*, *Cowal* and *Bute*, with much more spacious lounges.

Glen Sannox was the first passenger ship to be equipped with inflatable liferafts in place of buoyant apparatus and lifeboats, there being only two of the latter. Radar was installed from the outset. She was in 1964 the first member of the C.S.P. Clyde fleet to have the red lion emblem on her funnel (introduced at Stranraer by *Caledonian Princess*); and in 1965 was the first to be given the new colour scheme of "monastral" blue hull, retaining at first the white band at main-deck level, though this was soon removed.

Modifications made in 1970 included removal of all superstructure aft, and the fitting of a stern ramp (the lift being retained). In this condition she was employed mainly on the Dunoon route, and later on the Wemyss Bay-Rothesay run, using the stern ramp at Wemyss Bay and the side ramps at Rothesay from May, 1977. She first became a West Highland steamer on 29th April, 1974, on taking up the Oban-Craignure service, for which she had a certificate for 817 passengers, her first run to Tobermory being on 18th July that year, for Tobermory Games. She included Colonsay in her schedule, and, exceptionally, Gigha in February, 1979.

Early in 1977, she was sent to Hall Russell's yard at Aberdeen to be re-engined with German diesels, returning to the Dunoon or Rothesay route. In the summer of 1978, she took over the cruises from the *Queen Mary*, with white lines round the hull and with cafe tables under sunshades (or umbrellas!), a mobile bar on the car-deck, and moveable companionways to that deck from the one above. In 1980, regular sailings from Glasgow were abandoned and instead on Saturdays she supplemented the Wemyss Bay-Rothesay sailings, with extra runs on certain Fridays from Ardrossan to Brodick and back to Gourock. In winter she is normally on the Mull Ferry from Oban to Craignure, but in January-February, 1981, and later she also relieved on the Islay services from Kennacraig.

T.S.M.V. "Kyleakin" (II)/**"Kyleakin II"**/**"Largs."** The last of the turntable type ferryboats for service to Skye to be built was similar to *Lochalsh* (II) and came from the Troon yard, entering service in July, 1960. These were the largest of the Kyle ferries of this type, subsequent vessels being fitted with ramps only. Superseded at Kyle of Lochalsh by the larger ferries, this one was sent to Troon for conversion to bow-loading (as *Coruisk*), and in April, 1972, under the name *Largs*, took up the Cumbrae Slip service, for which she was latterly stand-by vessel. Her new name revived that of the Wemyss Bay Railway steamer of 1864, and also could be associated with a steamboat of 1822 on the Glasgow-Largs-Millport route. She was bought by Ardmaleish Boatbuilding Co., Bute.

T.S.M.V. "Portree" (II). A side-loading vehicle ferry of new design, capable of carrying nine cars, but with no covered passenger accommodation, was built at Port Glasgow in 1965. She differed from all the others in having her wheelhouse close to the bow. In 1970, however, this was removed, and a new bridge erected near the stern, as on the other ferries of this type; and she was converted to bow-loading by the installation of a hydraulic ramp and the removal of the side ramps and deck turntable. In this condition she was transferred from Kyle of Lochalsh to the service of Bute Ferry Co. Ltd. between Rhubodach and Colintraive.

T.S.M.V. "Broadford" (II). Similar in layout of her car deck, this boat differs from the foregoing in having from the outset her bridge in the traditional position aft. She entered service in 1967, and later had a small space under the bridge enclosed for covered passenger accommodation. In 1971 she joined her sister at Rhubodach, similarly converted. Both were sold late in 1986, to Mr Hooper of Sandbank.

M.V. "Rose"/"Keppel." It has not often occurred that a vessel from other parts has come to the Clyde for passenger service; but the Tilbury Ferry *Rose* sailed round the North of Scotland and, after modifications at Greenock, entered service between Largs and Millport on 12th June 1967, being later renamed as above. With Voith-Schneider propulsion she is easily manoeuvrable, but her speed does not rise to normal Clyde standards. She has a combined funnel and mast, yellow with black top, but without the lion emblem. Apart from a weekly call at Rothesday, she has not deviated much from her normal route. The Largs-Millport passenger service was withdrawn from the end of June, 1986, since which the *Keppel* has been based at Largs for cruises to destinations such as Rothesay, Tighnabruaich, Dunoon, Carrick Castle, Lochgoil, etc.

T.S.M.V. "Coruisk" (II). In July, 1969 a fifth ferryboat was added to the Kyle of Lochalsh fleet, similar to her immediate predecessor *Broadford*, but with covered passenger shelter as on *Lochalsh* and *Kyleakin*. The administration of the Skye ferries was reported to be transferred in 1969 to the Highland Omnibus Co. Ltd., Inverness, also a member of the S.T.G., with a local manager at Kyleakin; but this did not result in any operational change, and the Caledonian Company continued to own the ships.

The *Coruisk* was in September, 1971 converted to bow-loading, to carry six cars and 70 passengers on the new service between Largs and the Tattie Pier, Cumbrae (soon re-named Cumbrae Slip). This she inaugurated on 11th March, 1972, Fairlie Pier being then closed. She was sometimes relieved or assisted by *Portree* or *Broadford*, *Largs* or *Kilbrannan*, etc., and has herself relieved on other routes, including Iona-Fionnphort, Colintraive-Rhubodach, Scalpay, Tobermory-Mingary, and her original run, Kyle-Kyleakin. For Tobermory-Mingary the open launch *Marena* was sometimes chartered. The *Coruisk* was sold in September, 1986 to Euroyachts Ltd.

D.S.M.V. "Kyleakin" (III). The first of the large Kyle ferries was already under construction at Newport, Monmouthshire, when the announcement of their building was made, and it subsequently became clear that these were to be end-loading vessels, 116 feet in length, and with covered passenger accommodation at one side only, in the manner of the *Rosehaugh* at Kessock, Inverness. The new ship entered service at Kyle in August, 1970. A Caledonian MacBrayne funnel emblem appeared on her wheelhouse in December, 1983.

D.S.M.V. "Lochalsh" (III). The second Kyle ferry joined the fleet in 1971, and traffic queues were eliminated. She differs from the first in having tetrapod masts, unlike *Kyleakin* which has her navigation lights on a mast fixed to the wheelhouse at an angle so that the mast is on the centre line of the ship. The two ships have not deviated from the route for which they were built. They are normally overhauled at Stornoway. Radar was installed in March, 1984.

. . . .

On 1st January, 1969 The Caledonian Steam Packet Co. Ltd. became a wholly-owned subsidiary of the Scottish Transport Group; and in August the Company reported having acquired the share capital of Arran Piers Limited, a private company previously in the hands of the family of the late Duke and Duchess of Montrose, and in control of all piers and harbours on Arran. This acquisition prepared the way for the conversion by the Scottish Transport Group of the piers for end-loading ferry vessels, and a start was made almost at once with a survey for this purpose at Brodick. Later the same month, Mr. P. M. Thomas, Chairman of the S.T.G., stated that the ultra-modern Swedish 50-car drive-through ship *Stena Baltica* had been purchased, and was expected to be operating by Easter, 1970 on the Ardrossan-Brodick run. Arrangements were put in hand for an end-loading berth at Ardrossan, to the south-west of Winton Pier.

T.S.M.V. "Stena Baltica"/"Caledonia" (III). This was the first end-loading vehicle ferry in the C.S.P. fleet and as such marked a radical change in Clyde steamer design. She had belonged to the

Stena Line of Gothenburg, one of whose other ships—*Stena Nordica*—had already become known on the Stranraer-Larne run. *Stena Baltica* arrived at Greenock on Sunday, 11th January, 1970 having had her funnels already painted yellow with black top, and having been already registered at Glasgow. She was taken in hand by Scott-Lithgow Limited for overhaul; and, with a black hull and Caledonian boot-topping, she received the name *Caledonia* in April. She was not ready by Easter, but neither were the end-loading berths at Brodick or Adrossan: and she entered service on 29th May, 1970 by this time in full Caledonian livery, including red lions on the funnels and bow. On the same day *Iona* made her appearance on the Gourock-Dunoon station and the next day *Cowal* inaugurated the new Fairlie-Brodick-Tarbert car-ferry route. Various "teething" troubles in both *Caledonia* and *Iona* caused very considerable delays and inconvenience, but in due course they settled down. The end-loading of the former has, as expected, speeded up the car traffic; and it was then the passengers who caused delay in turn-round time!

1976 was the first season in which the *Caledonia* was used anywhere away from the Arran route, her first appearance at Oban being on 29th May that year. She has since been the regular summer ship on the Oban-Craignure run, exchanging places with the *Clansman*, which became the regular Arran summer vessel. The draught of the *Caledonia* precluded calling at Tobermory Pier. She was at Kyle in May, 1977 in connexion with a visit by the Duke of Edinburgh to an oil rig at Kishorn and on 29th October, 1983 she performed a charter sailing from Brodick to Tarbert and back, for the Clyde River Steamer Club.

CHAPTER IX

CALEDONIAN MACBRAYNE, LTD.

FROM 1st January, 1973, The Caledonian Steam Packet Co.,
Ltd. was re-named as above, and was to be responsible for all
major vehicle ferry operations of the Scottish Transport Group
without direct Government subsidy; and the two fleets began to
operate more or less as one, but with the crews remaining members of
their existing different trade unions. The MacBrayne ships were
transferred to this company, except eight, which remained the
property of David MacBrayne, Ltd., viz. *Loch Seaforth*, *Lochnell*,
Lochdunvegan, *Loch Carron*, *Claymore*, *Loch Toscaig*, *Scalpay*, and
Loch Arkaig. These were to continue operating cargo, passenger and
mail and minor ferry services. Bute Ferry Co., Ltd. was renamed
MacBrayne Haulage, Ltd., taking over the road haulage section of the
MacBrayne organisation, whose bus services passed to other members
of the S.T.G. Arran Piers, Ltd., a Caledonian subsidiary since
August, 1969, was re-named Caledonian MacBrayne Holdings, Ltd.,
to hold heritable property and other fixed assets; and to it many
members of the combined fleet were transferred, though continuing to
be operated by the parent company and later reverting to it.

M.V. "Tiger." An addition was made in 1973 to the fleet of "red"
boats at Iona, on the purchase of this one from Mr. Ritchie of
Gourock. She performed the Fionnphort service principally. Early in
1975 she was found to be unfit for further use and was put up for sale
at Timbacraft's yard at Shandon. Her name was painted in Gothic
lettering.

T.S.M.V. "Bruernish." When *Kilbrannan* and *Morvern* were
nearing completion six more similar craft were ordered from the same
builders, slightly longer to carry two additional cars of average size.
Names originally proposed for the six were *Bernera*, *Eriskay*, *Vatersay*, *Soay*, *Raasay* and *Staffa*, but most of these appear to have been
unavailable. Known as the "Small Island" Class, these ships have
become most useful members of the fleet on the shorter ferry
crossings. This vessel along with *Rhum* and *Coll* were completed in
1973. *Bruernish*, which takes her name, not from an island, but from a
peninsula in Barra, is the most widely travelled, including Lismore,
Fishnish, Mingary and Gigha among her calls, while all three have
relieved at Kyleakin.

During the building of the new landing places at Iona and
Fionnphort the *Bruernish* became the first MacBrayne ship for very
many years to use the pier at Bunessan, where she lay when not

engaged in carrying contractors' materials. In 1978 she was chartered to Howard Doris Ltd. for Kyle-Toscaig, which ended on 6th May, 1978 on the completion of the oil platform, but was taken up by Messrs. Maclean & MacRae, until 7th October. The *Bruernish* began the daily service between Kennacraig and Gigha on 5th February, 1979, with a certificate for 36 passengers. She has since been the regular vessel between Tayinloan and Gigha.

T.S.M.V. "Rhum." From her entry to service in April, 1974 this vessel has been the regular incumbent of the Claonaig-Lochranza station (in summer only), and has operated also from Largs, both to Cumbrae and, with calor-gas, to Brodick. In October, 1980 she made two trips between Inchmarnock and Kilmichael, Bute, with sheep and tractors during a farm removal; and in November the same year relieved the *Sound of Gigha* on the Port Askaig-Feolin route; she has also relieved at Scalpay and at Raasay. On charter to the C.R.S.C. on 15th May, 1982, she became the first passenger vessel to call at Carradale since 1939. In winter 1982-3 she was on duty at Colintraive-Rhubodach. From March, 1975 till early in 1981 the *Rhum* was distinguishable from her sisters by having her funnel red to the base.

T.S.M.V. "Coll" (II). In September, 1973 the *Coll* was fitted out for the Small Isles run during the overhaul of *Loch Arkaig*, being fitted with Radar and full VHF between the mast and a post on the wheelhouse; a fire-pump was installed and a ferry-door cut on the port side of the car deck. With a mobile crane on board she proceeded through the Crinan Canal, and performed Oban-Craignure for one day, with passengers only, taking up the Small Isles run from 19th November. The Portree-Raasay section was performed by *Rhum*. During a spell on Fishnish-Lochaline she released *Bruernish* for Tobermory-Mingary; and she has also done Western Ferries' Port Askaig-Feolin run on charter. During her time on the Small Isles route in April, 1979 she operated from Kyle to Canna only, while *Etive Shearwater* took the calls at Eigg, Rhum and Muck. *Coll* happened to be relieving on the Kennacraig-Gigha service when the new jetty at Tayinloan came into use, and so became the first vehicle ferry to operate on that route, from 11th November, 1980. She is the normal relief of the *Morvern* at Iona and of *Eigg* at Lismore. From summer 1986 she has been employed between Tobermory and Mingary.

D.S.M.V. "Jupiter" (III). Two much larger vehicle ferry vessels (in contemplation in various forms for quite a number of years) were ordered from Messrs. Lamont, intended for Gourock-Dunoon and Wemyss Bay-Rothesay, the first being launched in November, 1973 and completed in time to take up her intended run in the following spring. The design followed that of *Arran* (as altered) in having a flush vehicle deck aft, with not only a stern-loading ramp for use at Gourock, but also side-loading ramps for use at Dunoon; and there are main, saloon and upper decks forward with (in the case of *Jupiter* initially) a wheelhouse and bridge on the upper deck, afterwards altered (as in *Juno* from the outset) to have a flying-bridge above. The machinery consists of two Mirrlees-Blackstone 8-cylinder diesels driving fore and aft directional propellers, the exhausts being by two short thwart-ship funnels at the sides of the vehicle deck, and having tetrapod mainmasts joined to the funnels. A small foremast above the bridge supports the radar scanner. On the main deck level forward are a lounge, ticket-office and toilets, while on the deck above is another lounge with self-service cafeteria. The ships have great manoeuvrability and can spin round in their own length. When the *Juno* was completed in November, 1974, she was immediately required on the Dunoon run to give a frequent service along with *Jupiter*; and, since the departure of *Maid of Cumbrae*, the two have been the regular ships there, reliefs during overhauls having been provided by *Arran*, *Glen Sannox*, *Pioneer*, etc. In addition, one of the ships on the Dunoon route serves Kilcreggan, morning and evening. The *Jupiter* was in 1983 given necessary equipment to obtain a passenger certificate for Ardrossan or Wemyss Bay to Brodick, on which route she has provided extra capacity for passengers and vehicles.

T.S.M.V. "Pioneer" (III). For the Islay service this ship was built at Leith, reviving the name of one of the Greenock Railway Steam Packet Company's ships of 1844 (afterwards a well-known member of the Hutcheson/MacBrayne fleet) and also used for a previous Islay steamer, built in 1905. The new vessel followed the layout of the *Jupiter* and *Juno*, but without the upper lounge, and with higher bulwarks for the more exposed routes. The influence of the design of oil-rig supply ships is noticeable. She was intended in part to carry considerable quantities of whisky from Islay distilleries, and in addition is equipped with portable cattle pens on the vehicle deck to take 25 head of cattle. There are two passenger lounges, and that on the upper deck having cafeteria service, and that on the lower having a bar. The open vehicle deck can take 30 cars, or six 40ft. CRVs, and 9/10 cars. The main machinery is bridge-controlled. Navigational aids include wireless telegraphy, radio telephone, V.H.F., Radar, Echo sounder and public address system. The ship has twin controllable pitch propellers (by J. W. Berg, Sweden), twin rudders, retractable fin stabilisers (Denny Brown) and a bow thruster unit (British Pleuger), the stern ramp (by Cargospeed) being hydraulically controlled; and a hydraulic crane capable of lifting 3½ tons is provided at each side, for handling cargo at conventional piers. The absence of vibration is noticeable, despite her speed of 15·8 knots. Her Class IIA certificate allows for 273 passengers.

When launched the *Pioneer* with her tall red funnels with deep black tops looked like a traditional MacBrayne ship: unfortunately during fitting out the bases of the funnels became white (no doubt to harmonise with the superstructure) and this gave the impression of Laird Line funnels, which had not been seen for very many years.

West Loch Tarbert, which had been the mainland terminal for the Islay via Loch Fyne service since 1826, ceased to be used from 25th June, 1978, on the transfer to Kennacraig. In addition to her normal routes, the *Pioneer* has relieved on the Gourock-Dunoon-Kilcreggan, Wemyss Bay-Rothesay, Ardrossan-Brodick and Oban-Craignure stations; and, when superseded as regular Islay ship, in 1979 she had a lift installed (with ferry door cut in it) to operate the Mallaig-Armadale summer service (now her principal occupation) and to relieve on the Small Isles run. In November, 1980 she introduced a new service from Largs to Brodick on Friday evenings, continuing this up to Christmas each year till the advent of the *Isle of Arran*. On Wednesday, 11th June, 1981 she made her first visit to Iona, *Morvern* tendering.

T.S.M.V. "Suilven." To improve the Stornoway-Ullapool service, a ship under construction by Moss Rosenberg Vaerft A/S, Norway was purchased and launched by Mrs. C. B. Leith under the above name (new in the fleet) taken from the very prominent mountain near Lochinver. She arrived at Gourock in August, 1974, and has not deviated from her normal route where, with her speed of 15¼ knots, she is able to perform satisfactorily as immediate successor to the *Clansman* and with almost double her capacity, for 120 cars and 400 passengers. She has two complete decks, the lower of which is the vehicle deck, with hydraulically operated bow and stern ramps, and with hoistable car platforms which can be stowed away when not required. The engine-room is below the car deck, while on the uppermost complete deck are the passenger facilities, cafeteria, saloon, hall and toilets; also accommodation for 18 members of the crew. The bridge deck provides accommodation for nine officers, and also six 4-berth passenger cabins with shower and toilet. The propelling machinery (situated aft) consists of two Wichmann 7AX Diesels, each coupled to one variable pitch propeller, and with two bow thrusters for sideways manoeuvring. Stabilisers were fitted during her guarantee overhaul, in Garvel Graving Dock in November, 1974. She was the first of the fleet to have Caledonian MacBrayne on the side, this being done during her overhaul at Govan in November, 1983.

D.S.M.V. "Juno" (III). Both the Dunoon vessels have been chartered at various times and have sailed to such destinations as Tighnabruaich, Tarbert, Millport, Largs, and have cruised up Loch Long and on the Gareloch. For all these the display on the hull of "GOUROCK-DUNOON FERRY" was incongruous, and was removed from *Jupiter* in 1983, but kept by *Juno* till changed to "Caledonian MacBrayne" in 1985.

T.S.M.V. "Eigg" (II). The remaining three Burnett-Corless "Small Island" class vessels were completed at intervals between 1975 and 1976. This, the fifth of the series, inaugurated a temporary twice-daily service between Portree and Raasay on 18th March, 1975, which had been given on an even less regular basis by *Rhum*, during the overhaul of *Loch Arkaig*. The *Eigg* made several landings on Sconser Beach in 1975, near the site of the present slipway. On 3rd October, 1976 she took some earth-moving equipment to Easdale and brought back some cattle. She visited also the pulp-mill at Corpach, and in April, 1981 made exceptional trips to Inverliever on Loch Etive, the following year commencing visits to Glen Sanda with quarry equipment. She has been fairly constantly on the Oban-Lismore route, apart from exceptional runs such as conveying sheep from Eigg to Glenuig. From 3rd January, 1985 she has used the new slipway at Achnacroish, Lismore.

M.V. "Kildonan" (II). Purchased in March, 1975 from Mr. Murdo McSween of Fort William, the *Silver Darling* ex *Falcon*, originally a demonstration launch of The Bergius Company, was re-named as above, for tender duties at Eigg. In September, 1979 she was transferred to Loch Aline for ferrying crew to the spare vessel moored in Miodar Bay, performing also passenger runs on the Lochaline-Fishnish station in May/June, 1981 during the absence of *Canna*. After a period of idleness she was sold in 1985 to Mr. James Cowie and taken to Ardmaleish on 19th April, minus her engine.

M.V. "Staffa" (VII). About two months after the last acquisition the motor launch *Silver Spray* was bought from Wm. H. Dick Ltd., Largs for the Fionnphort-Iona ferry and for tendering at Iona, later at Eigg; and finally at Tobermory for tendering, and for the Mingary service from 11th May, 1981. For this she had a wheelhouse with small landing platform erected above the engine casing. She was succeeded in this by the *Applecross* later the same month, and thereafter did little sailing.

T.S.M.V. "Canna." The sixth "Small Island" class ship performed the last scheduled sailing to Portree from Raasay on 15th April, 1976, and inaugurated the new slip at Sconser the next day. She also visited Fladda off the north east coast of Raasay, landing on the shingle beach. In March, 1983 she relieved at Largs and on 25th November, 1984 she took a digger to Eilean Shona in Loch Moidart. She, however, became associated particularly with the Fishnish-Lochaline station till superseded there by *Isle of Cumbrae*, in the summer of 1986 (and by a "Loch" class vessel in winter).

T.S.M.V. "Raasay." The last of the series began her public service by taking over from the *Kilbrannan* at Largs (the latter being absent at Tarbert in connexion with oil rig matters). She ultimately took up her own service for which she was named, on Friday, 9th July, 1976, giving in addition evening cruises round the island, and to the Great Harbour at Rona. She relieved at Claonaig in May, 1978.

D.S.M.V. "Isle of Cumbrae" (II). Following the design of the two large Kyle of Lochalsh ferries, but about two-thirds of their size, this drive-through ship was built at Troon for the Cumbrae Slip service from Largs. With directional propellers fore and aft she is as manoeuvrable as *Jupiter* and *Juno*, but with a speed of only 8·7 knots, which suffices for the short crossing. Her name was chosen by competition among the schoolchildren of Millport and, in addition to beinig appropriate, is an interesting revival of an old Buchanan name, borne by their paddle steamer which began life as the first *Jeanie Deans* of the North British S.P. Co., and for several years in the First War operated under charter to the G. & S.W.R. as *Isle of Cumbrae*, even performing short charters to the Caledonian and North British Companies, so that the name has associations with several of the constituents of Caledonian MacBrayne. She was the first to have a Cal-Mac funnel emblem on the wheelhouse. In August, 1986 she was transferred to Fishnish-Lochaline, where her greater vehicle capacity will be useful. She reverts to Cumbrae in winter.

D.S.M.V. "Saturn." The Wemyss Bay-Rothesay route did not get its new regular ship till 1978, the service being maintained principally by the *Glen Sannox* after the introduction of stern-loading at Wemyss Bay and side-loading by link-span at Rothesay. The new vessel was a product of the Ailsa yard at Troon, somewhat similar to *Jupiter* and *Juno*, but with a tripod mainmast at the rear of the saloon deck, which gives her a better-balanced profile. She seems now to have settled down, and has seldom deviated from her accustomed route, serving on occasion on that from Gourock to Dunoon and Kilcreggan and having performed a *Columba* centenary charter in 1978 to Ardrishaig for the Clyde River Steamer Club. The choice of a G.S.W.R.-type name not previously used is noteworthy.

·   ·   ·   ·   ·   ·   ·

From time to time small craft have been chartered for the Lismore run, including in March, 1979 the *Dumaras*, normally used for cruising among the islands with overnight accommodation for passengers which would not be required on the Lismore route!

T.S.M.V. "Claymore" (III). Named by Lady Kirkhill, wife of the Minister of State at the Scottish Office, when launched at Leith on 31st August, 1978, this ship is a development in design from that of the same builders' *Pioneer*, but with four decks above the car deck, the top one being the navigating bridge deck, containing bridge, wheelhouse, radio room and radio officers' cabin. Below this is the bridge deck, containing the navigation lights and officers' accommodation—six single cabins, each with toilet. On the boat deck below this is the crew's accommodation—six single and six double-berth cabins, plus open deck for passengers on three sides of the crew's accommodation. The next deck down is mainly occupied by the spacious combined saloon and cafeteria, with galley, stewardesses' accommodation, officers' mess and crew's mess also on this deck, extensions aft on each side containing the imposing funnels, which, being rounded fore and aft, are more pleasing in appearance than those of *Pioneer*. The lower saloon and bar are forward of the car deck, the arrangements at the stern being also similar to those of the 1974 vessel, but with a 36-ton lift hydraulically operated, something which the *Pioneer* had not when new. She has sleeping berths on the lower deck, in the manner of *Hebrides*, *Columba* and *Clansman*. She could carry 300 passengers on Class IIA certificate, or 500 on Class III, with capacity for 47 cars, or 23 cars and six 30-foot trailers; also there is provision for 240 head of cattle. The machinery comprises two Mirrlees Blackstone type ESL 16M 16-cylinder 4-stroke turbo-charged engines with three Volvo Penta 6-cylinder 4-stroke turbo-charged Diesels each driving Macfarlane alternators of 147 kW capacity. Unlike the *Pioneer*, whose bow-thrust is electrically driven, her bow-thrust unit has its own engine—a fourth Volvo Penta. She has her own effluent disposal unit, in the stabiliser compartment forward of the main engine room, beyond which is the passengers' sleeping accommodation—four cabins each with four berths and eight cabins each with two berths.

Claymore took over the Oban-Castlebay-Lochboisdale run from the *Iona* early in 1979, leaving the latter free for the Islay service. She has not deviated much from that route, apart from cattle, etc. runs to Islay and an exceptional charter from Govan to Rothesay on 7th June, 1986.

T.S.M.V. "Lochmor" (II). Launched at Troon on 11th June, 1979, this ship was named by Mrs. G. S. Sinclair, wife of the General Manager of Caledonian MacBrayne Ltd., reviving the name of one of the 1930 sisters, which had been the first vessel specifically allocated to the Small Isles run when it became separated from that to the Outer Isles. The machinery comprises two Volvo Penta TMD 120A Diesel engines: two Perkins auxiliary Diesel-driven 21 kW alternators provide power; and the propulsion machinery is controlled from the wheelhouse or bridge wings. Steering is by a short "gear stick" lever, although there is a traditional steering wheel—of metal—for emergency use. A two-ton folding hydraulic HIAB crane is positioned on the starboard side of the after deck for transferring cargo into the ferry-boats at Rhum, Eigg and Muck or the pier at Canna, additional ribbed belting being installed on either side of the hull where the ferry-boats come alongside; the after end of the main deck is at a lower level than the rest of that deck and is open for stowage of cargo including space for two cars (lifted on). Forward of the funnel is an open area, with an inflated rubber dinghy for six persons; and forward of this area is a large deckhouse containing the passenger entrance, and three companion-ways to the lower deck, giving access to the after saloon, forward saloon (with small counter and serving area containing a tea-urn) and to the separate cabins for the mate, engineer, seaman and greaser, who, along with the captain comprise the entire crew. The reason for the three separate companionways is of course that the hull is divided by watertight bulkheads. Above the deckhouse is a landing platform for use at low tides. The small tripod mast rises from this deck.

The ship's route in summer includes visits from Mallaig to Kyle three times a week, with cruises in summer to Loch Duich or to the Crowlin Islands and (until 1985) to Portree.

T.S.M.V. "Isle of Arran" (III). Although normally on the Arran run, this ship early in her career qualified as a West Highland one by acting as relief on the Stornoway-Ullapool station in her first and third winters in service. She has accommodation for 80 cars or 10 articulated lorries, and for 800 passengers, with a crew of 16. Loading is by bow and stern ramps: she is fitted with bow-thrust, twin rudders, with computerised control and monitoring system in the engine-room, and the usual modern navigational aids.

T.S.M.V. "Hebridean Isles." After the launch of the *Isle of Arran* in December, 1983 it was announced that the Government had authorised the Scottish Transport Group to invite tenders for the building of a new drive-through vessel to take the place of the *Hebrides* on the Uig-Lochmaddy-Tarbert triangle. It was reported that the contract had been awarded to Cochrane Shipbuilders Limited, Selby, where the launch took place—sideways into the River Ouse, with an enormous splash—on 4th July, 1985, the naming ceremony being performed by H.R.H. The Duchess of Kent, the first "Royal" launch for this fleet, famous as operators on the "Royal Route". A contribution towards the cost of the new ship having been made from the European Economic Community, she appropriately carries their emblem. She was handed over at King George V Dock, Hull on 2nd December, 1985. On completing her relieving duty on the Stornoway-Ullapool run, she moved to the Oban-Craignure station temporarily, taking up her own service on 8th May, 1986, using the new linkspans at Tarbert and Lochmaddy, but lift-loading at Uig where the linkspan was not ready. The hull of this ship is similar in design to that of the *Isle of Arran*, but the internal layout differs, particularly in having a lift in addition to bow- and stern-loading; and the funnels are placed farther aft.

The main machinery comprises two Mirrlees Blackstone M.B.275 8-cylinder 4-stroke unidirectional turbo-charged water-cooled

Diesels, which drive two Ulstein 4-bladed propellers (variable pitch) through Ulstein-type gearboxes, with reduction ratio of 1.97 to 1. Auxiliary power is provided by six Volvo Penta Diesels, electrical power being supplied by four Volvo TD 121 CHC Diesels working in parallel. There is an additional harbour set, while the bow-thruster is powered by a TMD Diesel rated at 300 hp heavy duty at 1800 rpm. The hydraulic equipment (by McGregor Navire) comprises the bow-visor operating gear, the bow and stern ramps, the lift with side ramps and integral turntables, and an electro-hydraulic power pack/pump unit with capstan and windlass and full cross connexion facilities for emergency operation. The ship is provided with stabilisers, by Brown Bros., Edinburgh.

The lift platform spans the vessel's width, and is fitted with two side ramps, and manually operated turntables. The bow ramp is in three sections, and the stern ramp in one section plus flap, designed for the same load as the bow ramp. Navigational aids include two Radar sets (Decca), R.T. W/T V.H.F. Echo Sounder, Gyro Compass Auto Pilot, Navstar Navigator with Navtex Recorder. She carries four lifeboats, two liferafts and buoyant apparatus for 260 persons, passenger capacities being 240 on Class II A certificate and 500 on Class III the crew being 24. The car capacity is approximately 80, or 10 articulated lorries. The non-smoking lounge on the port side contains 34 reclining seats, the bar lounge on starboard side 57 passenger seats, the cafeteria 102 passenger seats and the upper deck observation lounge 50 passenger seats. An invalid lift from car deck to passenger lounge is provided.

D.S.M.V. "Loch Striven." At the launch of the *Hebridean Isles* it was announced that the Company was considering the building of two 12-car ferries for the Largs-Cumbrae station, and shortly afterwards it was confirmed that the order for these had gone to R. Dunston (Hessle) Ltd., followed by an order for other two similar ferries from the same builders, the design being developed from that of the *Isle of Cumbrae*, but with covered passenger accommodation on both sides and only two vehicle lanes, to accommodate twelve cars or one articulated lorry. The passenger lounges at the sides provide covered cushioned seating accommodation, and there is open deck space above.

Loading is by hinged articulated ramps at each end, operated hydraulically from the wheelhouse, or manually in emergency. Ramps of Kvaerner manufacture are fitted on *Loch Striven* and *Loch Linnhe*. On the starboard side above the promenade deck is a small wheelhouse (painted as a funnel), surmounted by a lattice mast of tubular steel inclined inwards to the centre-line. Equipment includes a deckhead-mounted Racal Decca radar, a Cooke shelf-type compass, a Sailor VHF radio telephone, and electric whistle control and a Minerva alarm panel for fire detection and extinguishing systems; also

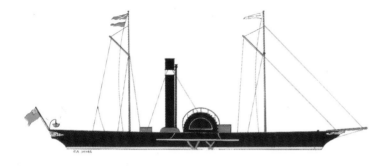

From Drawing by John A. Innes

70   P.S. *Duntroon Castle*

From Painting by John Nicholson based on a photograph

71   P.S. *Glencoe* ex *Mary Jane*

Leaving Kyle of Lochalsh c.1930

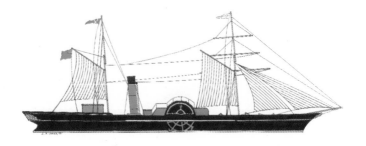

From Drawing by John A. Innes

72   P.S. *Chevalier* (I)

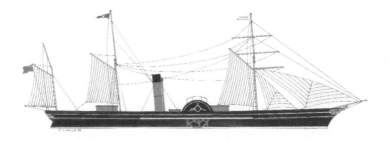

From Drawing by John A. Innes

73   P.S. *Clansman* (I)

From Drawing by John A. Innes

74   P.S. *Iona* (II)

From hand-coloured photograph, C.L.D.D. Collection

75   P.S. *Iona* (III)

Approaching Rothesay

From hand-coloured photograph. C.L.D.D. Collection

76   S.S. *Claymore* (I)

Approaching Oban

G.E.L.

77   T.S.S. *King George V*

Leaving Oban for Isles of the Sea, 6/9/74

G.E.L.

78   T.S.M.V. *Loch Arkaig* and T.S.M.V. *Bute* (V)

At Mallaig, 2/7/75

G.E.L.

79   T.S.M.V. *Maid of Skelmorlie*

Leaving Rothesay on inward Loch Fyne Mail run, 11/10/69

80   T.S.M.V. *Hebrides* (II)
Leaving Tarbert, Harris, 22/6/83

81   T.S.M.V. *Columba* (II)
Re-embarking passengers from M.V. *Iona* (VI) off Martyr's Bay, Iona, 10/6/75

82   T.S.M.V. *Columba* (II)

At North Pier and T.S.M.V. *Clansman* (IV) at Railway Pier Ferry Berth, Oban, 1975

83   T.S.M.V. *Claymore* (II)

At North Pier, and T.S.M.V. *Glen Sannox* (III) at Railway Pier Ferry Berth, Oban, 1975

G.E.L.

84 T.S.M.V. *Glen Sannox* (III)

In Oban Bay, with Hutcheson Monument on Kerrera in background, 21/11/85

G.E.L.

85 T.S.M.V. *Caledonia* (III)

In Oban Bay, 6/8/85

G.E.L.

86   T.S.M.V. *Iona* (VII)

As built, approaching Castlebay, Barra, 12/6/74

John A. Innes

87   T.S.M.V. *Iona* (VII)

As altered, at North Pier and T.S.M.V. *Arran* as altered to end-loading,

at Railway Pier Ferry Berth, Oban, 1975

G.E.L.

88   D.S.M.V. *Lochalsh* (III)

Leaving Kyle for Kyleakin, 11/9/73

G.E.L.

89   T.S.M.V. *Pioneer* (III)

Arriving at Armadale, 2/8/79

G.E.L.

90   T.S.M.V. *Suilven*

Off Kyleakin about to take up Stornoway run, 27/8/74, with Eilean Bhan Lighthouse in background

G.E.L.

91   D.S.M.V. *Jupiter* (III)

Off Criagmore, with Buachille Fhinn and Castle Toward in background, 2/11/85

92　　　　　　　　　　T.S.M.V. *Eigg* (II)

Approaching Railway Pier, Oban, 21/11/85

93　　　　　　　　　　D.S.M.V. *Saturn*

At Ardrishaig on charter to the Clyde River Steamer Club to celebrate the

centenary of P.S. *Columba*, 29/4/78

94　　　　　T.S.M.V. *Canna*

Leaving Portree for Raasay, 31/3/76

95　　　　　T.S.M.V. *Claymore* (III)

Off Lismore, 1/6/85

96   T.S.M.V. *Lochmor* (II)
Passing Eilean Bhan Lighthouse, 17/7/81

97   T.S.M.V. *Isle of Arran* (III)
Approaching Ullapool from Stornoway, 9/10/84

98　　　　　　T.S.M.V. *Sound of Islay*

In West Loch Tarbert, 13/7/77

99　　　　　　T.S.M.V. *Sound of Jura*

At Kennacraig Pier, 14/8/74

G.E.L.

100   T.S.M.V. *Highland Seabird*

Leaving Fort William, 7/9/77

G.E.L.

101   P.S. *Waverley* (IV)

Arriving at Crinan, passing the Canal Sea Lock, 3/5/85

remote controls for the main engines' speeds, and handwheels on a console to control the Voith-Schneider cycloidal propulsion units, which assure precise navigation with positive thrust in any direction. Power is provided by two diagonally-aligned Volvo Penta high-speed Diesels, normally running at a constant speed, each driving one propulsion unit through a Fluidrive coupling to a Norgear gearbox. Speed is about 9.25 knots.

The European Economic Community being involved also in the funding of the new ships, it was appropriate that the launching ceremony of the first should be performed by Mrs. Beverley Mathijsen, wife of the Director General. The revival of "Loch" names is noteworthy, these having been almost standard in the MacBrayne fleet between 1929 and 1955, some of them dating back to 1876-7.

The *Loch Striven* sailed up the east coast from Hull to Inverness, then through the Caledonian Canal, at Fort Augustus passing the remains of the *Gairlochy*. She entered service between Largs and the Cumbrae Slip.

D.S.M.V. "Loch Linnhe." The second of the "Loch" class vessels was launched at Hessle on 22nd May, 1986, and was taken immediately to Hull for fitting out. She obtained a Class VIA certificate for 50 passengers and three crew for Lochaline-Fishnish, Lochranza-Claonaig, Oban-Lismore and Sconser-Raasay. She made her debut on the Fishnish-Lochaline route, and changed places with the *Isle of Cumbrae* in the week-end of 2nd/4th August, 1986, in winter reverting to her first route.

D.S.M.V. "Loch Riddon." The third of these ferries is employed principally on the Colintraive-Rhubodach run. This (and the fourth) differ from the first and second in having McGregor-Navire type ramps, with (like the others) remote or local control.

D.S.M.V. "Loch Ranza." It is intended that drive-through facilities will be introduced in 1987 on the Claonaig-Lochranza route when this ship enters service.

.   .   .   .

After much discussion, the order for the new vessel for Mull and Colonsay was placed with Ferguson-Ailsa Limited, on the lines of the *Isle of Arran*, without a lift or open vehicle deck, and with one funnel on the centre line. Unfortunatley the advent of new ships inevitably means the withdrawal of others, but that has always been so and has to be accepted.

G

CHAPTER X

CLYDE & CAMPBELTOWN SHIPPING COMPANY, LTD.

THIS Company, until 30th September, 1949, a subsidiary of David MacBrayne, Ltd., maintained (in modified form and in some instances by road transport) the cargo services to the Clyde Coast and Loch Fyne ports formerly carried on by Messrs. MacBrayne themselves and the Lochfyne & Glasgow Steam Packet Co. Ltd. (to Loch Fyne); by Messrs. Hill & Co. (to Rothesay, Millport, Arran and Loch Fyne); and by John Williamson to Dunoon, Holy Loch ports, Rothesday, etc. It also maintained cargo services to the West of Arran and Campbeltown, in its capacity as successor to the Campbeltown & Glasgow Steam Packet Joint Stock Co. Ltd., which was taken over by Clyde Cargo Steamers, Ltd. at midnight on 3rd/4th March, 1937. The last-named changed its name to Clyde & Campbeltown Shipping Co. Ltd. on 29th March in the same year.

Clyde Cargo Steamers, Ltd.

It was on 19th August, 1915, that this company was registered, to co-ordinate the Clyde cargo services of David MacBrayne, Ltd., John Williamson, Hill & Company and the Minard Castle Shipping Co. Ltd. (the successors of the Lochfyne & Glasgow S.P. Co. Ltd.), a joint advertisement by these four concerns having appeared on 1st July in that year, intimating restricted goods services from Glasgow to the Coast, Arran and Loch Fyne. Mr. J. D. Rodger, of Messrs. Hill, became managing director of the new company. At first each of the three steamers carried the funnel-colouring of one of the constituents, viz. *Bute 4* kept Messrs. Hill & Co.'s own colouring of red with black top; *Minard Castle* retained her owner's black funnel; and *Arran* had her funnel painted white with black top, to represent the Williamson interest. Shortly afterwards, however, black became standard for all, and remained so till changed in February, 1937, to red with black top, the same as the standard MacBrayne colouring. The house-flag of Clyde Cargo Steamers, Ltd. was blue, bearing the initials C.C.S. in white; that of the Campbeltown & Glasgow Company was a white pennant, bearing in red an Iona cross (representing the old Cross in the main street of Campbeltown), flown above a pennant having horizontal stripes of red, white and blue. Later the words "Royal Mail" were added, one on each side of the cross. The flag of Clyde & Campbeltown Shipping Co. Ltd. was a white pennant with the red Campbeltown cross, following by the initials C.C.S. in red.

Hill & Co.

It is understood that Messrs. Hill's first steamer was *Success*, built in 1876 to succeed a smack of the same name. She was sold in 1882 and re-registered at Greenock in the name of Wm. W. C. Smith, Glasgow, being re-sold in the following year to Thomas R. Lee, Sunderland and others, and wrecked in October, 1884.

The first *Bute* was launched on 22nd February, 1879, to the order of Messrs. Hill & Co., for the purpose of giving greater carrying facilities for goods between and among Glasgow, Rothesay, Largs, Millport and Arran. On 18th December, 1890, she was wrecked on the south-east headland of the Mull of Kintyre while on an exceptional run from Liverpool to Stornoway with a cargo of salt.

Messrs. Hill acquired the paddle steamers *Marquis of Lorne* and *Dunoon Castle* in 1882 and 1883 respectively, and to these the names *Cumbrae* and *Arran* were respectively given. They were employed in passenger services, the former principally from Fairlie Pier to Millport in connexion with the Glasgow & South Western Railway. *Arran* was sold to A. Campbell on 2nd July, 1884 (Mr. J. Hill retaining management of her till 10th November, 1885). She left the Hill fleet after sale in April, 1890 for service on the Thames and was broken up in 1896. *Cumbrae* remained till succeeded at Fairlie by the Railway Company's own steamers, in 1892; she was sold in 1894 and became a coal-hulk at Newry.

The screw steamer *Bute No. 2*, launched on 17th April, 1890, was named by Miss Ada Hill, daughter of the late Captain James Hill, and was intended for the Clyde passenger and cargo services. In July, 1891 she was sold to Carenero Railway & Navigation Co. Ltd., La Guayra, Venezuela, by whom she was re-named *Higuerote*, being then under the Venezuelan flag. (The company was later transferred to Amsterdam.) The ship was sold about 1901 to V. Crassus, La Guayra, and re-named *Ossun*; she was omitted from Lloyd's Register after 1931-2.

The third *Bute* was launched on 12th January, 1892, and, on trial on 30th January, attained a speed of 10½ knots. She was sold in 1899 to the Glasgow Steam Coaster Co. Ltd., and named *Dunard*, being owned by Kynoch-Arklow, Ltd., London, from 1916 to 1919, thereafter by The Channel Islands & South Coast Shipping Co. Ltd., Guernsey, till about 1925. She was lost during World War II.

S.S. "Bute 4." The fourth *Bute* was launched on 22nd January, 1898, and was one of the two vessels contributed by Messrs. Hill to the combined fleet of Clyde Cargo Steamers, Ltd. Similar in design to her immediate predecessor, she became very well known at the Clyde Coast ports, and remained in service till broken up at Ardrossan in 1935.

S.S. "Barmore"/"Arran" (II). The steamer *Barmore*, originally registered in the name of William Hay, Tarbert, Lochfyne, had passed to John McKinney (later McKinney & Rafferty), and in 1885 to Robert Thom, Rosneath, by whom she was used as a yacht. Sold in 1911 to Wm. Cooper & Sons, Kirkwall, she was in November, 1912, purchased by Messrs. Hill and re-named *Arran* in the following year. She passed to Clyde Cargo Steamers, Ltd. in 1915, and in August, 1917, was sold to John S. Boyle, Fish Merchant, Glasgow, passing in 1921 to John S. P. Begbie, Glasgow, and in 1923 to Roderick N. McInnes, there. She disappeared from the registers during 1924.

Minard Castle Shipping Co. Ltd.

This company had been registered in 1913 on a change in ownership of the steamer *Minard Castle* previously owned by the Lochfyne & Glasgow Steam Packet Co. Ltd., which dated from 1882 and was really the successor to the Jura Steamboat Company (Donald Dewar), owner from 1876 of the *Jura* of 1869 (a puffer of dimensions for the Crinan Canal).

S.S. "Minard Castle." Launched on 19th June, 1882, this steamer was intended to run in opposition to Messrs. MacBrayne's Loch Fyne steamers, a number of merchants connected with that district being interested in the owning company, the Lochfyne & Glasgow S.P. Co. Ltd. On trial on 12th July, 1882, she attained a speed of 12 knots. She was a very neat little steamer, built on the lines of the coastal and cross-channel passenger and cargo steamers of her day, with one funnel (amidships) and two tall masts.

In February, 1913, she was taken over by Mr. R. G. Campbell and was registered in name of James Kenneth, Irvine, being shortly afterwards transferred to Minard Castle Shipping Co. Ltd., with John MacCalman as Manager. She came under the control of Clyde Cargo Steamers, Ltd. in 1915, remaining registered, however, in name of the Minard Castle Company till 1922, when she was transferred to the parent company. During the coal strike in April and May, 1921, under the heading "Reduced Sailings—Williamson-Buchanan Steamers" *Minard Castle* or other steamer was advertised by John Williamson & Co. to sail from Glasgow (Bridge Wharf) at 11 a.m. on Tuesdays, Thursdays and Saturdays with goods and passengers for Kirn, Dunoon, Innellan and Rothesay, returning from Rothesay at 1 p.m. on the alternate days.

She was broken up at Port Glasgow about the end of 1926.

.   .   .   .

During the 1899 season the Lochfyne & Glasgow S.P. Co. Ltd.

had one other ship, viz. the paddle steamer *Sultana*, acquired from John Williamson, and employed on a passenger and cargo run from Glasgow *via* Dunoon, Fairlie, Millport, Skipness and Tarbert to Ardrishaig. She was sold on 27th March, 1900, to M. Clavel, Cherbourg, and scrapped about seven years later.

Clyde Cargo Steamers, Ltd., 1915-1937

S.S. "Lapwing"/"Cowal" (I). This ship, previously a member of the MacBrayne fleet, was acquired in 1918, and registered in name of Mr. J. D. Rodger from 23rd April in that year, being from 3rd July, 1923, in that of Clyde Cargo Steamers, Ltd. She was requisitioned by the Government and placed on the mail run from Penzance to the Scilly Isles under the management of the Hain Steamship Co. Ltd., St. Ives, and after a spell there, was for about nine months engaged in sailing between Plymouth and the Channel Islands. About 1920 she returned to the Clyde, and was extensively altered, being converted into a pure cargo-carrier. The main mast was removed, and independent cranes fitted fore and aft instead of the one original derrick forward. On 25th January, 1926, her name was changed to *Cowal*. She was sold in April, 1930 and scrapped in 1931, her register being closed on 9th April in that year.

S.S. "Jane." Launched on 8th June, 1901, for Andrew Bremner, Wick, this trawler was bought by Duncan MacIver, Stornoway in 1919 and in 1924 was purchased by Clyde Cargo Steamers, Ltd. from Duncan MacIver, Ltd. for the purpose of developing an express service to Rothesay. She was sold in May, 1926, to Chas. F. Paton, Glasgow, and in 1930 to John Best (Edinburgh) Ltd., passing in 1932 to Peter C. McLeod, Alloa, and later the same year to Guyton & Co. Ltd., Great Yarmouth. Her name disappeared from the registers about 1934.

S.S. "Lintie." Built in 1909 for Steel & Bennie, Ltd., this vessel had been employed in their Glasgow-Greenock cargo trade. She was acquired by Clyde Cargo Steamers, Ltd., in the spring of 1925, and was employed on the Holy Loch, etc., cargo run for them, for less than a year only, being sold later in 1925 to Lough Sand & Gravel Co., and later registered in name of J. Shiels, Belfast. In 1935 she passed to Charles M. Murdoch, Dundee, and in 1938 to Tay Sand Co. Ltd., Dundee.

S.S. "Minard." This steamer, which was launched on 1st December, 1925, ran trials on 19th January, 1926, and perpetuated the name of *Minard Castle* in a modified form. After passing to the British Transport Commission she carried the yellow funnel with black top and after sale in April, 1955 was broken up by Smith & Houston Ltd., at Port Glasgow.

S.S. "Arran" (III). Third of the name, this steamer was similar to *Bute 4*, and succeeded *Jane* in the fleet. She was wrecked on Barmore Island, Loch Fyne, on 31st December, 1932, near the point where *Chevalier* had stranded six years earlier.

S.S. "Ardyne." A similar steamer to *Minard* was added in 1928. These were handsome little ships, with machinery amidships and independent cranes for the handling of cargo. Both originally had certificates for fifty passengers, but after the second war carried only twelve. Sold at the same time as *Minard, Ardyne* was used by John Lee, Belfast for transport of sand and gravel, but in July the same year was scrapped at Troon.

S.S. "Arran" (IV)/**"Kildonan"**(I). To take the place of the previous *Arran* a new vessel of this name was built by the Ardrossan Dockyard Ltd., and was launched on 31st July, 1933. She was somewhat similar to her predecessor, but with a cruiser stern.

With the development of road transport to places on the mainland the cargo services were gradually cut down, and they ceased altogether to certain ports, such as those on the Holy Loch and Largs. As above-mentioned, *Bute 4* was withdrawn in 1935, but was not replaced. In 1953 *Arran* was re-named *Kildonan*, to make way for the C.S.P. Co.'s car ferry and after being laid up at Greenock in 1957, was scrapped in the following year, at Port Glasgow.

Campbeltown & Glasgow Steam Packet Joint Stock Co. Ltd.

Formed in 1826 by some local merchants and others, and with its headquarters at Campbeltown, this concern was registered as unlimited in 1867 and as a limited company in 1883. A fuller account of its history will be found in the Centenary History of the Campbeltown & Glasgow Steam Packet Joint Stock Company, Ltd., published by the proprietors of the *Campbeltown Courier* in April, 1927. The Campbeltown steamers were distinguishable by their funnels which were black, red and black in approximately equal portions. The hulls were black, with pink waterline.

The Company's first steamer was *Duke of Lancaster*, built at Liverpool in 1822 and purchased when about four years old. In 1835 she was given an extensive overhaul, and in 1836 instituted an extended service to Larne and Islay. From 1827 calls were made also at Ayr; but from 1841 this and the Larne and Islay sailings were (except on special occasions) discontinued. *Duke of Lancaster* was sold on 30th May, 1845, and broken up.

The second steamer of the fleet, and the first actually built for the company, was *St. Kiaran*, which was sold in 1848 to J. Davidson & Co., Leith, to sail to Copenhagen, later returning to the Clyde for R. P. Stephens, and still later passing to Joseph Ibbotson, Goole.

A similar steamer to the foregoing, but built of iron, was *Duke of Cornwall*, which appeared in 1842. After a spell laid up in Bowling Harbour, she was sold on 20th October, 1866, for scrapping.

P.S. *Celt*, built in 1848, was a fine iron steamer, and long a favourite on the Campbeltown route. She had a clipper bow, one funnel (aft), two masts and large paddle-boxes, each ornamented by a gilt figure of a hand holding a dirk. She was sold in April, 1868 for scrapping but was given a new boiler and foredeck, and became a tug on the River Hooghly at Calcutta. A somewhat similar steamer, but with straight stem, was *Druid*, constructed in 1857 and sold in 1868 to John Robertson, Shipbuilder, Greenock (presumably in part payment for *Kintyre*). She was converted into a three-masted schooner, and was last heard of on 5th October, 1880, when she left Irvine with coal for Lisbon, and is believed to have foundered in the Bay of Biscay.

Encouraged by the success of an opposition company in the running of day trips to Campbeltown, the Campbeltown & Glasgow Company had the paddle steamer *Gael* built for this purpose in 1867. Her maiden voyage was made on 17th April in that year, and a dinner was held on board to celebrate her advent. She is said to have attained a speed of 16 knots on this run, and from the first became extremely popular. Originally flush-decked, *Gael* was fitted with a deck-saloon (with alleyways) aft in 1879, the furnishings of it and of the saloon below (which then became the dining saloon) being on the most lavish scale of the time. She was also re-boilered, and improvements were made to the paddles. It is understood that a surface condenser was installed in place of one of the jet pattern.

Strange to relate, on her resumption of duty the *Gael's* popularity deserted her. The improvements in accommodation did not come up to expectations; the speed was unsatisfactory; and her coal consumption proved far greater than had been anticipated. This was a grave disappointment to her owners; and, after only a few seasons more, she was sold in 1883 to the Great Western Railway Company, in whose name she was registered at Milford. During 1884-5 she was on the Weymouth-Cherbourg route, and during 1886-9 (or some part of this period) she was on the Bristol Channel, plying, it is understood, between Portishead and Ilfracombe. It appears that she also functioned on the Weymouth-Channel Islands and Penzance-Scilly Isles stations, presumably on charter. In 1891 she was purchased by Mr. MacBrayne, and the remainder of her history will be found commencing on page 70.

The first screw steamer for the Campbeltown fleet was *Kintyre* launched on 10th June, 1868, and one of the prettiest ships ever seen on

the Clyde, with a beautiful clipper bow and graceful lines, a single
funnel and two masts. Fitted originally with simple machinery, this
was compounded in 1882. She had an extensive overhaul in 1893,
being re-boilered and having the quarter-deck opened up so as to give
more deck and passenger accommodation. Unfortunately she was
sunk off Skelmorlie on 18th September, 1907, by the steamer *Maori*,
then running trials. In recent years her wreck has been visited by
divers.

Another beautiful yacht-like steamer was *Kinloch*. Ordered on
12th December, 1877, she was designed by Mr. Robertson, Junior,
son of the builder of *Kintyre*, and was launched by Messrs. Inglis on
30th May, 1878, being completed on 9th July in that year. Fitted with
compound machinery from the outset, she was re-boilered in 1890.
She remained on the Campbeltown route till superseded by *Dalriada*
in 1926, being sold in May of that year to the Channel Islands Packet
Company, Ltd., for service between the Channel Islands and France.
She was broken up at Bo'ness in 1928. When the *Kinloch* was amissing
in a fog on 17th November, 1909 a steamer named *Nightingale* was
chartered to take 12 passengers and cargo to Campbeltown.

S.S. "Davaar." the older of the two steamers in the fleet when it
was absorbed in 1937 was *Davaar*, which had been built to take the
place of *Gael* in the day excursion service. She had been launched at
Govan on 17th May, 1885, and was similar to, but somewhat larger
than *Kinloch* with a narrow deck-saloon aft, having alleyways outside.
She also was designed by Mr. Robertson, Junior. In March, 1896 her
forecastle deck was extended by 12 ft. and saloon stair covered.

Originally *Davaar* had two funnels, but in 1903 she was re-
boilered and re-appeared with only one, of considerably greater
diameter than those previously carried. At the same time a new
saloon the full width of the hull was fitted and the promenade-deck
extended to the stern. It is generally agreed that her appearance was
enhanced by the alterations, one of the few instances of such
improvement when changes are made from the original design.

After the loss of *Kintyre*, the service was carried on by *Kinloch*
and *Davaar* alone, one leaving Glasgow and the other Campbeltown,
each morning. The day excursion traffic was by this time in the hands
of Turbine Steamers, Ltd., and not much was done in this direction by
the old company till the appearance of *Dalriada* in 1926.

During July and August, 1915, the passenger service was operated from Ardrossan, a goods service being run from Glasgow on
three days per week. From 1st September, 1915, however, Wemyss
Bay became the terminus for the passenger sailings, which continued
till connexions *via* Prince's Pier and Gourock were resumed on 1st
April, 1919.

Davaar and *Kinloch* carried on till the latter was succeeded in
1926 by *Dalriada*; thereafter *Dalriada* and *Davaar* maintained the

service till the outbreak of the second war, having carried the red funnel with black top from 1937. *Davaar* left Campbeltown on 2nd October, 1939 on what was stated to be her last run. She was then laid up in East India Harbour, Greenock; but in January, 1940, she returned to service when *Dalriada* had to be withdrawn after damage by collision. She then had a black funnel and black saloon. The passenger service came to an end on 16th March, 1940. In July of that year *Davaar* was requisitioned and sent to Newhaven, where she was kept with steam up, ready to be sunk as a blockship. Fortunately this was not necessary; but she was beached near Newhaven Harbour, and scrapped in July, 1943.

S.S. "Dalriada." This steamer, launched on 16th March, 1926, broke the tradition of the clipper bow. She had not the yacht-like appearance of some of her predecessors, but was fitted with a slanting stem, two masts, and a very large funnel. She broke the record of all the previous steamers of the Company by doing the run from Gourock to Campbeltown in less than three hours on 30th April, 1926, and could attain about 17 knots. She has been stated to have been the fastest single-screw steamer in the world, but it has also been claimed that the London & Edinburgh Shipping Company's *Royal Fusilier* and *Royal Archer* were capable of 17½ knots.

In addition to the regular sailings, *Dalriada* made extra runs on Saturday afternoons in summer, giving afternoon excursions to Campbeltown or Carradale and back. She maintained the Campbeltown services from 2nd October, 1939, alone, her funnel being painted black from about the middle of that month, and her saloon a few days later. Early in January, 1940, she was in collision with a destroyer, and went to Messrs. Lamont's slip for repair. She was laid up in East India Harbour, Greenock till April, 1941, when she went to work as a salvage vessel. She was sunk in the Edinburgh Channel, in the Thames Estuary, on 19th June, 1942; and about four years later her wreck was blown up to clear the channel.

Clyde & Campbeltown Shipping Co. Ltd.

S.S. "Marie." The first steamer acquired after the absorption of the old Campbeltown Company, and the change of name to the above style, was the small vessel *Marie*, purchased in June, 1939, from Messrs. McKinney & Rafferty, Fish Salesmen, Glasgow. (She had been on charter from time to time to Clyde Cargo Steamers, Ltd.) In 1947 she was extensively overhauled, but was sold to Norwegian owners in 1949.

During part of 1945 and 1946 the motor vessel *Empire Tulip* was chartered from the Ministry of Transport for the Campbeltown cargo service.

From 31st December, 1948, the Company's steamers ceased to call at Kirn, Tighnabruaich, Ormidale, Tarbert and Ardrishaig, road transport, provided either by the Company, or by Messrs. Mitchell of Strone, being available as an alternative at these places, and cargo for Kirn being landed by the Company's steamers at Dunoon.

A proposal by David MacBrayne Limited to acquire all the assets of the Clyde & Campbeltown Shipping Co., Ltd. was deferred in December, 1947. A Government notice served on that company recorded October, 1948 was for nationalisation of road haulage; but in view of the difficulty of segregating land and sea activities it was recommended that both be taken over, or the notice withdrawn. In November, 1949 it was agreed that all shares in the Clyde & Campbeltown Company be transferred to the British Transport Commission at a price to be agreed. This was back-dated to 1st October, the C. & C.S. Co., Ltd. becoming a subsidiary of the B.T.S., through the Railway Executive, the shares being transferred to The Caledonian S.P. Co. Ltd. The steamers thereafter had Caledonian funnels.

From 1st October, 1949, the services to Millport and Brodick were operated from Ardrossan, the only other steamer service retained being that from Glasgow to Rothesay. The fleet consisted of *Minard*, *Ardyne* and *Arran*. Road transport was substituted for the Dunoon and Campbeltown calls.

Other owners commenced services to take the places of those abandoned by this Company, but these did not long continue.

The Arran service ceased when the car-carrying vessel *Glen Sannox* was placed on the run in 1957. The cargo steamers were sold, and the company was without ships till after its change of name on 31st December, 1959 to Caledonian Steam Packet Company (Irish Services) Limited. It then took over operation of the Stranraer-Larne services. Further changes of name occurred—to British Transport Ship Management (Scotland) Limited from 1st September, 1971 and to Sealink (Scotland) Limited in March, 1980.

CHAPTER XI

VARIOUS WEST HIGHLAND FLEETS

PERIOD 1820-1840. The early months of 1822 witnessed an extension of the West Highland services, a steamer called *Argyll*, which had been plying between Glasgow and Inveraray, being despatched on 7th February to Stornoway via Campbeltown and the Mull of Kintyre. In 1823, this vessel was re-engined, and performed an excursion to Campbeltown, Dublin and Plymouth—a big undertaking for a steamer at that time. On her return, she sailed for a time to Staffa and Iona, and in the following year was placed on the Londonderry route.

Mr. Colin McKenzie, in May 1834, advertised that the steamer *Rothsay* would sail for Inverness and Edinburgh, visiting Iona and Staffa *en route*. In 1836, he instituted a service to the West Highlands with the steeple-engined steamer *St. Mungo*, which created a record by reaching Islay in 11 hours from the Broomielaw; after about a month she was sold to Mr. Hugh Price to ply between Glasgow and Ardrossan.

P.S. *Gazelle*, previously owned by Messrs. Burns (*see* C.C.S., Chapter I) sailed for a time in the summer of 1838 to Inverness for Mr. John Fleming, while Mr. Alexander Graham continued to run the steamer *St. Mun* to Tarbert (Loch Fyne) in connexion with *Maid of Islay* from West Loch Tarbert to Islay.

A steamer called *Dolphin* (built by Messrs. Caird in 1834) appeared in the Loch Fyne trade in 1835, and in the following year was sold, plying, in 1836, to Tobermory, Barra, South and North Uist and the Isle of Skye, for Mr. Malcolm McLeod. Her dimensions were 96·9 feet × 16·4 feet × 8·6 feet.

PERIOD 1840-1860

DONALD CAMERON. In 1844, a service (with Oban as its starting point) was inaugurated to Strontian, Tobermory, Skye and Uist, in connexion with the steamers from Glasgow, with *Dumbuck*, a wooden paddle steamer previously engaged in the Glasgow-Dumbarton service, to which she returned after only four months in the West Highlands.

SIR JAMES MATHIESON. When Mr. Mathieson, as he then was, purchased the estate of Lewis in 1844, there was no steam communication with the mainland. He offered various firms a subsidy of £500 annually to run a steamer between Glasgow and Stornoway, but no one was prepared to take the risk. He then took shares in the *Falcon*, a steamboat which ran from Ardrossan to Stornoway, but ceased in

October, 1845. Mr. Mathieson then built at his own expense the *Mary Jane*, named after his wife, and built by Messrs. Tod & McGregor. (This steamer, from 1857, was well known in the Hutcheson/Mac-Brayne fleet, under her original name till 1875 and thereafter as *Glencoe* till broken up at Ardrossan in 1931) (*see* Chapter II). It was on 4th June 1846 that *Mary Jane* arrived at Stornoway on her first trip, after a passage of 28 hours. A large crowd assembled on the beach and evinced their delight at seeing a steamer which was intended to keep their island in regular steam communication with Glasgow. She had been running only a month when a mail diligence was put on to connect with her at Balmacarra and run right across Scotland to Dingwall parallel with the route now served by the Skye Line of British Railways. The steamer's calls included Oban, Tobermory, Armadale, Balmacarra, Kyleakin, Portree and Stornoway. The *Mary Jane* was soon found to be too small and on 29th September, 1848, a larger steamer, called *Marquis of Stafford* (owned by Mr. Mathieson and the Duke of Sutherland), was launched by Messrs. John Reid & Co., Port Glasgow. She took up her station in March 1849, Lochinver and Ullapool on the mainland being among her calls; but she was probably rather large for the trade, as she was shortly laid up. Her name appeared on several occasions afterwards alternately in the notices of sailings and in the advertisements of vessels for sale, but she is not traceable after October 1851. Mr. John Ramsay of Kildalton then took up the traffic with the *Islay*.

For many years a sailing packet conveyed the mails twice a week from Stornoway to Poolewe. After many years of discussion, the Post Office offered a subsidy of £1300 for the conveyance of the mails. No one would take this, until Mr. Mathieson took it himself, for ten years from 1st October, 1871, when the paddle steamer *Ondine*, built at London in 1847, was acquired and placed on the run from Stornoway to Ullapool, from which a coach connected at Garve (on the newly opened railway from Dingwall). *Ondine*, which had one funnel aft of the paddle-boxes and two masts, continued to sail till about 1877, after which the Stornoway service was worked by Messrs. Hutcheson through Ullapool, thereafter to Strome-Ferry, to connect with the Dingwall & Skye Railway.

WILLIAM ROBERTSON. Already in 1851 established in Renfrew as a coal merchant, Mr. Robertson (probably as agent) entered in the Highland trade in 1871 with the screw steamer *Marchioness of Lorne*, which sailed (till sold in July 1872) from Glasgow every Wednesday for Ardrishaig, Lochgilphead, Crinan Canal, Oban, Sound of Mull, Tobermory, Tiree and Coll; and, in alternate weeks, to Salen (Loch Sunart) or Strontian. He was agent for S.S. *Celt*, built at Whiteinch in 1868, which sailed to Lochindaal, Islay. She was sold in 1876 to Absalom Kerr and John Esplin, of Leith. Thereafter this fleet was not much connected with the West Highlands, except passing through. It developed into the "Gem" Line of William Robertson (Shipowners) Limited.

PERIOD 1860-1870.

About 1866, several operators entered the Highland trade, among them Messrs. D. Cowan & Co., with *Norseman*, running between Glasgow and Fort William; Messrs. James Wright & Co., with *Argyle* to the Outer Hebrides; and Mr. John Wilson with *Chieftain's Bride* to Tiree and Iona. A little iron paddle steamer *Carradale*, only 61·6 feet × 15 feet, of 28·26 tons register, with side-lever engine, two tubular boilers, two funnels athwartships, fore and aft masts, built in 1860, was advertised for sale in August 1861. She had two small cabins, and could be beached safely. In June 1866, she went ashore on Luing, afterwards trading on the Forth as a screw steamer. Another in the fleet of Messrs. D. Cowan & Co. was *Corsair*, launched on 19th June 1867 by Messrs. H. Murray & Co. as consort to *Norseman*. During the summer of 1868, Messrs. Cowan were agents for the very small screw steamer *Chase*, plying to Strontian, then owned by Duncan Colquhoun, Tiree, previously by Norman Buchanan, but sold in June 1869 to Thomas Ross, Glasgow. *Corsair* left the fleet in March 1871 and was succeeded by S.S. *Swan* (owned by John Lorne Stewart, of Campbeltown), which in that year sailed from Glasgow to Mull, Tiree and Skye via the Crinan Canal.

PERIOD 1870-1920

THE HIGHLAND RAILWAY CO. The Dingwall & Skye Railway having reached Strome Ferry, and having constructed the pier there, inaugurated sailings therefrom to Portree (daily) and to Stornoway (weekly), with the screw steamers *Jura* (1857) and *Oscar* (1850), both bought from Messrs. William Sloan & Co., Glasgow, in May/June, 1870. In the following winter the Stornoway sailings ceased, but were resumed in the summer of 1871. At times when these were not in operation, it was possible to reach Stornoway by changing at Portree into one of the Hutcheson/MacBrayne ships from Glasgow, the *Clydesdale* or *Clansman*, and later also the *Claymore*. In November, 1870 the *Oscar* ran aground at Applecross and was succeeded by P. S. *Carham*; and S.S. *Ferret*, purchased from Messrs. G. & J. Burns, took the place of *Jura*. In 1877 the Dingwall & Skye Railway Company sold the *Carham* and *Ferret*, together with the ferryboat plying across Loch Carron, to the Highland Railway Company, who in that year had built for them the screw steamer *John o'Groat* for the Scrabster–Stromness route. From 1880 the railway company abandoned the shipping services from Strome Ferry, having arranged for these to be provided by Messrs. MacBrayne, and two years later they withdrew from the Orkney service, which has since been maintained by the North of Scotland & Orkney & Shetland S.N. Co. Ltd., and its successors, P. & O. Ferries. Strome Ferry was afterwards operated by Inverness-shire County Council, until it became redundant on the opening of the road along the south side of Loch Carron. For further particulars of the

Highland Railway ships reference may be made to "R.O.S." and to "The Skye Railway", by John Thomas.

In May 1869, the small iron steamer *Jura* was launched by Messrs. Scott & Linton, Dumbarton, for Mr. Archibald McKenzie, who entered the West Highland trade. She was auctioned in January 1871, and went to Mr. A. G. Colvil for service in Irish waters. From 1876, she was owned by Donald Dewar, of Lochgilphead (Jura Steamboat Co.), predecessors of the Minard Castle Company. She was sometimes chartered by Messrs. MacBrayne.

J. & J. MACFARLANE. About 1874 this firm started a goods service with the screw steamer *Lyle*. It was they, also, who owned the *Trojan*, which during 1886-87 opened the "Island" route from Oban, while on charter to the Highland Fisheries Co. Ltd. (*see* Chapter III).

JOHN G. STEWART. S.S. *Loch Nell*, built in 1877 and owned by Mr. Wm. Sim, trading as the West Highland Carrying Company, was purchased by Mr. John G. Stewart in the early 'eighties, and remained in the West Highland trade till sold in March 1920 to Sessions & Son Ltd., Cardiff. S.S. *Nevis*, built in 1880, was acquired about 1887, and was sold in March 1913 to Messrs. Little, being then named *Capra*; as such she returned to her former owner during the First War. *Loch Etive* (I), built at Maryhill in 1877, remained in service till 1910. In 1904, *Loch Doon* was built, being sold in December 1920 to Oilfields of Egypt Ltd. *Loch Etive* (II) and *Loch Leven* were built in 1910, the former being sold to the British Aluminium Co. Ltd., and the latter in September 1919 to the Fort Shipping Co., passing in 1928 to Messrs. R. Cameron & Co., Glasgow, for whom she eventually sailed as *Kyle Rona*. Mr. Stewart had also a vessel called *Lochaber*, built in 1901 and sold in December 1915 to Mr. J. Leslie, Dundee. The final acquisition was *Islandmagee*, built in 1900 and purchased in February 1927; she afterwards became the property of Messrs. J. A. Landsborough & Co.

COLIN B. TURNER. Two new ventures in the Highland trade began in 1893: the steam yacht *Erne*, owned by Mr. Colin B. Turner, of Fauldtrees, Rothesay, made weekly trips to the Highlands and Islands, first from Rothesay, and later from Oban, calling at any ports desired by the passengers. This would probably have developed greatly, but for the early death of the owner.

A J. MACLEAN, Tiroran, Mull. (W. CRAIG) Weekly trips from the Broomielaw to Strontian were started about the same time by S.S. *Inniemore*, ex *Cambria*, dating from 1866.

J. & A. GARDNER LTD. Messrs. Gardner are the owners of extensive granite quarries at Bonawe, on Loch Etive; and for the transport of their products they operate a number of motor ships, some of which also carry general cargo, including sand for optical glass manufacture, from Loch Aline. The ships' funnels are black with white band, and hulls are mostly grey; but some are black. The houseflag is blue, with a large red G; and most of the names are those of saints associated with the district around Loch Etive. The *Saint*

Kentigern of 1973 has a bow-loading platform, and was on occasion chartered by David MacBrayne Ltd. for the Glasgow-Stornoway service, as were some of this company's steam vessels in the past, such as *Saint Barchan*, *Saint Enoch*, etc. The company also operated a motor-car ferry across Loch Etive at Bonawe, a special motor ferry-boat named *Deirdre* (after the heroine of the ancient Gaelic poem) having been constructed for this purpose by H. McLean & Sons Ltd., Govan.

PERIOD 1920-1940

MINISTRY OF FOOD. In 1920, the Ministry of Food operated a service from Mallaig and Kyle to the West Coast of Ross, Skye, Small Isles, etc., with the steam drifter *Rosedale*. This was a temporary measure, pending the return to normal working of the MacBrayne steamers after the war.

ERISKAY SHIPPING CO. LTD.—This company, in 1922, ran a service from Glasgow to the Hebrides with M.V. *Eriskay*, and the new steamers *Economy* and *Eriskaig*.

RODERICK CUNNINGHAM (SCALPAY) LTD. Owners of *Isle of Tiree*, *Eilean Glas*, etc. This company is best known for supplying calor gas to many of the Western Islands.

G. G. JACKSON & CO. LTD. A new service to Port Ellen, Craighouse, Ardlussa, Luing, Loch Aline, Salen (Mull), Tobermory, Mingary, Mallaig, Armadale, Kyle of Lochalsh, Portree, Gairloch, Aultbea, Ullapool and Baden Tarbet was instituted in October 1936 by Messrs. G. G. Jackson & Co., with the chartered steamer *Hamilton*. A short time afterwards the Point Steamship Co. Ltd. (under the management of Messrs. Colin McPhail, Urquhart & Co.) was registered, its first steamers being *Rubaan* and *Rumore*. (It should be noted that the prefix "Ru-" stands for Gaelic Ruadha=Point, hence the name of the company.) In 1937 *Rustoer* was added to the fleet and later the same year was transferred as *Isle Ornsay* to the Island Steamship Co. Ltd., another subsidiary. From the beginning of 1937, Lochinver and Stornoway were included among the ports of call. *Rumore* was lost in February 1948; and in that year Messrs. Jackson retired from the West Highland trade. *Isle Ornsay* was subsequently used (in 1939) to take material to South Uist for the construction of the bridge over the South Ford to Benbecula.

The passenger service between Mallaig and Armadale was carried on by Alexander MacLennan (Mallaig) Ltd., who operated also the mail service to Inverie and Loch Nevis, the fleet having included *Enterprise*, two vessels named *Bounty*, *Seagull*, *Royal Scot* and *Ossianic*, the last-named being succeeded on the ferry service by the *Blaven*, purpose built for this, at the yard of Hugh McLean, Renfrew in 1939. In 1968 she was sold to one of the Ullapool owners. Messrs. MacLennan then gave up boat-owning.

Another Mallaig owner, Mr. Bruce Watt, continued and since his death his son has carried on the operation of various boats. The fleet had included two named *Islander*, *Islerona*, *Clansman*, *Chieftain*, and *Highlander*, and the fishing-boat-type *Western Isles*, already mentioned as being chartered by David MacBrayne Ltd., and used for day (and longer) trips from Mallaig.

PERIOD 1940-1986

For many years trips have been run from Oban to destinations such as Grasspoint, Duart Castle, Port Appin, etc. by various operators, among whom one of the best known is Mrs. Henrietta Spencer, with boats such as *Island Lass, Island Queen,* etc.

The former Clyde Trust tug and tender *Clyde*, built in 1961, after disposal appeared on passenger excursions in the West Highlands, first at Ullapool, then, from 1974, at Portree, giving short trips to Rona and to Loch Ainort via Raasay, etc., in the ownership of Mr. Kennedy, till sold in 1984 for service between Strood and Southend for the Invicta Line. When at Ullapool she operated to the Summer Isles, later additions to the fleets there being *Etive Shearwater* (Maclean Marine) (from Loch Etive) and *Summer Queen* ex *Whitby* (Mackenzie Marine). The former of these sails from Arisaig to Eigg and Muck for Arisaig Marine, who began operations with the *Royal Scot*.

The Kyle Rhea-Glenelg vehicle ferry has for many years been operated by Mr. Murdo Mackenzie, now in summer only, with turntable ferries such as *Appin Chief*, *Glen Mallie*, etc.

Mr. Murdo McSween of Caol, Fort William, operated cruises with *Silver Darling*, *Barecatann* and *Maid of Bute*, the last-named being now on the Firth of Forth sailing to Inchcolm as the *Maid of the Forth*. Short cruises from Fort William are now provided by another operator with *Lochaber Lady*.

An interesting development in 1976 was the introduction of sailings to Staffa from Ulva Ferry, by Staffa Marine, with the fibre-glass *Laird of Staffa*, fitted out on the Clyde, with two inflatable dinghies as tenders, supplemented by the *Countess of Kempock* and *Flotta Owl* of Offshore Workboats Ltd., (O.W.L.), a company primarily concerned with providing tender services at Strome Ferry and Loch Kishorn during the oil-rig construction at the latter but which in 1978 operated its above named vessels from Oban to Mull etc.

Mr. D. A. MacAskill, Berneray, operated the passenger ferry service between North Uist and Berneray, and Berneray-Leverburgh (Harris) with various motor launches, including *Castle Moil*, *June Gibson*, *Sheilann*, and employs the *Endeavour of Berneray* on the Harris link, the connexion with North Uist being now provided by the Islands Council's vehicle ferry.

Following the re-organisation of local government in 1975 various ferry fleets became grouped by regions. Strathclyde inherited from

Argyll County Council the Luing ferry, on which the *Belnahua* ("corner" loading) is now the principal vessel, while the Highland Region took over Ballachulish (soon superseded by the bridge), Corran-Ardgour, Fort William-Camusnagaul, the last-named being for pedestrians only (previously operated by *Eilidh* and *North Wind*, now by *Cailin an Aiseig*. Ballachulish Ferry Co., Ltd. had had a number of turntable ferries, commencing with *Glencoe*, followed by *Maid of Glencoe* (I) and (II), *Queen of Glen Albyn*, *Mamore*, *Appin Chief*, *Glen Mallie*, *Glen Duror*, *Glen Loy* and culminating with *Glenachulish*, built by the Ailsa Co. at Troon in 1969. Dornie Ferry was superseded by a bridge in the 1930s, and Strome Ferry by a by-pass road in 1971. Corran-Ardgour had used turntable ferries including *North Argyll*, *Maid of Glengour*, *Garven*, *Ben Keil*, *Gleann Mhor*, and the largest turntable ferry of them all, carrying nine cars, *Lochaber* of 1974, now superseded by the transfer to Corran of the *Rosehaugh* from Inverness, and the *Maid of Glencoul* of 1975 from Kylesku, following the opening of the bridge there. Kessock Ferry across the Beauly Firth had steamboats from early times, including the *Maid of Morven* in the 1840s and in more recent times the *Maud*, *Lowestoft Belle*, *Hope* (from Alloa), *St. Mawes* (from Falmouth), the motor vessels *Black Isle* (twin-hulled), *Eilean Dubh*, *Inbhir Nis* and *Rosehaugh*. The Kessock Ferry also is now superseded by a bridge.

From the earliest years of steam navigation, the Caledonian Canal had a passenger steamer service. This had lapsed with the departure in 1939 of the *Gondolier*; and it was not until 1948 that passenger sailings, this time restricted to the eastern end of the Canal and Loch Ness, were revived.

The Fairmile "B" type vessel, No. 525, *T.S.M.V. Lenrodian*. built in 1942, was acquired by Mr. L. S. J. Wilkinson of Inverness in February, 1948, and next month was transferred to Lochness Cruises, Ltd., by whom she was operated for two seasons from Muirtown Wharf, Inverness, along the Canal to Loch Ness, turning off Castle Urquhart, and with a whole day sail to Fort Augustus twice each week. Evening cruises also were given. After two seasons the services ceased, and the ship was advertised for sale in 1950.

After employment for the S.M.T. Company from South Queensferry, and a spell on the Millport-Largs station, this motor vessel *Cramond Brig* cruised from Muirtown in 1958.

Apart from the two seasons of excursions by *Lenrodian* and one by *Cramond Brig*, there had been no sailings on Loch Ness for over 20 years when the welcome announcement was made by British Waterways that they intended to operate cruises from Inverness in the summer of 1961. A regular programme was provided that year, and each year since, by *Scot II*. Built in 1931 as successor to another ice-breaking tug (also named *Scot*, constructed in 1876), *Scot II* was sent to Leith towards the end of 1960 and converted from steam to Diesel, being at the same time fitted out for passenger cruising. The funnel, originally buff with black top, now became white with yellow band and pale blue top, while the hull was black to main deck level, then off-white above, with a yellow line. She commenced for her owners—British Waterways—operating from Muirtown Wharf, Inverness, in forenoon, afternoon and evening cruises, the shorter trips turning in Abriachan Bay, and the longer runs taking her to Drumnadrochit Bay. A charter by the Coastal Cruising Association on 7th May, 1966 took *Scot II* the whole length of the MacBrayne "swift steamer" stretch of the Canal, from Banavie to Fort Augustus and Inverness, an opportunity appreciated by many who had not been able to do this in the days of the *Gondolier*.

Built by Wm. Weatherhead & Son (1954) Ltd., Cockenzie, *Jessie Ellen* was designed for summer service on Loch Ness and winter service in the Orkneys. She had a passenger certificate for fifty-nine and commenced plying from Muirtown Wharf in 1961, in direct competition with *Scot II*. Her owner, Mr. James Newlands, operated her on her original route till 1968. She spent the 1969 season based at Helensburgh, and in 1970 was acquired by Mr. Donald Kennedy for service on Loch Etive. When superseded there, she reverted to Orkney.

Four cruising vessels, *Jacobite Lady*, *Jacobite Chieftain*, *Jacobite Clansman* and *Jacobite Princess* were placed on the Canal, two based at Inverness and two at Banavie for sailings therefrom and from Fort William, though the latter two seem to have ceased operating at the south end of the Canal after the 1976 season.

Inverness County Council in addition to having an interest in mainland ferries was responsible for ordering a "Rotork" sea truck for Vatersay, etc. This craft, built at Poole and named *A'Bhirlinn Bhatarsach*, seems not to have done much sailing. The successors to the County Council in the islands are Comhairle nan Eilean (Western Isles Islands Council), who have now two vehicle-carrying vessels, *Eilean na h-Oige* on the Ludaig (North Uist)-Eriskay run and *Eilean Bhearnaraigh* on that between Newton Ferry (North Uist) and Berneray. These are twin-screw bow-loading vessels, rather like the "Small Island" class of Caledonian MacBrayne. The first of them was built at Stornoway, and the other was the last construction at the yard of George Brown (Marine) Ltd., Greenock. For passengers from Castlebay to Vatersay, etc. the Council has the small motor launches *Solas* and *Ban Righ nan Tonn*, the latter being built of fibre-glass, pressed in Jersey. On the Sound of Barra run (for passengers only), between Eoligarry and Ludag, Mr. Donald Campbell operates the boat with the unlikely name of *Very Likely*, in 1986 superseded by *Most Likely II*.

CHAPTER XII

WESTERN FERRIES LTD.

W ITH the intention of providing more frequent services in the West of Scotland, and at lower cost than those existing, Western Ferries, Ltd. was formed in July, 1967, this to be achieved with simple, unsophisticated ships and terminals, combined with low crewing, on the lines of ferry operation in Norway.

T.S.M.V. "Sound of Islay." The first member of the new fleet was launched at Port Glasgow on 27th February, 1968, for a twice-daily service between Kennacraig on West Loch Tarbert and Port Askaig, Islay, once daily to Gigha, which commenced in April, it being intended to be later extended to Jura. Carrying 20 cars and six lorries or a mixture, the ship had a service speed of 10·75 knots, horse-power being kept low to achieve low crew costs in accordance with the Company's policy. She was fitted with twin rudders controlled by hydraulic steering-gear, and had a bow-thrust unit to assist in man-oeuvring. Two small saloons were provided for passengers (80 in summer, 35 in winter) and it was interesting to note how much had been put into a small space, all forward, since the vessel's main purpose was to carry vehicles on her open flush deck aft. Later in 1968 proposals were made by the company to provide a larger vessel and to establish an "overland" route to Islay, via Jura, with a subsidy from public funds; but this was rejected by Mr. William Ross, Secretary of State for Scotland, who was opposed to fragmenting the service and considered that the proposals of David MacBrayne, Ltd. and Argyll County Council for improving the approach roads to Port Askaig on Islay, and between Feolin and Craighouse on Jura, would result in a much better service than these islands had had up to that time. In August the company stated that they would continue to operate without a subsidy, and that plans for a second ship were at an advanced stage. In September, 1969 it was announced that her owners were considering using her on a new ferry route on the Clyde, between Hunter's Quay (where they already owned the pier) and McInroy's Point, near the Cloch Lighthouse, if planning permission could be obtained: this service was later instituted, but not with this ship. She was registered initially at Glasgow, but re-registered at Campbeltown in May, 1970, from which year till 1973 she was engaged in a summer run from Campbeltown to Red Bay, Cushendall, County Antrim, linking Kintyre with Ulster, with great expectations of increasing tourism and commercial traffic, which, however, did not materialise to an extent sufficient to justify the costs of running the service. (She did this run also in winter, 1970-1, but for freight only, not having a passenger certificate for this route in winter.) In November, 1971 it was announced that she would be available for contract, in which, or on charter work, she became engaged from early in 1972, including taking construction equipment from Ardrossan to Campbeltown. A berth was made for her at Rothesay, and in April she towed thither from Faslane a link-span that had been intended for Colonsay. This enabled her to unload at any state of the tide, and she conveyed many hoppers of granite chips from Furnace, Loch Fyne to Rothesay. Her Irish sailings did not commence till June, finishing in September. During October-December, 1972, she was on charter to David MacBrayne, Ltd. for the Portree and Small Isles. Her Irish runs were resumed in 1973, but ceased in September, and. have not since been operated. After a trip to Orkney in July, 1974, she assisted on the Clyde-Argyll route with lorries, from 30th being engaged regularly on the Ardyne run from McInroy's Point, reverting to Kennacraig-Islay on the departure of *Sound of Jura*. The terminal at Kennacraig was taken over by Strathclyde Regional Council, and the land there bought by Caledonian MacBrayne, Ltd. with a view to their service being transferred there in 1978. Western Ferries' service to Islay was suspended from 30th September, 1981 and the ship sold.

T.S.M.V. "Sound of Gigha." For the short crossing between Port Askaig and Feolin, Jura, the Company bought the *Isle of Gigha* from Eilean Sea Services—a vessel on the lines of a landing craft, capable of bow-loading on beaches, dating from 1966, and the prototype of the sort of craft envisaged when Western Ferries, Ltd. was formed. Overhauled at Port Glasgow, she took up her regular run on 1st March, 1969, and has remained thereon, except during periods when off for re-fit, when various chartered vessels have been employed, including *Cara Lass* from the Gigha-Tayinloan route, *Southern Star*, from Arrochar Boat-Hiring Company (both for passengers only), *Kilbrannan* from Caledonian MacBrayne in 1972, carrying vehicles also, the next such vessel being Caledonian MacBrayne's *Coll* in 1978; while in 1979 it was intended to use the landing-craft-type *Spanish John* of Inverie Estates. In 1973 it was estimated that the Jura service was incurring an annual loss of £8000, not including depreciation; and in September, Islay District Council arranged to contribute £1250, with a similar amount from Argyll County Council. The subsidy was substantially increased and continued by Strathclyde Regional Council, which, however, would not provide any subsidy for the mainland to Islay service of Western Ferries.

T.S.M.V. "Sound of Jura." In September, 1969 it was recorded that an order had been placed in Norway for a second ship for the Kennacraig-Islay service, after the contract had been put out to tender to yards in Scotland and Norway, the successful tender, on price and delivery date, being from Hatlo Verksted, Ulsteinvik. She was to carry 35 vehicles and 200 passengers; and, fitted with twin rudders and bow-thrust unit, would have a service speed of 14 knots, which would enable her to do three trips per day, or even four. She was the first drive-through seagoing vessel on the West Coast (though often used as a stern-loader only). Based on a Norwegian standard ferry design, modified for Scottish use, the ship had seating for 50 passengers in a carpeted observation lounge on the boat-deck and, like *Sound of Islay*, had vending machines for refreshments: also play-pens and a private room for mothers with young children. From September, 1970, she began calling (and bow-loading) at a link-span at the north end of Gigha, which was wrecked in a storm in January, 1972 and not replaced. It was assumed that Western Ferries would be the only operators to Islay, Gigha, Jura and Colonsay, as David MacBrayne, Ltd. had indicated withdrawal from 31st March. The proposed terminal at Scalasaig, Colonsay would not be ready before June; and, since the *Sound of Jura* had not a lift, crane loading would have been necessary there. It was then agreed that the MacBrayne services would continue till September, after which a further extension was made. In January, 1973, the *Sound of Jura* was fitted with an auto-pilot; and during overhaul in February next year her exhaust uptakes were painted blue, as on the *Sound of Islay*. In October and November, 1975, she made exceptional runs from Ardrossan to Portavadie with materials for the oil-rig construction site. No subsidy for the mainland-Islay service of Western Ferries being forthcoming either from Central or Local Government, the Company announced in July, 1976 that it could no longer run this ship in competition with the MacBrayne vessel then being subsidised to the extent of about £500,000 per year. The intention was to continue with *Sound of Islay* only, concentrating on freight; and the *Sound of Jura* was sold to the Mexican Government. She left Troon, after overhaul and under the name *Quintana Roo*, in September, 1976.

In September and October, 1972, negotiations were in progress for a take-over of Western Ferries, Ltd. by the Scottish Transport Group. Opposition to this was voiced in Islay and Jura, but on 7th October, 1972 it was announced that the principal shareholders were likely to accept. On 1st November, however, a new bid for the company was announced, by Dornoch Shipping Co., Ltd., after a three-week campaign by Sir William Lithgow. This was accepted and the new arrangement took effect from 1st January, 1973. The operating company then became Western Ferries (Argyll) Ltd.

D.S.M.V. "Sound of Shuna" and **D.S.M.V. "Sound of Scarba."** In December, 1972, following the acquisition of the shares in the company by Dornoch Shipping, Sir William Lithgow, Chairman of Western Ferries, announced the purchase of two double-ended Swedish car ferries, subject to satisfactory survey and safe arrival on the Clyde. These were *Olandsund IV* and *Olandsund III*, with capacities of 27 and 22 cars respectively, to be towed across the North Sea early next year from the sound between the Swedish mainland and Oland Island in the Baltic, where they had become redundant following the opening of a bridge. Both were delayed at Stavanger by weather, then were towed to Inverness, proceeding under their own power by the Caledonian Canal to Corpach, and so to the Clyde by the Mull of Kintyre, *Olandsund IV* arriving at Hunter's Quay in March, 1973. Her sister was further delayed at Inverness by the temporary closure of the Caledonian Canal till April, and called at Kennacraig the following month and berthed at Kilmun. They were overhauled by Scott-Lithgow, Ltd. in their Cartsburn Yard and dry-docked in the Garvel Graving Dock, Greenock. They emerged renamed respectively as above. *Sound of Shuna*, after trials in April, 1973 and tests of the link-spans in May, opened the service between McInroy's Point and Hunter's Quay on Sunday, 3rd June, 1973, being joined by her sister on 14th July. A half-hourly service was then given, fares being competitive with those on the Gourock-Dunoon route. The new route was at first advertised as "Clyde Cross". but has since become known as the Clyde-Argyll Ferry. A dolphin structure protected the link-span on the Renfrewshire coast, as did Hunter's Quay Pier on the north side, Kilmun being used for any spare vessel. The McInroy's Point span was wrecked by a severe gale on 27th September, 1973, and the service was suspended for nearly two weeks. In November, indication was given of inaugurating a service from McInroy's Point to Rothesay, but weather prevented the transfer of a link-span from Kennacraig to Rothesay. During overhaul in March, 1974 the red of the hull on *Sound of Scarba* was extended to the top of the bulwarks of the car-deck, making a useful distinguishing mark from the *Sound of Shuna*.

D.S.M.V. "Sound of Sanda." To provide a relief and extra vessel for the Clyde-Argyll route, the Company purchased the former Southern Railway Lymington-Yarmouth vehicle ferry *Lymington*, built by Wm. Denny & Bros., Ltd. at Dumbarton in 1938, one of the first in Britain with Voith-Schneider propulsion. After being berthed at Kilmun Pier for a time in April, 1974, she was overhauled and dry-docked at Greenock, during which much replating was done and her lifeboat superseded by two liferafts. She took up service in August. In common with the other members of this fleet, she has the name across the front of the bridge, in Scandinavian style, and carries the Company's colours—poppy-red hull, white superstructure, dark-blue funnels, which in her case bear the emblem of a red circle with tangential lines above and below in opposite directions, ending each in an arrowhead, representing "roll-on, roll-off". On occasions such as Cowal Games Day and the September Holiday Week-end, all three vessels have been in use, giving a 20-minute service.

T.S.M.V. "Highland Seabird." In April, 1976 the Company indicated that it hoped to introduce a catamaran, which it was believed scored over other advanced craft, such as hydrofoils and hovercraft, for their reliability in heavy seas and ability to use existing piers. The twin-hulled vessel (the first in Clyde service since the *Alliance* of 1857) was of welded aluminium construction and had a comfortable full-width carpeted lounge seating 160, with access to the open deck aft. Equipment included VHF and radiotelephone, two radars, echo-sounders and gyro-compass, and a loud-speaker system. She had a Class IIA passenger certificate for short international journeys. She had thus much more sophisticated equipment than indicated when the Company began. Chartered for a five-month proving period, she was based initially at Rothesay, operating to Dunoon, Helensburgh and Greenock (Customhouse Quay), intended to visit Glasgow Broomielaw at week-ends, and on Sundays, cruising as far as Tarbert Loch Fyne, this sometimes becoming a Round Bute cruise. The up-river trips were soon abandoned on account of the potential danger from floating timber. Before entering regular service she broke the Glasgow-Dunoon record time of 49 minutes by rail and steamer, set up by the *Duchess of Fife* over 50 years earlier, by establishing the new record of 42 minutes 38 seconds. By regular services connecting with trains at Greenock Central, the journeys from Dunoon and Rothesay to Glasgow could be completed in one and one-and-a-half hours respectively. In October, 1976, she was chartered by the Highlands & Islands Development Board to visit various ports, giving short runs at each. Setting out from Greenock, she called at Brodick and Campbeltown, then round the Mull of Kintyre to Port Askaig, Colonsay and Oban, Fort William, Tobermory, Tarbert-Harris and Portree. Although more than 60,000 passengers were carried during the season, overhead expenses made the service uneconomic; and it had been the intention of the Norwegian owners to sell the craft to French owners for the Cartaret-Channel Islands run in the 1977 season. That, however, fell through, and Western Ferries were given the option to retain her for the ensuing year. After talks with the H.I.D.B. it was arranged that the *Highland Seabird* would be based at Oban: she would cruise on various West Highland routes, including that to Fort William (which had last had a steamer service, by *King George V*, in 1974), Tobermory, Iona and Crinan. The last-named had not had passenger steamer calls since the withdrawal of the through "Royal Route" service by the Crinan Canal at the end of the 1928 season. From October, 1977 to May, 1978 she was chartered to Howard Doris, Ltd., to convey workers to the oil platform then under construction at Loch Kishorn, being based at Strome Ferry. As a result of a successful year, Western Ferries were able, in March, 1978, to purchase the vessel outright. For the 1978 summer season the *Highland Seabird* added a long-distance excursion on Saturday and Sunday from Oban to Moville and Portrush, with coach connexions by Highland Omnibuses from Inverness and Fort William to Oban and from Portrush via Coleraine to Belfast and rail to Dublin; also from Oban to Cairnryan for the Townsend-Thoresen sailing to Larne, and *vice versa*. From 1979 she could call at certain states of the tide at the new jetty at Iona, and so avoid the necessity of being tendered to by the MacBrayne red boats or the *Morvern*. A public excursion from Campbeltown to Ayr was given on 18th September, 1978. During 1978 she made connexion to Iona and Staffa (weather permitting) by the dinghies of Staffa Marine. The Irish services were in 1979 restricted to Sundays only, and were not resumed in 1980; but in the latter year an interesting occurrence in the spring was the charter of the *Highland Seabird* by Sealink (U.K.), Ltd. for the Portsmouth-Ryde passenger service, following which Western Ferries operated a few cruises in the neighbourhood of the Isle of Wight.

After being laid up at Renfrew she was sold in 1985 to French owners.

D.S.M.V. "Sound of Seil." A second former member of the Lymington fleet – *Freshwater* – was purchased, and re-named as above after an overhaul at Renfrew, entered the McInroy's Point service in June, 1986, being employed along with the *Sound of Shuna* on the principal runs.

APPENDIX I

GENERAL NOTES ON THE HUTCHESON/ MACBRAYNE STEAMERS

BEFORE concluding it is desired to make some remarks in connexion with the external appearance and lines of a large proportion of the older ships. A few other notes also are appended.

We all know that comparisons are odious, in spite of their everyday occurrence, and we also know that there is nothing so fickle or capricious as individual taste in the matter of beauty. However, readers will be liberal enough to allow us to give our own views which, incidentally, we know are shared by many.

We submit that in the paddle class, steamers like the *Ionas*, *Chevalier*, *Columba* and *Grenadier* were among the most beautiful creations of their kind ever put into water, their form and lines—enhanced considerably by the characteristic MacBrayne colouring—being almost perfect and a joy to the eye.

Pride of craftsmanship was not subordinated to undue pecuniary considerations, and in the details of design of such items as bows, sterns, paddle boxes, waste steam pipe tops and a host of other things, one could not fail to observe the most painstaking care.

There was such dignity too and a remarkable sense of balance. In the *tout ensemble* there was nothing harsh, and nothing jarred. On a fine sunny day when the West Highland coast scenery in summer is unsurpassed, we can visualise few more impressive and beautiful sights than one of these paddlers under way at close range. The combination of colouring in these circumstances was superb.

In the case of the screw vessels there was of course less scope for adornment and fine lines, on account of the services they performed—namely all the year round trading, by day and night—mainly with cargo.

Nevertheless, even under such conditions inimical to aesthetic considerations, there were some very notable examples, headed unquestionably by the *Claymore* of 1881. She was a real beauty and with a coat of white enamel would have passed anywhere as a private yacht. It is strange to think of this stately craft, whose demise in 1931 was the cause of widespread regret at home and abroad, and to contrast her with the modern shipyard product to perform the same service. It is but fair to say that internally these old vessels, according to present-day ideas, left much to be desired and it is in this direction that the up-to-date vessels show a marked superiority over the old.

Mention must also be made of the Company's last effort to maintain the old standards of beauty, in the *Chieftain* of 1907. As given elsewhere, her career on the West Coast was relatively short.

We deplore genuinely the dwindling sentiment concerning ships, both on the part of those who earn their living in the building, owning and manning of them, and the general public who observe and travel in them.

This sentiment we feel sure went a long way in the old days— however unconsciously—in making men proud of doing a job well, and towards their general contentment. These views may be deemed very old-fashioned, as many business men today insist that sentiment has no place in business.

We do feel that good is bound to ensue from the Company's point of view by getting passengers interested in the ships themselves so that they do not regard them merely as floating contrivances in which to move from place to place. If the latter point of view is predominant, then travellers only make use of the vessels when they cannot avoid doing so, and much business is lost. On the other hand extravagant phraseology in publicity probably does more harm than good in the long run.

The durability of the ships is a point which must have struck our readers on many occasions. The iron vessels were notorious in this respect, but those constructed of steel at a later period were but little inferior. One rarely reads of a set of engines and boilers requiring a new hull, unless it be the result of a wreck; it is nearly always the other way round if any such renewal occurs.

On the machinery side the life of engines and boilers was also very remarkable in many instances. It must be remembered that all cases of renewal of machinery were not the result of wear and unserviceability. It was not uncommon to re-engine steamers with more economical types before the earlier sets were worn out, on account of the ultimate savings which were obtained in fuel consumption on service.

About 1929-31 the MacBrayne fleet was a living museum of marine engineering. Reviewing the types of engine represented, there was the *Glencoe* with ancient single-cylinder steeple paddle engine, the *Iona* (III) and her two-cylinder simple oscillating engines, the *Linnet* with twin sets of two-cylinder simple screw machinery, all four cylinders being inclined together like an inverted letter "V", *Claymore* having a heavy two-cylinder compound inverted engine, the *Fusilier* and her large single-crank diagonal paddle engine, *Pioneer* (II) with the familiar two-crank compound diagonal type, the *Clydesdale* (II) and her set of triple-expansion engines, the *Comet* with twin sets of four-cylinder oil engines, the *Lochinvar* having three sets of six-cylinder motors, the *Lochness*(III) with two sets of triple-expansion machinery and oil-fired boilers, the *Lochshiel* having one six-cylinder motor, the *Lochearn* with a pair of motors similar to the *Lochshiel* and lastly the *Lochfyne* and her elaborate Diesel-electric installation, to quote but one example of each. Readers will no doubt agree that this is a fairly historical and representative collection of types, all of which could at that time be witnessed at work in their respective spheres of activity. If we go back to 1927 we embrace the compound oscillating machinery of the *Grenadier*, but lose the examples of oil engine and electric practice, as well as *Lochness* (III).

We can think of no other part of the world where such a state of affairs existed, and feel sure this must have been unique.

We have already mentioned the inherent noise of internal combustion machinery and we wonder what is the reaction of passengers to this. To those who have been "brought up on steam" since their early days the new noise is most irritating, and they almost without exception prefer the soft rhythm of the steam engine. But the rising generation has been brought up on internal-combustion noises on land, sea, and in the air from its infancy, we think therefore that it takes to these as a matter of course.

One small item has undergone an alteration in recent years and that is the Company's jersey as worn by the seamen. It used to look particularly smart with the name of the ship and the Royal Mail and Company's flags all very neatly woven into the fabric. The style has now been modified and is in our view much less attractive.

This brings us to the Company's flag and funnel. The MacBrayne house-flag is an attractive one: a blue pennant carrying red and white crosses. It looks extremely well when flown but is not at present in use.

The funnel position was curious and interesting, but in our view unsatisfactory. The Company had a Napier/Cunard/Burns ancestry, and appropriately enough adopted scarlet funnels with narrow black hoops (one hoop being sufficient for small ships, whereas the Cunard standard is three), and black tops. With the passage of time it became the practice (whether with official sanction or not is unknown) to wash over these hoops, so that a plain red funnel with black top resulted. This, however, was not universal, and certain individual ships retained black hoops—possibly because the master was proud of this detail, and appreciated the significance of it. Old photographs of the steamers bear out this. Later still the hoop was omitted from the funnels of all ships built for the Company; and, in the case of ships bought in, which had hoops already, these were invariably washed over red. Hence from about 1906 the Cunard/Burns link disappeared—in our view a great pity. But that is not the whole picture; for, McCallum, Orme & Co. Ltd., who, of course, traded in the same area, wishing to find a simple mode of rendering their red funnel slightly different from that of David MacBrayne, Ltd., hit on the idea of adding a black hoop, as previously mentioned; so that we had therefore the odd position of a concern forsaking the uniform to which it is entitled, and of which it ought to be proud, while the feature in question was adopted by another company merely to make a difference! The black hoop appeared on the red funnel depicted on the jacket of the first and second editions of this book; for this we were criticised in certain quarters after the appearance of the first edition in 1935, but we point out that the funnel as shown was correct in the past, and it is also as we feel it ought then to have remained.

It is extremely easy—too easy in fact—to level destructive criticism at the operations of an individual or a corporation. Constructive criticism on the other hand is another matter. The Company has frequently been the target for the former and it is probably true to say that some of it was deserved. On the other hand, much of the criticism cited has been based on very incomplete knowledge of all the difficulties encountered in running regular mail, passenger and cargo services in the West Highlands.

Experience has shown that before the advent of vehicle-carrying ships the 1,000-ton vessel of normal draught of about 15 to 16 feet was the limit which was a practicable proposition, and many of the services would not bear the cost of a vessel of this size. It is fairly obvious that the size of the ships and the frequency of service must bear some close relation to the volume of traffic to be transported, whether this be mails, passengers, or freight.

The most significant fact in this connexion was that in 1928, prior to the formation of the then new Company, not one other body or individual was prepared to step into the breach if Messrs. Mac-Brayne withdrew from the trade until in the end the L.M.&S. Railway Company and Coast Lines Ltd. took it over.

The introduction from 1964 of vehicle-carrying ships of greater tonnage and later using link-spans for end-loading resulted in greatly improved facilities, while the bow-loading vessels of the "small island" class proved invaluable for short crossings and helped to reduce the costs of operation.

Whilst this book is devoted to ships, it should be noted that the activities of the Company were not confined to water-borne traffic. They wisely took up road transport and co-ordinated it with many of the steamer and train services, but it is not proposed to deal with this branch of their operations.

Air powers were obtained in 1928, but have not been utilised.

When hovercraft and hydrofoils become fully reliable in weather conditions such as are likely to occur in the West Highlands, it is possible they may be introduced: though the initial attempt in the use of hovercraft on the Firth of Clyde was not particularly encouraging, and the catamaran *Highland Seabird*, while quite successful, proved uneconomic on her scheduled services in the Highlands.

The "Loch" class small ferries should give greatly improved service, with their drive-through facilities and passenger accommodation superior to that on their predecessors on the short-distance routes.

Intentions for the future include the building, about 1989, of a successor to *Iona* for the Islay route; of a Ro-Ro ship for Mallaig-Armadale in 1992; of a successor to the *Suilven* on the Stornoway mail run about 1994: also further "Loch" class small ferries, of capacities to be determined according to traffic requirements. In 1991-2 new vessels will be required for Kyle-Kyleakin, unless an earlier decision to build a bridge there may have made these unnecessary.

FLEET LISTS

Notes: The printing of ships's names in bold capitals indicates that these vessels were members of the Hutcheson/MacBrayne/ Caledonian MacBrayne or Clyde Cargo/Clyde & Campbeltown fleets; ordinary capitals that they were members only of an immediately absorbed fleet, and not taken over; Roman type that they were members only of a fleet absorbed by such, and not taken over; italics capitals that they reached only one degree farther from the main fleet; and small italics still one degree farther removed therefrom.

Where a full date is given in the "building" space, this is the date of launching.

FLEETS

OF THE

GLASGOW & HIGHLAND ROYAL MAIL STEAMERS

CITY OF GLASGOW STEAM PACKET COMPANY (I) 1831 - 30/9/1840
James Donaldson, Robert Ure, David Chapman, Robert Napier, James Thomson
Became part of Clyde Steam Navigation Co. 1/10/1840

CITY OF GLASGOW STEAM PACKET COMPANY (II) 2/1844 - 4/1851
James Donaldson, David Chapman, Archibald MacConnell, David MacIver, Charles MacIver
Thomson & MacConnell, Agents. 1838 - 12/1850

Dates: Built Acqd. Displ.	Name	Type	Shipbuilders Enginebuilders	L.	B.	D.	G.T.	N.H.P.	Machinery	Remarks
1882 1831 7/1834	CITY OF GLASGOW (I)	Wood P.S.	Greenock	123'6"	22'0"	12'6"	300	300		3m.
1832 8/1832 8/1836	JOHN WOOD	"	John Wood & Co. Port Glasgow	132'7"	21'6½"	14'0"	370	340		
1833 5/1833 1840	VULCAN	"	John Wood & Co. Robert Napier	141'0"	22'10"	14'4"	450	480 IHP		
16/2/1835 5/1835 1842	CITY OF GLASGOW (II)	"	"	156'0"	24'4"	16'7½"	650	230 / 560 IHP		2m.
1/6/1837 2/1838 1850	COMMODORE (II)	"	R. Steele & Sons Caird & Co.	172'6"	24'3"	17'5"	705 387.11 NT	620 IHP		
10/1839 1840	ADMIRAL	"	John Wood & Co.	188'0"	24'6"	19'4"	930	900		

James Donaldson, James Thomson & Archibald MacConnell 1834 - 20/9/1840

Became part of City of Glasgow S.P. Company (II) in 1834

								99	90		
1/1828 1828 1831	Frolic	Wood P.S.	..								
1822 1832 6/1849 11/7/1849 1850	TOWARD CASTLE	..		J. Lang & W. Denny, Dumbarton	114'0" 115'6"	16'8½" 17'1"	9'4" 10'10"	163 NT	150	(1) S.L., 1 cyl. 54"-54" (2) St. 1 cyl.	Len' 1831 NE1831 Eng. ex *Brenda* fitted 1838 NB 10/1838 Re. acqd. 11/7/49
18/2/1835 1835 22/7/1836	Arab	..		Wood & Mills, Dunglass	132'9"	23'11"	12'11"	275 NT	220		
1836 1/1837 12/1850	TARTAR	..		Wood & Mills, Little Miln	148'0'	21'3'	13·7'	383	340		
1837 9/1837 31/12/1838	Circassian	..		Chas. Wood, Dumbarton	139·4'	19·2'	13·0'	302	220		2m. Sold foreign

TOBERMORY STEAM BOAT COMPANY

Archibald McEachern, Agent

Absorbed by Thomson & MacConnell *in 4/1838*

								99			
1836 11/1836 6/1839	Tobermory	Wood P.S.		Scott & Co., Greenock	80·1' •	11·7'	8·2'	80·47			Regd. Greenock, 1836-8

THOMSON & MacCONNELL

James Thomson and Archibald MacConnell
Archibald MacConnell and David Chapman
Clyde Steam Navigation Co. (II) 1/10/40
Steamers transferred to City of Glasgow S.P. Co. (II) in 3/1844, but Thomson & MacConnell
continued as Agents till 12/1850; agency then to G. & J. Burns till the transfer to
David Hutcheson & Co. in 1851

Dates: Built Acqd. Displ.	Name	Type	Shipbuilders Enginebuilders	L.	B.	D.	G.T.	N.H.P.	Machinery	Remarks
1817 3/1828 1832	Highland Chieftain	Wood P.S.	As below							Archbd. MacConnell; to W. Young
1838 3/4/1840 18/3/1841	Royal Victoria	Iron P.S.	Barr & McNab	106-8'	13-2'	7-3'	58-47 NT			To R. Napier
1839 5/1841 5/1853	SHANDON	Wood P.S.	John Wood & Co. R. Napier	134-9'	16-5'	9-4' 10-9'	186 165	170	S.L. 1 cyl. 50"-45"	Len. 1840 from 119-9' From R. Napier

ROBERT NAPIER

William Napier, Jnr., Agent, 12/1835 - 1838
Thomson & MacConnell, Agents, 1838 - 1844
Absorbed into City of Glasgow S.P. Co. (II), 3/1844

Dates: Built Acqd. Displ.	Name	Type	Shipbuilders Enginebuilders	L.	B.	D.	G.T.	N.H.P.	Machinery	Remarks
1825 16/6/1832 1/5/1833	Benlomond	Wood P.S.	See below							From Benlomond Steam Boat Co. To Alex. Allan, Snr. and others. NB 1833
1827		Wood	Denny							

GLASGOW & CALEDONIAN CANAL STEAMSHIP COMPANY, 1824 - 1828

DUNCAN McINNES. 13/5/1828 - 5/1835

ARCHIBALD McEACHERN and others, 1828 - 5/1835

D. WRIGHT & CO.. 5/1835 - 12/1835

Taken over by Robert Napier, 31/12/1835

Name	Dates	Type	Builder	Length	Breadth	Depth	Tons	HP	Engine	Remarks
Ben Nevis (I)	1824 1824 8/1831	Wood P.S.	Jas. Lang	82'9"	13'3"	9'2"	45		1 cyl.	1 dk. 2m. Regd. Stornoway 28/10/29
Commodore (I)	1824 — —	,,								
Highland Chieftain ex Duke of Wellington	1817 12/1824 9/1826	,,	A. McLachlan D. McArthur & Co.	71'4"	14'10"	5'5"	53·6	16		Trustees of Highland Chieftain Steamboat Co. 1828 to Archd. Mac-Connell, as above
MAID OF MORVEN	1826 1/1827 10/3/41	,,	John Wood & Co.. Port Glasgow Duncan McArthur	85'4"	14'7"	8'8"	52·5	32		A. McEachern and others. Trs. of Maid of Morven Steam Boat Co. R. Napier from 31/12/1835. NB 1836
Benlomond	1825 1828 16/6/32	,,	Jas. Lang Robert Napier	90'11"	16'0"	8'0"	70·3	35	1 cyl. 33½"-36"	A. McEachern and others, Trustees of Benlomond Steam Boat Co. NB 1833 To Robert Napier

Henry Bell
Henry Bell, Thomson and others
Robert Stewart, Agent, 8/1822 - 1825
Alex Laird, Agent, 1825 - 1832
Absorbed into fleet of A. McEachern, 1832

Dates: Built Acqd. Displ.	Name	Type	Shipbuilders Enginebuilders	L.	B.	D.	G.T.	N.H.P.	Machinery	Remarks
24/7/1811 8/1812 12/12/1820	*Comet (I)*	Wood P.S.	John Wood, Port Glasgow John Robertson	43'6" 65'6" 73'10"	11'4" 11'6"	5'9" 5'3" 7'0"	24·6 29·9		(1) ½ S.L. 1 cyl. 11" - 16" (2) ½ S.L. 1 cyl. 12½" - 16"	NE 10/1812 Regd. Port Glasgow 13/5/13 Len '19 NE '19 Regd. Greenock 10/2/ 1820
1820 1/1828	*Stirling Castle*	'' ''								
1817 11/1820 2/8/1821 23/5/1822 1824	*HIGHLAND CHIEFTAIN* ex. *Duke of Wellington*	'' ''	A. McLachlan D. McArthur	77·3' 81'0"	14·8'	5·4' 7'5"	53·5	32 16 20 34	S. 1 cyl.	From Dumbarton Steamboat Co. Len. 1820 by Wm. Denny and re-named. To J. McColl & Co. then to R. Stewart, Stranraer; then 1824 to Glasgow & Caledonian Canal S.P. Co.
1821 6/7/1821 25/10/25	*Comet (II)*	'' ''	Jas. Lang D. McArthur & Co. Camlachie				94	25		
1821 3/1822	Highlander	'' ''	John Wood	78'6"	14'4"	8'2"	51·2			Regd. Tobermory.

Dates	Name	Hull	Builder / Engine maker	Length	Breadth	Depth	Tonnage	HP	Engine	Notes
1832 10/1832 1848	**STAFFA (I)**	Wood P.S.	Robt. Barclay D. Napier	81'8" 79·4'	13'2" 10·5'	8'11" 4·6'	46·7 NT			NB 1836
1832 2/1833 1834	*Inverness*	"	Robt. Barclay	82'6"	12'1"	8'9"	43·5 NT	87		
1828 1834 1834-5	*Colonsay* (1) ex *Glasgow*	"	R. Duncan & Co., Greenock	130'0"	21'6"	12'3"	181	560 IHP		

ROBERT NAPIER (contd.) 21/12/1835 - 4/1844
Shandon & Glasgow S.P. Co.
Absorbed into City of Glasgow S.P. Co. (II) 4/1844.

Dates	Name	Hull	Builder / Engine maker	Length	Breadth	Depth	Tonnage	HP	Engine	Notes
1836 9/1836 4/1845	**BRENDA (I)**	Wood P.S.	A. McFarlane, Jnr. & Co. Dumbarton J. & W. Napier	123·6'	16·0'	9·0'	160	100	(1) St. 1 cyl. (2) S.L. 54"-54"	1m./2m.('44) Engine ex *Toward Castle* fitted 1838.
1839 1839 5/1841	Shandon	"	John Wood & Co. R. Napier	134·9'	16·5'	9·4'	165	170	S.L.	R. Napier & R. B. Clelland (Shandon & Glasgow S.P. Co.) To T. & McC. 5/1841.
1839 1839 1850	Superb	Iron P.S.								(Shandon & Glasgow S.P. Co.)
1834 22/12/40 25/2/41	James Oswald	Wood P.S.	J. Scott & Sons	101'8"	14'9"	8'4"	68 NT			
1838 18/3/41 1841	Royal Victoria / Victoria	Iron P.S.	Barr & McNab	106·8'	13·2'	7·3'	58·47 NT			From T. & McC. To G.P. & G. Rly. Co.

WILLIAM YOUNG and OTHERS, 1832 - 1835
GEORGE BURNS and WILLIAM YOUNG 18/4/1835 - 9/5/1835
GEORGE BURNS, 9/5/1835 - 8/1844
GLASGOW & LIVERPOOL STEAM SHIPPING CO., 8/1844 - 1845
G. & J. BURNS
(Highland Steamers only)

Dates: Built Acqd. Displ.	Name	Type	Shipbuilders Enginebuilders	L.	B.	D.	G.T.	N.H.P.	Machinery	Remarks
1817 1832 2/1834	Highland Chieftain ex Duke of Wellington	Wood P.S.	A. McLachlan D. McArthur & Co.	81'0"	14'10"	7'5"	53·6 NT	34		Len'
1832 1834 4/1846	INVERNESS	"	Robt. Barclay	82'6"	12'10"	8'9"	70	87		
1834 1834 11/1850	ROB ROY	"	R. Duncan & Co.	83'3"	12'11"	9'3"	42·2 NT			
2/1835 5/1835 1848	HELEN McGREGOR	"	R. Duncan & Co., Greenock Murdoch & Aitken	81'4" 82'0"	13'11"	10'2"	49·7 NT	35	St. 1 cyl. 37¼"-42"	Engine to *Lapwing*
1839 c.1847	THORNWOOD	Trackboat						—	Nil	On Crinan Canal
27/7/44 1844 1862	DOLPHIN (I)	Iron P.S.	R. Napier	161·0' 170·2'	23·0' 21·2'	10·8' 10·5'	121 238	100	St. 1 cyl. 53⅜"-48"	
1845 1845	CULLODEN	"	Caird & Co.	145·0'	16·5'	8·6'	149		St. 1 cyl.	

NORTH BRITISH STEAM NAVIGATION COMPANY, 1835 - 1845
(James Martin, James Burns and George Burns)

Dates	Name	Type	Builder	Length	Beam	Depth	Tonnage	HP	Notes
1834 1834 16/4/1838	GLEN ALBYN	Wood P.S.	John Scott & Co. Greenock	121'4"	19'4½"	12'7"	200 NT	165	
1833 1838 1845	ANTELOPE	"	Robt. Barclay	137'1"	19'0"	11'10"	273 NT	230	

JOHN McCOLL, ALEXANDER PATRICK and OTHERS
JAMES EWING
CASTLE STEAM PACKET COMPANY, 1832 - 1842
GLASGOW CASTLE STEAM PACKET COMPANY, 1842 - 1846
(Taken over by Glasgow & Liverpool Shipping Company, G. & J. Burns, 6/1846)

Dates	Name	Type	Builder	Length	Beam	Depth	Tonnage	HP	Notes
1814 1814 1814-6	Inverary Castle (I)	Wood P.S.	John Wood	84'0'	17'0'		112	40	
2/1815 1815 1819	Dumbarton Castle	"	Archbd. McLachlan D. McArthur & Co., Camlachie	87'0'	16'5'	7'7'	108	30	2 cyls.
2/1816 1816 11/1830	Rothesay Castle (I)	"	Wm. Denny, D. McArthur & Co.	92'11" 98'	16'1"	8'10" 9'2½"	74-7	34	1 cyl.	Len. 3/1821.
1820 1820 2/1838	Inverary Castle (II)	"	John & Charles Wood	95'6'	16'0'	9'5"	70-1	40	L. 1 cyl. 2 copper flue boilers
1817 1821 1822	Highland Chieftain	"	See above						From Bell, Thomson & Co. J. McColl To. R. Stewart

GLASGOW CASTLE STEAM PACKET Co. (contd.)

Dates: Built Acqd. Displ.	Name	Type	Shipbuilders Enginebuilders	L.	B.	D.	G.T.	N.H.P.	Machinery	Remarks
3/1822 1822 1831	Toward Castle	"	J. Lang & W. Denny D. McArthur & Co.	101.8' 115'6"	16·7' 17'1"	9'0" 10'10"	130 79 NT	45	St. 1 cyl.	Len. 1826 2 boilers.
1826 8/1826 2/1851	DUNOON CASTLE	"	W. Denny D. McArthur & Co.	106·7'	18·1'	8·6'	151	55 60	L. 1 cyl.	
1830 6/1830 12/1843	Arran Castle	"	John Wood R. Napier	103'8"	16'0"	8'8"	81·7	50		
1832 1832 4/1838	Windsor Castle (I)	"	" "	110'1"	16'0"	9'9"	151	80		
1835 6/1835 4/1838	Edinburgh Castle (I)	"	Hunter & Dow. Glasgow	117'6"	16'8"	10'5"	103·9			
1836 1836 22/3/38	Tarbert Castle (I)	"	Wood & Mills, Dunglass	122·2'	18·9'	10·0'	100-82			
1837 9/1837 5/1851	ROTHSAY CASTLE (II)	Iron P.S.	Tod & McGregor	133·8'	17·0'	8·6'	180	92	St. 1 cyl. 52⅝"-48"	NB 1845
4/1838 1838 7/1/39	Tarbert Castle (II)	"	Hedderwick & Rankin Tod & McGregor					90	St. 1 cyl. 50'-48"	Engine to *Inverary Castle* (III)
1838 1838	Windsor Castle (II)	"	Tod & McGregor	128·9'	16·5'	8·0'	151	80	St. 1 cyl.	

Dates	Name	Type	Builder	Length	Beam	Depth	Tonnage	HP	Engine	Notes
1839 11/1839 12/2/1851	INVERARY CASTLE (III)	Iron P.S.	Tod & McGregor	136·1'	19·4'	8·6'	120	113 90	St. 1 cyl. 50"-48" ex *Tarbert Castle*, made '38	NB '50
1842 9/1842 5/1853	**DUNTROON CASTLE**	"	Anderson & Gilmour, Govan	140·1' 144·0'	21·0'	10·2'	176 247	130	St. 2 cyls. 44"-54" 1 horiz.	
3/3/44 1844 1851	CARDIFF CASTLE	"	Caird & Co.	170·3'	19·0'	9·3'	96-57 NT	74 84	S.D. 2 cyls.	
26/6/44 1844 1851	CRAIGNISH CASTLE	"	::	170·3'	19·0'	9·3'	111 NT	70	S.D. 2 cyls.	
1844 1844 8/3/60 23/3/60 12/1927	EDINBURGH CASTLE (II) / GLENGARRY (5/75)	::	Smith & Rodger	138·1' 148·5'	15·8' 16·3'	7·5' 7·2'	114 124	45 55	St. 1 cyl. 36"-42".	NB '63. 20lb Len. 6/75
1824 1/1845 10/1846	MAID OF ISLAY	Wood P.S.	John Wood & Co. (1) Claud Girdwood (2) D. Napier	94·2"	18'5	11'4½"	140	50 60		NE Len.
1833 11/4/45 4/11/45	ALERT	Wood P.S.	Jas. Lang, Dumbarton	61·5'	14·2	8·0'	44·17'			
1836 1845 c.1846	VALE OF LEVEN	Iron P.S.	Tod & McGregor R. Napier				112			
24/5/45 6/1845 c.1846	WINDSOR CASTLE (II)	::	Tod & McGregor Meadowside						St. 1 cyl. 63".	
1846 1846 1851	DUNROBIN CASTLE	::	::	162·6'	19·0'	8·9'	120	450 IHP		:: ex *Windsor Castle* ('45)

G. & J. BURNS (contd.) 1846 - 6/1849
(Highland Steamers only)

Dates: Built Acqd. Displ.	Name	Type	Shipbuilders Enginebuilders	L.	B.	D.	G.T.	N.H.P.	Machinery	Remarks
1844 2/1847 8/1895	PIONEER (I)	Iron P.S.	Barr & McNab, Paisley	159·8' 186·6'	17·8' 18·2'	8·8' 9·2'	196 144 209	91 95	St. 1 cyl. 53"-51⅝ 22lb.	NB '62 and '84 1m./2m./1m. Len. '74
1844 2/1847 4/185	PILOT	"	"	137·4'	15·8'	7·9'	192	210 HP	St. 1 cyl.	1m.
1845 2/1847 1/1851	PETREL	"	"	165·5' 168·6'	17·4' 18·0'	8·7' 8·4'	162	60 320 IHP	St. 1 cyl. 54"-51⅝	2m.
— 1847 c.1866	MAID OF PERTH	Iron Trackboat	Blackhill				—	Nil	Nil	On Crinan Canal
1847 1847 c.1888-9	SUNBEAM	"	"	80·0'	13·0'		—	Nil	Nil	"
7/4/48 1848 1882	CYGNET (1) (Launched as BEN NEVIS (II))	Iron P.S.	Wood & Reid, Port Glasgow (1) J. & G. Thomson, Clydebank Foundry, Finnieston (2) Barclay, Curle & Co.	77·5'	14·5'	10·0'	107·41	50 50	(1) St. 1 cyl. 37½"-42" (2) St. 1 cyl. 41"-42"; 18lb.	NB '73 NE.
1848 1848 1859	LAPWING (I)	"	John Reid & Co. Murdoch & Aitken	82·7'	14·6'	10·0'	109.92	44	St. 1 cyl. 37¼"-42" ex Helen McGregor (made 1835)	
1848 1848 2/1853	PLOVER (I)	"	T. Wingate & Co.	159·9'	16·0'	7·6'	99.26	80	St. 1 cyl.	

(The three steamers absorbed into the Burns fleet, 6/1849)

								IHP		
1844 19/12/45 1850	QUEEN OF BEAUTY	Iron P.S.	T. Wingate & Co. (1) R. Napier (2) D. Napier	135·8' 137·8'	16·1'	8·0'	89·99 NT 140	240 104	(1) (2) S.L. 1 cyl. 30"-36" ex Leven	Chain-floats removed 1/46. Engine made '24, ex Leven, fitted '46. Contemporary reports state that she was rebuilt as Merlin (see below).
1826 1846 1850	MAID OF MORVEN	Wood P.S.	John Wood Duncan McArthur	85·4'	14·7'	8·8'	52·5 57·1	32		
1837 7/3/46 1855	GLENCOE (1) ex Loch Lomond / CURLEW ('49)	Iron P.S.	David Napier Glasgow	92·9' 95·0'	15·1' 15·2'	7·0' 8·2'	54·17 NT 92·36	135		1½ dk. 2m./1m.
	G. & J. BURNS, etc. (contd.) 6/1849 - 2/1851									
1847 1850 25/6/1851	LOCHFINE	Iron S.S.	Denny Bros... Dumbarton	74·5'	18·0'	7·6'	83	18	S. 2 cyls.	
1850 1850 1/1851	MERLIN	Iron P.S.	T. Wingate & Co.	150·8'	16·1'	8·0'	159	104		Stated by builders to be "new" in 1850; probably incorporated parts of Queen of Beauty (see above).
	DAVID HUTCHESON & CO. 2/1851 - 2/1857									
1852 1852 27/9/89	MOUNTAINEER (1)	Iron P.S.	J. & G. Thomson Govan	174·3' 184·1' 195·6'	17·6' 19·0' 18·2'	7·9' 8·3' 8·2'	173 190 188	120	St. 1 cyl. 57"-48" 26 lb.	NB '61 and '82 Len. '69 and '71
24/3/53 1853 11/1854	CHEVALIER (1)	"	"	176·9'	22·0'	10·9'	329	180	S.O. 2 cyls.	1¼ dk. 2m.

DAVID HUTCHESON & CO. (contd.)

Dates: Built Acqd. Displ.	Name	Type	Shipbuilders Enginebuilders	L.	B.	D.	G.T.	N.H.P.	Machinery	Remarks
1769 5/1854 c.1855	TWO FRIENDS	Wood Sloop	Burntisland	41·7'	13·34'	7·5'	—	—	—	
1844 5/1854 1855	ROBERT	Wood Smack	Dundee	45·7'	15·2'	8·6'	47·82			
1855 4/1855 10/1862	IONA (I)	Iron P.S.	,,	225·2' 232' OL	20·4'	9·0'	325	220 120	S.O. 2 cyls.	
1855 1855 21/7/1869	CLANSMAN (I)	,,	,,	191·3' 208·3'	25·7' 23·2'	12·8' 12·7'	414 462	180		3m. Len. '65

WILLIAM ROXBURGH
GLASGOW & LOCHFINE STEAM PACKET COMPANY
(Thomas Brownlie and William Roxburgh)
(D. Roxburgh & Co., Agents)
Taken over by D. Hutcheson & Co., 12th February, 1857

Dates: Built Acqd. Displ.	Name	Type	Shipbuilders Enginebuilders	L.	B.	D.	G.T.	N.H.P.	Machinery	Remarks
1847 1847 25/12/49	Lochfine	Iron S.S.	Denny Bros. Dumbarton	74·5'	18·0'	7·6'	83	18	S. 2 cyls.	2m. Wm. Roxburgh
1846 4/1851 3/8/1931	MARY JANE / GLENCOE (II) ('75)	Iron P.S.	Tod & McGregor, Meadowside	149·5' 153·0' 165·4'	19·3' 20·2'	9·5' 9·3' 9·4'	211 193 226	120 177	St. 1 cyl. 56"·54"	Regd. 8/1851 Len. '65 and '75 NB '83: 01 ex *Fusilier* (made '88); and 5/28 ex *Grenadier* (made '02)

Dates	Ship	Hull/Type	Builder	Length	Breadth	Depth	Tonnage	HP	Engine	Notes
8/1851 9/1895	**INVERARY CASTLE / INVERARAY CASTLE (8/74)**	..	Mavisbank	158·5' 172·9'	20·2' 20·5'	9·3'	209 230	90	50"-48" (ex *Tarbert Castle*, made 1838)	Len. '62 and '73
1826 9/1851 11/1854	Dunoon Castle	Wood P.S.	W. Denny D. McArthur & Co.	107'4"	18'0½"	8'6"	100·1	60		
1852 11/1852 1/12/58	**DUKE OF ARGYLL**	Iron P.S.	Scott, Sinclair & Co. Greenock	166·7' 209·4'	20·2' 20·9'	10·6' 10·0'	101 NT 391	176	1 cyl.	Len. 6/1855

GLASGOW & HIGHLAND STEAM PACKET COMPANY (Henry Ainslie and Others), 1849 - 1852
DAVID STIRLING and Others 1852 - 1857
Taken over by David Hutcheson & Co. 28/3/1857

Dates	Ship	Hull/Type	Builder	Length	Breadth	Depth	Tonnage	HP	Engine	Notes
1/8/1849 1849 21/12/58 1/1/59 1879 1879 1/2/1883	**MAID OF LORN / PLOVER (II)** (2/59)	Iron P.S.	T. Wingate & Co. R. Napier	83·0' 82·5' 83·8'	14·7' 13·6' 14·8'	8·4' 8·9'	120 110	59	St. 1 cyl. 43"-42" 18lb. Return flue boiler	NE '69 & '78

DAVID HUTCHESON & Co. (contd.) 3/1857 - 1875

Dates	Ship	Hull/Type	Builder	Length	Breadth	Depth	Tonnage	HP	Engine	Notes
1851 1858 1861	**STORK**	Iron P.S.	Wm. Denny & Bros.	190·7'	23·1'	12·0'	396	250		1¼ dk. 3m.
10/1860 1861 1861	**FINGAL (I)**	Iron S.S.	J. & G. Thomson	178·0'	25·0'	18·0'	352	120		
1861 1861 1863	**FAIRY**	Iron P.S.	..	149·4'	21·0'	6·9'	151	75	S.O. 2 cyls.	

DAVID HUTCHESON & CO. (contd.)

Dates: Built Acqd. Displ.	Name	Type	Shipbuilders Enginebuilders	L.	B.	D.	G.T.	N.H.P.	Machinery	Remarks
1862 1862 1/1905	CLYDESDALE (II)	Iron S.S.	J. & G. Thomson (1) ,, (2) Hutson & Son	180·2' 196·7'	24·1	13·2' 13·5'	403 447 446 468	120 128	(1) S. 2 cyls. 40"-30" (2) C. 2 cyls. 26½", 53"-30"	Len. NB '69 and '98 Cpd. '98
1863 19/5/63 24/11/1863	IONA (II)	Iron P.S.	J. & G. Thomson	249·2'	25·0'	9·1'	368 372	180	S.O. 2 cyls. 50"-48'	
1863 1863 1863	OSSIAN	Iron S.S.	,,	153·0'	23·0'	12·0'				May have become *Staffa*
1863 8/1863 8/1886	STAFFA (II)	Iron S.S.	J. & G. Thomson (1) J. & G. Thomson (2) Barclay Curle & Co.	153OL 148·1' 148·4'	23·1'	11·2'	268 273 294	100 85 90	(1) S. 2 cyls. (2) C. 2 cyls. 25", 44"-33"	NE & B '73
10/5/64 1864 3/1936	IONA (III)	Iron P.S.	J. & G. Thomson	255·5'	25·6'	9·0'	393 396	180 280	S.O. 2 cyls. 50½"-51"	NB '75 and '91
1866 1866 1939	GONDOLIER	,,	,,	148·2'	20·2'	7·8'	173 250	80	S.O. 2 cyls. 33"-39" 22lb.	2 loco boilers; '30 1 haystack ex *Grenadier*, made '02
1866 1866 3/1927	CHEVALIER (II)	,,	,,	211·0'	22·2'	9·3'	292 334 302	150 199	S.O. 2 cyls. 42"-54" 40lb.	NB '86 and '01
1866 1866 12/9/29	LINNET	Iron T.S.S.		86·0'	16·2'	2·8'	33 34	50 IHP	S. 4 cyls.	NB '94
1849 2/1868	DOLPHIN (II)	Iron	Tod & McGregor	167·0'	20·8'	10·0'	325	160		

Dates	Name	Type	Builder	Length	Breadth	Depth	Tonnage	HP	Engine	Notes
1870 7/1909	CLANSMAN (II)	S.S.	J. & G. Thomson	211·3'	27·3'	13·4'	597 619	150 171	32½" (later 33½"), 58½"-36"	
9/1863 1876 1882	QUEEN OF THE LAKE	Wood S.S.	Duncan Young at Bravallich, Port Sonachan A. Campbell & Son	80·0'	15·4'	5·7'	51	15	S. 2 cyls. 10"-12"	
1876 1876 5/1924	LOCHAWE	Iron S.S	A. & J. Inglis Muir & Caldwell	100·2'	16·8'	8·8'	97	30 100 IHP	S. 2 cyls. 14"-20"	

WALTER FREDERICK CAMPBELL of Islay
JAMES MORRISON and Others
JOHN RAMSAY, WILLIAM MUTTER and ALEX MacEWAN
C. MORRISON, T. G. BUCHANAN and JOHN RAMSAY
Taken over by David Hutcheson & Co.. 1876

Dates	Name	Type	Builder	Length	Breadth	Depth	Tonnage	HP	Engine	Notes
1815 1825 1834	Maid of Islay (I) ex Waterloo / Maid of Islay No.1	Wood P.S.	John Hunter, Port Glasgow James Cook	72·0' 100·5'	16·0' 15'11"	9'0"	90 79 NT	20		Re-built by Wm. Simons & Co. Greenock, 1826, 2m. Unofficialy called *Maid of the Mist*
1824 1827 7/1846	Maid of Islay No. 2 / Maid of Islay (II)	..	John Wood & Co. (1) Claude Girdwood (2) D. Napier	82' 94·2'	18' 18·4'	11·4'	92 140	50 60		Len.
1845 1845 —	Mogul	Wood Sail	Wm. Simons & Co.							3m square rigged
1836 1846 20/10/49	Modern Athens	Wood P.S.	David Adamson, Dundee P. Borrie, Dundee	115' 119·7'	10½' 17·7'	10·8'	119·02 122·5 NT	120	S.L. 2 cyls. 43"-48"	1 dk. & poop 2m
1849 10/1849 1866	Islay (I)	Iron P.S.	Tod & McGregor	167·0'	20·8'	10·6'	325	150 160	2 cyls.	

WALTER FREDERICK CAMPBELL of Islay (contd.)

Dates: Built Acqd. Displ.	Name	Type	Shipbuilders Enginebuilders	L.	B.	D.	G.T.	N.H.P.	Machinery	Remarks
1850 7/1853 —	City of Worcester	Iron S.S.	Govan	97·1'	20·3'	7·9'	130			1¼ dk. 2m
1867 1867 19/12/90	ISLAY (II)	Iron P.S.	Barclay, Curle & Co.	192·7' 206·6'	23·4'	10·6' 10·7'	362 395 401	145	St. 2 cyls. 46"-60"	Len. '82
			DAVID HUTCHESON & CO. (contd.) 1875 - 1879 **DAVID MACBRAYNE 6/1879 - 1905** **DAVID MACBRAYNE, LTD. 1905 - 1911**							
1877 25/6/1877 1907	LOCHIEL (I)	Iron S.S.	A. & J. Inglis Muir & Caldwell	139·8'	18·2'	9·2'	262 212 217	50	C. 2 cyls. 19", 34-24"	
1877 8/11/1877 1/1917	(LOCHNESS) /FINGAL (II)	..	..	115·3'	18·1'	7·3'	124	30 RHP	C. 2 cyls. 15", 26"-20"	Re-named while fitting out
11/4/78 1878 26/2/1936	COLUMBA (I)	Steel P.S.	J. & G. Thomson, Clydebank	301·4'	27·1'	9·4'	543 548 562 602	351 2200 IHP	S.O. 2 cyls. 53"-66" 50/55 lb.	NB '00
14/7/81 10/1881 12/5/31	CLAYMORE (I)	Iron S.S.	J. & G. Thomson	227·0'	29·6'	14·5'	726 720 760 776	208 1400 IHP	C. 2 cyls. 32", 61"-45"	
1883 1883	CAVALIER		Aitken & Mansel, Glasgow	151·1'	25·1'	11·8'	369 353	113	C. 2 cyls. 74" 48"-39"	

4/1928

Date	Name	Builder	Type	Length	Breadth	Depth	Tonnage	HP	Engine	Notes
							357			90/95lb.
1853 24/4/85 7/1912	**LOCHNESS (I)** ex Lough Foyle ex Lochgoil	J. Barr	Iron P.S.	153·0'	16·4'	6·9'	121	80	St. 1 cyl. 45"-42"	NB '76 Shortened, '85 from 163·9'
1880 5/10/85 16/5/16	**ETHEL** ex Obokh ex Ethel / **CLANSMAN (III)** (10/1910)	Workman, Clark & Co., Belfast J. Rowan & Son, Ltd., Glasgow	Iron S.S.	150·1'	21·7'	10·7'	281 287 300	60	C. 2 cyls. 19", 38"-30"	
1878 12/3/87 5/5/1917	**HANDA** ex Aros Castle	Blackwood & Gordon, Port Glasgow	..	84·2'	20·1'	9·5'	146	35 RHP	C. 2 cyls. 16", 28"-21"	
1883 5/1887 1913	**MABEL**	T. B. Seath & Co.	..	45·0'	10·0'	5·0'	30 28	35 IHP	1 cyl. & flywheel	Vertical boiler. 25lb.
1870 4/10/87 1904	**COUNTESS OF KELLIE**	A. Stephen & Sons, Kelvinhaugh. Glasgow Muir & Caldwell	Iron P.S. /S.S. ('87)	81·1'	19·5'	6·5'	68 74	30 20 95 IHP	(1) (2) C. 2 cyls.	NE '87
1860 11/1887 12/12/1893	**GLADIATOR**	M. Pearse & Co.. Stockton Dunsmuir & Jackson	Iron S.S.	192·8'	27·8'	15·7'	659 668	80	C. 2 cyls. 23", 42"-30"	3m NE and B '81
1873 19/1/88 7/4/94	**UDEA**	Schlesinger, Davis & Co.. Newcastle (1) Christie. Gutch & Co.. Stockton (2)	..	110·5'	18·1'	10·1'	157	30	(1) S. 2 cyls. 22"-20" (2) C. 2 cyls. 14", 27"-20"	NB '80 NE&B '92
1861 24/2/88 1909	**STAFFA (III)** ex Adela	W. Simons & Co.. Renfrew Portilla. White & Co.. Seville	..	141·8' 134·5'	19·1'	10·0'	211 197 188	60 RHP	C. 2 cyls. 16½, 32⁵/16"-24"	NE '70 NB '84 Shortened '91

DAVID MACBRAYNE, etc. (contd.)

Dates: Built Acqd. Displ.	Name	Type	Shipbuilders Enginebuilders	L.	B.	D.	G.T.	N.H.P.	Machinery	Remarks
14/4/88 6/1888 25/7/1934	FUSILIER	Iron & Steel P.S.	McArthur & Co., Paisley Hutson & Corbett, Glasgow	202·0'	21·6'	· 8·1'	251 280	133 142	D. 1 cyl. 49"–60"	NB '01
1850 17/9/88 6/12/95	PELICAN	Iron S.S.	E. Pike, Cork J. Dickinson, Sunderland	205·6'	28·3'	15·8'	638	140	C. 2 cyls. 29", 54"-33"	Cpd.
1854 17/9/88 16/11/90	FALCON	''	E. Pike, Cork Palmer's S.B. Co., Jarrow	211·0'	28·0'	15·9"	613	100	C. 2 cyls. 26", 48"-30"	Cpd. '83
— 14/1/89 1894	MARGARET	''	D. M. Cumming, Blackhill	66·5'	13·5'	4·5'	60	25		
1884 13/2/89 20/8/17	TEXA ex James Mutter	''	Scott & Co., Bowling W. King & Co., Glasgow	100·0' 118·4'	19·1'	8·8'	157 185 186	35	C. 2 cyls. 16", 28"-22"	Len. '91 NB '97
1870 18/7/89 1/1897	LOANDA	''	J. Elder & Co., Glasgow	279·1'	31·1'	23·5'	1475	221	C. 2 cyls. 38", 68"-33"	
1878 30/8/89 1904	FLOWERDALE ex Recovery	Iron T.S.S.	Barrow S.B. Co. Ltd., Barrow	177·0'	25·1'	14·7'	488 485 539	150	C. 4 cyls. 23", 42"-24"	
— 1889 1900	MAUD	Iron S.S.	T. B. Seath & Co.				10	10		Launch
1858	HERO	Iron	T. Wingate & Co.						St. 1 cyl.	

Name	Dates	Type	Builder	Length	Beam	Depth	Tonnage	HP	Engine	Notes
ISLAY (III) ex Princess Louise	30/12/90 1902	::	Glasgow	211·4	24·1	12·4	497 539	200 347	34'-60"	NB '78
GREAT WESTERN / LOVEDALE ('93)	1867 9/4/91 1904	::	W. Simons & Co., Renfrew	220·4'	25·2'	12·4'	466 459	190 237	S.O. 2 cyls. 48"-45"	NB '93
GAEL	1867 19/5/91 1925	::	Robertson & Co., Greenock Rankin & Blackmore, Greenock	211·0'	23·2'	10·6'	419 361	150 247	S.O. 2 cyls. 45"-63"	NB '79 and '92
CYGNUS / BRIGADIER ('92)	1854 21/7/91 7/12/96	::	J. Henderson & Sons, Renfrew (1) McNabb & Clark, Greenock (2) Hutson & Corbett	182·0'	21·4'	9·7'	250 275 264	120	S.O. 2 cyls. 42¾"-42"	NB '74 and '92
CARABINIER ex Albert Edward	1878 10/10/93 1/1909	::	Oswald, Mordaunt & Co., Southampton	169·4'	20·5'	9·0'	269 299	120	C.O. 2 cyls. 26", 50"-51"	
HIBERNIAN	1875 13/7/94 12/8/94	Iron S.S.	H. Murray & Co., Port Glasgow Kemp & Hume, Glasgow	145·3'	22·7'	11·8'	334	47	C. 2 cyls. 18½", 32"-23"	NB '84
AGGIE	1893 c.1894	Steel & Iron S.S.	J. Fullerton & Co., Paisley Ross & Duncan	110·2'	20·5'	9·5'	183	45 RHP	C. 2 cyls. 16", 32"-24"	Chartered 1894 et seq.
GAIRLOCHY ex Ardmore ex Sultan	1861 10/9/94 12/1919	Iron P.S.	Barclay, Curle & Co. J. Barr	176·0' 148·3'	16·6'	6·6'	124 142	60	St. 1 cyl. 45"-42⅝ ex Wellington, made '53	NB '77 Shortened '95
JESSIE	— 1895 —	S.S.								Launch
GLENDALE ex La Belgique ex Flamingo ex Paris	1875 8/9/02 7/1905	Iron P.S.	J. Elder & Co., Govan	220·0'	25·2'	11·0'	481 491 511	335 220	C.O. 2 cyls. 41", 72"-60"	NB '88

DAVID MACBRAYNE, etc. (contd.)

Dates: Built Acqd. Displ.	Name	Type	Shipbuilders Enginebuilders	L.	B.	D.	G.T.	N.H.P.	Machinery	Remarks
1903 1903 1918	LAPWING (II)	Steel S.S.	Scott & Co., Bowling Hutson & Sons	135·2'	21·2'	9·4'	211	64 RHP	C. 2 cyls. 19", 36"-27'	
30/1/04 1904 1/1/27	SHEILA	"	A. & J. Inglis, Ltd.	150·2'	23·1'	10·5'	280 256 263	76 RHP	T. 3 cyls. 13½", 23½", 36"-27'	
17/5/04 1904 23/3/1946	PLOVER (III) / LOCH ALINE ('34)	"	Scott & Co., Bowling Barrow S.B. Co., Ltd.	136·8'	21·1'	9·4'	208 187 191 192 229	77 RHP	C. 2 cyls. 23½, 42"-24" (ex port eng. of *Flowerdale*, made '78)	
14/6/04 1904 17/9/30	CYGNET (II)	"	A. & J. Inglis, Ltd. Barrow S.B. Co., Ltd.	135·0'	21·1'	9·4'	191 201	72 RHP	C. 2 cyls. 23½, 42"-24" (ex starboard eng. of *Flowerdale*, made '78)	
1904 1904 11/12/29	BRENDA (II)	"	Scott & Sons, Bowling J. Fisher & Co., Paisley	82·0'	19·1'	7·8'	115	20 RHP	C. 2 cyls. 11", 22"-14" (ex a yacht, made '88)	
2/1905 1905 31/1/1945	PIONEER (II)	Steel P.S.	A. & J. Inglis Ltd.	160·0'	22·1'	8·3'	241	84	C.D. 2 cyls. 20", 38"-48"	
18/5/05 1905 2/1953	CLYDESDALE (II)	Steel S.S.	Scott & Sons, Bowling Ross & Duncan	151·1'	26·1'	12·4'	394 401 412	85 RHP	T. 3 cyls. 15", 25½", 41"-30'	

Name	Dates	Type	Builder / Engine builder	Length	Breadth	Depth	Tonnage	HP	Engines	Notes
COMET (III) ex Win	1907 5/1947	T.S.M.V.	Co., London (1) L. Gardner & Sons, Manchester (2) L. Gardner & Sons. Ltd.	65·0'	14·1'	5·1'	43	144 / 180 BHP	paraffin mtrs. NE '28 (2) Two semi-Diesel, 8 cyls. 8½"-9½" / Two 4 cyl. paraffin mtrs.. 11"-14"	
SCOUT	11/4/07 1907 8/1913	,,	Ailsa S.B. Co., Ltd., Troon Griffin Eng. Co., Ltd., Bath	100·0'	18·0'	5·9'	82	260 IHP	T. 3 cyls. 21½", 35", 58"-36"	
CHIEFTAIN	11/5/07 1907 5/6/19	Steel S.S.	Ailsa S.B. Co., Ltd., Troon Clyde S.B. & E. Co. Ltd., Port Glasgow	241·7'	33·1'	11·1'	1081 982 1088	257	T. 3 cyls.	
LOCHINVAR	1908 1908 6/1960	Steel Tr.S.M.V. /T.S.M.V. ('49)	Scott & Sons, Bowling (1) L. Gardner & Sons, Manchester (3) Davey, Paxman & Co. (Colchester) Ltd.	145·2'	24·1'	7·5'	178 201 216	288 BHP / 64 / 330 BHP	(1) Three 6 cyl. paraffin mtrs. (2) Three 4 cyl. oil engines, 9½"-10¾" (3) 4 S.C.S.A. 12 cyls. 7"-7¾" geared 2·5:1	NE '26 and NE made '47, fitted '49
LOCHIEL (II)	30/5/08 1908 7/1918	Steel S.S.	Scott & Sons, Bowling Ross & Duncan	135·4'	22·1'	9·2'	241	74 RHP	C. 2 cyls. 17", 36"-24"	
NELLIE / STAFFA (IV) (4/10)	1892 1908 7/4/16	,,	J. H. Gimour, Irvine Muir & Houston	80·0'	19·1'	7·7'	89	25	C. 2 cyls. 12", 24"-18"	NB '08
DIRK	18/6/09 1909 1918	,,	Scott & Sons, Bowling Ross & Duncan	125·3'	19·6'	8·6'	181	70 RHP	C. 2 cyls. 15", 32"-24"	
MOUNTAINEER (III)	10/2/10 1910 9/1938	Steel P.S.	A. & J. Inglis. Ltd.	180·0'	20·1'	7·7'	235	86 RHP	C.D. 2 cyls. 20½", 38½"-48"	

LOCH LEVEN SHIPPING COMPANY, 1905 - 1908
J. D. Sutherland. R. P. Grant and John P. Grant
LOCH LEVEN SHIPPING COMPANY, LTD. 5/1908 - 1911
Taken over by David MacBrayne, Ltd, 1/7/1911

Dates: Built Acqd. Displ.	Name	Type	Shipbuilders Enginebuilders	L.	B.	D.	G.T.	N.H.P.	Machinery	Remarks
1905 1905 1908	Glencoe	Wood M.V.	A. M. Dickie & Sons, Tarbert Albion Motors. Ltd.	25-0'	6-0'	3-5'			Albion mtr., 2 cyls.	Launch
1906 1906 c.1917	CONA	"	James Adam & Sons, Gourock Albion Motors. Ltd.	35-0'	7-0'	4-0'			··	Launch-26 passgrs
1907 c1908	Dolphin	"								Launch-34 passgrs
1896 6/1908 10/1/29	LOUGH NEAGH QUEEN ex Clutha No.12 / **LOCH LEVEN QUEEN** (10/1908) / **LOCHNESS** (II) (1912)	Steel T.S.S.	Russell & Co., Port Glasgow Muir & Houston	87-1'	17-1'	5-8'	82	20	C. 4 cyls. 7½", 15"-10"	
			DAVID MACBRAYNE, LTD. (contd.) 1911 - 1928 DAVID MACBRAYNE (1928) LTD. 1928 - 1934							
1897 1914 1917	**COUNTESS OF MAYO**	Steel S.S.	T. B. Seath & Co., Rutherglen J. Fisher, Paisley	70-2'	14-1'	7-3'	46	90 IHP	C. 2 cyls. 9½", 20"-12"	
1888 20/5/14 22/7/15	**DUKE OF ABERCORN** ex Britannia	Steel T.S.S.	Grangemouth Dockyard Co. Ltd.	120-4'	19-0'	7-0'	144	50 IHP	C. 4 cyls. 12", 24"-18"	

KATE	8/6/14 6/6/17	Bristol	S.S.	60·1'	10·3'	5·4'	18	11		
1906 1919 7/10/1938	DEVONIA / LOCHIEL (III) (1920)	Scott of Kinghorn, Ltd.	Steel S.S.	140·2'	23·1'	10·5'	314 326 318	52 RHP	C. 2 cyls. 16½", 36"-27"	
1913 1928 21/4/1938	C. & B. No.1 / LOCHGORM (I) ('30) / IONA (IV) ('36)	Dan S.B. Co., Ipswich Penman & Co., Ltd.	Steel M.V.	60·3'	13·5'	5·2'	37	45 BHP		
1891 18/5/29 7/1948	LOCHDUNVEGAN (I) ex Denbigh Coast ex Kelvindale ex Grouse	Caird & Co.	Steel S.S.	175·4'	28·0'	11·9'	411	85 RHP	T. 3 cyls. (1) 15¼", 24½", 40½"-30" (2) 15¼", 25", 40⅜"-30"	NB '23 Cyls. rebored 3/23 and 11/31
6/6/29 12/7/29 21/7/55	LOCHNESS (III)	Harland & Wolff, Ltd. Govan J. G. Kincaid & Co. Ltd., Greenock	Steel T.S.S.	200·3'	34·1'	10·5'	777	150	T. 6 cyls. 14", 23", 38"-27"	
8/8/29 20/9/29 4/1/52	LOCHSHIEL (I)	H. Robb, Ltd., Leith L. Gardner & Sons, Ltd., Manchester	Steel M.V.	105·8'	26·1'	8·5'	208	300 BHP	6 cyls. 12½"-15"	
29/4/30 4/7/30 26/8/64	LOCHEARN	Ardrossan Dockyard Ltd. (1) L. Gardner & Sons, Ltd. (2) Davey, Paxman & Co. (Colchester) Ltd.	Steel T.S.M.V.	155·7'	29·1'	9·0'	542	600 BHP 660 BHP	(1) 2 S.C.S.A., 12 cyls. 12½"-15" (2) 4 S.C.S.A. 24 cyls. 7"-73" geared 3'33:1	NE 7/48 and subsequent interchanges
15/5/30 5/7/30 26/8/64	LOCHMOR (I)	‥	‥	‥	‥	‥	‥	‥	‥	NE made 1/44 fitted 4/49 and subsequent interchanges
1871 16/2/31 21/6/1937	LOCHBROOM (I) ex City of London	J. Elder & Co., Govan	Iron S.S.	241·9'	30·5'	16·7'	1139	1800 IHP	C. 2 cyls. 46", 80"-39"	NB '82 and '01

DAVID MACBRAYNE, (1928) LTD. etc. (contd.)

Dates: Built Acqd. Displ.	Name	Type	Shipbuilders Enginebuilders	L.	B.	D.	G.T.	N.H.P.	Machinery	Remarks
1931 28/5/31 1/1970	LOCHFYNE	Steel T.S.M.V.	Wm. Denny & Bros. Ltd., Dumbarton (1) Davey, Paxman & Co. Ltd. Metropolitan Vickers Elec. Co. Ltd. Manchester (2) British Polar Engines Ltd.	209·9'	30·1'	7·9'	748 754	Dsls. 2000 IHP Mtrs. 1340 SHP 247 NHP	(1) Two sets of 5 cyl. 4 str. Diesel. $15\frac{7}{8}''$-20": 330 r.p.m. Generators - 2DC, 520V, 540 kW. Motors-2DC, 438 r.p.m. (2) 2 S.C.S.A. 8 cyls. $13\frac{3}{8}''$-$22\frac{7}{16}''$	NE '53
— 1931/2 1964	MINGARY / KILCHOAN	Wood M.V.	— The Bergius Co. Ltd.	26·0'	7·6'	2·0'		15	Kelvin-Ricardo	Ferry at Kilchoan, Glenelg, Rodel, etc.
1932 1932 26/4/48	DUMB BARGE No.1	Wood	—	24·0'	7·5'	2·5'				Ferry at Rodel (may have been named *Rodel*)
1932 1932 1939	STAFFA (V)	Wood M.V.	Carse & Holmes, Ltd., Glasgow The Bergius Co., Ltd.	32·0'	9·0'	2·5'	—	14	Kelvin Paraffin Motor	Ferry at Iona/Staffa
1933 1933 9/1942 19/5/46 16/9/1961	FINGAL (III)	::	::	::	::	::	::	::	::	::
1933 1933 1/1956	DUMB BARGE No.2	Wood	—	24·0'	7·5'	2·5'				Ferry at Stockinish
— 1933	GLENELG	Wood M.V.	— The Bergius Co., Ltd.	26·0'	7·6'	2·0'		15	Kelvin-Ricardo	Apparently sold, then reacquired as *Kellin*

Dates	Name	Builder / Engine builder	Material & Type	Length	Breadth	Depth	Tonnage	H.P.	Engines	Notes
— 1891 1893	Marchioness of Lorn		Steel S.S.							
1894 1894 1898	Princess Louise (I)	H. McIntyre, Kelliebank, Alloa	Steel S.S.	75·0'	15·1'	7·5'	66	17	2 cyls.	
1898 1898 4/1939	PRINCESS LOUISE (II)	Ritchie, Graham & Milne, Whiteinch Campbell & Calderwood, Paisley	..	95·1'	17·1'	8·2'	106	30	C. 2 cyls. 13¼", 26"·18"	NB '19
1884 1901 1919	Countess of Bantry	Workman, Clark & Co. Ltd., Belfast W. Kemp. Glasgow	Iron S.S.	91·6'	17·0'	9·0'	86 90	30	C. 2 cyls. 14", 27"·20"	NB '93

DAVID MACBRAYNE (1928) LTD. 1934 - 1935
DAVID MACBRAYNE LTD. 1935 - 31/12/47

Dates	Name	Builder / Engine builder	Material & Type	Length	Breadth	Depth	Tonnage	H.P.	Engines	Notes
15/3/34 29/6/34	LOCHNEVIS	Wm. Denny & Bros., Ltd. (1) Davey, Paxman & Co., Ltd. (2) National Gas & Oil Eng. Co. Ltd., Ashton-under- Lyne	Steel T.S.M.V.	175·0'	31·0'	10·5'	568 573 (8/61)	(1) Dsls 1300 BHP Mtrs. 1050 SHP (2) 1560 BHP	(1) Two sets of 6 cyl., 4 str. Diesels. 13": 16":500 r.p.m. (2) 2 oil engs. 4 S.A... each 6 cyls. 305-381mm Generators 2DC. 500 V 420 kW, Motors-2DC. 400 r.p.m.	NE 3/1957
— 17/5/35 7/44 24/5/46 22/12/55	SOAY ex Ripple	J. White, Glasgow The Bergius Co., Ltd.	Wood M.V.	32·0'	10·6'	3·0'	—	15	Kelvin P.2	Ferry at Loch Scavaig, Staffa/Iona, Glenelg, etc.

DAVID MACBRAYNE, LTD. etc. (contd.)

Name	Dates: Built Acqd. Displ.	Type	Shipbuilders Enginebuilders	L.	B.	D.	G.T.	N.H.P.	Machinery	Remarks
QUEEN ALEXANDRA / SAINT COLUMBA (5/36)	1912 3/10/35 12/1958	Steel Tr.S.S.	Wm. Denny & Bros. Denny & Co.	270-3'	32-1'	11-0'	792 827 851	3000 SHP	3 turbs. D.D.	Oil fuel 1937
KING GEORGE V	1926 3/10/35 3/4/75	Steel T.S.S.	Wm. Denny & Bros., Ltd. Parsons Marine Steam Turbine Co. Ltd.	260-6'	32-1"	10-6'	797 796 801 815 985 (7/62)	3500 SHP	6 turbs. S.R.G.	NB '29 and '35. Oil fuel 1938. To Caledonian MacBrayne Ltd., as at 1/1/73, later to Caledonian MacBrayne Holdings, Ltd.
LOCHGORM (II) ex Lairdspool ex Lily	1896 11/12/1936 5/6/51	Steel S.S.	Blackwood & Gordon. Port Glasgow	190-5'	29-3'	13-3'	635 126	126	T. 3 cyls. (1) 15", 24½" 40"-30" (2) 15", 24½" 40½"-30'	NB 12/1920 LP cyl. re-bored 1947
LOCHGARRY ex Lairdsrock ex Vulture	1898 1/1/1937 21/1/42	..	A. & J. Inglis	265-0'	33-6'	15-9'	1670	367	T. 3 cyls. 28", 46", 74"-45"	NB '24
GARRY	1937 1937 20/3/69	Wood M.V.	H. McLean. Govan Kelvin-Ricardo	25-0'	7-5'	2-5'	—	15	Kelvin-Ricardo	Ferry and cruise launch at Fort William; later at Rodel and Loch Shiel.
KYLE	1916 1/2/38 31/3/41	..	The Bergius Co. Ltd.	32-0'	9-0'	2-5'	6 NT	14	4 S.C.S.A. 2 cyls. Kelvin Paraffin	Ferry ex Kyle-Kyleakin
LOCHBUIE (I)	1938 6/1938 3/1947	Steel T.S.M.V.	Nicolas Witsen & Vis. Amsterdam M.A.N. Augsburg &	59-4'	12-5'	4-9'	40	260 BHP	4 S.C.S.A. 12 cyls.	

Name	Dates	Material/Type	Builder / Engineer	Length	Breadth	Depth	Tonnage	Power	Engines	Notes
LOCHIEL (IV)	1939 3/1970	··	Ltd. Davey, Paxman & Co. (Colchester) Ltd.	183·7'	32·1'	7·7'	580 603 577	140	16 cyls. 9½"-17"	Chartered
ULSTER STAR ex Dynamic ex Lismore ex Broom ex James Crombie	1904 1942 7/1947	Steel S.S.	Ramage & Ferguson. Ltd., Leith	186·4'	28·1'	13·8'	576 626	132 135	T. 3 cyls. 17", 27" 45"-33"	Chartered
ROBINA	1914 12/6/46 1948	Steel T.S.S.	Ardrossan Dockyard & S.B. Co. Ltd. McKie & Baxter	159·6'	26·1'	8·8'	306	79	2 x T.3 cyls. 10½", 17" 28"-18"	Chartered
LOCH SEAFORTH	19/5/47 1947 5/1973	Steel T.S.M.V.	Wm. Denny & Bros. Ltd. Sulzer Bros.. Ltd., Winterthur	229·4'	36·1'	11·2'	1089 1126	217	2 S.C.S.A. 12 cyls. 14½"-23⅝"	Retained by David MacBrayne Ltd. at 1/1/73
LOCHNELL ex Galen	1941 6/1947 10/6/81	Wood T.S.M.V.	Jas. A. Silver. Ltd., Rosneath The Bergius Co.. Ltd.	51·5'	14·1'	4·9'	31	60 BHP 6	8 cyls. 4¼"-6⅝"	NE '58. Retained by David MacBrayne Ltd. at 1/1/73

McCALLUM, ORME & CO., LTD. 1929 - 31/12/47

Controlled by David MacBrayne. Ltd. from 10/1947 and absorbed on 1/1/1948

ANDREW ROSS - ANDREW McKENZIE ROSS

JOHN McCALLUM & CO. 1875 - 1929

WESTERN ISLES STEAM PACKET CO., LTD.

Name	Dates	Material/Type	Builder / Engineer	Length	Breadth	Depth	Tonnage	Power	Engines	Notes
Jean	1831 1873 c.1875	Wood Schooner	Dumbarton					78 NT	—	
Saint Clair of the Isles ex Lisboa	1860 c.1873 3/1875	Iron P.S.	J. Reid & Co. Port Glasgow Macnab & Co.. Greenock	185·5' 190·8'	24·2'	11·7' 11·2'	358	120	S.O. 2 cyls. 43"-48"	Len' NB '73

JOHN McCALLUM & CO. etc. (contd.)

Dates: Built Acqd. Displ.	Name	Type	Shipbuilders Enginebuilders	L.	B.	D.	G.T.	N.H.P.	Machinery	Remarks
1874 1874 1890	Lady Ambrosine	Iron S.S.	J. & R. Swan, Dumbarton W. King & Co.	85·0' 105·0'	19·5'	9·1' 8·8'	116 111 136	30	C. 2 cyls. 13½", 20"-24"	Len '85 NB '85
1876 4/1876 22/10/80	Saint Clair	,,	Birrell, Dumbarton Walker, Henderson & Co.	84·1'	20·0'	8·0'	130	33	C. 2 cyls. 16", 27"-22"	
30/4/81 1881 6/1917	Hebridean (I)	,,	T. B. Seath & Co., Rutherglen W. King & Co.	139·8'	23·6'	12·0'	330 314 322 331	70 RHP	C. 2 cyls. 22", 40"-30"	NB '10
1877 1889 1890	John o' Groat ex Fé ex John o' Groat	,,	Gourlay Bros., Dundee	174·8'	24·8"	12·9'	388	116	C. 2 cyls. 28", 52"-33"	
1870 12/1890 12/1896	Quiraing ex La Valette ex South Western	,,	Blackwood & Gordon, Port Glasgow	190·5'	26·3'	12·8'	460	120	C. 2 cyls. 28⅜", 50⅜"-30"	NB '83
24/3/98 1898 1/8/55	HEBRIDES (I)	Steel S.S.	Ailsa S.B. Co., Ltd., Troon A. & J. Inglis	180·0'	28·1'	13·2'	585	90 RHP	T. 3 cyls. 16", 26", 42"-30"	NB 2/37
1914-18		Wood								Loch Eport
1914-18		Wood								Loch Eport
		Wood							Kelvin	Engine fitted

Dates	Name	Builder	Type	Length	Breadth	Depth	Tonnage	HP	Engine	Engine builder / Owner
1902 3/1926 17/1/1949	**RESPECT**	— St. Monance	Wood M.V.				54			Aux. Motor– Loch Eport

ORME BROS. & CO. 1853 - 1853

Dates	Name	Builder	Type	Length	Breadth	Depth	Tonnage	HP	Engine	Engine builder / Owner
1852 1/1853 1853	Queen	T. Wingate & Co., Glasgow	Iron S.S.	144·5'	19·3'	11·0'	275	70	S. 2 cyls.	Jas Orme, Martin Orme, Laurence Orme

WILLIAM LANG 1860 - 1/1861

Dates	Name	Builder	Type	Length	Breadth	Depth	Tonnage	HP	Engine	Engine builder / Owner
1860 10/1860 12/1862	Queen of the Isles	— Port Glasgow	Steel S.S.	116·0'	20·4'	10·0'	156·5	40	S. 2 cyls.	W. Lang

THE GREAT WEST OF SCOTLAND FISHERY CO., LTD. 1858 - 1/1861
(Martin Orme, Manager)
(Steamer taken over 1/1861)

Dates	Name	Builder	Type	Length	Breadth	Depth	Tonnage	HP	Engine	Engine builder / Owner
1858 1858 26/5/68	Islesman	Robert Napier	Iron S.S. & Sail	107·7' 106·0' 130·5'	20·1' 20·0' 19·8'	11·5' 11·4'	116 142 173	80	S. 2 cyls.	Len. 4/1861 W. Lang

WILLIAM LANG - MARTIN ORME (contd.) 1/1861 - 1912
MARTIN ORME & CO. 1/1913 - 1929

Dates	Name	Builder	Type	Length	Breadth	Depth	Tonnage	HP	Engine	Engine builder / Owner
1860 1/1861 3/1/63	Chieftain	John Reid & Co., Port Glasgow Hastie, Greenock	Iron S.S.	85·4'	19·1'	9·2'	87	35	S. 2 cyls. 16"-20"	W. Lang

MARTIN ORME & CO. (contd.)

Dates: Built Acqd. Displ.	Name	Type	Shipbuilders Enginebuilders	L.	B.	D.	G.T.	N.H.P.	Machinery	Remarks
1868 1868 4/1875	Dunvegan Castle	Iron S.S. & Sails	Blackwood & Gordon, Port Glasgow	140·5' 154·5'	20·6'	11·0'	229 254	60	S. 2 cyls. 32"-30"	W. Lang / M. Orme Len.
1871 1871 17/4/75	Talisman	Iron S.S.	"	170·0'	23·0'	12·6'	310	90	C. 2 cyls. 32", 44"-30"	W. Lang, M. Orme & Thos. Blackwood
1875 1875 4/1948	DUNARA CASTLE	"	"	180·4'	24·5'	12·5'	423 454 450 454 450 457	130 123	(1) S. 2 cyls. 42"-30" (2) C. 2 cyls. 30", 52"-30"	W. Lang M. Orme Cpd. '82 NB '82 and '94
1878 1878 1887	Aros Castle	"	"	84·2'	20·1'	9·5'	140	35	C. 2 cyls. 16", 28"-21"	W. Lang / M. Orme

JACK BROS. - JAMES JACK - ALEXANDER JACK
1926 - 1935
(Taken over by McCallum, Orme & Co., Ltd. 1935)

Dates: Built Acqd. Displ.	Name	Type	Shipbuilders Enginebuilders	L.	B.	D.	G.T.	N.H.P.	Machinery	Remarks
1918 c.1926 1933-5	Rose Valley	Wood S.S.	Herd & Mackenzie, Findochty, Yeamann & Baggeson, Dundee	87·0'	20·0'	10·1'	100	42 RHP	T. 3 cyls. 9½", 15½, 26" -18"	(A. Jack)
1887 1926 1931	Sagitarius	Iron S.S.	Earle's Co., Ltd. Hull	119·1'	20·2'	10·6'	195	45 RHP	T. 3 cyls. 11½", 17", 30"-18"	
1897 1929	CHALLENGER	Steel S.S.	Hall, Russell & Co., Ltd. Aberdeen	107·5'	20·1'	10·6'	151	50	C. 2 cyls. 17" 34"-24"	(I. Jack)

Dates	Name	Material / Type	Builder	Length	Breadth	Depth	BHP	Engine / RHP	Notes
13/3/33 — 27/6/49	ex Dunsmore —	Wood —							at Finsberg

McCALLUM, ORME & CO., LTD. 1935 - 1947

Dates	Name	Material / Type	Builder	Length	Breadth	Depth	BHP	Engine	Notes
— 1946	Thistle	Wood M.V.							
— 18/11/49	ARINAGOUR	ʺ							To David MacBrayne Ltd. 11/12/45
— 14/3/1949	NORA	ʺ							To David MacBrayne Ltd. 11/12/45
— 31/8/51	ARDGOIL / ERISKAY (I)	ʺ	The Bergius Co., Ltd.	26·0'	7·6'	2·6'		Kelvin Poppet	Ferry at Kallin / Gramsdale:Eriskay Foundered 19/12/49
1918 c.1939 4/1949	GLASSARD ex Bounty	ʺ	The Bergius Co., Ltd.	32·3'				4 S.C.S.A.. 2 cyls. 5½-7" Petrol-Paraffin	Colonsay Ferry
1905 1944 9/10/1948	JANET B.	ʺ	Eyemouth	60·4'	18·6'	7·0'	40 / 50 BHP		Aux. motor

DAVID MACBRAYNE, LTD. (Contd.) 1/1/48 - 31/12/72

Dates	Name	Material / Type	Builder	Length	Breadth	Depth	BHP	Engine	Notes
1923 1948 1/1968	KALLIN ex Glenelg	Wood M.V.	The Bergius Co., Ltd.	26·0'	7·6'	2·0'	15 BHP	Kelvin-Ricardo	Gramsdale

DAVID MACBRAYNE, LTD. etc. (contd.)

Dates: Built Acqd. Displ.	Name	Type	Shipbuilders Enginebuilders	L.	B.	D.	G.T.	N.H.P.	Machinery	Remarks
1948 — 7/4/67	MARNE	..	..	30·0'	9·5'	4·0'		..	Kelvin Poppet	Gramsdale: then Eriskay till 1965
1945 27/3/47 13/7/71	LOCHBROOM (II)	Steel M.V.	Scott & Sons. Ltd. Bowling British Polar Engines, Ltd.	144·0'	27·1'	7·7'	413 325	84	2 S.C.S.A. 5 cyls. 9 3/16 - 16" 9/16" (made and fitted '48)	Launched as *Empire Maysong*; To have had T. 3 cyls. 9", 16", 26"-18" by White's Marine Eng. Co., Ltd. Newcastle
1942 3/1949 6/5/68	LOCHBUIE (II) ex G. S. Pinnace R213	Wood Tr.S.M.V. /T.S.M.V. ('50)	Groves & Gutteridge, East Cowes F. Perkins, Ltd. Peterborough	58·1'	14·0'	5·1'	33 37	300 BHP 200 BHP	18/12 cyls. 4 3/8"-5"	
1948 3/1949 4/1963	LOCH FRISA ex Marleen	Steel S.S.	Morton Eng. & Drydock Co. Ltd. Quebec Canadian Vickers, Ltd., Montreal	143·6'	27·1'	15·6 7·6'	338 519 329 (3/51)	73 MN	T. 3 cyls. 9", 16", 26"-18"	Launched as *Ottowa Maycliff*; Oil fuel. 2 dks/1 dk. & shltr. dk., 3/51
1946 3/1949 1956	DUMB BARGE No.3	Wood —	Quebec	24·0'	7·5'	2·5'		—	Hand propelled	Iona (ex lifeboat from *Marleen*)
1943 1950 3/4/64 3/1973 4/8/79	CRAIGNURE ex Silver Crest	Wood M.V.	— The Bergius Co.. Ltd.	36·1'	10·0'	3·0'	15	30 BHP	Kelvin F-4	Craignure: / Lismore / Iona/Staffa
1950 1950	IONA (V)		J. Barr & Son (Craigendoran) Ltd	34·9'	10·5'	4·5'	15	22	Kelvin J.2 4 S C S A	Iona/Staffa

Name	Dates	Builder / Engine	Type	Length	Breadth	Depth	Tonnage	BHP	Engine	Notes
STAFFA (II)	1950 13/4/67	··	··	··	··	··	··	··	··	'65 to Eigg; '66 to Lochboisdale
ÖRNEN / LOCHDUNVEGAN (II) (12/50)	1948 8/1950 11/1973	Akt. Lindholmens Varv, Gothenburg A/B Atlas Diesel, Stockholm	Steel M.V.	179·7' 180·1'	30·6'	9·6'	562 528	188	2 S.C.S.A. 5 cyls. 13⅜"-22⁷⁄₁₆"	Variable pitch propeller *
LOCH CARRON	24/10/50 4/1951 5/1977	Ardrossan Dockyard Ltd. British Polar Engines Ltd.	··	194·8'	34·1'	9·8'	650 683	850 BHP	2 S.C.S.A. 6 cyls. 13⅜"-22⁷⁄₁₆	*
COLL (I)	1951 1951 11/6/67	J. Barr & Sons (Craigendoran) Ltd. The Bergius Co., Ltd.	Wood M.V.	34·9'	10·5'	4·5'	BHP 22		Kelvin J.2	Coll
COLONSAY (II) / ERISKAY (II) ('65)	1951 1951 11/2/69	··	··	··	··	··	··	··	··	Colonsay; '65 to Eriskay
ROSALIND / LOCHSHIEL (II) (12/53)	10/1953 10/1953 28/4/70	··	··	45·3'	12·0'	4·1'	16	66 BHP	Kelvin Diesel, Type K3	Loch Shiel; Iona from 1962
(CELIA) / LOCHAILORT	5/1954 1/6/54 1969	··	··	··	··	··	14	··	··	Loch Shiel
CLAYMORE (II)	10/3/55 16/6/1955 4/1976	Wm. Denny & Bros., Ltd.	Steel T.S.M.V.	185·5'	35·0'	11·2'	1024	72	2 S.C.S.A. (2) each 8 cyls. 360-600mm	*
LOCH ARD	23/5/55 22/6/1955 4/1971	Ferguson Bros. (Port Glasgow) Ltd. British Polar Engines Ltd.	Steel M.V.	175·6'	34·1'	9·1'	611	1000 BHP	2 S.C.S.A. 6 cyls. 340 x 570 mm.	
LOCH TOSCAIG ex Irene Julia ex M.F.V. 1003	1945 7/1955 12/1975	J. Bolson & Co., Ltd. Poole The Bergius Co., Ltd.	Wood M.V.	61·0'	17·8'	7·6'	49	132		*

* Retained by David MacBrayne Ltd. at 1/1/73

DAVID MACBRAYNE, LTD. etc. (contd.)

Dates: Built Acqd. Displ.	Name	Type	Shipbuilders Enginebuilders	L.	B.	D.	G.T.	N.H.P.	Machinery	Remarks
1956 1956	ULVA	··	Timbacraft Ltd., Shandon The Bergius Co. Ltd.	35·0'	10·5'	4·5'		22 20 SHP	(1) Kelvin J.2 (2) Kelvin P4R	Iona/Staffa Eigg NE 9/83
1942 9/1959 10/1979	LOCH ARKAIG	Wood T.S.M.V.	J. Bolson & Son, Ltd., Poole The Bergius Co. Ltd.	113·0' OL	22·0'	8·5'	230 179	240 BHP	2 oil engines, each 8 cyls. 6½"-7¼"	Ex inshore mines-weeper. NE '60 *
1947 12/1961 10/1971	LOCH EYNORT ex Valonia	Wood M.V.	Wivenhoe Shipyard, Ltd. Crossley Bros., Ltd.	91·5'	22·3'	9·8'	135 117		2 S.C.S.A. 4 cyls. 12½"-13½"	
1962 1962	IONA (VI)	··	Timbacraft Ltd. The Bergius Co. Ltd.	34·3'	10·5'	4·5'		22 20 SHP	(1) Kelvin J.2 (2) Kelvin P4R	Iona-Staffa NE 1/84
1944 12/1963 9/3/69 4/1973 25/10/85	APPLECROSS ex Highlander	··	··	40·0'	11·3'	3·0'			Kelvin Diesel J.4 NE '64	
20/11/63 4/1964 11/1985	HEBRIDES (II)	Steel T.S.M.V.	Hall, Russell & Co., Ltd., Aberdeen Crossley Bros., Ltd. Manchester	220·0 235·0 OL	46'3"	13'0"	2104 1420†		2 x 2 S.C.S.A. each 8 cyls. 10½"-13½" Bow-thrust propellor fwd.	Car carrier: Chartered from Secy. of State for Scotland. Ownership transferred to David MacBrayne Ltd., 10/1973 and to Caledonian MacBrayne Holdings, Ltd., 4/1974; operated by Caledonian MacBrayne, Ltd. and ownership also to

Name	Dates	Builder / Type	Length	Breadth	Depth	Tonnage	Engine	Notes
	14/8/84	:		46 5	1 6	1420†	:	Chartered from Secy. of State for Scotland. Charter transferred to Caledonian MacBrayne Ltd 1/1976 to Caledonian MacBrayne Holdings Ltd. and ownership transferred from Secretary of State to David MacBrayne Ltd., and 1980 to Caledonian MacBrayne Ltd. Len. '73 to 266'; superstructure raised to permit drive-through with bow and stern loading.
COLUMBA (II)	12/3/64 30/7/64	:	235'0"	46'3"	13'0"	2104 1420†	:	Car carrier. Chartered from Secy. of State for Scotland. Ownership transferred to David MacBrayne Ltd., 10/1973 and to Caledonian MacBrayne Holdings, Ltd., 4/1974; operated by Caledonian MacBrayne, Ltd. and ownership also to them by 1980.
SCALPAY (I) ex Maid of Glencoe	1957 2/1965 1/11/1971	Wood M.V. J. Noble, Fraserburgh	45.5'			24		Turntable ferry: Scalpay-Kyles-Scalpay
EIGG (I) ex A'Mhaighdean Mhara ex Chieftain	1923 13/5/66 1978	Wood M.V.	32.0'	11.4'	3.5'	20	Kelvin Diesel P4R fitted by MacLean & MacRae	Eigg: converted lifeboat from P&O *Mooltan*

* - Retained by David MacBrayne Ltd., at 1/1/1973
† - Tonnage change in 1972 on new regulations excluding car deck

DAVID MACBRAYNE, LTD. etc. (contd.)

Dates: Built Acqd. Displ.	Name	Type	Shipbuilders Enginebuilders	L.	B.	D.	G.T.	N.H.P.	Machinery	Remarks
1953 8/11/69 1980	ARRAN (V)	Steel T.S.M.V.	Wm. Denny & Bros., Ltd. British Polar Engines, Ltd.	178·8'	35·1'	7·3'	568	393	2x2 S.C.S.A. each 6 cyls. 13⅜"-22⅐6"	David MacBrayne Ltd. 8/11/69, then back to C.S.P.Co. Ltd. 2/1970; remained on charter to David MacBrayne Ltd; converted to stern-loading. 3/1973
22/1/70 5/1970	IONA (VII)	,,	Ailsa S.B.Co. Ltd. Troon English Diesels Ltd. Packman Engine Division, Colchester	230·0'	44·0'	15·0'	1192 1324	1600 BHP	2x4 S.C.S.A. each 12 cyls. 5½"x6½" Bow thrust fwd. Denny-Brown retractable stabilisers.	To Caledonian MacBrayne Ltd., as at 1/1/73, later to Caledonian MacBrayne Holdings, Ltd., and to Caledonian MacBrayne. Ltd., 2/1974.
1956 1971 11/1979	SCALPAY (II) ex Lochalsh II ex Lochalsh (II)	,,	W. Denny & Bros., Ltd., Dumbarton Gleniffer Eng. Co.	40·2'	17·5'	5·0'	23·78	6 36 BHP	3 cyls. 4⅜"x6"	Ren. 11/1971 *
19/5/72 1972	KILBRANNAN	,,	James Lamont & Co., Ltd. Port Glasgow English Electric Diesels Ltd., (Kelvin), Glasgow	63·0'	21·0'	6·9'	65	300 BHP	(2) 4 S.C.S.A. each 6 cyls. 5"x5⅜" rev. red. gear	Launched for David MacBrayne. Ltd. Registered in name of Caledonian MacBrayne Services.
18/12/72 1973	MORVERN	,,	,,	63·0'	21·0'	6·9'	64	300 BHP	,,	Registered in name of Caledonian MacBrayne Services.

(also CALEDONIA, which was on MacBrayne serive in 1969)

(For previous ships see ''C.R.O.S.'')

Dates	Name	Type	Builder	Length	Breadth	Depth	Tonnage	HP	Engines	Notes
1933 1933 6/1978	QUEEN MARY / QUEEN MARY II / QUEEN MARY	Steel Tr.S.S.	Wm. Denny & Bros. Ltd.	252·5'	35·1'	10·1'	870 821 1014	350	3 steam turbines D.D.	To C.S.P. 3/10/35 Re-named 1934 and 5/1976 NB '57 - WT, oil fired
1934 1934 1970	CALEDONIA (II)	Steel P.S.	Wm. Denny & Bros. Ltd.	223·6'	30·1'	9·4'	624	193	TD 3 cyls. 20" 31½" & 50"x60"	NB 1955
1947 1947 8/8/74	WAVERLEY	..	A. & J. Inglis Ltd. Rankin & Blackmore, Ltd.	239·6'	30·3'	8·6'	693	2100 BHP	TD 3 cyls. 24", 39" & 62"x66"	To C.S.P. 5/11/51
3/3/53 1953 9/3/82	MAID OF THE LOCH	..	A. & J. Inglis Ltd. Glasgow (erected at Balloch) Rankin & Blackmore, Ltd.	191·0'	28·1'	7·1'	555 295 NT	1060 IHP 57	CD 2 cyls. 24" & 48"x51"	To C.S.P.Co. 5/1957
17/2/53 5/1953 2/1973	MAID OF ASHTON	Steel T.S.M.V.	Yarrow & Co. Ltd. British Polar Engines Ltd.	161·3'	28·2'	8·9'	508 233 NT	650 BHP at 425 RPM	2x2 S.C.S.A. each 6 cyls. 9⅞"x16½"	..
4/3/53 6/1953 4/1974	MAID OF ARGYLL	..	A. & J. Inglis Ltd. Glasgow British Polar Engines, Ltd.	..	..	..	508	40 MN 105 HP	..	
2/4/53 1953 4/1973	MAID OF SKELMORLIE	..	..	..	..	..	..	..	..	
13/5/53 7/1953 8/1978	MAID OF CUMBRAE	..	Ardossan Dockyard Ltd. British Polar Engines, Ltd.	..	..	..	..	..	..	Converted to car ferry, stern and side loading. 3/1972

THE CALEDONIAN STEAM PACKET CO. LTD. (contd.)

Dates: Built Acqd. Displ.	Name	Type	Shipbuilders Enginebuilders	L.	B.	D.	G.T.	N.H.P.	Machinery	Remarks
20/1/54 1954 1979	COWAL (II)	..	Ailsa S.B. Co., Ltd., Troon British Polar Engines Ltd.	178·8'	35·1'	7·3'	569	393	2x2 S.C.S.A. each 6 cyls. 13⅜"-27⁷⁄₁₆"	
28/9/54 11/1954 5/11/79	BUTE (VI)	..	..	..	..	..	568 199·09 NT	..	..	
30/5/57 6/1957	GLEN SANNOX (III)	..	Ailsa S.B. Co., Ltd., Troon (1) Sulzer Bros., Winterthur (2) Wichmann Moter- enfabrik, fitted by Hall Russell & Co., Ltd., Aberdeen	243·9'	44·1'	9·4'	1107 1269	2400 BHP 864	(1) 2x2 S.C.S.A. each 8 cyls. 420-500mm (2) 2x2 S.C.S.A. each 8 cyls. 450-500mm	Converted to stern- loading but retaining lift for side-loading 1970; thw. forward from 10/1972.
9/6/60 1960 11/1983	KYLEAKIN (II) / KYLEAKIN II / LARGS	..	Ailsa S.B. Co., Ltd., Troon Gleniffer Eng. Co., Ltd.	82·5'	21'	6'	60			Ren. 670. Converted to bow-loading.
1965 7/1965 3/11/86	PORTREE (II)	..	Jas. Lamont & Co., Ltd (1) Gleniffer Engs. Ltd., Glasgow (2) Gardner Engs. Ltd., Manchester	76' OL	21'	4'	65			To Rhubodach Ferry 1970: NE '70
1966 10/1966 3/11/86	BROADFORD (II)	..	Jas. Lamont & Co. Gleniffer Engs. Ltd.	..	..	..	64			To Rhubodach Ferry 1971
1961 5/1967	ROSE	Steel M.V.	White's Shipyard, Southampton	110·0' OL	27'	5'	214			Dir. Prop. Voith-Schneider

Date	Name	Material/Type	Builder	Length	Breadth	Depth	Tonnage	BHP	Engine	Notes
7/1969	CORUISK (II)	T.S.M.V.	English Electric Diesels (Kelvin), Glasgow	80·0'	21'	4'	60			
1966 12/1969	STENA BALTICA / CALEDONIA (III)	:	A/S Langesunds Mek. Verk. M.A.N. Augsburg	183·0'	40·0'	10'4½"	1157	2670 BHP	2x4 S.C.S.A. eacg 9 cyls. 300-450mm	Ren. 4/4/70 Engine made '64 fitted '66
7/1970 1970	KYLEAKIN (III)	Steel D.S.M.V.	Newport S.B. & E. Co. Ltd. Newport, Mon. Gardner & Sons Ltd.	112·0'	42·3'	4'1¼"			2x4 S.C.S.A. each 8 cyls. 5½"-7¾"	Dir. Props. Voith-Schneider
1971 1971	LOCHALSH (III)	:	:	:	:	:	:	:	:	:
	CALEDONIAN MACBRAYNE LTD. **DAVID MACBRAYNE, LTD.** (from 1/1/1973)									
1904 3/1973 1975	TIGER ex *Shona* ex *Elizabeth of Buckhaven*	Wood M.V.							(Test engines for lifeboat of No. 534)	Ferry at Iona
22/3/73 1973	BRUERNISH	Steel T.S.M.V.	James Lamont & Co., Ltd. Port Glasgow English Electric Diesels Ltd.. (Kelvin). Glasgow	68·0'	21·0'	6·9'	69 71	300 BHP	2x4 S.C.S.A. each 6 cyls. 5"x5⅝" rev. red. gear	
23/5/73 6/1973	RHUM	:	:	:	:	:	:	:	:	
2/8/73 18/9/73	COLL (II)	:	:	:	:	:	:	:	:	
27/11/73 3/1974	JUPITER (III)	Steel D.S.M.V.	James Lamont & Co., Ltd. Port Glasgow Mirrlees Blackstone, Ltd.. Stockport	217·9'	43·9'	12·9'	849		2x4 S.C.S.A. each 8 cyls. 8¾"x11½"	2 dir. props. Voith-Schneider

CALEDONIAN MACBRAYNE, etc. (contd.)

Dates: Built Acqd. Displ.	Name	Type	Shipbuilders Enginebuilders	L.	B.	D.	G.T.	N.H.P.	Machinery	Remarks
1/4/74 6/8/74	PIONEER (III)	Steel T.S.M.V.	Robb Caledon Shipbuilders. Ltd., Leith Mirrlees Blackstone. Ltd., Stamford	200·2'	44·2'	13·2'	1071	3400 BHP	2x4 S.C.S.A. each 16 cyls. 222x292 mm S.R.G.	Cont.-pitch props. Thw. fwd.
19/4/74 8/1974	SULVEN	Steel T.S.M.V.	Moss Rosenberg Vaerft A/S. near Oslo Wichman Motorenfabrik	255·7'	50·8'	12·5'	1908	3500 BHP	2x2 S.C.S.A each 7 cyls. 300x450 mm.	Cont.-pitch props 2 thw. fwd. (each 300 BHP)
16/9/74 11/1974	JUNO (III)	Steel D.S.M.V.	As JUPITER, supra	217·9'	43·9'	12·9'	854		As JUPITER	2 dir. props. Voith-Schneider
12/12/74 3/1975	[CANNA]/EIGG (II)	Steel T.S.M.V.	As BRUERNISH. supra	68·0'	21·0'	6·9'	69	300 BHP	2x4 S.C.S.A. each 6 cyls. 5"x5⅞" rev. red. geared	
1923 28/3/75 11/3/85	KILDONAN (II) ex Silver Darling ex Falcon	Wood M.V.	Bergius Co., Ltd., Glasgow	68·0'	21·0'					Ferry at Eigg
1934 20/5/75 1981	STAFFA (VII) ex Silver Spray	..	Munro, Blairmore Gardner	34·0'	9·0'	2·5'				Ferry at Iona/Eigg and Tobermory/Mingary
31/10/75 23/3/76	[EIGG]/[RAASAY]/ CANNA	Steel T.S.M.V.	As BRUERNISH. supra	68·0'	21·0'	6·9'	69	300 BHP	As BRUERNISH	As BRUERNISH
23/3/76 4/1976	[VATERSAY]/[PABBAY]/	..	..	..	..					

Dates	Name	Material / Type	Builder / Engine builder	Length	Breadth	Depth	Tonnage	BHP	Engines	Notes
22/12/76 3/1977	ISLE OF CUMBRAE (II)	Steel D.S.M.V.	Ailsa S.B. Co., Ltd., Troon L. Gardner & Sons, Ltd.	32.0m 125' O.L.	10.0m 33'	2.39m	201		2x4 S.C.S.A each 8 cyls. 140x197 mm	2 dir. props. Voith-Schneider
30/6/77 27/1/78	SATURN	Steel D.S.M.V.	Ailsa S.B. Co., Ltd., Troon Mirrlees Blackstone, Ltd., Stockport	66.5m 227' O.L.	13.4m 46'	4.0m	851	4880 BHP	2x2 S.C.S.A. each 8 cyls. 222x292 mm.	2 dir. props. Voith-Schneider
31/8/78 12/1978	CLAYMORE (III)	Steel T.S.M.V.	Robb Caledon S.B. Ltd., Leith Mirrlees Blackstone, Ltd., Stamford	229.6'	50.8'	15.7'	1580 1631	3400 BHP	2x4 S.C.S.A. each 16 cyls. 222x292 mm. geared to two screw shafts	2 cont. pitch props. Thw. fwd.
11/6/79 1979	LOCHMOR (II)	"	Ailsa S.B. Co., Ltd., Troon A/B Volvo Penta. Gothenburg	92.8'	25'	12.2'	189	520 BHP	2x4 S.C.S.A. each 6 cyls. 130x150 mm. rev. red. geared.	
2/12/83 1984	ISLE OF ARRAN (III)	"	Ferguson Ailsa Ltd., Port Glasgow Mirrlees Blackstone (Stockport) Ltd.	78.01m 81.5m 267' O.L.	15.8m 52'	4.98m	3296	4690 BHP	2x4 S.C.S.A. each 8 cyls. 275x305 mm. with clutches, flex. couplings & SRG:	2 cont. pitch props. fwd.
4/7/85 1985	HEBRIDEAN ISLES	"	Cochrane (Shipbuilders) Ltd., Selby Mirrlees Blackstone (Stockport) Ltd.	84.9m	15.8m	5.0m	3040	2x 2310 BHP	"	
8/5/86 7/1986	LOCH STRIVEN	Steel D.S.M.V.	R. Dunston (Hessle) Ltd. Volvo Penta. Gothenburg, Sweden	30.2m	10.0m	2.6m	206			
22/5/86 7/1986	LOCH LINNHE	Steel D.S.M.V.	"	30.2m	10.0m	2.6m	206			

CALEDONIAN MACBRAYNE, etc. (contd.)

Dates: Built Acqd. Displ.	Name	Type	Shipbuilders Enginebuilders	L.	B.	D.	G.T.	N.H.P.	Machinery	Remarks
19/8/86 1986	LOCH RIDDON	Steel D.S.M.V.	R. Dunston (Hessle) Ltd. Volvo Penta	30·2m	10.0m	2.6m	206			Building
17/12/86 1986	LOCH RANZA	Steel D.S.M.V.	,,	30·2m	10.0m	2.6m	206			Building
		Steel T.S.M.V.	Ferguson Ailsa Ltd., Port Glasgow Mirrlees Blackstone (Stockport) Ltd.	78·01m	15.8m	4·98m			As Isle of Arran *supra*	Building

FLEET

OF

CLYDE & CAMPBELTOWN SHIPPING COMPANY, LTD.

(Controlled by David MacBrayne, Ltd., from 3/1937 to 30/9/49; transferred to British Transport Commission, Railway Executive, 1/10/49)

CLYDE CARGO STEAMERS LTD
J. HILL & COMPANY 1871 - 1915
J. RODGER - J. D. RODGER

Dates	Name	Builder	Material	Length	Breadth	Depth	Tonnage	Power	Engine	Notes
1871 8/1871 c.1896	SUCCESS (I)	Robert McLea, Rothesay	Wood							Jas. Hill Duncan Hill and Jas. Hill, Jr.
8/1876 1876 1882	SUCCESS (II)	Murdoch & Murray, Port Glasgow Kesson & Campbell	Iron S.S.	66·6'	17·7'	8·'	69	20	S. 2 cyls. 10"-12"	
22/2/79 1879 18/12/90	BUTE (I)	Scott & Macgill, Bowling W. King & Co.	".."	95·1'	19·0'	9·2'	143	35	C. 2 cyls. 16", 28"-22"	
1863 14/3/82 16/3/94	CUMBRAE ex Marquis of Lorne ex Victory	Barclay, Curle & Co. J. Barr, Glasgow	Iron P.S.	176·7'	17·6'	6·8'	126	75 RHP	St. 1 cyl. 54"-42"	NB '67 and '79 Ren. 207/82
1867 1/3/83 2/7/84	ARRAN (I) ex Dunoon Castle	T. Wingate & Co., Glasgow	".."	191·7'	18·2'	7·5'	171	90 85	St. 1 cyl. 50"-45"	NB '83 Ren. 307/83
17/4/90 1890 17/7/91	BUTE No. 2	Scott & Co. Bowling W. Kemp	Iron T.S.S.	116·4'	22·0'	8·7'	170	38	C. 4 cyls. 12", 23"-18"	
12/1/92 1892 4/1899	BUTE (III)	J. Fullerton & Co., Paisley Cameron, Mills & Co.	Steel S.S.	110·0'	20·0'	9·0'	158	43 RHP	C. 2 cyls. 16", 32"-26"	
21/1/98 1898 1935	BUTE 4	".."	".."	115·0'	21·1'	..	174	..	C. 2 cyls. 16", 32"-24"	NB '19, fitted 2/1924
1879 11/1912	BARMORE	J. Fullerton & Co.	Iron P.S.	110·3'	18·0'	..	126	45	C. 2 cyls.	NB 1/1889

LOCHFYNE & GLASGOW STEAM PACKET COMPANY, LTD. 18.. 1...
MINARD CASTLE SHIPPING COMPANY, LTD. 2/1913 - 1922

Dates	Name	Type	Builder	Length	Breadth	Depth	Tonnage	HP	Engine	Notes
1869 1876 3/4/1913	JURA	Iron S.S.	Dumbarton	82·0'	17·3'	7·9'	69	16		
19/6/82 7/1882 11/1926	MINARD CASTLE	Steel S.S.	J. Fullerton & Co. W. Kemp	140·2'	22·0'	10·4'	223 246	80 RHP	C. 2 cyls. 23', 42"·30"	NB '89
1868 7/1899 23/7/00	SULTANA	Iron P.S.	W. Robertson & Co. W. King & Co.	188·1'	18·3'	7·3'	173	136	D. 1 cyl. 49"·54"	NB '86

CLYDE CARGO STEAMERS, LTD. 1915 - 1937

Dates	Name	Type	Builder	Length	Breadth	Depth	Tonnage	HP	Engine	Notes
1903 23/4/18 4/1931	LAPWING / COWAL (25/1/26)	Steel S.S.	Scott & Co., Bowling Hutson & Sons, Ltd.	135·2'	21·2'	9·4'	211 284 194	64 RHP	C. 2 cyls. 19", 36"·27"	J. D. Rodger till 3/7/23
1901 1924 5/1926	JANE	"	Ardrossan D.D. & S.B. Co., Ltd. Fisher & Co., Paisley	91·8'	19·1'	7·5'	104	24 RHP	C. 2 cyls. 12", 24"·18"	
1909 c.3/1925 1925	LINTIE	"	Geo. Brown & Co., Greenock Gauldie, Gillespie & Co., Glasgow	110·1'	20·6'	8·8'	172 174 167	30 RHP	C. 2 cyls. 11", 24"·16"	
1/12/25 1/1926 4/1955	MINARD	"	Scott & Sons, Bowling Aitchison Blair, Ltd., Clydebank	143·1'	25·1'	9·7'	241	53 RHP	C. 2 cyls. 17½", 36"·24"	
26/1/26 1926 31/12/32	ARRAN (III)	"	Ayrshire Dkyd. Co., Ltd., Irvine Aitchison Blair. Ltd.	99·7'	21·1'	8·3'	132	34 RHP	C. 2 cyls. 14", 29"·21"	

CLYDE CARGO STEAMERS. LTD. (contd.)

Dates: Built Acqd. Displ.	Name	Type	Shipbuilders Enginebuilders	L.	B.	D.	G.T.	N.H.P.	Machinery	Remarks
1928 1928 4/1955	**ARDYNE**	..	Scott & Sons, Bowling Aitchison Blair, Ltd.	135·1'	25·1'	9·2'	242	53 RHP	C. 2 cyls. 17½",36"-24"	
31/7/33 1933 2/1958	**ARRAN (IV) / KILDONAN (I)** (30/4/53)	..	Ardrossan Dockyard, Ltd. Aitchison Blair, Ltd.	120·4'	23·1'	8·6'	208	..	C. 2 cyls. 15', 32"-24"	

CAMPBELTOWN & GLASGOW STEAM PACKET JOINT STOCK COMPANY. 1826 - 1883

CAMPBELTOWN & GLASGOW STEAM PACKET JOINT STOCK CO., LTD. 1883 - 1937

Absorbed 3 ; 4/3/1937 by Clyde Cargo Steamers, Ltd. whose name became CLYDE & CAMPBELTOWN SHIPPING CO. LTD.

Dates: Built Acqd. Displ.	Name	Type	Shipbuilders Enginebuilders	L.	B.	D.	G.T.	N.H.P.	Machinery	Remarks
1822 2/1826 30/5/45	DUKE OF LANCASTER	Wood P.S.	Mottershead & Hayes, Liverpool Fawcett & Co., Liverpool	103·5'	17·0'	9·5'	91 NT	50	S.L. 2 cyls.	
1835 1835 1848	ST. KIARAN	..	R. Duncan, Greenock J. & W. Napier	115·8'	19·1'	11·9'	128·7 NT	110		
1842 1842 20/10/66	DUKE OF CORNWALL	Iron P.S.	Caird & Co., Greenock J. & W. Napier	121·7" 122·9'	19·2" 18·2'	9·9" 9·5'	211	90	St. 1 cyl. 45"·45"	NB 1847
1848 1848 4/1868	CELT	..	Wm. Denny, Dumbarton T. Wingate & Co.	155·9' 164·8'	20·3' 21·3'	10·3' 10·4'	252 251	140	St. 1 cyl. 62"·56"	
1857 1857 15/9/68	DRUID	..	Barclay, Curle & Co. Tod & McGregor	160·1' 160·0'	20·6' 21·6'	9·7' 9·6'	229 220	150	S. 2 cyls. 44"·52"	

Name	Dates	Builder	Material	Length	Beam	Depth	Tonnage	HP	Engine	Notes
GAEL	1867 / 4/1867 / 1884	Robertson & Co., Greenock / Rankin & Blackmore	..	211·0'	23·2'	10·6'	347 / 403	160 / 150	S.C. 2 cyls. 45"-63"	NB '79
KINTYRE	10/6/68 / 1868 / 18/9/07	Robertson & Co. (1) Blackwood Gordon (2) Kincaid, Donald & Co., Greenock	Iron S.S.	184·7'	22·9'	11·5'	299 / 314	90 / 90 RHP	(1) S. 2 cyls. 36"-30" (2) C. 2 cyls. 26", 48"-30"	NE '82 / NB '82 and '93
KINLOCH	30/5/78 / 1878 / 5/1926	A. & J. Inglis	..	205·0'	24·1'	12·7'	425 / 428 / 480 / 427	135 / 158	C. 2 cyls. 29", 54"-42"	NB '90 and '14
DAVAAR	17/5/85 / 1885 / 7/1943	London & Glasgow Co., Ltd., Govan	Steel S.S.	217·8'	27·0'	12·9'	543 / 516 / 568 / 535 / 495	182	C. 2 cyls. 29", 58"-42"	NB '03
DALRIADA	16/3/26 / 1926 / 19/6/42	R. Duncan & Co., Ltd., Port Glasgow / D. Rowan & Co., Ltd.	..	230·0'	34·7'	14·8'	758	348	T. 4 cyls. 22", 35½" (2) 40"-33"	

CLYDE & CAMPBELTOWN SHIPPING CO., LTD. (contd.) 1/4/1937 - 1/10/49

Name	Dates	Builder	Material	Length	Beam	Depth	Tonnage	HP	Engine	Notes
MARIE	1904 / 6/1939 / 4/1949	W. Chalmers & Co., Rutherglen / Ross & Duncan	Steel P.S.	82·8'	19·8'	8·1'	105	36 RHP	C. 2 cyls. 13", 28"-18"	NB 6/1925
EMPIRE TULIP	1939 / 1945 / 1946	N.V. Delfzijl, Gebr., Saldes Appingedammer Brow Motorenfbk	Steel M.V.	126·4'	23·5'	7·3'	288	195 BHP	2 S.A. 4 cyls. 9⁷⁄₁₆" - 14³⁄₁₆"	Chartered

FLEET

OF

WESTERN FERRIES LIMITED

and Associates

WESTERN FERRIES, LTD.
WESTERN FERRIES (ARGYLL) LTD.
WESTERN FERRIES (CLYDE) LTD.

Dates	Name	Type	Builder / Engines	Length	Beam	Depth	Tonnage	Power	Engines	Notes
27/2/68 1968 1981	**SOUND OF ISLAY**	Steel T.S.M.V.	Ferguson Bros. (Port Glasgow) Ltd. Bergius Kelvin Co. Ltd.	125.1'	30.0'	7.5'	276 280	640 SHP	2x4 S.A., 370-500 mm. 6½"-7¼" S.R. red. gear	10¾ kn
1966 1/1969	**SOUND OF GIGHA** ex Isle of Gigha	"	Bideford. N. Devon (1) Thorneycroft (2) A/B Scania. Vabis. Sodertalje	25.95m	5.88m	1.524m	65		(1) (2) As SOUND OF SCARBA	From Eilean Sea Services, Ltd. Regd. Campbeltown
18/4/69 1969 9/1976	**SOUND OF JURA**	"	Hatlo Werksted A/S. Ulsteinwik. Norway Lister Blackstone Marine. Ltd., Dursley	149.9'	36.1'	13.2'	558	2000 BHP	2x4 S.A., each 8 cyls. 8¼"-11¾"	Regd. Campbeltown. 14kn. Cont.-pitch props. Thw. fwd.
1962 12/1972	**SOUND OF SHUNA** ex Olandsund IV	Steel D.S.M.V.	A/B Asi Verken. Amal. Sweden (1) Albin Motor. Kristinehamn (2) A/B Scania. Vabis. Sodertalje	131.4'	29.5'	11.5'	244	600 BHP	(1) 4x4 S.A., each 6 cyls. 120-145 mm. geared to 3 screw shafts (2) As S. of SCARBA°	Dornoch Shipping Co. From R/A Olandsund. Kalmar, Sweden. 2 Dir. Props.
1960 12/1972	**SOUND OF SCARBA** ex Olandsund III	Steel D.S.M.V.	A/B Asi Verken. Amal. Sweden A/B Scania Vabis Sodertalje	10.6m	13.5m		175		4x4 S.A., each 6 cyls. 127-135 mm.°	Dornoch Shipping Co. From R/A Olandsund. Kalmar, Sweden. 2 Dir. Props.
1/1/38 3/1974	**SOUND OF SANDA** ex Lymington	Steel D.S.M.V.	Wm. Denny & Bros., Ltd. W. H. Allen, Sons & Co., Ltd., Bedford	132.1' 148.0' OL	26.1'	3.0'	275	400 BHP	2x4 S.A., each 6 cyls. 230-300 mm.	2 Dir. Props.
1976 1976 1985	**HIGHLAND SEABIRD**	Aluminium T.S.M.V. Cata-	Westermoen Hydrofoils AS, Mandal Mercedes M.T.U.	89.0'	29.0'		200	2200		Cruising speed 27 kn.

....../.. 10/1981 1984	**FARRINGFORD**	Steel P.M.V.	Wm. Denny & Bros. Ltd., English Electric Co., Ltd., Stafford	162-0'	28-1'	8-6'	489	4 S.A. 12 cyls. 10"-12"	Diesel electric
1959 1/1986	**SOUND OF SEIL** ex Freshwater	Steel D.S.M.V.	Ailsa S.B. Co. Ltd., Troon Crossley Bros. Ltd.	145-0'	30-0'	10-0'	363	640 BHP	Dir. props. Voith-Schneider

FLEETS
(as at 31st December, 1986)

CALEDONIAN MACBRAYNE, LTD.
- T.S.M.V. *Glen Sannox*
- M.V. *Keppel*
- T.S.M.V. *Caledonia*
- M.V. *Ulva* (ferryboat)
- M.V. *Iona* (ferryboat)
- D.S.M.V. *Kyleakin*
- D.S.M.V. *Lochalsh*
- T.S.M.V. *Columba*
- T.S.M.V. *Iona*
- T.S.M.V. *Kilbrannan*
- T.S.M.V. *Morvern*
- T.S.M.V. *Bruernish*
- T.S.M.V. *Rhum*
- T.S.M.V. *Coll*
- D.S.M.V. *Jupiter*
- D.S.M.V. *Juno*
- T.S.M.V. *Pioneer*
- T.S.M.V. *Suilven*
- T.S.M.V. *Eigg*
- T.S.M.V. *Canna*
- T.S.M.V. *Raasay*
- D.S.M.V. *Isle of Cumbraë*
- D.S.M.V. *Saturn*
- T.S.M.V. *Claymore*
- T.S.M.V. *Lochmor*
- T.S.M.V. *Isle of Arran*
- T.S.M.V. *Hebridean Isles*
- D.S.M.V. *Loch Striven*
- D.S.M.V. *Loch Linnhe*
- D.S.M.V. *Loch Riddon*
- D.S.M.V. *Loch Ranza*

WESTERN FERRIES (ARGYLL) LTD.
- T.S.M.V. *Sound of Gigha*
- D.S.M.V. *Sound of Shuna*
- D.S.M.V. *Sound of Scarba*
- D.S.M.V. *Sound of Sanda*
- D.S.M.V. *Sound of Seil*

Addenda et Corrigenda
(to 8th December, 1987)

P. 177. At end add:— The second royal launch in the history of the fleet took place at Port Glasgow on Tuesday, 8th December, 1987, from the Newark Yard of Appledore Ferguson Shipbuilders Limited (as the builders are now styled), when the vessel for Craignure and Colonsay was named *Isle of Mull* by H.R.H. Princess Alexandra. The ship differs from recent additions to the West Highland fleet in having one funnel on the centre line aft of amidships, and is arranged for end-loading only, with a totally enclosed vehicle deck, partially divided longitudinally by the engine-room casing. She is intended to obtain a certificate for 1000 passengers.

The same builders have an order from Caledonian MacBrayne for a vessel similar to *Hebridean Isles*, for the route from Oban to Coll, Tiree, Loch Boisdale and Barra, for completion in 1989, when it is expected that the *Claymore* will be transferred to Islay.

P.13, para. 1 and p.14, para. 5, penultimate line in each case:— Amend "Lochfyne" to "Lochfine".

P.18, para. 4, penultimate line and p.30, para. 2, line 6:— Amend "instituted" to "re-commenced".

P.21. The engine of the *Leven* is now re-located on ground adjacent to the Denny Tank, Dumbarton, owned by the Scottish Maritime Trust, Irvine.

P.30, line 4. The saloon was fitted in 1874.

P.51, para. 7, line 6:— Amend 1900 to 1899.

P.70, para. 5, line 3:— For "But" read "By".

P.104, para. 6, line 4:— For "She" substitute "*Lochfyne*".

P.112. para. 4, line 10:— For "caried" read "varied".

P.113, para. 1. At end add:— She was subsequently scrapped.

P.117, para. 1, line 4:— Amend "drives" to "drove".

P.122, line 28:— For "In this" read "At Toscaig". At end add:— She has since been sold to a Paisley owner, who intends operating cruises in connection with the Glasgow Garden Festival, 1988.

P.130, para. 4, line 11:— For "with" read "was".

P.138, para. 3, line 3:— For "0" read "5".

P.139, para. 3:— For "commenced" read "commended".

P.149, para. 3, line 8:— Insert "once" between "she" and "performed".

P.157. The name "Railway Steam Packet Company" was used from 1844.

P.160, end:—Delete "Glasgow-Inverness".

P.165, line 1:— Between "as" and "*Coruisk*" insert "for".

P.167. At end add:— "She did call at Tobermory on Sunday, 26th April, 1987 after the pier had been rebuilt. She is understood to have been sold after the 1987 season".

P.178, line 8:— Delete "d", to read "Rothesay".

P.193, para. 4, line 2:— For "this" read "the".

P.235 Insert under *Lochnevis*:— disposal date—3/1970.

BIBLIOGRAPHY

An t-Aiseag an Iar (The Passage West). Domhnall E. Meek (Clò-beag, Glasgow, 1977).
Australian Steamships, Dickson Gregory (The Richards Press, London, 1928).
Blockade Runner, the Narrative of a, John Wilkinson (Sheldon & Co., New York, 1877).
Sir George Burns, Bart., Edwin Hodder (Hodder & Stoughton, London, 1892).
G. & J. Burns, Papers, (Strathclyde Regional Archives).
Chamber of Commerce Papers, Parliamentary Returns.
Caledonian Railway Centenary, Stephenson Locomotive Society.
Caledonian Steam Packet Company Ltd., The Sixtieth Anniversary of, Rev. William C. Galbraith (Clyde River Steamer Club, 1949).
The Caledonian Steam Packet Company Limited, Iain C. MacArthur (Clyde River Steamer Club, 1972).
Classic Scottish Paddle Steamers, A. J. S. Paterson (David & Charles, Newton Abbot, 1982).
The Clyde Passenger Steamer, 1812-1901, James Williamson (James MacLehose & Sons, Glasgow).
About Clyde Steamers and Skippers, Senex Afloat (Gillespie Bros. Ltd., Glasgow, 1886).
The Clyde Puffer, Dan MacDonald (David & Charles, Newton Abbot, 1977).
Clyde and Other Coastal Steamers, Duckworth and Langmuir (T. Stephenson & Sons Ltd., 2nd Edition, 1977).
Clyde River Steamers of the Last Fifty Years, Andrew McQueen (Gowans & Gray, Glasgow, 1923).
Clyde River and Other Steamers, Duckworth and Langmuir (Brown, Son & Ferguson Ltd., Glasgow: 3rd Edition, 1973).
Supplement to Clyde River and Other Steamers, Duckworth and Langmuir (Brown, Son & Ferguson Ltd., Glasgow, 1982).
Clyde Shipping Company Limited, A History, Alan D. Cuthbert (privately printed by Robert MacLehose and Company Limited at the University Press, Glasgow, 1956).
The Coastwise Trade of the United Kingdom, Sir Alfred Read (George Thompson, London, 1925).
Cross Channel and Coastal Paddle Steamers, Frank Burtt (Richard Tiling, London, 1934).
Echoes of Old Clyde Paddle Wheels, Andrew McQueen (Gowans & Gray, Glasgow, 1924)
Early American Steamers, Eric Heyl.
The Floating Post Offices of the Clyde, James Mackay, Dumfries, 1979.
Glasgow Harbour Report Book, (Strathclyde Regional Archives).
Golden Years of the Clyde Steamer, A. J. S. Paterson (David & Charles, Newton Abbot, 1969).

Hebridean and Clyde Ferries, Caledonian MacBrayne Ltd., 1985.

History of Steam Navigation, John Kennedy (Chas. Birchall, Liverpool, 1906).

The History and Development of Machinery for Paddle Steamers, G. E. Barr (Paper No. 1150 of The Institution of Engineers and Shipbuilders in Scotland, Glasgow, 1951).

Kirkintilloch Shipbuilding, A. I. Bowman, (Strathkelvin District Libraries, Bishopbriggs, 1983).

Loch Maree and the Voyage of the Mabel, John H. Dickson (Northern Chronicle, Inverness).

Loch Lomond Steamboat Companies, Donald Macleod (Bennet & Thomson, Dumbarton, 1888).

The Story of the MacBrayne Line, David MacBrayne Limited, 1936 (private circulation).

MacBrayne Centenary, David MacBrayne Limited, 1951 (private circulation).

Sir James Mathieson of the Lewes, Alexander Mackenzie, F.S.A., reprinted from the Celtic Magazine, 1882.

Movern Transformed, Philip Gaskell (Cambridge University Press, 1980).

Napier Papers, (Glasgow University Archives).

The Native Steamboat Companion, Quentin Dalrymple (Edinburgh, 1845).

The Northern Highlands in the Nineteenth Century, James Brown – Volume I, 1880-1824 (Robert Carruthers & Sons, Inverness)

Northwards by Sea, Gordon Donaldson (published by the author, Edinburgh, 1966).

Pacific Steamers, Will Lawson (Brown, Son & Ferguson Ltd., 1927).

Puffer Ahoy!, G. W. Burrows (Brown, Son & Ferguson Ltd., 1981).

The Royal Route; Glasgow and the Highlands, D. MacBrayne 1879-1939; (issued most years).

Ship Registers.

The Skye Railway, John Thomas (David & Charles, Newton Abbot, 1977)

Song of the Clyde, Fred M. Walker (Patrick Stephens Ltd., Cambridge, 1984).

The Steamboat Companion, (James Lumsden & Sons, Glasgow, 1820).

The Short Sea Route, Fraser G. Machaffie (T. Stephenson & Sons, Ltd., Prescot, 1975).

Steamers of the Forth, Ian Brodie (David & Charles, Newton Abbot, 1976).

Railway and Other Steamers, Duckworth and Langmuir (T. Stephenson & Sons Ltd., 2nd Edition, 1968).

Victorian Summer of the Clyde Steamer, A. J. S. Paterson (David & Charles, Newton Abbot, 1972).

West Coast Steamers, Duckworth and Langmuir (T. Stephenson & Sons Ltd., 3rd Edition, 1966).

Wotherspoon Collection (In the track of the Comet) (Mitchell Library, Glasgow).

PERIODICALS

The American Neptune
Bulletin
Buteman
Clyde Steamers
Cruising Monthly
The Engineer
Fairplay
Greenock Telegraph
Glasgow Herald
Evening Times
Evening News
Evening Citizen
Chamber of Commerce Journal
Lloyd's List
*Lloyd's Register of British
  and Foreign Shipping*
Marine News
Marine Week

Mercantile Navy List
Mitchell's Steam Shipping Journal
Motor Ship
Nautical Magazine
North British Daily Mail
Oban Times
Railway Magazine
Railway and Travel Monthly
Scotsman
Sea Breezes
The Shipbuilder
Shipbuilding and Shippng Record
Shipping World
Syren and Shipping
Ship Ahoy
Ships Illustrated
Ships Monthly
*West Highland Steamer Club
  Reviews and Newsletters*

INDEX

K